"This is a valuable book, well written and a pleasure to read. It sheds light on aspects of Winston Churchill's career that are overlooked by those who see him simply as the man who delivered victory in 1945.

Adrian Phillips knows what many historians, dazzled by the myth, fail to see: Churchill was always vulnerable, right up to the end of the war. He was mistrusted by much of his party and disliked by the establishment. In these circumstances, he depended on the clutch of supporters, some of them slightly dodgy and unreliable but all, like him, mavericks, whom Hugh Dalton described as Churchill's 'camarilla'.

Phillips concentrates on their role to give a new and important perspective on Churchill's erratic political career and brings the disparate elements into a cohesive narrative, thematic as much as chronological.

This is a novel approach, a revealing one and one which is far from uncritical. But still it is clear that whatever may be said against him, Churchill remains a very great man – indeed, perhaps all the more so for being revealed in three dimensions."

Walter Reid, author of *Fighting Retreat: Churchill and India*

"A well-researched and lively foray into the curious cast of colourful characters spanning Churchill's remarkable career. Phillips's enjoyable account of friendship, feuds and Whitehall machinations helps us see Churchill in a new light."

Professor Rory Cormac, University of Nottingham

WINSTON'S BANDITS

Churchill and His Maverick Friends

ADRIAN PHILLIPS

Biteback Publishing

First published in Great Britain in 2024 by
Biteback Publishing Ltd, London
Copyright © Adrian Phillips 2024

Adrian Phillips has asserted his right under the Copyright, Designs and Patents Act 1988
to be identified as the author of this work.

ISBN 978-1-78590-789-0

10 9 8 7 6 5 4 3 2 1

A CIP catalogue record for this book is available from the British Library.

Set in Adobe Caslon Pro and Goudy Oldstyle

Printed and bound in Great Britain by
CPI Group (UK) Ltd, Croydon CR0 4YY

For Sheila

'My own relationship with Churchill is of negligible importance,
except insofar as it sheds a light on his character.'
BOB BOOTHBY, 1976

CONTENTS

DRAMATIS PERSONAE

This section aims to provide sufficient information to situate individuals within the narrative of the book. It makes no attempt to provide a balanced assessment of their careers and, still less, an exhaustive list of their titles, honours and decorations. The titles and ranks used in the text are those held at the periods in which they are discussed. Readers seeking fuller information are directed to the relevant entries in the *Oxford Dictionary of National Biography* and *Who Was Who*, respectively.

Amery, Leopold (1873–1955)
Conservative MP and passionate imperialist. At Harrow School with Churchill, who once threw him into the swimming pool. Out of office through the 1930s but was not deeply engaged over India or appeasement. Made devastating contribution to the Norway debate in May 1940 when he used Cromwell's words on Chamberlain, 'Depart, I say, and let us have done with you. In the name of God, go.' India office minister outside Cabinet in Churchill government.

Anderson, Sir John (1882–1958)
Civil servant turned MP and minister. Governor of Bengal 1932–37. Joined Chamberlain government. Lord Privy Seal, 1938–39; Home Secretary and Minister of Home Security, 1939–40; Lord President of the Council, 1940–43; Chancellor of the Exchequer, 1943–45. Highly influential in domestic policy.

Attlee, Clement (1883–1967)
Labour politician. Leader of the Opposition, 1935–40; Lord Privy Seal, 1940–42; Secretary of State for Dominion Affairs, 1942–43; Lord President of the Council, 1943–45; Deputy Prime Minister, 1942–45; Prime Minister and First Lord of the Treasury, 1945–51. Led the Labour Party into the National government under Churchill and then into its landslide victory in the 1945 general election.

Baldwin, Stanley (1867–1947)
Conservative politician. Financial Secretary to the Treasury, 1917–21; President of the Board of Trade, 1921–22; Chancellor of the Exchequer, 1922–23; Prime Minister, 1923–24, 1924–29 and 1935–37; Lord Privy Seal, 1932–34 (de facto Deputy Prime Minister); leader of the Conservative Party 1923–37. The dominant inter-war politician. Accused Beaverbrook of seeking 'power without responsibility; the prerogative of the harlot' when he tried to impose his empire free trade policy on the Conservative Party in opposition.

Beaverbrook, Lord (1879–1964)
Financier, press proprietor and politician. Minister of Information, 1918; newspaper titles included *Daily Express* and *London Evening Standard*; Minister for Aircraft Production, 1940–41; Minister of State, 1941; Minister of Supply, 1941–42; Lord Privy Seal, September 1943– July 1945. Personal friend of Churchill but favoured appeasement.

Bevin, Ernest (1881–1951)
Trade union leader and Labour politician. Minister of Labour and National Service 1940–45. One of the dominant figures in the Labour Party, rival to Herbert Morrison.

Blackett, Patrick (1897–1974)
Scientist. Professor of physics, Birkbeck College, 1933–37; Langworthy Professor of physics, University of Manchester, 1937–53. Nobel Prize for Physics, 1948. From 1935, was a member of Tizard's air defence committee.

Scientist RAF Coastal Command from March 1941 and then the Admiralty from January 1942 to the summer of 1945. Advised on anti-U-boat warfare and argued for its importance. Lindemann preferred using air resources to attack German cities and frowned on Blackett's left-wing politics.

Bonar Law, Andrew (1858–1923)
Anglo-Canadian politician and industrialist. Leader of the Conservative Party, 1911–21; Prime Minister, 1922–23. Closely allied to Beaverbrook.

Boothby, Bob (1900–86)
MP East Aberdeenshire, 1924–58; parliamentary private secretary to Churchill as Chancellor of the Exchequer, 1926–29; Parliamentary Secretary, Ministry of Food, 1940–41; military service as RAF staff officer; a British delegate to the Consultative Assembly of the Council of Europe, 1949–57.

Bracken, Brendan (1901–58)
Press publisher and Conservative politician. MP North Paddington, 1929–45; MP Bournemouth, November 1945–February 1950; MP East Bournemouth and Christchurch, 1950–51; parliamentary private secretary to the Prime Minister, 1940–41; Minister of Information, 1941–45; First Lord of the Admiralty, 1945; director of Eyre & Spottiswoode Ltd; chairman of *Financial News*; managing director of *Economist*; chairman of Union Corporation.

Bridges, Sir Edward (1892–1969)
Cabinet Secretary 1938–46; Permanent Secretary to Treasury and head of the civil service 1945–56.

Bruce-Gardner, Sir Charles (1887–1960)
Industrialist. Industrial adviser to Bank of England 1930–38; chairman of the Society of British Aircraft Constructors, 1938–43. Trusted by Chamberlain and Wilson to run the programme of air rearmament, he was accordingly influential.

Bruce Lockhart, Robert (1887–1970)
Journalist and public servant. Editorial staff, *Evening Standard*, 1929–37; Political Intelligence Department, Foreign Office, 1939–40; Deputy Under-Secretary of State, Foreign Office; director-general of Political Warfare Executive, 1941–45. Knew Beaverbrook well from working for him as a journalist and worked closely with Bracken as Minister of Information.

Butler, Richard 'Rab' (1902–82)
Conservative politician. Under-Secretary of State, India Office, 1932–37, where he fought Churchill over the India Bill; Parliamentary Secretary, Ministry of Labour, 1937–38; Under-Secretary of State for Foreign Affairs, 1938–41, where he presented the policy of appeasement, which he supported vigorously, to the House of Commons; Minister of Education, 1941–45. Recognised the importance of progressive policies for post-war Britain.

Cadogan, Sir Alexander 'Alec' (1884–1968)
Permanent Secretary to Foreign Office, 1938–46.

Cartland, Ronald (1907–40)
Conservative MP for King's Norton, Birmingham. Opposed appeasement and killed in action age thirty-three. Brother of the romantic novelist Barbara Cartland.

Chamberlain, Sir Austen (1863–1937)
Conservative politician. Half-brother of Neville Chamberlain. Financial Secretary to Treasury, 1900–02; Postmaster General, 1902–03; Chancellor of the Exchequer, 1903–06; Secretary of State for India, 1915–17; resigned, 1917; Member of the War Cabinet, April 1918; Chancellor of the Exchequer, January 1919–21; Lord Privy Seal and Leader of the House of Commons, 1921–22; Secretary of State for Foreign Affairs, November 1924–June 1929; negotiated Locarno Pact for which he was awarded Nobel Peace Prize and Knighthood of the

Garter; First Lord of the Admiralty in National government August–October 1931.

Chamberlain, Neville (1869–1940)

Conservative politician. Chancellor of the Exchequer 1931–37; Prime Minister, 1937–40; Lord President of the Council, 1940. Attempted to bring peace to Europe through a policy of positive engagement with Hitler and Mussolini, usually known as appeasement, but was also convinced of the need to rearm.

Channon, Henry 'Chips' (1887–1958)

Conservative MP. Parliamentary private secretary to Rab Butler, 1938–41. Strong supporter of appeasement. Socialite and diarist.

Churchill, Clementine 'Clemmie' (1885–1977)

Married Churchill in 1908

Churchill, Pamela (née Digby, later Harriman) (1920–97)

Married Randolph Churchill in 1939, divorced in 1946. Married Averell Harriman in 1971.

Churchill, Randolph (1911–68)

Journalist and author. MP for Preston, 1940–45.

Churchill, Winston (1874–1965)

Politician. Secretary of State for War and Secretary of State for Air (posts held simultaneously), 1919–21; backbench MP 1929–39. Fell out with the National government over its policy of granting limited autonomy to India. Recognised the danger of Hitler earlier than most and campaigned for rearmament, especially in the air.

Colville, John 'Jock' (1915–87)

Junior personal secretary to Chamberlain, 1939–40, then to Churchill, 1940–41, 1943–45; served RAF 1941–44.

Cooper, Alfred Duff (1890–1954)
Conservative MP. First Lord of the Admiralty, 1937–38; resigned in protest at Munich agreement; Minister of Information, 1940–41

Cripps, Sir Stafford, Baronet (1889–1952)
Socialist politician and barrister. Opposed rearmament and expelled by Labour Party in 1939 for advocating 'united front' with the Communist Party. Ambassador to the USSR, 1940–42, where it was believed that his credentials as an extreme left-winger would be well received, but they were not and he gradually adopted a more realistic approach to Stalin; Lord Privy Seal and Leader of House of Commons, 1942; failed to reach agreement on autonomy with Indian leaders; Minister of Aircraft Production, 1942–45.

Crow, Alwyn (1894–1965)
Director of ballistic research, Woolwich, 1919–39; chief superintendent, projectile development, 1939–40; director and controller of projectile development, 1940–45. Key ally of Lindemann and Churchill in promoting anti-aircraft rockets.

Cunliffe-Lister, Philip *see* **Swinton**

Cherwell Lord *see* **Lindemann**

Dalton, Hugh (1887–1962)
Labour politician. MP for Bishop Auckland, 1929–31 and 1935–59. One of the first Labour leaders to accept rearmament. Minister of Economic Warfare, 1940–42; President of the Board of Trade, 1942–45.

Davidson, J. C. C. (1889–1970)
Conservative politician. Parliamentary private secretary to Baldwin; President of the Board of Trade, 1921–22; parliamentary private secretary to Bonar Law, 1922–23; Chancellor, Duchy of Lancaster,

1923–24; Parliamentary Secretary to the Admiralty, November 1924–27; chairman of the Unionist Party, 1927–30; Chancellor, Duchy of Lancaster, 1931–37; hon. adviser, commercial relations, 1940; and controller of production, Ministry of Information, 1941. Baldwin's close confidant.

Dawson, Geoffrey (1874–1944)

Editor of *The Times*, 1912–19, 1923–41. Tried to advise government during the 1936 abdication crisis, but his influence is often exaggerated. Important support of Chamberlain's appeasement policy.

Dowding, Sir Hugh (1882–1970)

RAF officer. Rose to command a wing of the Royal Flying Corps. Air officer commanding Fighting Area, Air Defence of Great Britain, 1929; Air Member for Supply and Research, 1930; Air Member for Research and Development, 1935; air officer commanding-in-chief, Fighter Command, 1936–40. Devised and implemented integrated air defence system which made full use of technology such as radar. Despised by the leadership of the RAF who believed that only bombing could protect against bombing.

Dunglass, Lord 'Alec' (1903–95)

Conservative MP. Parliamentary private secretary to Chamberlain, 1936–40; Prime Minister, 1963–64 (as Sir Alec Douglas-Home).

Eden, Anthony (1897–1977)

Conservative politician. Foreign Secretary, 1935–38; resigned after being bypassed by Chamberlain in pursuit of appeasement policy; Foreign Secretary again, 1940–45; Leader of the House of Commons, 1942–45; de facto Deputy Prime Minister.

Einzig, Paul (1897–1973)

Journalist. *Financial News* and *The Banker*.

Ellington, Sir Edward (1887–1967)
RAF officer. Chief of Air Staff, 1933–37; Inspector General RAF, 1937–40. Opposed rearmament because he believed the danger of Nazi Germany was exaggerated and feared diluting the quality of the RAF. Opposed national radar system because he felt it offered bad value.

Fisher, Sir Warren (1887–1948)
Civil servant. Head of the civil service/Permanent Secretary to Treasury, 1919–39. One of the dominant Whitehall figures between the wars.

Freeman, Sir Wilfrid (1888–1953)
RAF officer. Air Member for Research and Development, 1936; Air Member for Development and Production, 1938; transferred with his department to the Ministry of Aircraft Production, where he resisted Beaverbrook's policies until he returned to the RAF as Vice-Chief of Air Staff in November 1940; Chief Executive, Ministry of Aircraft Production, 1942–45. Clearly understood the industrial and technological dimension to air warfare.

Halifax, Lord (1881–1959)
Conservative politician. Foreign Secretary, 1938–40.

Hankey, Sir Maurice (1877–1963)
Administrator. Secretary to Committee for Imperial Defence, 1912–38; Secretary to the Cabinet, 1917–38; member of War Cabinet as Lord Hankey, 1939–42. Dominant figure in the military establishment and Whitehall between the wars.

Harriman, Averell (1891–1986)
US businessman and close associate of Franklin Roosevelt, who sent him to Britain, Egypt and the USSR as a special envoy. Lover and much later husband of Pamela Churchill (née Digby), then married to Randolph Churchill.

Harris, Arthur 'Bert' (1892–1984)
RAF officer. Group captain and deputy director of plans on Air Staff, 1934–37. Highly influential despite comparatively junior rank. Air officer commanding-in-chief Bomber Command, 1942–45, where he advocated for a policy of bombing German cities to the exclusion of other forms of air warfare.

Harrod, Roy (1900–78)
Economist. Student of Christ Church, Oxford, 1924–67, where he was a friend of Lindemann. Served on Churchill's private statistical staff in Admiralty, 1940, and in Prime Minister's office, full-time, 1940–42, and subsequently in advisory capacity; also statistical adviser to Admiralty, 1943–45.

Harvie-Watt, George (1903–89)
Conservative politician and Territorial Army officer; assistant government whip, 1938–40; lieutenant colonel commanding 31st Battalion RE TA, 1938–41; promoted to brigadier to command 6th Anti-Aircraft Brigade, 1941; parliamentary private secretary to Churchill, July 1941–July 1945. Unabashed at Churchill's change of allegiance, Harvie-Watt was an efficient and loyal assistant but never part of Churchill's inner circle.

Hoare, Sir Samuel Baronet (1880–1959)
Politician. Secretary of State for Air, 1922–24 and November 1924–June 1929; with seat in Cabinet, 1923–24, 1924–29 and (briefly) 1940; Secretary of State for India, 1931–35, when he oversaw the tortuous passage through Parliament of the India Act in the teeth of opposition of Churchill and 'diehards'. Enthusiastic supporter of Trenchard during his second term as Chief of Air Staff.

Hore-Belisha, Leslie (1893–1957)
National Liberal MP. War Secretary 1937–40. Continued to entertain hopes of high office and remained an MP until he lost his seat in the 1945 election.

Imay, Hastings (1887–1965)
Soldier and administrator. Took over the military side of Hankey's functions in 1938. Deputy secretary, Committee of Imperial Defence, 1936–38, and secretary, 1938; chief of staff to Minister of Defence (Winston Churchill), 1940–45; deputy secretary (military) to War Cabinet, 1940–45. Smoothed Churchill's often fraught relationship with service chiefs. A key figure in the wartime administration.

Jones, R. V. (1911–97)
Scientist and intelligence officer. Worked in the Clarendon Laboratory, Oxford, with Lindemann, under whose auspices he went on to work on air defence problems before being attached to the Secret Intelligence Service in 1939 to work on German technology. Deeply involved in British attempts to understand the V-weapons.

Keynes, John Maynard, Lord Keynes from 1944 (1883–1946)
Economist and public servant. Contributed much to the debate on post-war economic arrangements, notably to prevent recurrence of mass unemployment. Negotiated financial package with the US which created the International Monetary Fund.

Korda, Alexander (1893–1956)
Film producer. City contact of Bracken. Helped the Churchill family in their media careers.

Lindemann, Frederick, Lord Cherwell from 1941 (1886–1957)
Scientist and politician. Experimental pilot and researcher in the Royal Flying Corps in the First World War. Fellow of Wadham College, 1919, and professor of experimental philosophy, Oxford; student of Christ Church from 1921; headed Churchill's Statistical Section, 1939-1945; Paymaster General, 1942–45 and 1951–53; again professor of experimental philosophy, Oxford, 1953–56. Note on Lindemann: After he was made a peer in 1941, Lindemann was generally known as Cherwell after his title, but as the narrative moves back and forth

between both periods, he has been referred to as Lindemann through-out for the sake of clarity. His usual and widespread nickname 'Prof' is also used.

Lloyd, Geoffrey (1902–84)

Conservative politician. Harrow School. Parliamentary Under-Secretary, Home Office, 1935–39; Secretary for Mines, 1939–40; Secretary for Petroleum, 1940–42; chairman of Oil Control Board, 1939–45; Minister in charge of Petroleum Warfare Department, 1940–45; Parliamentary Secretary (Petroleum), Ministry of Fuel and Power, 1942–45; Minister of Information, 1945. Likely candidate for a promotion favoured by Churchill but not by Bracken, who told Churchill that he only preferred him because he had gone to 'that old Borstal of yours'.

Lloyd, Lord (1879–1941)

Conservative politician. Governor of Bombay, 1918–23; MP East-bourne, 1924–25; made peer in 1925; High Commissioner for Egypt and Sudan, 1925–29; Secretary of State for the Colonies, 1940–41. Along with Churchill, the most high-profile politician to support the campaign against the India Act.

Lloyd George, David (1863–1945)

Liberal politician. Chancellor of the Exchequer, 1908–15, where he worked closely with Churchill on social legislation; Minister of Munitions, 1915–16; Secretary of State for War, 1916; Prime Minister and First Lord of the Treasury, 1916–22. Deposed as Prime Minister by Carlton House coup led by Bonar Law and Baldwin but continued to hold great ambitions. Persistent critic of successive governments. Ambiguous attitude to Hitler; suspected of ambitions to lead a British surrender government in 1940.

Londonderry, Lord (1878–1949)

Politician. Secretary of State for Air, 1931–35. Supported Ellington.

Replaced by Swinton to bring urgency to rearmament and became enthusiastic appeaser. Cousin of Churchill.

Low, David (1891–1963)
Leading political cartoonist of the 1930s. Drew for Beaverbrook's *Evening Standard*. Criticised both governments and Churchill's India campaign. Beaverbrook claimed – improbably – to exercise no control over his work.

Ludlow-Hewitt, Sir Edgar (1886–1973)
RAF officer. Air officer commanding-in-chief, Bomber Command, 1937; Inspector General RAF, 1940.

Lyttelton, Oliver (1893–1972)
Businessman and later politician. Managing director of the British Metal Corporation; controller of non-ferrous metals, 1939–40; Conservative MP, 1940–54; President of the Board of Trade, 1940–41; Minister of State in Cairo and member of the War Cabinet, 1941–42; Minister of War Production and member of the War Cabinet, 1942–45. City contact of Bracken and technocrat minister. Gave political direction to the war effort in the Middle East.

MacDonald, James Ramsay (1866–1937)
Labour politician. Prime Minister, 1924 and 1929–35.

Macmillan, Harold (1894–1986)
Conservative politician. Opponent of appeasement. His wife Dorothy had a long and agonised affair with Boothby. Parliamentary Secretary, Ministry of Supply, 1940–42, where he encouraged Beaverbrook's ambitions.

Maisky, Ivan (1884–1975)
Soviet ambassador to London, 1932–43.

Margesson, Captain David (1890–1965)

Conservative MP and Chief Whip, 1931–40. One of the most formidable whips ever; savagely punished dissidents from Chamberlain's appeasement policies. Transferred his allegiance to Churchill, for whom he was Secretary of State for War, 1940–42.

Monckton, Sir Walter (1891–1965)

Attorney General to Prince of Wales, 1932–36; Attorney General to the Duchy of Cornwall, 1936–47. Liaised between King (later Duke of Windsor) and government. Director-general of the Press and Censorship Bureau, 1939–40; subsequently director-general of Ministry of Information Affairs, 1940, 1940–41; director-general of British Propaganda and Information Services Cairo, 1941–42.

Morrison, Herbert (1888–1965)

Labour politician. Minister of Supply, 1940; Home Secretary and Minister of Home Security, 1940–45; member of the War Cabinet, 1942–45. Rival of Ernest Bevin.

Morton, Desmond (1891–1971)

Intelligence officer. Director of Industrial Intelligence Centre, 1929–39, where he fed Churchill with data on German rearmament; principal assistant secretary, Ministry of Economic Warfare, 1939; personal assistant to Prime Minister on intelligence matters, 1940–46.

Newall, Sir Cyril (1886–1963)

RAF officer. Rose to command Independent Air Force in the First World War, awarded CB and Albert Medal; air officer commanding RAF Middle East, 1931; Air Member for Supply and Organisation, 1935; Chief of Air Staff, 1937–40; Governor General of New Zealand, 1941–46. Removed as Chief of Air Staff in putsch organised by Beaverbrook, Trenchard and Salmond.

Nicolson, Harold (1886–1968)

National Labour MP so theoretically a government supporter but opposed to appeasement. Parliamentary Secretary to Ministry of Information, 1940–41; governor of the BBC, 1941–46.

Nuffield, Lord (1877–1963)

Industrialist. Founder and owner of Morris motor company and other enterprises. Picked by Kingsley Wood to manage Spitfire shadow factory at Castle Bromwich and the RAF Civilian Repair Organisation. Removed from both missions by Beaverbrook.

Portal, Sir Charles 'Peter' (1893–1971)

RAF officer. Air Member for Personnel on the Air Council, 1939–40; Air officer commanding-in-chief Bomber Command, 1940; Chief of the Air Staff, 1940–45.

Reith, Sir John (1889–1971)

Public servant. First general manager of the BBC, 1922, then managing director, 1923, and director-general, 1927–38; chairman of Imperial Airways, 1938–39; first chairman of British Overseas Airways Corporation, 1939–40; Minister of Information, 1940; Minister of Transport, 1940; first Minister of Works, 1940–42, leading to Ministry of Works and Planning; lieutenant-commander, Royal Naval Volunteer Reserve (RNVR), Coastal Forces, 1942; extra naval assistant to 3rd Sea Lord, 1943; captain, RNVR; director of Combined Operations Material Department, Admiralty, 1943–45.

Rothermere, Lord (Harold Harmsworth) (1868–1940)

Newspaper proprietor and politician. Secretary of State for Air, 1917–18. Appeaser but strong advocate of air rearmament.

Runciman, Lord (1870–1949)

British politician. Headed the British mission to Czechoslovakia, July–September 1938.

Salmond, Sir John (1881–1968)
RAF officer. Air officer commanding-in-chief, Air Defence of Great Britain, 1925–28; Chief of the Air Staff, 1930–33. Plotted with Beaverbrook and Trenchard to remove Newall and Dowding from office.

Sandys, Duncan (1908–87)
Conservative politician. Diplomatic Service, 1930; MP Norwood division of Lambeth, 1935–45, Streatham, 1950–February 1974; commissioned in Territorial Army (Royal Artillery) lieutenant-colonel, 1941; Financial Secretary to War Office, 1941–43; Parliamentary Secretary, Ministry of Supply, responsible for armament production, 1943–44; chairman, War Cabinet Committee for defence against German flying bombs and rockets, 1943–45; Minister of Works, 1944–45; Minister of Supply, October 1951–October 1954; Minister of Housing and Local Government, October 1954–January 1957; Minister of Defence, January 1957–October 1959; Minister of Aviation, October 1959–July 1960; Secretary of State for Commonwealth Relations, July 1960–October 1964; chairman Lonrho, 1972–84. Married Diana Churchill in 1935, divorced in 1960.

Simon, Sir John (1873–1954)
Politician and lawyer. Foreign Secretary, 1931–35; Home Secretary, 1935–37; Chancellor of Exchequer, 1937–40. One of the top figures in Chamberlain's government.

Sinclair, Sir Archibald Baronet (1890–1970)
Politician. Leader of the Opposition, Liberal Party, 1935–45. Close to Churchill, whose adjutant he had been during the First World War when Churchill commanded a battalion in combat on the Western Front. Swung Liberal Party in favour of rearmament. Secretary of State for Air, 1940–45. Whipping boy for Beaverbrook and Churchill.

Singleton, Justice Sir John (1885–1957)
Judge, 1934–48. Conducted inquiries on behalf of Winston Churchill

during the war on controversial topics: manufacture of stabilised bomb sights (Beaverbrook wrongly thought this was into the wider behaviour of RAF leadership); estimates of Luftwaffe strength; the effectiveness of bombing Germany; and supply of Churchill tanks).

Smith F. E., Lord Birkenhead (1872–1930)

Barrister and Conservative politician. Lord High Chancellor of Great Britain, 1919–22; Secretary for India, 1924–28. Despite notional party differences, a great friend of Churchill. Also a reactionary over India.

Spears, Edward (1886–1974)

Army officer, Conservative MP and businessman. Friend of Churchill who encountered him during the First World War where he conducted high-level liaison with the French Army. Intermittent opponent of appeasement but also linked to Sir Joseph Ball, Chamberlain's personal adviser. Major-general, 1940; Churchill's personal representative with the French Prime Minister and Minister of Defence, May–June 1940; head of British mission to General de Gaulle, June 1940, and to Syria and Lebanon, July 1941; head of Spears mission, Syria and Lebanon, July 1941; First Minister to Republics of Syria and Lebanon, 1942–44. Fell out badly with de Gaulle.

Strakosch, Sir Henry (1871–1943)

Financier. City contact of Bracken. Rescued Churchill from the financial consequences of unwise investments in US equities during the Great Slump.

Stuart, James (1891–1971)

Conservative MP. Deputy Chief Whip, 1935–41; government Chief Whip, 1941–45. Another of Chamberlain's whips who transferred their allegiance to Churchill.

Swinton, Lord (1884–1972)
Politician. Born Philip Lloyd-Graeme and adopted surname Cunliffe-Lister in 1924. Secretary of State for Air, 1935–38; Minister of Civil Aviation, 1944–45.

Tallents, Sir Stephen (1884–1958)
Publicist and public servant. Secretary to Empire Marketing Board, 1926–33; public relations officer, General Post Office, 1933–35; director-general designate, Ministry of Information, 1936–39; controller public relations of the BBC, 1935–40, and overseas services, 1940–41.

Taylor, A. J. P. (1906–90)
Historian. Began with a low opinion of Beaverbrook but gradually was won over to a positive view. He became a well-paid columnist on the *Sunday Express* and the first (and last) director of the Beaverbrook Library.

Tedder, Sir Arthur (1890–1967)
RAF officer, director-general of Research and Development, 1938–40; air officer commanding-in-chief Middle East, 1941–43; air commander-in-chief Mediterranean Air Command, 1943; Deputy Supreme Commander under General Eisenhower, 1943–45.

Tizard, Sir Henry (1885–1959)
Scientist, science administrator and government adviser. Experimental Royal Flying Corps pilot and assistant controller of experiments and research during the First World War. Rector of Imperial College London, 1929–42; chairman Committee of Imperial Defence committee for the scientific study of air defence, 1935–40. Advocate of radar and other scientific aids. Feuded with Lindemann.

Trenchard, Sir Hugh (1873–1956)
RAF officer. General Officer Commanding Royal Flying Corps, France, 1915; Chief of Air Staff, 1918; General Officer Commanding

Independent Air Force, March 1918; Chief of Air Staff, 1919; commissioner, Metropolitan Police Force, 1931–35. Trenchard was raised to the peerage in 1930. He was a passionate advocate of the view that future wars would be won by bombing. Conspired with Beaverbrook and Salmond against Newall and Dowding.

Wardlaw-Milne, Sir John (1879–1967)
Conservative politician. MP for Kidderminster, 1922–45.

Watson-Watt, Robert (1892–1973)
Government scientist. Superintendent radio department of the National Physical Laboratory, 1933; appointed to lead development of RDF (now called radar) at Air Ministry, 1935. Often erroneously considered the inventor of radar.

Waugh, Evelyn (1901–66)
Writer. Moved in London high society in the 1920s and 1930s. Military service in Layforce in 1941, together with Randolph Churchill, who took him on his mission to the Yugoslav partisan forces in 1944. Consistently helped by Bracken as Minister of Information, whom he caricatured as Rex Mottram in *Brideshead Revisited*.

Wavell, Sir Archibald (1883–1950)
Army officer. Commander-in-chief, Middle East, 1939–41; commander-in-chief, India, 1941–43; Supreme Commander, South-West Pacific, January–March 1942; Viceroy and Governor General of India, 1943–47. Churchill's bête noire amongst the generals.

Westminster, Duke of, 'Bendor' (1879–1953)
Aristocrat. Friend of Churchill but pro-appeasement.

Wilson, Sir Horace (1882–1979)
Civil servant. Personal civil service adviser to Baldwin then

Chamberlain, based at 10 Downing Street, 1935–40; head of the civil service, 1939–42. The éminence grise of the Chamberlain government who resolutely fought anyone who opposed appeasement. Sidelined by Churchill when he became Prime Minister.

Wimperis, Harry (1876–1960)
Government scientist. Director of scientific research, Air Ministry, 1925–37. Early advocate of radar.

Winterton, Lord (1883–1962)
Conservative politician. Under-Secretary for India, 1922–24 and November 1924–29; Chancellor of Duchy of Lancaster, 1937–39; deputy to Secretary of State for Air, March–May 1938. Diehard over India. Incompetent Air Minister.

Wood, Sir Kingsley (1881–1943)
Politician. Postmaster General, 1931; Minister of Health, 1935; Secretary of State for Air in succession to Swinton, 1938–40. Had earned a great reputation promoting the public telephone service but left the practicalities of air rearmament to his subordinates. Delivered the decisive advice to Chamberlain that he should resign in May 1940. Chancellor of the Exchequer 1940–43.

Zuckerman, Solly (1904–93)
Demonstrator and lecturer in human anatomy, 1934–45, Oxford University; Oxford Extra-Mural Unit of Ministry of Home Security, 1940–41; scientific adviser to Combined Operations Headquarters, 1941–43; adviser RAF Middle East, 1943–44; scientific adviser on planning Allied Expeditionary Air Force, 1944–46

INTRODUCTION: FRIENDSHIP AND CHURCHILL

It is a truism to describe Winston Churchill as a towering figure. No one doubts his stature. Even the most enthusiastic of his many detractors has never claimed that he was insignificant, although every aspect of his greatness has been held up to critical examination and been found wanting by some.

The aura and reputation of the great figures of history can often mask the human being which lies behind. The scale of the events and ideas with which they are associated can make us lose sight of the fact that they were subject to the same instincts and needs as us all. Churchill stands out amongst the big people of history as most obviously cut from ordinary human cloth, not least because it is easy to understand what he was thinking. If ever a huge personality wore their heart on their sleeve, it was Churchill. We can read the intentions and opinions which lay behind his achievements with unusual clarity. We can understand him. It is easy to believe we know him as a person. He is arguably one of the most human of history's big names.

The importance of friendship is one of the defining characteristics of humanity. It is one that Churchill shared to an immense extent, a facet of his warm and emotional character. The company of people he liked, or in whom he found something to like, was an elemental pleasure to him. What he wanted and expected of others ran the full gamut of needs and desires. To those that met them, he was capable of profound loyalty which went far beyond any calculation of self-interest. Friendships are often asymmetric and unbalanced, but that does not make them any the less a key part of the lives of the individuals involved. Looking at Churchill, the historical figure, somehow distinct from the individual, will only give part of the story.

The size of Churchill's personality and the scale of the historical events with which he was involved cast long shadows which can easily obscure those around him. To thrive, those around powerful figures must often abase themselves and flatten their own personalities, make themselves insignificant. The reverse is true of Churchill. His greatest friends were strong, distinct personalities. Churchill's ambition and self-confidence translated into egoism, not uncommon in senior politicians, if not the rule, but this is different to the vanity of power. The cut and thrust of conversations were some of Churchill's great joys in life and were something that cautious sycophants could not give. They work by feeding self-regard. Churchill wanted and needed something quite different.

The friends whom this book examines resembled Churchill in their openness and accessibility. All were incomplete personalities; all maintained barriers of some kind; but none effaced themselves. What you saw was what you got. It might have been baffling or repulsive, but it was not the product of compromise. It would be naive to suppose that the friends did not adjust their behaviour to get the best from Churchill's volatile personality, but their integrity stayed intact.

Throughout his life, Churchill was noted as a foul-weather friend, willing to stick by acquaintances when they were going through difficult periods. It is one of his most attractive characteristics. Often it was repaid by a degree of loyalty and affection that is not necessarily the common coin of politics. In a similar vein, Churchill's wilderness friends appeared to transcend unappealing calculations of self-interest. It would be foolish to assert that there was no self-interest whatever in what drew Frederick Lindemann and Brendan Bracken to Churchill; part of his appeal was the same magnetism and strength of personality that made him such a force in politics.

A graph of Churchill's political standing would show sharp fluctuations from top-level influence at a national scale to near insignificance, taking in almost every intermediate stage. The classic pattern of steady rise to power and the associated accumulation of subsidiary figures that goes with it is not Churchill's story. The friends discussed in this book were with him all the way, closer at some times than at others, but still part of his life.

Churchill was a man of strong ideas, but he was also a flexible, pragmatic politician: 'It is better to be both right and consistent. But if you have to choose – you must choose to be right.'[1] Notoriously, he changed his political party allegiance twice, but his life was defined by big, simple causes which he followed faithfully. Two were catastrophically wrong – opposing autonomy for India and supporting King Edward VIII in the abdication crisis – but one was entirely right: that Britain needed to rearm to be able to survive against a Germany ruled by Hitler. Many of Churchill's detractors wish to obfuscate this and elevate Neville Chamberlain's reputation to do so. Certainly, it is easy to find flaws in the detail of Churchill's proposed policies, both conceptually and in terms of practical politics, but it is impossible to claim that Chamberlain was correct to believe that a peaceful modus vivendi with Hitler was the best way forwards.

In all three causes – India, rearmament and the abdication – some friends were involved, supporting Churchill, with one exception where a friend saw his error and tried to save him from himself. His lost causes – India and Edward VIII – were, at least in hindsight, doomed from the start in themselves, so it is idle to ask whether the friends weakened Churchill here. Churchill's stance on his lost causes, though, created a vicious circle in which the standing of his supporters suffered as much as his and compromised the seriousness with which he was treated over his ultimately winning cause, rearmament.

Compromise, fudge and half-measures did not belong in his make-up. If he suppressed a belief for the sake of expediency, he did so with clarity and commitment, distasteful though this might have been. Above all, Churchill knew that Britain had to have a truly national government to fight the Second World War and was willing to set aside his visceral hatred of socialism to achieve this. He similarly acquiesced in alliance with the Soviet Union for pragmatic reasons but saw clear limits to what was possible and necessary, unlike one of his friends. He was just as clearsighted on how an alliance with the USA was key to victory, but here he could be wholehearted as well. As the war was coming to an end, he reverted to his principled opposition to socialism with the encouragement of two friends.

When Churchill attained power in 1940, his friends stayed with him (one, not for long). He brought them into his government in the widest sense, because he needed them. He gave them power and made some sacrifices to do so, but he knew he needed other politicians, bureaucrats and military men just as much as them, so the friends had power but not control. Churchill never doubted the importance of democracy, and his wartime regime gave a voice not only to his friends but to the military and political establishments as well. The three-party wartime national government did not make politics disappear as if by magic, and Churchill's personal position was complex and he needed allies. Like any Prime Minister, he wanted people whom he could trust personally at key positions in the machinery of government. In turn, his friends did not supplant established structures however much they might have disliked them.

* * *

This book looks closely at four of Churchill's friends and two members of his family who were also part of his public life – Max Aitken (Lord Beaverbrook), Frederick Lindemann (Lord Cherwell), Brendan Bracken, Bob Boothby, Randolph Churchill and Duncan Sandys. The intensity of the relationships varied; two came practically to an end, but the others lasted for their lifetimes. All were substantial figures in their own right, although only one would have anything more than a tiny fraction of his historical standing without Churchill.

Lord Beaverbrook's friendship with Churchill was the most uneven and erratic of the group, which rather reflects Beaverbrook's own ambivalent personality. He had tasted power and craved it but only on his own terms. He relished politics, but he was not a working politician.

He could never make the bridge between his easy existence as the autocratic owner of a large profitable business and the contingency and compromises of government. The balance of power in Beaverbrook's relationship with Churchill was the most complex of the group. Even when Churchill was Prime Minister, Beaverbrook enjoyed an unmatched personal standing with him. Churchill needed the psychological boost of Beaverbrook and his optimism and positivity.

By contrast, the mutual loyalty and commitment between Churchill and two of his friends, Professor Frederick Lindemann and Brendan Bracken, was unshakeable and stayed constant both in power and out. Lindemann was a friend who only gradually became a colleague as their common belief in the importance of rearmament came to dominate Churchill's political life. Churchill revered him for his intelligence and clarity of thought. Lindemann was his closest and most consistent wartime colleague. Bracken successfully aspired to become Churchill's colleague and doggedly supported him through thick and thin. He helped Churchill dig himself into a hole over India and then dig himself out in the fight against appeasement. He showed his loyalty to Churchill when he sacrificed his position as a close colleague to take an unloved and unpromising wartime ministerial job. Bracken was utterly loyal but anything but slavish. At the risk of delving into amateur psychology, Bracken appears as something of the kind of son whom Churchill wanted.

The fight for rearmament and against appeasement was by far the most important cause of Churchill's life. It had to be sustained against the overwhelming hostility of most of British public and political opinion, which took immense moral courage on his part and those of his allies to challenge. It was the acid test of loyalty and united all the figures in this book except for Beaverbrook. Churchill's son Randolph faithfully supported his father over India to their mutual cost. Randolph's hugely flawed personality made him a disappointment and then a burden to his father. Bob Boothby rekindled his friendship and collaboration with Churchill when he recognised independently the threat which Hitler posed and the vital importance of standing up to him. Boothby was too much of a friend to Churchill to let him commit suicide over the abdication, but he paid a personal cost for having done so. He was also a professional politician and hedged his bets too often to earn the benefits of unconditional loyalty. Duncan Sandys, who married Churchill's daughter Diana, had no difficulty backing his father-in-law over appeasement and reaped the benefits in the form of wartime political preferment.

But the friends were anything but a cohesive group. Beaverbrook and Lindemann were notoriously prone to long and savage vendettas and conducted a venomous feud with each other for most of the war. Sandys also fell foul of Lindemann over one of the professor's pet projects and their dislike and distrust deeply marked Britain's preparations to fight Germany's V-weapons. Beaverbrook was jealous of Bracken and competed for Churchill's loyalty.[2] But they did join forces when Churchill swung back to his traditional anti-socialism at the end of the war as a return to party politics loomed.

This story of Churchill and his friends is anything but the complete story of Churchill, but it covers some of the most important episodes in his career. No attempt has been made to manufacture a flattering or unduly respectful picture of what happened. They, as much as he did, made mistakes, but this does not detract from any of them. The friends and the friendships were a vital part of Churchill's life and his story.

1

RETURN TRIP TO
THE WILDERNESS

Winston Churchill made his first foray into the political wilderness during the First World War, and he liked it no better than either of his next ones. It was the first break in a meteoric political career that had seen him elected to Parliament at the age of twenty-five, a Cabinet minister at thirty-three and the holder of one of the great offices of state at thirty-five. Becoming the First Lord of the Admiralty and the political head of Britain's premier fighting service in 1911 as the First World War approached and then broke out seemed a step forwards in his career, a move towards being a great war leader like his ancestor, 1st Duke of Marlborough. The first months of the war appeared to bear this out. At first, the mobilisation of the Royal Navy for war had gone with impeccable smoothness. The pretensions of Imperial Germany to challenge Britain's global maritime predominance appeared to evaporate almost overnight. Britain's army was ferried to France to join the land war with Germany entirely unhampered. A minor defeat at the Battle of Coronel off the coast of Chile was swiftly and massively avenged at the Battle of the Falkland Islands. Moreover, Coronel fell squarely into the tradition of British heroic defeats with the commanding admiral losing his life. Even the Royal Navy's one conspicuous embarrassment was not a defeat but its failure to sink two German warships that seemed to be at its mercy. These ships, the *Goeben* and the *Emden*, were able to flee to safety in Turkey and this contributed to Turkey's decision to enter the war on Germany's side.

Here things began to go seriously wrong for Churchill. He believed

that Turkey could be defeated easily and quickly by forcing the Darda-
nelles Strait and attacking the capital, Istanbul. He won Cabinet approval for the plan, but the initial, purely naval attack was beaten off.
Next the British tried an amphibious operation against the Gallipoli
Peninsula, but this degenerated into a bloody stalemate of trench warfare just as the larger campaign in France had done. Neither phase
of the attack was well thought out or planned, so Churchill's grand
strategic calculation was never put to the test. Churchill certainly deserves blame for this episode, but he also served as a useful political
scapegoat. It was almost inevitable that he would be removed from
the Admiralty. His demotion to the minor, non-departmental job of
Chancellor of the Duchy of Lancaster was little short of an outright
dismissal from government. The arrival of the Conservatives in government, albeit as junior partners in the coalition, in May 1915 further
undermined Churchill's position. Churchill may well simply have
judged that he would have been sacked entirely and anticipated this
by resigning voluntarily, going to France as a mere infantry battalion
commander. His qualification for this was minimal: after school he
had served as a cavalry subaltern and then been a minor officer on
the staff of Kitchener in the invasion of Sudan, but the move fulfilled
his craving to command in combat operation. In the early days of the
war, he had seriously proposed leaving his political responsibilities to
take personal command of the British defence of Antwerp. These aspirations cemented a growing reputation for impulsiveness if not downright instability. Churchill's departure for France was also unsound
political tactics. To parlay a spectacular resignation into a spectacular
return to office, he would have needed a substantial body of support
amongst the rank and file of the governing party or with other ministers. Churchill never tried to recruit the mundane claque of less gifted
followers that is indispensable to the first element and he also managed
to inspire passionate distrust and hostility from more conventional
politicians. He had defected from the Conservatives, for whom he had
first been elected to Parliament 1900, to the Liberals in 1904 and had
rapidly been rewarded with ministerial office. The Conservative leader

Andrew Bonar Law detested Churchill. Not merely did Churchill lack support, he also faced powerful positive opposition. Bonar Law was a dangerous enemy and had held the principal position since 1911, when he emerged as a middle-way candidate in a leadership election marred by two divisive issues: Unionism and tariff reform. His rivals were Walter Long, who was seen as a firm, albeit moderate, Unionist, and Austen Chamberlain, who was an advocate of tariff reform. Bonar Law went on to lead the Conservatives until 1923. His importance as party leader eclipsed his career as a minister. He was Chancellor of the Exchequer in David Lloyd George's government, but the office is far less important in wartime than peace. Bonar Law did become Prime Minister but terminal cancer limited his time in Downing Street to a few months.

When Lloyd George replaced Herbert Asquith as Prime Minister in late 1916, Churchill had some reason to hope his political fortunes had turned. Churchill had been a close ally of Lloyd George in Asquith's pre-war Liberal administration. They had been partners at the radical wing of the government, promoting measures of economic reform and social justice. They also shared a deep strain of unconventionality and personal sympathy, strong but short of outright friendship. Churchill had actively spoken out on Lloyd George's side during the Marconi scandal of 1912 which could easily have ended Lloyd George's career. Lloyd George certainly wanted to bring Churchill into his new government. He would be far more of a loyal personal follower than his Conservative allies in the coup against Asquith, and he had political talents manifestly lacking amongst the mainstream Conservative mediocrities and a growing number of technocrats who featured ever more in the wartime government. But Lloyd George faced severe headwinds. It was Bonar Law's decision to back Lloyd George that decided Asquith's fate. To secure the support of the Conservatives for his government, Lloyd George had specifically promised Bonar Law that he would not bring Churchill back as a minister. Lloyd George would need to get his feet far more firmly under the table before he contemplated seriously taking the risk of Churchill's return.

The bad news came to Churchill through Max Aitken, Lord Beaverbrook. He had been one of the many players in the removal of Herbert Asquith from office. In his book *Politicians and the War*, Beaverbrook later claimed to have been a major force in the coup, but his contribution was far from decisive. Beaverbrook consistently imagined that his power and influence was greater than it was in fact. Like Beaverbrook, Bonar Law had grown up in Canada and, more important than this shared heritage, the two men had extensive business dealings which had begun whilst they were still in Canada and were highly lucrative to Bonar Law. These continued after Bonar Law entered the Cabinet and were the major, if not the dominant, part of the relationship. Beaverbrook's generally adulatory biographer A. J. P. Taylor estimated the benefit to Bonar Law at the then colossal sum of £10,000 per year. Even in the gentler ethical standards of the era, the relationship was questionable. Beaverbrook's personal political standing was modest, but as Bonar Law's jackal, he was a power in the land. Beaverbrook had built a fortune in his native Canada through obscure financial dealings, which many in the Canadian business and political establishment labelled as dishonest and corrupt. He had come to Britain with hopes of parlaying this fortune into political influence. To begin with, he pursued the conventional path of winning a seat in the House of Commons, but the world of Parliament was never one that appealed to him or that offered a profitable field of action for his talents. He was happy to swap the House of Commons for the House of Lords and took the peerage under which he is best known. He far preferred the world of hidden influence and intrigue.

As Lloyd George was forming his government on 5 December 1916, Beaverbrook and Churchill had dinner together in the company of the lawyer and politician F. E. Smith, an intimate ally of Churchill.[1] Beaverbrook later claimed in his memoir *Politicians and the War* that he had been charged by Lloyd George with hinting to Churchill that he would be left out of the new government. According to Beaverbrook, Churchill became violently angry as well as being predictably disappointed. Whatever the truth, Churchill described it as one of the toughest moments of his life. It may have helped set the tone for their future relationship. Even if Beaverbrook was only acting as Bonar Law's messenger, he was still in the position of power. The episode might have been bitter, but it did not deter Churchill from persisting with Lloyd George. He gave him striking and effective support in a secret parliamentary debate on the conduct of the war. By July 1917, Lloyd George was confident enough to bring Churchill back into the government as the Minister of Munitions. This was a key job in the war government and had been held by another Liberal, Christopher Addison, who was one of Lloyd George's closest and most loyal allies. Addison left the Ministry of Munitions willingly to take up the question of post-war reconstruction. The Conservative reaction was the only potential obstacle. By Beaverbrook's later and suspect account, Lloyd George chose not to tell Bonar Law directly and, with a degree of symmetry, sent Beaverbrook to bring the bad news to him. Beaverbrook claimed that Lloyd George had used the pretext that as Beaverbrook had been advocating Churchill's return to the new Prime Minister, the task was rightfully his. Beaverbrook reported that Bonar Law believed that the appointment might come at a heavy price to Lloyd George – 'Lloyd George's throne will shake' – but Bonar Law rode out pressure from his backbenchers and refused to make an issue of Churchill's return.[2]

Churchill remained as a minister for as long as Lloyd George held office and the pattern of master–servant relationship endured. Churchill paid the penalty of having a weak political constituency of his own. As opposition to Lloyd George amongst the Conservatives grew, ultimately to fatal levels, Churchill had no real alternative but to tie his fortunes to those of Lloyd George. Bonar Law's mainstream Conservatives did not need defections from what came to be labelled 'the thieves' kitchen' of the coalition government;[3] they just wanted their leader to pull his support.

2

THE TWO RONIN

Once he had been brought back into government, Winston Churchill remained a minister as long as David Lloyd George's coalition endured. He could share the kudos that it earned as the government that won the war. Lloyd George reaped the reward for military triumph in the shape of a resounding win for the coalition at the 'coupon' general election of December 1918 held immediately after the Armistice. The victory masked a severe deterioration in Lloyd George's political position and, by extension, Churchill's. Churchill held his seat at Dundee by a comparatively narrow margin. The true victors in terms of solid political coin were Andrew Bonar Law's Conservatives, who increased their number of MPs by more than one third and provided even more of the parliamentary bedrock on which Lloyd George's power rested. The Conservatives won 379 seats and the Liberals only 127. The Conservative MPs were becoming ever-more disenchanted with the coalition and the dubious characters who appeared to dominate the Cabinet. Lloyd George had split the Liberal Party by turning against Herbert Asquith and it remained split. But worse for Lloyd George and Churchill was that those Liberals elected to support the coalition did not form a cohesive group. Neither Lloyd George nor his ministerial allies succeeded, despite lavishly financed attempts in Lloyd George's case, in building significant independent constituencies for themselves. Lloyd George funded his party-building from the blatant sale of honours, many to conspicuously unworthy recipients. Lloyd George's touts offended the Conservatives by approaching potential buyers whom they regarded as their party's preserve.

Lloyd George's peacetime government was tumultuous and

unstable. Even his personal allies did not constitute a harmonious bloc. His old ally from his days of radical social measures, Christopher Addison, failed as Minister of Health, attracted Conservative ire for heavy government spending and was increasingly out of step with the government's rightward drift. He resigned and began a bitter public feud against his old friend. Lloyd George controversially appointed F. E. Smith as Lord High Chancellor, but Smith's increasingly drink-fuelled wilful behaviour dented the government's image. Perversely, Churchill's most important achievement came when he reversed his previous hard-line stance and shepherded through Irish independence, which was only reluctantly accepted by most Conservatives.

Churchill was a key figure in the second coalition government. After the Armistice in 1918, he was put in charge of shrinking the army and the Royal Air Force to meet peacetime requirements. Next in 1921, he was Secretary of State for the Colonies, handling uprisings in Ireland and Iraq. Churchill fought battles against Lloyd George, notably over recognising the Soviet Union, and won some of them, but he could do nothing to uncouple his fate from Lloyd George. They would stand or fall together. But being trapped by a common destiny is not the same as creating a common front stronger than the individuals. For all their occasional and deep disputes over policy, Lloyd George and Churchill were close. Churchill classed himself as Lloyd George's 'principal lieutenant'. The problems of peace offered far less scope for either to build a heroic reputation. The urgent need to win the war had been the justification for Lloyd George to be wartime coalition leader and his sometimes-questionable expedients; the challenges of post-war Britain offered no such get-out clause. Lloyd George was one of the leading figures in the succession of summit conferences which sought to rebuild a lasting European order after the war, but his international status was of little help at home. He still needed the votes of the Conservative MPs to govern.

Whilst Lloyd George battled unavailingly to replicate his achievements of wartime, Bonar Law bided his time. His political capital remained intact. Conservative grandees such as Lord Curzon and

Austen Chamberlain were loyal to him. As well as the backbench mediocrities, he could count on the continuing support of Lord Beaverbrook. His newspaper empire was not yet the mighty beast that it was to become, but in the frantic haggling and plotting of the peacetime coalition, Beaverbrook had his part to play. His authority and influence stemmed wholly from his relationship with Bonar Law, but it was powerful nonetheless. As a senior minister, Churchill outranked Beaverbrook in the ostensible pecking order, but in the hidden balance of power, the future belonged to the Canadian. That the peacetime coalition survived as long as it did may have been due to the accident of Bonar Law's health which forced him to step down from politics, resigning the leadership of the Conservative Party in March 1921. He was replaced by Sir Austen Chamberlain who proved inept and ineffectual. He also offered the Conservative rank and file a convenient lightning rod for their unhappiness at the Irish settlement.

By the autumn of 1921, Bonar Law's health had recovered almost completely and he returned to politics. The turn of the year found Churchill, Beaverbrook, Lloyd George and Bonar Law all at Cannes, moving from one luxury hotel to the next. Lloyd George had practically run through his political capital and the cracks in the rickety edifice of his coalition were all too apparent. The instability and uncertainty that resulted were Beaverbrook's natural hunting ground. Beaverbrook had established himself as the indispensable middleman between Bonar Law, Churchill and Lloyd George. Lloyd George had pulled off a last-minute escape from the Irish trap with a deal that was pragmatic and inevitable, albeit distasteful to most Tories and anathema to Bonar Law. Lloyd George had brought F. E. Smith, now Lord Birkenhead, and Churchill into the discussion about Ireland to draw their fangs. Lloyd George's only hope of salvation lay in a general election in which Beaverbrook's newspapers would have played a major role. Best of all for Beaverbrook, Bonar Law's star was rising and he had only to bide his time to win big from a restoration of conventional party politics. Beaverbrook did not hold back from making plain how much he expected deference from the full-time politicians.

As Churchill reported to his wife, Clementine 'Clemmie' Churchill, with some amusement, Beaverbrook was being *exigeant* (demanding):

> Today I move to the Negresco [hotel]. Nice to stay with Max for a couple of days ... My dear, he was furious with me for urging him to come out here & then not being at the Mont-Fleury when he arrived! Such a to-do. The PM anxiously pacifying him. Bonar stroking him.[1]

Lloyd George's final error was the Chanak crisis, an exercise in diplomatic adventurism, which brought Britain to the brink of war with Turkey. In October 1922, the Conservative backbenchers staged an open revolt. At a meeting in the Carlton Club, they pulled the party's support from the coalition and drove Lloyd George from office. Austen Chamberlain also paid the price for his loyalty to the coalition and he was replaced as party leader by Bonar Law. The relics of the coalition government disintegrated rapidly. Senior Conservative coalition ministers refused to serve in Bonar Law's government. He was left with what Churchill dubbed a 'second eleven' Cabinet because it did not feature the high-profile Conservative figures of Austen Chamberlain and Birkenhead. Churchill himself did not feature either; he was still nominally a Liberal and, worse, in the general election that followed Lloyd George's ousting, he lost his parliamentary seat at Dundee to a combination of Labour and a local prohibitionist candidate, who won both seats for the two-member constituency.

A page had turned in British politics. Lloyd George had been removed from power and he was never to return. The two wings of the Liberal Party, split since Lloyd George's rise to Prime Minister in 1916, reunited but out of weakness rather than genuine reconciliation. The enduring mutual suspicion of Lloyd George and Herbert Asquith was a fatal obstacle to either ever regaining high political office or any hope of a serious recovery in the Liberal Party's standing. Thus began the era of dominance by the Conservatives, who would be by far the strongest force in British politics until the Second World War. Moreover, there was no room for the glamorous figures of Lloyd George's coalitions. It was the low-key instincts of Conservative Party backbench MPs who set the tone.

But Bonar Law and Beaverbrook had only 211 days in which to enjoy this revolution. Bonar Law was stricken with terminal throat cancer and forced to resign as PM in May 1923. He died soon afterwards. Beaverbrook had never been under serious consideration for a seat in Bonar Law's Cabinet, even if he had wanted one, but he was perfectly positioned to operate as a hidden string-puller with the support of his friend and business partner. Beaverbrook gave an unwitting picture of how he might have imagined his contribution to a long-lasting Bonar Law premiership many years later when he came to promote his own version of the 1936 abdication crisis in his book *The Abdication of King Edward VIII*. It features Beaverbrook's bitter complaints at the relationship between then PM Stanley Baldwin and the editor of *The Times*, Geoffrey Dawson. Beaverbrook painted Dawson as Baldwin's intimate adviser whose counsel had been sought ahead of each step in the crisis, long before he ever discussed anything with ministers. Dawson would dearly have loved to be treated as a journalistic statesman in the crisis and was a regular visitor to 10 Downing Street, which provided a foundation of factual events on which Beaverbrook could build a fantasy of a PM working hand in glove with his journalistic consigliere. Baldwin did indulge Dawson; *The Times* was a significant force and Baldwin only very rarely shut the door completely, but all he truly wanted or needed was a dependable mouthpiece to communicate with the public as and when he felt the moment arrived. Lord Camrose's *Daily Telegraph* fitted the bill admirably. The image of Dawson as a powerful conservative establishment player in the abdication has endured to this day, but it is no more than a double fantasy: Beaverbrook's vision of himself as Bonar Law's trusted adviser, projected onto a hate-figure journalist in contact with a hate-figure politician. Bonar Law's resignation and death meant that it is pure speculation as to whether he would have indulged Beaverbrook to this extent.

By the end of 1923, both Churchill and Beaverbrook were ronin

– masterless men who had lost the leaders who gave the final seal of authority to their doings. Each had to set out to build autonomous careers. Beaverbrook had his growing and financially successful newspaper on which to fall back. It was powerful and absorbing. Other men would have been perfectly content to devote their lives and efforts to it alone, but Beaverbrook had glimpsed the paradise of top-level power. For the rest of his life, he tried to regain this status. If he could not exercise power, he worked mischief. Disrupting the plans and lives of others was one of Beaverbrook's pleasures in life. Delivered with impish grins, some found this charming, but many found it hateful. At its worst, Beaverbrook's instinct took the form of savage, outright vendettas against individuals who had challenged him or otherwise attracted his ire conducted through his newspaper empire.

Churchill's absence from the House of Commons meant that his second excursion into the political desert was more comprehensive than his first, but it was much less of an ordeal and in some ways positively constructive. It opened another phase in his life. He was no longer the young man in a hurry but still had far to go to reach elder-statesman status. The loss of a minister's salary stimulated Churchill's activity as a highly paid writer and science and politics overlapped in Churchill's journalism. The future shape of warfare in an age of technology was a favoured theme. His first book had been published at the age of twenty-three and authorship came naturally to him and was almost as much an integral part of his career as politics itself. Moreover, he could now turn his hand to writing history, with himself naturally at the centre. In 1923, he completed the first of two volumes of *The World Crisis*, his account of the First World War. The project featured a then gigantic publisher's advance of £5,000. By coincidence, £5,000 was also the fee he was to receive for his sole foray into the world of big business. He was commissioned to advise on, in practice to lobby in favour of, a merger between Royal Dutch Shell and Burmah's Anglo-Persian Oil, in which the government had a major holding. As First Lord of the Admiralty, Churchill had been instrumental in switching the Royal Navy to oil power from coal, so he knew fully the strategic issues involved. The money was all the more important as Churchill had just bought a large house, Chartwell, with all the costs it involved. Churchill's desire to go further than his father, Lord Randolph, who had fallen victim to his own political misjudgement and then illness lay close to his heart. The reputation of his great ancestor, 1st Duke of Marlborough, illuminated his view of British history. On a more mundane level, Chartwell soon became the focus of Churchill's social life. Good company and the pleasures of the table and the bottle were central to Churchill's existence. His restless spirit never allowed him to stand still and as his political career slipped into a more settled pattern, he found hobbies to give him new challenges. He even contributed a little to the redevelopment of Chartwell through his surprising passion for bricklaying. Chartwell also provided him with a full-scale artist's studio for his other new passion, painting. Paint and easel became a routine feature of his luggage for his frequent journeys abroad.

Politics did not remain in the background for very long and Churchill's first objective was to return to Parliament. Another general election was called in December 1923 as the new Prime Minister, Stanley Baldwin, who had surged from comparative obscurity to succeed Bonar Law sought a firm electoral mandate for his purely Conservative government. Baldwin doubled up on his call for political renewal by adding tariffs to his platform. This sharpened the distinction from the Liberals and briefly cast Churchill in a firmly Liberal light as he stood for them at Leicester West. It was his last hurrah as a Liberal. His time as a coalitionist had stretched his Liberal allegiance to breaking point, but he had now backed away from the principle of free trade. Churchill lost at Leicester, so it is impossible to tell whether he would have reconciled himself to the decision of the Liberal Party leadership to support the Labour Party, which had doubled its number of seats and formed a coalition government with the Liberals. Churchill reacted with horror to what he saw as a disastrous move which sparked his final break with the Liberals. Within months, Churchill was courting the Conservative candidacy for a by-election in the Westminster Abbey constituency. He was still too divisive a figure for him to be fully accepted by all the party's leaders and he stood as an independent, albeit presenting himself as closer to the Conservatives than the Liberals. Briefly, the idea was floated of him leading a breakaway group of anti-Labour liberals, but when Ramsay MacDonald fell as Prime Minister, in his turn triggering the third general election in barely two years, Churchill and the Conservative leaders cobbled together a formulation for him to stand as a 'Constitutionalist' with Conservative backing. He was elected for Epping (which eventually became Woodford), the seat he was to hold until he retired; but he always stood at some distance from the Conservative Party.

When Stanley Baldwin formed his government after winning a healthy majority for the Conservatives, he did not leave the former coalitionist ministers out in the cold where they might have caused difficulties. Austen Chamberlain was given the Foreign Office where he earned the Garter and a Nobel Peace Prize for his contribution to the Locarno Treaty. This did not diminish his sense of his own importance. Lord Birkenhead was made Secretary for India, where he could indulge his reactionary instincts without an excessive workload. Baldwin wanted to separate Churchill comprehensively from the Liberals and he made sure of this. Baldwin was fortunate that there were no high-profile pure Conservative aspirants for the Chancellorship of the Exchequer. Rather to his own surprise, Churchill was offered the job and accepted with alacrity. It was a high office, but it was not one that offered Churchill scope for mischief. It was not a brief that played to Churchill's strength or interests. Baldwin boasted that the Exchequer would restrict Churchill's field of activities to finance, in particular keeping him out of labour relations questions on which he was dangerously hawkish.[2] Under a Conservative government, he was never going to repeat the radical work that he and Lloyd George had done before the First World War. Moreover, the Treasury was not an office where he was going to win any spurs. The parlous state of Britain's finances after paying for the war left little room for manoeuvre.

Consciously or otherwise, Baldwin had set Churchill up perfectly to fail as a minister. Churchill held the Exchequer longer than any other ministry, but he achieved the least there. He was back at the top level of government, but his career was stalling. Churchill remained a ronin. His relationship to Baldwin was utterly unlike his to Lloyd George. From a complex blend of politics spiced with personal sympathy and shared political objectives, he had slipped into an employer/employee relationship with little more than hostility to socialism in common.

Beaverbrook still held something of the upper hand in his relationship with Churchill. The rising MP Victor Cazalet described a dinner at the *Daily Express* office with the two: 'W hates criticism and will do anything to get into favour with [Beaverbrook]. I hate to see a great man like that lick B's boots. After dinner there was a show in a poor cinema. Winston sat through the programme, he never would have done under any other circumstances.'[3]

Churchill's political assets were wasting, but Beaverbrook's press power was staying intact.

3

AN AUSTRALIAN ON THE MAKE

Winston Churchill's second foray into the wilderness had brought him a new friend who was to remain his devoted ally for the rest of his career. It was the Leicester West by-election campaign that brought Churchill and Brendan Bracken together. Bracken volunteered to help Churchill and his assistance was gratefully received. Bracken spotted the opportunity to make himself useful to a prominent politician and seized it with both hands. It is of a piece with his doings up to that point. It was only the latest gambit in a series by a man who had come from almost nowhere to make a name for himself in the higher reaches of British society.

Bracken took great efforts to mask the hard facts of his own biography. This is almost the first in the many mysteries that surround him. When the facts were finally established, they included nothing discreditable that a ruthless adventurer would have wanted to suppress out of fear that knowledge of this would have held him back in business or society. Bracken simply preferred that people did not know. He was born in 1901 in Templemore, a small town in the west of Ireland, then still part of the British Empire albeit facing an active movement for independence. Bracken's family were Roman Catholic and his father was a very active member of the Irish Republican Brotherhood. Bracken's father was a reasonably prosperous builder and mason, but he died in 1904, throwing Brendan's family life into disarray. His mother moved the family to Dublin where the boy attended in quick succession St Patrick's National School, Drumcondra, until 1910, and then the O'Connell School, run by the Christian Brothers. He was an intelligent pupil but apparently undisciplined, so the famously ferocious methods of the Christian Brothers may have motivated the move. If that was the plan, it did not succeed and Brendan was sent to an even more constrictive establishment, a Jesuit boarding school at the age of fourteen. This triggered yet more rebellion, with Brendan running away and staying at hotels on credit. In 1916, Patrick Laffan, a friend of his mother whom she later married, came up with the drastic solution of sending the boy to his brother in New South Wales, where he had a sheep station. Laffan may also have wanted to remove a potential obstacle to his romantic intentions towards the widowed Mrs Bracken. In Australia, Brendan Bracken's life became almost entirely that of a drifter. He did not settle down on the sheep station and worked briefly at a number of schools. To escape becoming an outright vagrant, he stayed at convents where he developed one of his most striking characteristics: he had lost whatever Catholic faith he had had but acquired a deep interest in the history and rituals of the church that stayed with him for the rest of his life. He eventually returned to Ireland in 1919 to find his mother remarried and bogged down in a squabble with her family over money. That marked the end of his Irish life and he moved to Britain. In later years, he generously supported family members when he could fully afford to, but to all intents and purposes, he no longer had a family. His life was a blank canvas that he could paint to his heart's content.

Bracken's most breathtakingly ambitious piece of self-invention came in 1920. He had moved from one minor school teaching job to another in the style of the shiftless, hard-up young men of the Evelyn Waugh novels, but he had somehow amassed a respectable stock of cash. This he used to enrol himself as a pupil at the moderately prestigious public school Sedbergh in the north of England. He was nineteen years old but improbably passed himself off as sixteen; he was already tall and far more an adult than a boy. A public-school education was the marker of belonging to the higher class of British society, but Bracken's exercise in manufacturing British class status did not succeed. He did not try too hard to develop the fiction. According to one story, he paid his first (and, as it proved, only) term's fees in cash direct to the headmaster. He was not a popular boy; his opinionated stance grated in a remorselessly conformist culture. He took no part in sports, that other vital aspect of the male identity in Britain. He left Sedbergh with no formal qualification, but he listed the school in the line for education in his *Who's Who* entry, along with 'Sydney', as though the city were a school. Despite the brief and ambiguous direct relationship with the school, Bracken stayed in touch and publicly advertised his relationship to Sedbergh in direct contrast to the veil he drew over his Irish and family roots.

Bracken was a striking and unmistakable figure. He was tall and well built, just the right side of gangling. Observers sometimes referred to his 'negroid' appearance and compared him to a 'golliwog'.[1] His wavy hair was bright red and unkempt. His features were strong but the most noticeable was a nose broken in a childhood riding accident which had never reset properly. He was badly short-sighted and always wore spectacles. His teeth were noticeably bad. He smoked constantly and never appeared to take exercise but was capable of epic walks.[2] He kept pace with Churchill's sustained drinking and showed similarly little ill-effects. He was sociable and affable; most people with whom he came into contact liked him, but there is no sign that he formed close friendships.

In his early years in Britain, Bracken stayed with a number of families. The Sedbergh name helped him win more substantial teaching work as he set out to climb society. Practically everyone with whom he came into contact remembers the same forceful, often engaging personality, given to huge and transparently false fictions about himself. These were not the calculated and plausible lies of a confidence trickster but betrayed a strained relationship between their author and reality. No one was taken in and few, in his early days, took this amiss; it was almost part of his charm. Often enough he disseminated his fictions by implication, rather than direct statements. The question of his home country is typical. He had returned to Europe with, intentionally or otherwise, an Australian accent; he let many people think that he came from Australia originally. Perhaps as Ireland was winning its independence through an outright revolution that morphed into a savage civil war, he thought he would somehow seem less British if his Irish background were known. He kept his pose as a pseudo-Australian well into the war and affected anger at slighting references to it as a penal colony.[3] Even after Bracken's death, it was only with the publication of biographies of him by Andrew Boyle and Irishman Charles Lysaght that his Irish origins were universally known.

After Sedbergh, Bracken set out to make his way up in literary London by toiling away at some of the myriad journals that made up that world. He trod the well-worn path to the fringes of the political world by helping with the League of Nations Union, which brought him into contact with more prominent figures such as MP Oliver Locker-Lampson.[4] More unusually, Bracken attended debates at the House of Commons. The politician who caught his eye most firmly was Winston Churchill, a master of parliamentary speech-making. He supposedly enthused to friends that Churchill was 'the man of the future', a brave prediction considering that his political career rested solely on the shaky foundations of Lloyd George's faltering and fractious coalition government.

Bracken presented himself voluntarily as Churchill's helper in the campaign for Leicester West in the December 1923 by-election. He had picked his moment well. Churchill had no particular links to the area or constituency and so no natural body of potential local supporters. It was some distance from London, so his circle of friends and allies was not readily going to supply helpers. Bracken did not hesitate. He appears to have been a constant presence at Churchill's side through the campaign. He worked to drum up favourable press coverage with brazen effrontery. Bracken's efforts were unavailing and Churchill was defeated. But Bracken was not daunted by Churchill's defeat at Leicester and stepped up to serve as his campaign assistant in the Westminster Abbey by-election three months later. The two by-elections were very different. Leicester had been fought out in acrimony and provincial isolation; Westminster Abbey was conducted with a certain good fellowship in a distinctly metropolitan setting.

The Conservative Party machine was deployed against Churchill, so Bracken's assistance in the basic organisation of his campaign was all the more valuable. Churchill's London circle was a constant presence and accidentally or otherwise, Bracken found himself moving amongst the top level of society and politics. Beaverbrook also put himself firmly behind Churchill's cause, which helped place Bracken on the press lord's radar screen. Bracken was at Churchill's side as the votes were counted and first misinformed him that he had won but soon had to correct this.

Bracken was a regular visitor at the Churchills' London house. Whilst the works at Chartwell were being completed, the Churchills' main base was their house on Sussex Square. During the Westminster by-election campaign, Bracken became a familiar face there; rather too familiar as one of the servants was non-plussed to find 'Mr Bracken' fast asleep on the sofa and had to seek counsel of her employers as to what to do. Bracken was anything but the standard image of the oleaginous climber; he took remarkable liberties with his patron. Once, when he was unable to find a match, he lit his cigarette from the end of a cigar that Churchill was smoking to Churchill's irritation: 'Brendan, I have known men to be shot for less than that.'[5] Bracken's irruption into the family circle was unwelcome to Clementine Churchill, whose instinct seems to have been to disapprove of her husband's friends on principle. As a high-living, brash adventurer, Bracken was an inevitable target. Bracken's particular sin was to condone, and perhaps actually to foster, the rumour that he was Churchill's illegitimate son. He appropriated Churchill family photographs to decorate his own room, implying truth in the rumour. As Churchill had had until he became bald, Bracken had distinctly red hair. Mischievously, Churchill never denied the story outright and it was still doing the rounds in the Second World War.[6] He even teased Clemmie when she confronted him with the tale, pretending that the chronology supported the possibility.[7]

Bracken was set to rise on Churchill's coat-tails, but he was anything but a self-abasing sycophant. The friendship that burgeoned between the two was not that of master and servant. Bracken was one of the few people who regularly challenged outright things that Churchill said, which made for frequent ferocious arguments.

When Churchill stood again for Epping, he had secured the de facto support of the Conservative Party, so Bracken's help was of rather less importance in getting Churchill finally back into Parliament. Churchill's elevation to the Treasury also curtailed his contact with Bracken. The scale of his workload curbed his free time and, long before the era of the 'special adviser', the Treasury's dauntingly self-sufficient world was anything but propitious for interventions by even the most conventional outsider and still less someone as wild and individualistic as Bracken.

As well as helping Churchill in his efforts to return to mainstream politics, Bracken had anointed himself as Churchill's literary agent. It was a world of which he knew something. He succeeded in placing a number of articles at gratifyingly high fees, all the more useful given the costs of Chartwell and the absence of a ministerial salary. But Bracken over-stepped the limit and placed an article on economics written by Churchill as his own work, taking the fee. This triggered the first of what were to be numerous rows between the two, almost as though between a married couple, that ran deep but were never permanent. This was another reason why the Churchill and Bracken relationship ebbed during Churchill's Exchequer years. Bracken became something of a distant observer of his friend's doings but a supportive one. He published an article praising Churchill's fateful decision to return Britain to the gold standard in response to pressure from orthodox and conservative financial and Treasury circles.[8] Bracken may well have been supportive rather than sincere, as he was soon ferociously critical of the tight-money policy embodied in the return to the gold standard. This was Churchill's most important decision as Chancellor and one that contributed to the severity of the Great Slump in Britain.

4

A DUCAL PROFESSOR

Winston Churchill's friendship with Brendan Bracken was rooted in his political career, but his friendship with the Oxford scientist Frederick Lindemann, which also blossomed in the 1920s, was essentially social. Churchill's fascination with science and his admiration of Lindemann's intellect were the bedrock of the relationship. Lindemann's motivations are less easy to grasp, although he later professed admiration for Churchill's intellect. Lindemann was an avid participant in the social life of the higher reaches of the British establishment so susceptible to Churchill's ducal heritage. According to one of Lindemann's close colleagues, they were also bound by sporting prowess: Churchill in polo; Lindemann in tennis. Whatever attracted Lindemann to Churchill, it was strong enough to overcome radically different lifestyles and, as with Bracken, national backgrounds.

Like Bracken, Frederick Lindemann was not born in Britain. His family were well established in the Palatinate and his father made his fortune as the owner of the waterworks in Speyer and Pirmasens. Soon after the Franco-Prussian War of 1870, the father moved to Britain, having married the American widow of a wealthy British banker called Davidson. He settled in Sidmouth and was naturalised as a British subject, so his sons were born British, the only nationality they held. Frederick, however, was born in Baden-Baden because his mother happened to be taking the waters there. The elder Lindemann remained German enough to eschew the traditional step in adopting a British identity for his family of sending his sons to a British public school, where they would have focused on the classics and team sport, and then to an Oxbridge college. Instead, after they had attended a minor and undistinguished preparatory school in Scotland, Blair Lodge, he sent them instead to the *Realgymnasium* and then *Hochschule* of Darmstadt where they received the mathematical and science-focused education typical of Germany. Frederick Lindemann extended the German and scientific aspect of his education by going on to university in Berlin. He obtained a physics doctorate under one of the day's leading physicists and Nobel Prize winner, Professor Walther Nernst. Lindemann's wealth meant he could afford to live at Berlin's leading hotel, the Adlon. Here he pursued his studies amongst the physicists working at the cutting edge of the discipline. But for the outbreak of the First World War, he might have remained in Germany, albeit as part of the international scientific community.

Lindemann's German heritage imposed a double burden on him. He had no German accent, but his surname was obviously not British. Anything German became deeply suspect during the First World War. Even during the Second World War, he was sneeringly referred to as 'Baron Berlin'.[1] A further layer of confusion arose when some faint or imaginary family connection with Alsace was played up to dilute his Germanness, in keeping with common post-First World War practice (for example, 'Alsatian' was adopted as a euphemism for the German Shepherd dog breed). The 2nd Lord Birkenhead, son of Churchill's friend and Lindemann's biographer, wrongly asserted in a misguided attempt to shield his subject from the imputation of Germanness that the family came from Alsace-Lorraine,[*] but then went on to relate that they originated in an entirely different region, the Palatinate, on the French border but entirely German in culture. Birkenhead gave the birthplace of his grandfather and great-uncle as Jägersburg, which he misleadingly described as being French soil; the Palatinate was one of the numerous places briefly annexed to France under Napoleon. A German surname was also frequently a sign of being a Jew. Lindemann vigorously shared the contemporary dislike of Jews even though the prejudice never spilled over into political or even personal

---

[*] An immediately suspect conflation as Alsace and Lorraine were always distinct regions, albeit subject to the same political destiny.

antisemitism. He rallied to the support of Jewish colleagues driven out of Nazi Germany, most notably Albert Einstein. There is no firm evidence of Jewish ancestry, although his junior colleague and friend Roy Harrod did suspect some. The nationalist prejudice against Lindemann was fed by ignorance of his admittedly complicated family history. Like Bracken, he made no effort to broadcast the truth, albeit without engaging in the Irishman's deliberate encouragement of false alternatives. Lindemann's resolute refusal to disclose anything still appeared to be an attempt to mystify his family past.[2] Churchill was untroubled by Lindemann's heritage and reacted furiously when an MP questioned his national loyalty during the Second World War when he had become Churchill's closest adviser.[3]

Lindemann attempted to obtain an army commission during the First World War but was turned down because of his eyesight. Instead, he joined the Royal Aircraft Establishment at Farnborough, working on the development of British military aviation. He learned to fly and his most notable achievement was to work out theoretically how an aircraft might be rescued from a spin, which up till then had almost invariably led to the machine crashing, and then trying out this method of recovery by deliberately putting his aircraft into a spin. He was correct and he survived; his method became the standard procedure, saving countless pilots' lives afterwards. The episode proves that he was a brave man, but it had the malign consequence of reinforcing an overwhelming confidence in his ability to produce a solution to a practical question from scientific theory which stayed with him for the remainder of his life.

Lindemann cut a mildly eccentric figure as an experimental pilot because he maintained impeccable and conservative standards of dress whilst flying. He invariably wore an immaculate suit and bowler hat, often with a stiff collar. Outdoors, he usually sported a rolled umbrella. It is hard to imagine how he could have adapted his fastidious standards to life in the trenches. In later life, he wore a Christ Church Oxford tie, the only heavyweight club tie to which he was entitled. His hair was cropped short and he had a faint moustache.

The first half of the twentieth century was a golden age for physics, with huge strides in atomic and quantum studies. Lindemann was in the right discipline. He could hold his own with the great figures of the era and his career took him to the secretaryship of the prestigious Solvay conference in 1911. After his service in the First World War, Lindemann was elected as Oxford professor of experimental philosophy (physics), in part with the help of an Oxford academic, Henry Tizard, who had become friends with him as a fellow test pilot and researcher at the Royal Aircraft Establishment. The professorship came with a fellowship of Wadham College, but Lindemann also secured his election as a student (the equivalent of fellow at other Oxbridge colleges) of Christ Church, the grandest college at Oxford. He was a regular participant in the college's famously combative and competitive high table, but he had little time for its essentially inward-looking intellectual life. He was too outspoken and acerbic to relish or thrive in the labyrinthine and serpentine world of British academic institutional politics. His main work at Oxford was to lift the Clarendon Laboratory from the neglected somnolence into which it had fallen and to save Oxford from the reputation of being almost exclusively dedicated to the study of humanities. The Clarendon became a leading force in low-temperature physics, but for all Lindemann's effort, it never rivalled the global standing of the Cavendish Laboratory at Cambridge, which was one of the powerhouses of the new era of physics research under the guidance of the New Zealander Professor Sir Ernest Rutherford. As Lindemann's career in academic administration developed, his own scientific career withered. Rutherford described him crushingly as a 'scientist manqué'.[4] His Christ Church colleague Roy Harrod felt that Lindemann had 'lost caste' amongst his scientific colleagues as his research work had lost ground to administrative work at the Clarendon.[5] As his direct scientific career faded, Lindemann pursued as a hobby a study of prime numbers. Lindemann's combative instincts and high-handedness led him into a series of acrimonious and largely pointless squabbles with other dons at Oxford. He saw people as being either for him or against him, and remorselessly conducted vendettas against the latter. He was aware of the dislike that he inspired, but this did not disturb him.[6]

Lindemann's inherited wealth would easily have allowed him to live in a grand house of his own, but he preferred to live in Christ Church where his rooms were furnished tastelessly and decorated with pictures from his mother, notably saccharine sentimental paintings of kittens by Henriëtte Ronner.[7] He did, though, employ a full-time servant as his valet and chauffeur for his Rolls-Royce. James Harvey was a constant figure in his life for thirty years. Photography and golf were Lindemann's hobbies.

Lindemann was a radically different character from Bracken, but they were the same in one important respect: full sexual relationships did not feature in either of their lives. As a student in Berlin, Lindemann slept with a number of women, in keeping with the mores of the place and time, but by the time he got to England, this had faded away. There are a couple of signs that he might have conducted a very discreet sex life, but there is no trace of any long-term relationship. In this respect, he might be the mirror image of Bracken's well-observed but unconsummated relationships with women.

Churchill met Lindemann in an appropriately ducal setting: Eaton Hall, the home of one of Churchill's steadiest friends Bendor, Duke of Westminster.[8] They were fellow guests at the Duke's house when Lindemann partnered Clemmie Churchill in a game of tennis. Lindemann was an enthusiastic and highly skilled tennis player, reaching international standard. He won the Swedish tennis championship and also played the German Kaiser. The Duke of Westminster was a horrible man who successfully engineered the legal and social punishment of his brother-in-law, Lord Beauchamp, for homosexuality. Beauchamp's true sin was to be socially and politically successful in a way that eluded the thuggish Duke. The Duke's later support for good relations with Nazi Germany verged on treason, but this brought only a mild rebuke from Churchill. Lindemann was a man of considerable wealth and relished contact with elevated social circles, but it is rather difficult to understand what other attraction he could have found in a traditional sporting British aristocrat like the Duke, devoid of anything approaching intellectual interests.

Lindemann was soon established as a firm friend of the Churchill family and a regular visitor to Chartwell as the Churchills made it their home. Churchill and Lindemann overcame a gulf between their lifestyles to get on so well. Unlike Beaverbrook or Bracken, Lindemann did not share Churchill's fondness for fine food and copious drink. He had been a strict vegetarian since his mother briefly and fervently adopted the practice during his childhood. When she changed her mind, Lindemann remained a vegetarian. He seemed to live off egg whites prepared to minutely detailed recipes. He did not smoke, whilst Churchill smoked large cigars regularly and Bracken smoked cigarettes heavily. He was in principle a teetotaller, although he did once admit to Churchill that a human could safely drink 10cc of brandy per day; Churchill thereafter enforced this on him as minimum daily consumption.[9] Lindemann's charm lay in his conversation.

Even if he did not share the sybaritic pleasures of Churchill and his other guests, Lindemann was a lively talker. Churchill particularly appreciated Lindemann's ability to explain complex scientific issues clearly and comprehensibly. Churchill's education was limited, if not downright minimal, and his grasp of science was accordingly weak, but he did understand fully the growing importance of science in the modern world. He knew from personal experience how it had transformed warfare during the First World War and was certain it would continue to do so. Churchill's professional collaboration with Lindemann began when he was commissioned to write an article for *Nash's Pall Mall Magazine* on the future of warfare in 1924. Churchill sought Lindemann's advice on how technology might change the next war. His starting point was the widespread belief at that time that electric death rays would wreak havoc and destruction at a distance or immobilise the electric circuitry of machinery. Churchill quoted Lindemann, whom he described simply as a 'German', declaring that the next war would be fought with electricity. He also warned of the dangers of chemical and biological warfare in a forceful and pessimis-tic piece entitled 'Shall We All Commit Suicide?' Churchill was also entirely sceptical that what he sneered at as the so-called Peace Treaty would be effective. He recognised clearly that Germany's defeat was only temporary and the country 'cannot be kept in permanent subju-gation'. Lindemann's German heritage did not make him in any way sympathetic to German national aspirations to restore past glories, and he was to warn early of the threat that the country might pose to European peace. The League of Nations seized on the article as propaganda for its project of harmonious relations between nations and issued it as a pamphlet in the USA where 250,000 were distrib-uted in a fortnight. Some of the theses advanced by Churchill with Lindemann's advice proved incorrect, but on balance, the article en-capsulated the vision that drove Churchill's predictions of the future and was extremely prescient.

Lindemann shared Churchill's fear and distrust of socialism. During the General Strike of 1926, Churchill was one of the Cabinet members who wanted the hardest possible line taken against the strik-ers. Lindemann considered the strike to be undemocratic.[10] The strikers provided a relatively innocuous outlet for his energies by forcing the closure of the newspapers, thus creating an opening for a government newspaper opposed to the strike, the *British Gazette*, which Churchill organised and edited. Prime Minister Stanley Baldwin saw the danger of an outright confrontation with the strikers and was happy to see Churchill's energies channelled into such an unthreatening project. Lindemann supported Churchill and dragooned his students and the Clarendon staff into helping with the printing and distribution of the *British Gazette*.[11] One night, Lindemann stayed until dawn to get an edition out.

5

A GOLDEN YOUTH

Robert Boothby started life with a great fund of advantages and appeared to be obviously destined for great things. Unlike Lord Beaverbrook, Brendan Bracken or Frederick Lindemann, Boothby easily fitted the mould of a privileged British man for whom success in life was there for the taking. His father, Sir Robert Tuite Boothby, was a well-placed figure in Scotland's financial elite: manager of the Scottish Provident Institution, a major insurance company, and a director of the Bank of Scotland. Born in 1900, the young Robert was able to escape the slaughter of the trenches. He attended Eton and Magdalen College, Oxford. His academic achievement at Oxford was slight, but he was a great social success; his voracious sexual appetite was soon noted. Thanks in part to his father's friendship with Stanley Baldwin, he was elected as Conservative MP for Aberdeen and Kincardine East (later East Aberdeenshire) in 1924. He was to hold the seat for thirty-four years, until he stepped down with a firm reputation as a dedicated constituency MP who worked hard for the people he represented. The local fishing community was a distinct feature of his constituency and he strived constantly for their interests. His good looks and charm won him a happy position in the golden high society that reappeared as the horrors of the First World War were sloughed off. The great fortunes were still largely intact and famous hostesses such as Lady 'Emerald' Cunard, Sibyl Colefax and Maggie Greville held sway over a vibrant social scene in London.

Boothby had an early break of fortune in his political career when Churchill picked him as his parliamentary private secretary. Churchill had become disenchanted with Sir Clive Morrison-Bell who held the job and lit on Boothby. Hitherto, they had had no significant contact, but in 1926, Boothby had written him a long letter setting out his vision for economic policy.[1] For a young MP, it was a major distinction to become parliamentary private secretary to the Chancellor of the Exchequer and a high rung on the ladder of a parliamentary career. He frequently appeared in newspapers in photographs of the Chancellor, a respectful pace behind his master. He worked hard to help Churchill compose his speeches; he later described his master as not a natural orator but by then Boothby was deeply disenchanted with him.[2] Boothby was helped in his work by his comfortable understanding of economic and financial policy, where he was able to fill a gap in Churchill's intellectual armoury. In the other ministries that he held, Churchill could take a commanding grip of policy with a clear eye on the key issues. The Chancellorship was the exception and Churchill's advisers were able to exert an unusually decisive influence on him. To his later immense regret, Churchill bowed to the overwhelming majority of Britain's financial establishment in readopting the gold standard in 1926. Boothby opposed the decision but does not appear to have tried to swing his master against it.

The early years of the relationship were unclouded; Boothby was a frequent guest at Chartwell and Churchill classed him as a friend.[3] Churchill bestowed on Boothby the high accolade of inviting him to join the Other Club, the select dining club founded by Churchill and Birkenhead, where he was the youngest member amongst eminent figures from politics, journalism and elsewhere. He earned the more dubious distinction of coldness from Clemmie, who was generally hostile to her husband's livelier friends. Along with Beaverbrook, Boothby was judged to 'push luck too far'.[4]

Boothby was allowed considerable freedom as parliamentary private secretary to form and express his own views. Together with three other promising and gifted young Conservative MPs – Harold Macmillan, Oliver Stanley and John Loder – he published a book *Industry and the State: A Conservative View* in 1927 which argued for state intervention in businesses in defiance of the laissez-faire norms of the day and his party. The authors were the core of a group of young, progressively minded Conservative MPs nicknamed the YMCA. Boothby was also an early disciple of John Maynard Keynes's expansionary approach to the economy and a ferocious critic of the extreme fiscal rigour manifested in the return to the gold standard and championed by the dominant conservative forces in British finance led by Montagu Norman, governor of the Bank of England, with the support of the Treasury.[5] Boothby was violently hostile to Norman, whom he accused of favouring the profits of City businesses over the interests of British industry. Churchill's professional advisers at the Treasury, together with most politicians, solidly supported the return to gold; Beaverbrook was a rare exception which helps explain the respect in which Churchill was to hold his views later.[6] With hindsight, Churchill admitted that the return to the gold standard was an error and wrote to Boothby a few years later of Norman: 'Surely it will become a public necessity to get rid of Montagu Norman. No man has ever been stultified as he has been in his fourteen years of policy.'[7]

On one score, though, Churchill was never reconciled to Boothby's view: his sympathy for the Bolshevik regime in the Soviet Union, then also a distinctly minority view and almost unique amongst Conservatives. Boothby's tolerance of Bolshevism was in part motivated by local political considerations; the Soviet Union was a major export market for fish caught by his constituents who suffered from the trade embargo imposed by the British government. Here, though, Churchill had rather less tolerance:

> You must not mind my chaff about the Bolsheviks. It has a serious under-side however. I do not want to see you get mixed up with these snakes or their servitors in this country just for the sake of herrings, & so prejudice what I daresay will be a prosperous political career.[8]

Boothby persisted in defending the interests of his constituents and even offered to resign as Churchill's parliamentary private secretary to prevent a public disagreement on the issue.[9]

Boothby had solid career reasons to cultivate his relationship with Churchill, who was still a figure at the front rank of politics, but his affection for David Lloyd George is far less easy to explain in terms of self-interest. Boothby was vocal in apparently genuine respect and admiration of the former Prime Minister, writing that 'the greatest man produced by this country in our time was unquestionably David Lloyd George'.[10] Lloyd George appeared an ever-more isolated figure after his expulsion from power by the Carlton Club coup in 1922; mainstream hostility and suspicion towards him had not softened. The Conservative leadership frowned on the friendship, but Boothby was not deterred. The only other new MP who enjoyed a similar relationship with Lloyd George was Harold Macmillan. Boothby was given a privileged snapshot of the relationship between Churchill and Lloyd George. In 1927, as Churchill was writing *The World Crisis*, his personal account of the First World War, points arose which he wanted to discuss with Lloyd George. They had drifted apart and Churchill asked Boothby as a friend of Lloyd George to arrange a meeting. When Boothby asked him how it had gone, according to Boothby's later account, 'It could not have gone better ... Within five minutes the old relationship between us was completely re-established. The relationship between Master and Servant. And I was the Servant.' As with much of Boothby's version of things, this must be taken with a good pinch of salt, but he repeated the story a number of times so Churchill probably did acknowledge that Lloyd George was the stronger party at least at the start. Boothby split his loyalty between Lloyd Geoge and Churchill, and it did not work to Boothby's advantage when he later appeared to support Lloyd George's title to a share in government.

As well as the question of relations with the Soviet Union, Boothby also offered to resign over a personal matter, which he discussed with Churchill. His MP's salary and other investment income were not enough to fund the extravagant lifestyle that he was leading in high society. He wanted to accept the offer of a job with London Stock Exchange brokers Chase, Henderson and Tennant but saw the danger of

a conflict of interest with Churchill's position as Chancellor. Churchill did not and Boothby conducted the two jobs simultaneously and
part-time. It was a poor decision and one that stored up trouble for
the future. Boothby had a good abstract grasp of economics, but this
was not enough to make him money. He was overly given to outright
speculation in securities and he lost heavily. Nor was he prepared to put
in the time and effort on mundane work to build a career in the industry. In the words of a friend and partner, 'The City bored him stiff.'[II]
His hostility to the tight-money policy in general and to Montagu
Norman in person was another obstacle to a successful City career; it
set him at odds with the prevailing ethos. He accused Norman in the
House of Commons of using 'power without responsibility.' The City
was not an environment where he thrived at a personal level. He was
as out of sympathy with the regular financial market practitioners of
the day as he was with the mundane Conservative MPs.

When Stanley Baldwin's government fell in 1929, Churchill lost
office and with him so did Boothby. His early promise in life began
to recede; he began to look like the proverbial politician with a great
future behind him. Life in opposition demands a different set of
skills to life in government. There was much to criticise in the way
Ramsay MacDonald's Labour government addressed the onset of the
Great Slump, but neither the Conservatives, now in opposition still
under Baldwin, nor its individual members had either the taste or
the skill to flay it in the House of Commons. Boothby distinguished
himself neither as a star performer against MacDonald nor as a loyal
Conservative foot soldier. Nor did he affiliate himself to any of the
high-profile radical political alternatives that enlivened this low ebb
in British political life and presented themselves to Boothby. Beaverbrook had cultivated him as a rising star in the Commons and gently
tried to interest him in his attempt to hijack the Conservative Party
as a tool for his empire crusade. Boothby wisely had no interest. He
was even less receptive when his friend, Sir Oswald 'Tom' Mosley, by
then a minister in the Labour government, became so frustrated with
its inaction that he planned to break away and form the 'New Party',

embryo of the British Union of Fascists. Boothby advised Mosley firmly against the plan. There never seems to have been any thought that Boothby might join Churchill in his ferocious campaign against MacDonald's proposals to grant India some measure of autonomy. Boothby received no reward for holding back from any of the alternatives to the mainstream when MacDonald's Labour government fell in 1931 and was replaced by a 'National' government, also nominally led by MacDonald but firmly under the control of the Conservatives following their stunning victory in the election that followed the formation of the new government. It is uncertain why Boothby was left out. His biographer Robert Rhodes James believed that Baldwin still held him in enough regard to have given him a ministry had the government been a purely Conservative one. Boothby's association with Churchill and Lloyd George cannot have helped his cause. The arch tight-money advocate Philip Snowden remained Chancellor in the National government.

Boothby's personal life gave him no real consolation. He began an agonised love affair with Dorothy Macmillan, the wife of his fellow MP Harold Macmillan. It was to drag on through the 1930s, barely interrupted by Boothby's own brief and miserable marriage. He was seriously injured in a car accident which took him months to recover from. He developed something of a journalistic career, but his income from this source stood in the shade of Churchill's huge earnings from his writing. In February 1932, Churchill did propose that Boothby join him in covering the congress of the Democratic Party in the US later that year, which was to choose F. D. Roosevelt as the party's candidate, but nothing came of this.[12]

6

CHARTWELL

In 1922, Winston Churchill had bought Chartwell House in Kent, an estate dating back to the fourteenth century, situated on a high ridge with views stretching southwards over the Weald of Kent. He paid £5,000, but the house required extensive work, including extension and modernisation, for which the cost spiralled to £18,000 over the next two years. Chartwell became Churchill's true home for the rest of his life. It played a central part in his political career; he invited a huge range of figures from politics and public life there to enjoy copious food and drink. On the unencumbered roads of the era, it was an easy drive from central London.

Chartwell was a family home as well as Churchill's country retreat, and visitors met a growing and lively set of children. The Churchills' first child, Diana, was born in 1909, followed by their only son in 1911, named Randolph, in keeping with the family tradition of alternating the given names Winston and Randolph. They were followed by a further three daughters, Sarah, Marigold and Mary. Marigold died of septicaemia at the age of only two. Neither Frederick Lindemann nor Brendan Bracken had children of their own or lived in company where children were a regular presence, but both established happy and deep contact with the Churchill children. Both were noted for their generosity.

Despite his formidable appearance, Lindemann did especially well with the children.[1] His near-universal nickname of the 'Professor' was abbreviated to the more-easily pronounced 'Fesser' and his visits were a treat to be looked forward to.[2] Unlike many of their father's friends, Lindemann enjoyed their mother's approval. She was a keen tennis player herself and continued to relish his skill on the court. He did not share the penchant for drink and smoking which Clemmie deplored in her husband and was shared by Bracken, Lord Beaverbrook and Lord Birkenhead. One of Churchill's daughters recalled:

> He was part of our Chartwell life. It is hard to remember an occasion on which he was not present. His exterior was conventionally forbidding: the domed cranium, the close-cropped iron-grey hair which had receded as if the brain had pushed it away, the iron-grey moustache, the sallow complexion, the little sniff which took the place of what normally would have been a laugh, yet he could still exude a warmth that made scientific thinking unfrightening.[3]

Lindemann was present at the charming ceremony in which Mary laid the foundation stone of what was to become the 'Marycot', a tiny one-roomed cottage that Churchill was building for his daughters in the wall of the Chartwell garden using his newly developed skill of bricklaying. Lindemann presented her with a bouquet of flowers to mark what she ranked as her first 'public engagement'.[4] She delivered a speech in honour of the event to the delight of her father, ever appreciative of public speaking.

Churchill was grateful for Lindemann's scientific advice on the complex hydraulics of one of his cherished projects at Chartwell.[5] A series of ponds and a swimming pool drained into a large artificial lake. Lindemann also helped Churchill with articles on the role of women and great leaders of the past.

Churchill's nephew Johnny described Churchill's complete faith in Lindemann's judgement:

> He swore by Lindemann. Anything that was a query, which Winston did not know he would say, 'What do you think about that, Prof? What is that about?' If the Prof said it was all nonsense, Winston believed it was nonsense. He was a loner, Prof – almost an eccentric. He could not bear not to be right. Everything we said, Prof pulled to bits.[6]

Bracken, too, was a regular guest at Chartwell, albeit much less frequently than Lindemann, with thirty-four appearances in the guest book compared to 138.[7] The contrast between Bracken and Lindemann was strong enough to register on the children at an early age. Sarah Churchill described Bracken as being 'in complete contrast' to Lindemann.[8] Bracken too became part of the children's lives and they became accustomed to his visits on Sundays which were enough of an event for the day to be rechristened 'Brendan Day'.

One of Churchill's friends did not feature at all in the roll call of regular visitors to Chartwell: Lord Beaverbrook delighted in being a host but never in being a guest. He went on to apply the same rule to Chequers and Ditchley, the prime ministerial country retreats, during the war despite frequent invitations from Churchill.[9] As host, he could keep control over the proceedings which he did gleefully at his own country house, Cherkley, which swarmed with his courtiers and lackeys, the hub of his universe.

Churchill took undiluted pleasure in Chartwell, but his wife Clemmie had a more ambiguous attitude. She was a far stronger and more distinct personality than was usual for political wives of the era. Their relationship was intensely affectionate and she supported him wholeheartedly throughout his career, but she was fully prepared to disagree with him on questions of all kinds. Brought up in financially straitened circumstances, she was acutely conscious that Chartwell required extensive and costly renovation and rebuilding work as well as having heavy running costs. Clemmie was fully aware of Churchill's casual and overly optimistic approach to his finances and disapproved of the purchase of Chartwell, but Churchill himself was adamant and saw the house as a family seat that would be passed down to his son Randolph, now approaching maturity and inheritor of the dynastic ambitions that lay close to Churchill's heart. Clemmie also frowned on many of his friends, with the notable exception of Lindemann. She singled out the 'terrible Bs' – Birkenhead, Beaverbrook and Bracken – who led her husband astray into high-living and political misjudgements. Eventually, she warmed to Bracken, and Birkenhead died in 1930, but she never lost her distrust of Beaverbrook.

Lindemann and Bracken devoted their efforts to rather more practical help for Randolph, the only son and heir in whom Churchill invested so much hope and expectation. Mindful of the way in which his own father had neglected him in favour of his political career, Churchill was determined that Randolph would receive his full attention and support. Churchill talked to Randolph as an equal and he was allowed to stay up late to talk to important visitors. Stanley Baldwin's confidant, the assistant Cabinet Secretary Tom Jones, describes a dinner at Chartwell to which he had been summoned to discuss a national coal strike.[10] Randolph was about fifteen years old and Churchill even appeared to defer to his judgements, which were manifestly shaped by the ultra-hawkish views of Lindemann, who was also a guest. Churchill found Lindemann to be an especially good companion for Randolph.[11] Churchill invested huge dynastic hopes in his son and even imagined him following in his footsteps as Prime Minister, taking Pitt the Younger as a template.[12] Randolph's godfather was Birkenhead who was clearly expected to mentor his political career. It is little surprise that Randolph developed a vastly inflated opinion of his own talents. His relationship with his mother was ambiguous. Clemmie devoted her life to her husband's political career and expected her children to do likewise. Randolph was a severe disappointment to her.

Randolph was coming to the end of his not particularly happy time at Eton and was struggling to overcome his father's doubts about him going to Oxford, to which he aspired. Randolph's academic performance had been middling and his father wanted this to improve before contemplating a university education. Lindemann had already introduced him to the senior common room at Christ Church, where he had made a favourable impression. In his youth, Randolph was strikingly handsome, having inherited his mother's good looks, and was capable of talking with impressive intelligence. Lindemann supported his wish to become an undergraduate. Finally, his father relented and with the assistance of Lindemann, Randolph easily secured a place at Christ Church which he took up mid-year. He thus missed out on the usual process of forming friendships at the start of the first term of the academic year.

Randolph's time at Oxford was not a success. Before he went up, he had inspired dangerously vainglorious press stories that he would triumph and become president of the Oxford Union in a shorter space of time than anyone else ever. It was not to be. His first speech was lacklustre and his second major intervention was more notable for taking an extreme position against the government's Egyptian policy, alienating established Conservative sentiment. His father had solicited the help of his Cabinet colleague Lord Hailsham, the Lord Chancellor, to persuade his own son Quintin Hogg, who had just been elected president of the union, to look favourably on Randolph.[13] Even though Hogg classed Randolph as a friend, any assistance that might have come from this quarter failed to help. Hogg was a conventional Conservative Party careerist and unlikely to approve of someone who so openly set himself against the policies of Prime Minister Stanley Baldwin. Throughout his life, Randolph was burdened by an inability to concentrate and focus on mundane business such as regular study. He was also too abrasive a personality to settle in the university's enclosed social and political life. Randolph was querulous and arrogant which deterred other students. Unlike his father who had been an enthusiastic polo player, he had no sporting distinction. His only close friends were a small circle of upper-class yahoos in whose company he developed a fatal fondness for high-stakes gambling.

During his undergraduate days, Randolph was once again the beneficiary of Lindemann's generosity. Lindemann lent him money on the basis of some scheme that would supposedly return a phenomenal 2,500 per cent annually and give him an income of £10,000 per year.[14] Six years later, Randolph finally remembered to pay back what was presumably the original capital lent to him of £125, the astronomical rate of return quietly forgotten.[15]

Bracken also visited Randoph at university. He would arrive in his resplendent chauffeured Hispano-Suiza, whose blue carriage lamps (a trademark of the marque) particularly caught Randolph's eye, and whisk him to London for an evening of fun. Randolph was entertained lavishly. One evening, Bracken took Randolph with him to make some political speeches in Bath but realised that even high-speed driving was not going to be enough to get Randolph back to Christ Church in time to re-enter the college before the curfew on students, strictly enforced in those days, came into force. He delivered Randolph the following morning, complete with a doctor's certificate justifying his absence that he had managed to procure.

Randolph's studies were interrupted by two journeys to America. The first was in the company of his father when he could bathe in Churchill's reflected glory. The second was even less helpful in forming his character. He accepted an invitation from an American lecture agent to deliver a series of well-paid talks. He got away with minimal preparation for speaking, but his immense extravagance more than consumed his fees and he returned to Britain heavily in debt. Partly to try to earn money to cover his debts and partly because he felt that he had learned enough of life outside Oxford, Randolph decided to leave. Bracken urged Randolph to resume his studies for the sake of his prospects in business or politics, but he ignored this. Two of Lindemann's close colleagues at Christ Church also suggested that he remain at the university, but he would not change his mind.[16] He left without a degree after only four terms.

Randolph's relationship with Bracken evolved into a complex and intense love–hate relationship. He admired much in Bracken but resented much as well. He was deeply jealous of Bracken's closeness to his father, which he was never able to replicate. There is a distinct father–son aspect to Churchill's relationship with Bracken; he was close to very few men who were so much younger than he was. It was one of the ways in which Bracken had succeeded but Randolph had failed despite his advantages of birth and upbringing. The rumour condoned, if not fostered, by Bracken that Churchill was his real father provided a flashpoint.

Things came to a head on a holiday in Venice during the summer of 1932, in confrontations which showed both men at or near their worst and proved a deep embarrassment to the British community in the city, who feared it would show lively British social behaviour up as a form of hooliganism.

Tension began when Bracken showed Randolph the palazzo where he was staying. In one of his most outrageous and improbable fictions, Bracken claimed to have inherited it from his parents. When Randolph observed that the furniture was very Germanic, Bracken further embroidered the story to give his mother a German second husband. Randolph wasn't fooled and the discontent between the two men simmered. Randolph himself had already been displaying especially bad behaviour on that holiday, having launched into a drunken fist fight with a baronet during a party given by Henry 'Chips' Channon.[17] His aggressive mood continued at a lunch with Bracken at the Lido Taverno, where he provoked Bracken by calling him 'my brother'. This annoyed Bracken enough for him to attack Randolph. The fight continued on the beach and came to an end when Randolph pulled off Bracken's spectacles and threw them in the water, from which Bracken ineffectually tried to retrieve them, roaring with fury.

Similarly, Randolph gleefully peddled an anecdote of a put-down that the press baron Lord Rothermere delivered to Bracken. The two were at a dinner in London with other worthies including Churchill when talk turned to a piece of news that had just broken.[18] Rothermere and Bracken sent out for copies of their respective papers; a single copy of the *Daily Mail* was brought back for Rothermere, but Bracken was brought enough copies of the *Financial News* for one to be given to each guest, which Bracken did not allow to go unremarked. Rothermere riposted with the crack that Bracken had sent out for the full print of his paper. Randolph described Bracken as the 'greatest liar in God's creation because he doesn't mind being found out'.[19] He later delivered a verdict on Bracken's life that is widely repeated: 'a fantasist, whose fantasies came true.'[20]

After Oxford, Randolph went into journalism. He started in the improbable role of editing the house magazine of the ICI chemicals giant but went on to get a contract to write a highly paid weekly column for the *Daily Mail*, which belonged to the Harmsworth group, headed by Lord Rothermere. He scored a number of high-profile successes, including an interview with the former Kaiser. He was commissioned to cover the bloody Chaco War between Bolivia and Paraguay in 1935.

Randolph's relationship with his father was already coming under strain during his time at Oxford. Churchill complained:

> Your idle & lazy life is vy offensive to me. You appear to be leading a perfectly useless existence ... Your personal appearance has already deteriorated under the untidy slothful & self-indulgent conditions in which you choose to live ... I have tried ... to add to our natural ties those of companionship & comradeship. But you do not do your part.[21]

After one furious argument, Randolph stormed out on Churchill, who opened his heart to Lindemann and asked him, 'more in sorrow than anger ... "Tell me, am I as a parent responsible for all the biological and chemical reactions in my son?"'[22]

7

THE FINANCIAL PUBLISHER

During the election campaigns, Brendan Bracken's priority had been Winston Churchill's politics, but in the middle of the 1920s, he could return to his journalistic career. He became a leading light at one of Britain's oldest and best-established publishers, Eyre & Spottiswoode, founded as the King's printers in 1739 and devoted to relatively unadventurous operations such as bibles and prayer books. Major Simon J. S. Crosthwaite-Eyre, the head of the company, wanted to diversify from a lucrative quasi-monopoly which might not last much longer.[1] By 1926, Bracken was on the board, successfully advocating a radical strategy. The firm had developed *English Life* into one of Britain's leading magazines with a solid mixture of lifestyle and a loyal advertiser base. Bracken calculated that its growth had peaked and that the potential sale value of the title was not going to get any better as circulation plateaued. He pushed for it to be sold, which it was in 1926. Bracken's next move was to invest the proceeds in a new venture with potential. He identified bankers as the one major professional group not to be served by a dedicated journal and led Eyre & Spottiswoode to found *The Banker* in 1926. Bracken devoted great effort to promoting his progeny and personally cultivated leading figures in the financial world. His successes included Robert Boothby's father, on whom he called unannounced. His courtship of Montagu Norman, the all-powerful governor of the Bank of England, was assiduous but was rebuffed and *The Banker* became one of the few City journals to criticise Norman openly.[2] After a relatively brief period of start-up losses, *The Banker* was turning a useful profit considering its small circulation.

Bracken extended Eyre & Spottiswoode's commitment to the new sector further. After founding *The Banker*, he drove investments in two established publications which also served the financial world. The *Financial News* had long been the number two City daily behind the *Financial Times*. By the mid-1920s, it had settled as a feature of the business newspaper world, but it was still dogged by the legacy of a chequered past. It had never quite lived down its ties to dubious company promoters, a rabid campaign against the 'unseen hand' of German influence during the First World War (an absurd idea even measured against the demanding standards of British paranoia in this direction), a murky struggle for control and a court case alleging outright blackmail of financier politician Rufus Isaacs. Revenue from publishing prospectuses for company flotations was the key item in the finances of any newspaper in the sector, with accompanying conflict-of-interest pitfalls. The *Financial News* had been acquired by the Trireme Trust, the owners of Britain's oldest and staidest generalist daily the *Morning Post*, but only because it owned the Argus printing company; Trireme had no interest in publishing the *Financial News*. The *Morning Post* was moribund and losing money hand over fist, so the owners decided to sell the *Financial News* in early 1928. One of the *Financial News*'s star journalists was already working for Bracken on *The Banker* and provided the link. Paul Einzig had arrived in Britain as a semi-refugee from the disintegrating Austro-Hungarian Empire. He had no money and almost no friends and he had yet to master English, but he built up a formidable list of strong contacts at the highest levels of the financial world. There were concerns over the quality of his English well into his career, but it was content and not style that made his articles. Einzig was aware that an Anglo-Canadian financier MP who sported a dubious colonelcy – in every way a poor man's Lord Beaverbrook – was interested in buying the *Financial News* and he saw Bracken as a more suitable alternative. Bracken was fired up about the idea and ended up in a ruthless haggle over the price in which the Trireme Trust exploited fully the boost to the paper's profitability from a heady stock market boom. Eyre & Spottiswoode finally paid

£280,000, around £14 million in today's value. Bracken became chairman and took day-to-day control with a salary set at an initial £3,000, together with the ownership of 100 shares in the company worth £900 at Eyre & Spottiswoode's purchase price. This was healthy compensation but by no means a fortune. Bracken's finances are shrouded in mystery and uncertainty; Einzig believed quite incorrectly that he was a partner in Eyre & Spottiswoode. Like Churchill, his appearance of wealth went far beyond what an objective calculation of his net worth might have shown.

Bracken was more astute in guiding Eyre & Spottiswoode's next investment in financial journalism and overcoming serious obstacles in the way. He encountered both a serious rival and hostility to himself as a proprietor when he tried to buy the venerable *Economist* magazine. He settled for 50 per cent ownership and an agreement that left full control of the title with its own executives. Bracken next bought full ownership of the *Investors' Chronicle* for £100,000, which advised – and still advises – private investors on equity investments. His next purchase was the *Liverpool Journal of Commerce*, which cost £70,000. It lay on the fringes of the financial world as a shipping journal and, like the *Financial News*, it played second fiddle to the venerable leader in its sector, *Lloyd's List*. Bracken finessed his own run of tricks in financial publications by diversifying Eyre & Spottiswoode's journalistic exposure into an entirely unrelated area. To widespread surprise, he came up with the purchase of a journal for GP doctors, *The Practitioner*. Unlike the profession's leading publications *The Lancet* and the *British Medical Journal* which combined scientific erudition with rigorous professional conservatism, *The Practitioner* was avowedly a trade journal for people making a living in the sector. *The Practitioner* also carried extensive advertising from pharmaceutical companies.[3] Its profits had slipped from £8,000 to £5,000, so it could be bought for £50,000, the same as the half-share in *The Economist* and well below the cost of the *Financial News*. This was to prove a shrewd investment.

Bracken rounded off the assembly of this group of financial publications by the creation of a dedicated holding company for them,

Financial Newspaper Proprietors Ltd, which was floated on the stock exchange in July 1928. In time-honoured fashion, Eyre & Spottiswoode kept full control of the operation through the ownership of 25,000 management shares which had twenty times the votes of the 525,000 ordinary shares available to the public. Bracken chaired the new company and was in confident form for the future of the combined group when he presented its first set of results. Presciently, he noted how profits had been driven by revenue from publishing prospectuses for companies taking advantage of the market boom to issue new shares:

> This alliance will be of considerable advantage to the *Financial News*, and will not only lead to important administrative economies, but will also provide a basis for the development of your property upon a scale far beyond the resources of a single newspaper. Believing as we do in the great future which lies before this journal, we are nevertheless convinced that all schemes of development must be tempered by a careful regard for its distinctive character, which has won for it the confidence and esteem of a great number of readers in all parts of Great Britain and beyond the seas ... Upon this point I must observe that the recent spate of issues has contributed considerably to these profits. It is prudent to doubt the permanence of this condition of affairs. We do not rely upon this rather abnormal contribution to our revenues. Much otherwise.[4]

Bracken remained on the board of Eyre & Spottiswoode with the prestige and income that this brought, but he now had his own show to run. The administrative savings that he had promised his shareholders were elementary economies. These took the form of grouping the operations of three of the titles – *Financial News, Investors' Chronicle* and *The Banker* – into one house, a modern light and spacious building at 20 Bishopsgate.[5]

A new arrival at the *Financial News* described Bracken as 'a likable erratic figure' whose habit of forgetting to appear at meetings was part

of 'the casual style' allowable when 'one has the Bracken personality –
backed by the Bracken power and money'.[6] In reality, Bracken was not
wealthy, but his self-projection created that impression.

Bracken parlayed his management success at Eyre & Spottiswoode
into material success. He was granted a small holding in Eyre & Spottiswoode's equity. He acquired the lease on an elegant town house on
North Street near the Houses of Parliament. He claimed to have been
the driving force in renaming the road as Lord North Street, of which
he pretended to own half.[7] He travelled in a large, chauffeured Hispano-
Suiza car, luxurious and more ostentatious than a Rolls-Royce. He
was a living illustration of how to achieve success through a combination of 'other people's money' and 'positive mental attitude' – the
saws of self-help gurus down the ages. Bracken collected antiquities
and paintings enthusiastically to furnish the house.[8] His library was
described as 'a complete library of an eighteenth-century English no-
bleman'. When he left it to Sedbergh, his alma mater, it was said to be
worth the vast sum of £20,000.[9]

Bracken's work with Eyre & Spottiswoode established him firmly
as a force in the world of business journalism. He rounded this off
by putting his foot on the first rung of his own career in politics as
distinct from acting as Churchill's faithful assistant. There is no trace
of political activity after the Westminster Abbey by-election in 1924,
when he had been no more than a personal and unpaid assistant to
Churchill, but in 1929, he had become the official Conservative Party
candidate for Paddington North. Sir William Perring, the sitting MP,
had announced his intention of standing down, so the opening arose
in a routine and uncontentious fashion. Perring had secured only a
slender majority even in the Conservative landslide of 1924 and would
be facing a severe fight at the next general election. The choice of
Bracken as candidate seems to have been an exclusively local move
with no involvement from anyone senior in the Conservative Party
nationally, Churchill included. Sir Herbert Hunter, chairman of the
local association, knew that his party would need the most dynamic
candidate possible to give it a chance in a tough fight. Bracken secured

the nomination by the usual combination of courting the relevant hierarchy and financial donation to the local party. Rear-Admiral Murray Sueter, who had been a patron in one of Bracken's early forays into London's literary and political world, turned up to speak for him.

Paddington North was socially mixed, but this did not deter Bracken from parading his open hostility to socialism even when canvassing more deprived areas. He blamed unemployment on the General Strike and the ensuing protracted miners' strike. The campaign was distinctly rumbustious, with Labour supporters attempting to disrupt Bracken's meetings so vigorously that the Labour candidate offered to attend a meeting to restrain hecklers. Bracken fully justified Hunter's confidence in his commitment to the campaign and spoke at twenty open-air meetings in a fortnight. He even had to fight off the accusation circulated in a flyer that he was really a Polish Jew; Paddington was socially but not ethnically mixed.

Bracken's task was all the harder because the Liberals fielded a candidate likely to appeal to some Conservative voters: Reginald Myer, who was connected to the powerful banking house of Samuel Montagu. Now reunited under David Lloyd George, the Liberals had regained something of their old force, although Lloyd George himself concentrated his campaign on Wales. At the national level, the Conservatives were held back by Prime Minister Stanley Baldwin's uninspiring leadership, encapsulated in the party's leaden election slogan, 'Safety First'. Bracken had a low opinion of the contribution of either Baldwin or J. C. C. Davidson, his close ally, who was then party chairman. On election day in May 1929, Bracken's efforts paid off and he won with 13,876 votes just ahead of Labour's 13,348; the Liberals polled 6,723. He publicly thanked Beaverbrook for the support of his newspapers (albeit to a *Daily Express* reporter), which he contrasted with a disappointing performance by the rest of the press.

8

THE WINSTONIANS

Brendan Bracken's victory at Paddington North went against the trend of the national results in the general election of 1929. The Conservatives paid the price for Stanley Baldwin's errors and lost 152 seats and the majority in Parliament. Labour under Ramsay MacDonald gained 136 and became the largest party in Parliament. With the support of the Liberals, MacDonald became Prime Minister again, this time with a far more solid political position.

The new Labour government adopted causes which offended Winston Churchill's instinctive support for the British Empire. It dismissed Lord Lloyd, the British High Commissioner to Egypt, who had dragged his heels over loosening Britain's grip on the country. More important, it began to make moves to reform Britain's relationship with its colony in India. Churchill saw both choices as malign socialist policies from the outset. The leadership of the Conservative Party took a far more conciliatory approach, but Churchill took an extreme hostile position towards the proposals on India. This opened a rift with the mainstream Conservative Party which was not to heal until his wartime leadership recast the relationship completely. This mistaken decision was to shape his political destiny through the 1930s. It was one long step into the political wilderness where only his most faithful adherents were willing to follow him. He had broken with the Conservative front bench and struck out on his own. The arrival of the MacDonald government gave a fillip to the search for a response to the pressure which was building in India against British rule. A year after Baldwin's defeat in the 1929 election, Churchill had been the first high-profile MP to join the Indian Empire Society, which had been founded under the leadership of Sir Michael O'Dwyer, former lieutenant governor of the Punjab, in 1930 to oppose reform. O'Dwyer was a hard-line opponent of liberalisation of the British Raj and had strongly supported General Dyer for his actions during the 1919 Amritsar massacre. O'Dwyer was murdered in long-delayed revenge in 1940. A series of Round Table Conferences with Indian leaders began in London in 1930, broadly supported by the Conservative leadership. Churchill rejected this approach and, in early 1931, left the Conservative shadow Cabinet, which he followed up with a now notorious speech in his constituency: 'It is alarming and also nauseating to see Mr Gandhi, a seditious Middle Temple lawyer, now posing as a fakir of a type well known in the East, striding half-naked up the steps of the Vice-Regal palace ... to parley on equal terms with the representative of the King-Emperor.'[1]

Churchill's move into internal opposition might have been hastened by his growing financial difficulties. He had lost heavily on US share investments in the Great Crash of 1929, which spurred him towards more lucrative activities such as writing and lectures. In December 1931, he arrived in New York for a well-paid lecture tour in the US but was run over by a car and severely injured. Frederick Lindemann consoled him with a computation of the force of the accident which he had survived and the resilience of his body's frame.[2] Bracken was nearly in tears at the news and organised a collection amongst Churchill's friends, fronted by Archie Sinclair, to buy him an expensive car on his return.[3]

In the 1930s, the British position in India was confused and ambiguous. At one level, it was a relic of Victorian imperialism. Under the statute of Westminster, the white-governed possessions had won practical independence as dominions, bound to the mother country by almost nothing except for a common sovereign, but India stood apart, its statute barely changed since the previous century. British viceroys were drawn primarily from the ranks of the hereditary aristocracy. Government was split between areas under direct British rule and the notionally autonomous princely states, which covered half the land mass and a quarter of the population. These were ruled by hereditary princes of various grades, who had surrendered control over what passed for external affairs in exchange for British support at home. In practice, the British had often taken internal charge as well when they felt that the princes were not up to the job. Only 60,000 white soldiers, supplemented by 174,000 locals in India's British-led but autonomous army, were available to maintain British power, but this was a negligible force in the face of the potential challenge from the continent's fast-growing population of 320 million. Hitler admired Britain's ability to achieve control over so much with so few resources, but in practice, the Raj depended on acceptance far more than force. Like the Indian Army, the Indian civil service which administered those territories directly under British rule had a relatively small number of men of British origin in the top ranks and was largely local at lower levels. The judiciary and organisations like the Indian forest service showed similar patterns. The number of white British people who directed the continent was only in the thousands, but they held wildly disproportionate power and created a preeminent section of British society; almost all retired to their home country. Their salaries and pensions were paid by taxation on India. As early as the beginning of the nineteenth century, the Scots philosopher James Mill described the British Empire as 'a vast system of outdoor relief for the upper classes'. India was a major trading partner of Britain, but it was no longer a captive and easy market for British manufactured goods, and by 1931, the Indian government was making full use of its power and was levying a tariff of 25 per cent on imports. The newly constructed modernist and elegant government complex in New Delhi, designed by Sir Edwin Lutyens and completed in 1931, projected British self-confidence and faith that their rule would continue, but the current of history was turning against the project.

The first cracks in the edifice had come during the First World War, when the British government had accepted the need for 'the gradual development of self-governing institutions with a view to the progressive realisation of responsible government in India'. In total,

1.5 million Indians had volunteered to serve in the armed forces, over-whelmingly the army, during the war and India had been a major source of finance. The aspiration to 'responsible government' was anchored in the 1919 Government of India Act, which made baby steps including an elected (but largely powerless) lower house. The 1919 Act also made a large deposit in the store of grievances amongst hard-line 'diehard' Conservatives who were affronted that it was passed with no parliamentary debate by governmental fiat.

The 1919 Act conspicuously failed to satisfy Indians. Civil unrest such as that which culminated in the Amritsar massacre continued. Mahatma Gandhi's Congress Party grew in power and influence. Its communal inclusivity and programme of non-violent protest were strong advantages. When Baldwin succeeded MacDonald as Prime Minister, he extended his support for the Round Table Conference's work. He backed a scheme devised by the Conservative delegate on the conference, the ambitious young MP for Chelsea Sir Samuel Hoare, for a constitution rigged to hold Congress at bay and heavy representation for Muslims as a counterbalance to the Hindu majority. Hoare's plan worked its way slowly through the parliamentary mechanisms of a Select Committee and eventually emerged as a Bill that was to be debated and voted. Unlike in 1919, the diehards would have every opportunity to make their objections heard and to attempt to frustrate the measure.

The long-grinding attritional battle to pass what was to become the 1935 Government of India Act is one of the most epic pieces of parliamentary history. It lasted five years and consumed many hours of parliamentary time. Overall, 15.5 million words were spoken in the discussion, which covered 4,000 pages of Hansard, and 15,000 parliamentary questions were asked. Hoare bore the brunt of the work and earned a place in the higher councils of the government, despite the widespread distrust he garnered. Hoare inspired almost as much suspicion amongst mainstream Conservative supporters as amongst his opponents on the issue. At stake was Baldwin's authority over his own party and he was fully prepared to use every dirty trick in the book to uphold it. He was also determined to prevent India becoming a running sore as the Irish question had become in the second half of the nineteenth century, when it sucked the life out of much of British politics, leading ultimately to near civil war in Britain and civil war in Ireland.[4] Baldwin was also more farsighted than Churchill and believed that control should be surrendered gracefully: 'If you refuse [dominion status] you will infallibly lose India before two generations have passed.'[5] The India Bill episode was neatly sandwiched between two general elections, so it cannot be judged whether the British electorate was especially concerned. It arose as a by-election platform issue in Lancashire constituencies where India's ferocious 25 per cent tariffs on imported goods added further pain to a textile industry struggling with the Great Slump and, as we now know, long-term structural decline, but there is no sign that these concerns spread much more widely in the electorate.

The opponents of reform in India came to be called the diehards. The diehards were not a cohesive group with a distinctive or coherent positive ideology. Insofar as they had positive beliefs, it was that India was part of the eternal greatness of the British Empire and nothing that put this into question should be allowed. A simple question of career background also played a part. It has been calculated that fifty-two of the 1929 intake of Conservative MPs were former professional military, colonial or civil service officers; such men made up much of the local Conservative Party organisations as well.[6] Perhaps the strongest common bond was a traditional law-and-order hostility to the civil disobedience practised by Gandhi and his followers. The diehard label had originally been applied to opponents of constitutional reform in Ireland and there was some overlap of individuals. Both Churchill and Lord Birkenhead, who had opposed Indian reform in the 1920s, came out of this stable. There was also some trace of a broader agenda that lay behind the diehards' campaign on India. Lord Wolmer was rather in a minority when he fantasised that the India battle would 'lay the foundations of a new Conservative Party which is true to Conservative principles'.[7] Churchill's final break with the party leadership came in 1933, when he declined a seat on the Select Committee that was to shape the Bill and, together with Lord Lloyd, founded the India Defence League (IDL) to mobilise opposition to the Bill in the party organisation.

The issue of India was stronger on the ground in the Conservative organisations than at Westminster. At its peak, the IDL had 8,000 members, admittedly not exclusively party members. The threat of deselection against MPs who overstepped the mark in supporting the Bill was a constant presence, although it only occasionally came to the surface. There was no distinct body amongst Conservative MPs comparable to the pro-Brexit European Research Group, but the diehards could consistently muster around fifty MPs in their support against the various steps in the Bill and on one occasion, 118 voted against the government's 209 members. Arguably, the peak of the diehards' parliamentary power came when 245 Conservative MPs defied a three-line whip to abstain and voted for an amendment tabled by leading diehard Sir Henry Page Croft aimed at limiting the scope of the Bill.[8] The government never came remotely near defeat, but the size of the insurrection was a constant preoccupation. Baldwin was disadvantaged because there was no material grass-roots support for the Bill in the Conservative Party and precious little in the country as a whole. The Union of Britain and India (UBI), set up as a counter to the IDL, was largely a sham. Despite its claims to be non-party and independently financed, it was practically an arm of the Conservative Central Office.[9] In terms of membership, branches, prestige of officers and quality of its publications, the UBI was a pale shadow of the IDL. Rab Butler, who was in charge of the UBI, ran it from the start as 'some publicity campaign against Winston' but admitted that it was very difficult to find anyone distinguished to join it.[10] The personalisation of the issue is telling.

The balance between principle and opportunism is almost unguessable in any politician's career, none more so than Churchill's. Churchill's choice of the Indian issue on which to break with his party leadership was fateful. Fighting reform in India meshed with Churchill's conservative tendencies and he retained a deep emotional attachment to the Raj as an aspect of national grandeur. During the Second World War, he was clear that one of his war aims was to preserve the empire: 'I have not become the King's first minister in order to preside over the liquidation of the British Empire.' At a practical level, he repeatedly asserted that sectarian issues complicated self-government enormously and presented Britain as a force preventing violence between the Hindu, Muslim and Sikh communities in India. He had served in India briefly as a young cavalry subaltern at the height of the Raj but otherwise had no links to the region. He had never revisited the subcontinent and he had no particular friends or contacts amongst the Anglo-Indian community. Baldwin shrewdly captured Churchill's converging instincts at an early phase of the campaign: 'He wants the [Indian] Conference to bust up quickly and the Tory party to go back to pre-war and govern with a strong hand. He has become once more the subaltern of Hussars of '96.'[11]

It is hard to escape the conclusion that Churchill's strongest motive was political opportunism. Churchill set out his analysis to Sir Austen Chamberlain, whom he had invited to Chartwell in 1933 and was trying to win over to his scheme to use the issue to gain power:

> [Churchill] anticipates that he and his Indian Die-Hards will continue to hold about 1/3rd of the Party, that the India Bill will be carried but that a fight would leave such bitter memories that the Govt. will have to be reconstructed. Only Ramsay, S. B., Samuel (Sam) Hoare, Irwin [Edward Wood later Lord Halifax] and perhaps the Lord Chancellor are so committed that they would have to be reconstructed. Simon could stay and it would still be a National Government, but who is to lead it? Obviously I am the man! And so he led me up to a high place and showed me the kingdoms of the world. I was not greatly tempted.[12]

Churchill advertised his ambitions flagrantly and even boasted to party chairman and Baldwin ultra-loyalist J. C. C. Davidson, 'I am going to lead a Midlothian campaign against you, and the Government will be out … in a fortnight.'[13] It is hard to judge whether Churchill's misreading of the Conservative Party was worse than his misreading of Austen Chamberlain. Baldwin had already survived one well-supported challenge to his leadership in 1931, which in practice had anointed Neville Chamberlain as his successor and the controller of the party's policy. Down the years, it came as a constant surprise that a politician as uninspiring as Baldwin was able to outmanoeuvre far more glamorous figures. Contempt for Baldwin's persona too easily translated into a huge underestimate of his political skills. Churchill's opposition to the India Bill fed a vicious circle of doubts over his judgement, both in the choice of issue and in his willingness to fight the party's leadership over it.

Baldwin found it convenient to personalise the debate. He spotted early on that the diehards who had 'loathed' Churchill as Chancellor were now 'running round him'.[14] Baldwin presented the choice as lying between his judgement and Churchill's: 'My doubts and apprehensions would be increased many times if the course advocated by Mr Churchill or any of his friends was taken.'[15] To more biddable opponents, Baldwin displayed a respectful and conciliatory face. Supporters of the Bill constantly inveighed against the 'Winston crowd'.[16] At the extreme end of the spectrum, Baldwin's would-be tame journalist, the editor of *The Times* Geoffrey Dawson, invented the label 'Winstonians' who were 'all "traitors" to their party'.[17] Churchill probably did Baldwin a favour by providing him with a lightning rod to draw criticism into an ultimately harmless direction, but India set the seal on Baldwin's determination that Churchill should be a pariah. According to his long-term ally J. C. C. Davidson, 'I asked him bluntly what kept Churchill out [of government]. "India … He has gone about threatening to smash the Tory Party on India, and I did not mean to be smashed."'[18] Rab Butler judged that Churchill's goal of capturing the Conservative Party machine never had any prospect of succeeding because the members distrusted him personally.[19]

Churchill might have been the standard-bearer of the diehards, but they trusted him no more than the government did. Wolmer labelled him an 'Awful incubus' to the diehards.[20] In the view of Davidson:

In opposition to the Government of India Bill there were really two groups; there was the Tory Opposition and the Churchill Opposition, and although they were synchronized up to a point, it was only up to a point. Churchill wasn't really a Conservative, and he cut very little ice with the Conservative Party; in fact the diehard Tories who opposed us over India never regarded Churchill as a Conservative at all. Thus, although the Tory opponents of the Government's India policies welcomed Winston's support, they always rather apologized for the fact that Winston was in their camp.[21]

The *Morning Post* was the house journal of the typical diehards scattered throughout the Conservative Party organisation. It was a relic of a past age that has helped create the parody image of the crusty reactionary retired colonel or district commissioner. It featured a full page of 'Indian' news, although when it wrote of 'Indians', it meant members of the British Raj; the local inhabitants were referred to simply as 'natives'. Its circulation shrank with each of its death notices. The most serious journalistic support for Churchill's campaign came from the Harmsworths' *Daily Mail*.[22] Beaverbrook did not pick up the issue in his *Daily Express* even though it offered one on which to undermine Baldwin, whom he detested. Beaverbrook's imperial preoccupations focused on the 'white dominions'. More important, perhaps, the Bill's chief parliamentary shepherd, Samuel Hoare, was the closest to him of any minister, so compromising the Bill would harm Hoare's prospects and with them the possibility that Beaverbrook might ultimately help place a man in Downing Street who would elevate him to the role that he had fantasised he would hold under Andrew Bonar Law.

Churchill was facing an uneven and savage fight. He was the driving force behind parliamentary opposition to the Bill and its very public face, but he failed to create a distinct group which acknowledged him as its leader. The only high-level Conservative to fight the Bill wholeheartedly was Lord Lloyd, who had the double disadvantage in this kind of fight of having been more of an imperial pro-consul – Governor of Bombay 1918–23 and High Commissioner to Egypt

1925–29 – and sitting in the Lords from 1924. The IDL was distinctly middle-aged or older. The most effective and vigorous young diehard Conservative MP, Victor Raikes, never truly entered Churchill's orbit. Patrick Donner, who acted as the IDL's secretary, was not yet an MP. Clemmie Churchill seems to have been tepid about the project, to judge from her perfunctory interest in the gatherings of diehards at Chartwell.[23] Frederick Lindemann was a supporter but had then no position in politics.[24] Robert Boothby was entirely unsympathetic. Only Brendan Bracken shared fully his master's commitment.

9

THE DISCIPLE

As the 1920s drew to a close, Brendan Bracken stood on top of the world. He had come an immense distance for someone without important family or territorial support in the still closed and hierarchical British society of the era. At the age of twenty-eight, he was both an MP and the chairman, in practice chief executive, of a quoted company that was a major force in financial journalism. The continuing stock market boom held out the prospect of relentless prosperity. He had an elegant town house in a prestigious area that he was filling with valuable antiques.

Bracken was also back on firmly good terms with Winston Churchill and he was able to use his new seat in the House of Commons to extend the friendship. He was part of a group of Young Turk Conservative MPs, which included Robert Boothby – no longer formally tied to Churchill since he had ceased to be Chancellor – and Harold Macmillan, who were discontented and frustrated at Stanley Baldwin's lethargic and uninspiring leadership.

Bracken's self-invention as a powerhouse of financial journalism gave him a perhaps unpredictable edge over Churchill. Churchill was an enthusiastic, not especially successful stock market speculator and his intellectual grasp of financial markets was never better than shaky. As his ministerial record as Chancellor showed, he was comfortable with grand reform but not the minutiae of day-to-day economic management. Bracken's boundless self-confidence extended to the world of finance and lent him the appearance of a master of its intricacies. At a more mundane level, Bracken's contacts amongst powerful financiers and business figures would come as very welcome to Churchill.

As a young, first-term MP, Bracken threw himself into the doings of Parliament with his trademark vigour and forcefulness. His numerous interventions in debate and ministerial questions spanned the whole gamut of topics, but it was his engagement on the question of constitutional reform for India that stood out. Here he was a faithful second in Churchill's campaign against reform.

The Harmsworth press dynasty supplied more than journalistic support for Churchill over India. Through the intermediary of Bracken, they provided something of a financial lifeline. Bracken was lunching with Lord Rothermere and his son Esmond Harmsworth and seized the opportunity that was presented when Esmond proved to be taking an interest in the hands-on running of the *Daily Mail*. Hitherto, he had rather concentrated on the affairs of the Newspaper Proprietors' Association trade body. Bracken negotiated a deal giving Churchill a fee of £150 for a weekly article worth £7,800 over a year. Churchill insisted on complete freedom to choose the subject, which would not be exclusively topical political matters. Bracken headed him off from giving the Harmsworths exclusivity. In the event, the Harmsworths pulled their horns in and only signed Churchill for thirteen articles a year but still at the same very healthy fee.[1] Bracken also brokered a serialisation deal for Churchill's final and least commercially attractive book on the First World War, *The Eastern Front*.[2]

The income was all the more welcome given the scale of Churchill's losses on equity investments in the Great Crash of October 1929.

Bracken was just as ill-advised as Churchill himself in thinking that India was a winning issue that would turn round his chief's standing in the party and bring him back to power. Early in the campaign, he told Randolph Churchill:

[Churchill's] activities with regard to India ... have been altogether splendid. He has untied himself from Baldwin's apron, rallied all the fighters in the Tory Party, re-established himself as a potential leader & put heart into a great multitude here & in India. By a series of brilliant speeches in the House he has shown the Tories the quality of his genius

& the incredible drabness & futility of [Stanley Baldwin]. The boneless wonder speech is immortal.[3]

In July 1932, just before Churchill finally broke with the party, he was happy to discuss detailed and sensitive plans for his campaign with Bracken.[4] Bracken became a constant presence fighting on Churchill's behalf in the House and drew almost as much criticism as his chief from Baldwin: '[Churchill] had got with him sheets of typewritten invective against everybody and everything, and with all his stage army, including Randolph in the gallery, and the Bracken claque carefully dotted about the House.'[5] Bracken left the grand sweeping speeches to Churchill; his forte was constant harrying of ministers. Bracken spoke aggressively, complaining of the inadequacy of government answers to questions. He was often called to order. In one notably acrimonious exchange, Bracken revealed his tactics. Even though the MP concerned had accepted a government reply to a question, Bracken continued to press it. The Speaker rebuked, 'I hope Hon. Members will keep order, but I also hope that less provocative statements will be made.'

Bracken replied, 'There will be less provocation if Hon. Members will listen.'

Bracken steered close to outright abuse of ministers and the government's position: 'There are several ways of losing an empire and the Secretary of State is choosing a particularly bad way.' Under the MacDonald government, he had described William Wedgwood Benn, the India minister, as 'Gandhi's bell-hop'.[6] Bracken enthusiastically invented, often cuttingly effective, nicknames for his political opponents and occasionally for his allies. Ministers responded in kind. When a junior minister referred to him as Churchill's 'henchman Sancho Panza', Bracken sneered back – accurately, as it proved – that the minister was moved by ambition to reach the front bench but would not achieve this. His critic had been echoing Churchill's own attack on Ramsay MacDonald and John Simon returning from Geneva.[7] The most insidious and lasting epithet on Bracken came from

Baldwin, who called him Churchill's 'faithful chela', the Hindi word for disciple that had probably been suggested to him by his cousin, Rudyard Kipling. The imputation of religious subservience was all the more effective as it insinuated that Churchill operated on his followers in the same way as Gandhi, a particular bugbear for both Churchill and Bracken.

Bracken was deeply involved in Churchill's severest tactical miscalculation in his India campaign. Churchill had been presented with a prime example of government skulduggery when the Manchester Chamber of Commerce, which had initially come out against the Bill because of fears that it would hurt exports by the local textile industry, suddenly reversed its position. Bracken was one of the witnesses when Churchill spoke to a whistle-blower who gave him the inside story.[8] Churchill had been dealt an ace, but he misplayed it by trying to arraign the government for outright breach of parliamentary privilege rather than taking the easy win of pointing up publicly its misbehaviour. Baldwin spotted that Churchill had dug himself into a hole.[9] The episode also featured another parliamentary misstep when Churchill rose to the bait that his old sparring partner Leo Amery offered him by labelling his attitude with a Latin tag, one of Churchill's pet hates: '*Fiat justitia ruat caelum.*' When Churchill demanded, 'Translate', Amery had his answer ready, 'If I can trip up Sam [Hoare], the government's bust.' The House roared with laughter, giving Amery a long-delayed payback for Churchill having ducked him in the Harrow School swimming pool.

Bracken tried to help build up a coterie of supporters in the House. One beneficiary was Patrick Buchan-Hepburn, who had first hitched his star to Churchill's in the more promising days when he was at the Exchequer and had taken an unpaid private secretaryship. Churchill claimed that Bracken was able to fix a safe constituency for Buchan-Hepburn in the 1931 general election, when the Conservative landslide carried Buchan-Hepburn into Parliament as the member for the East Toxteth division of Liverpool. It was, though, Churchill who had supported him during the campaign and he appeared to be appropriately grateful. But Churchill and Bracken had judged their man wrong and once he was safely in Parliament he did not support them against the bill. Churchill complained that Buchan-Hepburn proved to be a 'very poor spirited creature. All he could do was profess his undying love and loyalty to Baldwin and to dissociate himself from my views on India.'[10] Four years later, Churchill still considered him a rat.[11]

As the India Act was reaching its final parliamentary stages, Randolph Churchill chose to complicate things both politically and personally for his father. Entirely on his own initiative, he stood as a candidate in a by-election in Liverpool Wavertree on an anti-Bill platform against the official Conservative candidate. There was a large local textile industry, so fears that the Bill would further harm exports to India were a potent force. Randolph was heavily backed by the Harmsworths, for whom he was working a journalist. By contrast, Beaverbrook's *Evening Standard* published a cartoon by its star cartoonist David Low portraying the 'Churchill Party' (Winston and Randolph) as hirelings of India's notoriously wealthy and unappealing princes whose overwhelming interest in the Bill was to protect their own status. Beaverbrook and Low pretended that Low enjoyed autonomy, but Beaverbrook exercised a powerful influence over the editorial content of his newspapers.[12] Churchill himself privately did not approve but spurred by family loyalty and pride in his son's efforts came out in support both financially and on the ground. Randolph's sisters were given little choice in the matter and were driven to the constituency to turn out for him despite the rowdy and often violent turn that his campaign took. Bracken threw himself into the battle with his customary vigour, helping Randolph develop the economic side to his platform, 'preparing through his financial papers *The Economist*, *The Banker* etc. a thoroughly sound statement'.[13] He did not neglect the more mundane logistical side of the campaign either.[14] After some hesitation, the IDL also endorsed Randolph, but none of the political heavyweight opponents of the Bill apart from his father backed him. More money came from the predictable sources of the

Duke of Westminster and the eccentric Lucy, Lady Houston.[15] Randolph split the Conservative vote, letting in the Labour candidate. It might all have been calculated to further harm Churchill's already badly dented reputation.

There was enough concern over the Churchills' doings for the constituency association for Epping to include a paragraph sharply critical of them in a report:

> India is in the forefront of our thoughts, and while no one doubts Mr Churchill's sincerity, is he, in the words of Sir Samuel Hoare, 'the only Gulliver in a land of pygmies?' The vast majority of thinking Conservatives consider that this Government Bill is a wise and constructive measure, and if the lamentable Wavertree by-election is to be regarded as a test of public opinion in regard to it, the result can only be construed as three to one in favour of the Bill: 32,000 votes were polled against Mr Randolph Churchill and 10,000 in his favour.[16]

The criticism was challenged but was upheld by the association's annual general meeting.

Randolph doubled down by backing an independent candidate at the Norwood by-election soon after. Again he did not consult his father beforehand and Churchill was furious at the potential damage to his own reputation.[17] Almost no one backed Randolph's efforts; even his employer Rothermere turned against him and Beaverbrook tried to persuade him to back down; only Lady Houston stayed true to Randolph's cause and she was as great a reputational drawback as she was a financial boon. Here at least he did not fatally damage the Conservative vote and the official candidate Duncan Sandys was elected.[18] Randolph's candidate, Richard J. Findlay, was an extreme right-winger whom even the India Defence League refused to back.[19] Findlay polled fewer votes than the majority by which the official Conservative candidate, Duncan Sandys, won the seat. By a small irony, Sandys soon became one of Churchill's handful of parliamentary backers and a member of the family when he married Churchill's daughter Diana.

The India Act was a titanic parliamentary effort, but it was an almost perfect example of the mountain labouring to bring forth a mouse. The Act might have met the needs of the House of Commons, but it came nowhere near settling unrest or the aspirations of the Indian people. It failed to attract any serious positive support in India – above all, Gandhi gave it scant attention. On the ground, the Bill never overcame the multiple contradictions it faced amidst conflicting interests and even its limited provisions never came into effect. It was submerged by the events of the Second World War and the process that led to full independence. Churchill was sucked into fighting a legislative Stalingrad that almost fatally damaged his career. He won no friends; the diehards were mainly on the other side of the barricades in his next great battle against appeasement.

By the time of the 1935 general election in November, India had faded into the background. Churchill actively hoped that Randolph would be able to return from covering the Chaco War in South America to fight the election.[20] Initially, Randolph threatened a rerun of his Wavertree campaign as an independent, but he was bought off with the Conservative Party's nomination as their official candidate for another constituency. West Toxteth was a far more mixed area and it had swung between the Conservatives and Labour: it was Labour in 1929, with a 3,679 majority; Conservative in 1932 by 5,635 votes; and Labour again at a by-election in 1935, with a majority of 5,343. The campaign was rowdy and violent. Even without the India issue, Randolph managed to cut the Labour majority to 2,004.

10

APPRENTICESHIP IN SURVIVAL

Whilst Brendan Bracken was undertaking the prolonged apprenticeship in parliamentary warfare red in tooth and claw presented by the India Bill, he was also fighting a savage battle for survival in his business career. The Great Slump triggered by the Wall Street Crash of 1929 spelt the end of the high hopes that he had entertained when Financial Newspapers had been founded. New share issue activity came to a near complete end and with it the lucrative business of publishing prospectuses. Having published 646 prospectuses in the 1928 boom, the total slumped to 381 in the following year and to 186 in 1930, which was not yet even the low point. The company's more subscription-based titles rode out the storm comparatively well, notably Bracken's diversification away from the financial world *The Practitioner*, but the *Financial News* was in peril. The *Financial News*'s difficulties were all the greater as it lagged behind the *Financial Times* considerably in circulation. Its losses in 1931–32 surged to £26,731 from £21,184 the previous year, before recovering to a still unsatisfactory £6,130. It was still in the red the year afterwards. It went from an exceptional seventy-four pages in 1928 to a dozen or so.

A number of expedients attracted Bracken's attention and enthusiasm as he desperately sought an avenue to survival only to be discarded. It was briefly considered merging the *Financial News* with the *Liverpool Journal of Commerce*.[1] Eventually, though, the *Liverpool Journal of Commerce* was sold for a much-needed cash injection. Bringing down the cost of printing the paper was a constant preoccupation. Staff wages were cut by as much as 33 per cent. The strain on Bracken was manifest and one journalist described his 'rat-like rushings' and relayed a story of him summoning another director for an urgent consultation at his house, where Bracken drank himself to sleep on the sofa. Bracken was inclined to involve himself too deeply in detail and some of the cost-cuts he imposed were seen as downright cheese-paring. Bracken pushed for one of the two assistant editorships to be cut, even whilst another senior journalist was desperate to resign.[2] A triumvirate of senior journalists became so concerned at his leadership that they plotted to force his removal, but their resolution weakened in the face of his personal charm: 'Bracken is such a lovable boy as well as such a dangerous bloody fool.'[3]

Bracken's task in managing the *Financial News* through this bruis-ing period was complicated by his deteriorating relationship with the newspaper's editor, Oscar Hobson. Bracken had appointed Hobson, who had been the financial editor of the *Manchester Guardian*, for his experience and skills in daily newspapers and they had worked happi-ly to begin with, but the partnership soured. Bracken tried to cut costs to the bone, but the editor resisted. Bracken was also deeply critical of Hobson's editorial approach and sent out a memo savagely critical of the quality of his work. Hobson was a resolute free trader at a time when the financial world was overwhelmingly in favour of tariffs, so curbing his independence might have won potentially influential friends in the City but Bracken stuck to the principle of editorial free-dom. He allowed Hobson editorial control even though he referred to him as 'that incorrigible Calvinist'.[4] Hobson opposed a scheme to control tin output which antagonised Oliver Lyttelton, a leading figure in mining finance and later government minister. Lyttelton had set up the Amalgamated Metals Corporation with open City and tacit government backing to challenge the German monopoly of trading in non-ferrous metals. Even though Lyttelton was a large potential advertiser and they had a great mutual friend in W. S. Robinson, the Australian mining financier, Bracken did not suppress Hobson's crit-icism. Hobson's dogmatic free trade stance was a flaw and this was obvious even to Collin Brooks, a senior journalist who tended to side with his editor in the fight and criticised Bracken's aggression towards

Hobson. Hobson stuck to his economic mantra even though he weakened his principles on other points. In the *Financial News*'s desperate state, Hobson was willing to suppress an unfavourable article on the flotation of the Decca company, one of the rare such deals in that period, and Brooks excoriated him for it. Hobson left the *Financial News* when his contract expired to mutual relief.

The combination of Bracken's standing in the journalistic world and his political position gave him an entrée into the rarified spheres at the top of the industry and he was able to brag of being privy to the gossip amongst the Beaverbrooks and Rothermeres of the world.[5] This seems to have given him rather grand ideas of his status as a top-level industry insider, controlling the destiny of senior journalists from titles where he had no connection. He genuinely sought out and found opportunities for Brooks and was happy to try to broker ambitious salary demands.[6] Bracken was not overawed by the grand figures who inhabited the world of finance and, after his early rebuff, was downright scabrous about Montagu Norman, the dominant and domineering governor of the Bank of England for the whole inter-war period. When Norman unexpectedly married a divorcee not quite half his age, he quipped, 'In future, he'll call himself Professor Foreskinner.'[7*] Norman received no more respectful treatment in a map of the different sections of the stock exchange drawn by artist Rex Whistler and published by the *Financial News*. In the area labelled 'Gilt Market', worshippers prostrate themselves before a bust which is adorned with Norman's trademark goatee beard and homburg hat.

As the economy recovered, the financial crisis passed. *Financial News* was able to bring its advertising rates up to the level of those commanded by *Financial Times* and it appears to have reached financial break-even in the second half of 1933.[8] By the late 1930s, prosperity had been far enough rebuilt for Bracken's salary to be put up to £5,000.[9] At the start of the slump, his pay had been cut from £3,000 to £2,000. It had been a brutal training in managing an organisation

---

* Norman, who loved to shroud his doings in secrecy, travelled under the alias Professor Skinner.

through a crisis and it was to stand Bracken in good stead before too long.

*   *   *

Brendan Bracken's fictional avatar, Rex Mottram in Evelyn Waugh's *Brideshead Revisited*, rounds off his assault on British aristocratic society with – an ultimately catastrophic – marriage to an earl's daughter. Marriage into the ruling class would have been a classic avenue for Bracken to establish himself more firmly as a member of the establishment, but Bracken never quite got there. Bracken had romantic or near-romantic attachments to two women, but neither progressed to a more intense relationship. In both cases, the women were connected to Winston Churchill or his circle.

In 1932, Bracken began to take an interest in Lady Pamela Smith, the younger daughter of Lord Birkenhead, who was then aged eighteen.[10] Lord Beaverbrook backed the relationship and Bracken pleased her with compliments of her late father. However, she remembered her father's dislike of the 'red charlatan' and when he hinted at marriage, she was entirely uninterested. His world was one of older men, not given to frivolity, and she stood Bracken down.

The next object of Bracken's affections was Churchill's goddaughter, Penelope 'Pempie' Dudley-Ward, the beautiful daughter of the Prince of Wales's long-term mistress and her Liberal MP husband. This attachment lasted some years and was still running in 1935. When Pempie lost her dog on a train back from the Côte d'Azur, Bracken paid for a detective to try to find it.[11] He also asked his City contact, the film producer Alexander Korda, to help her in her acting career.[12] She was, though, deterred by Bracken's ultimate unwillingness to let anyone else fully into his life. He never proposed to Pempie and she later regretted: 'He told everyone that he was in love with me but he never told me.'[13] She broke up with Bracken, which reduced him to tears according to one account. He kept a photograph of her at his bedside until he died.[14] He remained a bachelor and there is no sign of even casual sexual encounters. Bracken may have known his limits. Paul Einzig, the journalist with whom he worked closely, took a prurient interest in his boss's sexuality but 'strongly rejected' the idea that he was a 'poofta'.[15]

Bracken's contact Korda was also able to extend a financial lifeline to Churchill himself. On their tours of the US, both Churchill and Randolph had visited Hollywood and were taken with the glamour of the film industry. Charlie Chaplin had been a guest at Chartwell already in 1931. The technologies of sound and, soon, colour film were transforming film into the dominant – and hugely lucrative – entertainment medium of the age. Churchill was aware of the opportunities for himself, and Korda immediately spotted the potential of bringing a high-profile politician into his output and was willing to pay lavishly.[16] Randolph handled the details. Korda paid Churchill an advance of £1,250 in early 1935 on a projected film about the Silver Jubilee of George V, from which Churchill expected to earn £10,000. The project eventually fell through, but given the parlous state of Churchill's finances at that point, what he did earn was immensely welcome.

11

PARRYING THE KNOCK-OUT BLOW

In the first half of the 1930s, Winston Churchill's political energies were absorbed by the struggle over Indian constitutional reform. It was the area where he aimed to influence practical policy, but it was not the only one on which he challenged the government. He was also vocal in his twin campaigns in favour of rearmament and to alert the country to the danger of Germany.

Churchill did not believe that the Versailles Treaty had brought permanent peace to Europe and was looking for signs of danger in any resurgence in Germany even before the Nazis came to power. He saw French consciousness of the threat posed by Germany as a constant of power politics. When Germany and Austria signed a customs union in 1931, he denounced this as the harbinger of a military alliance.[1] He applied the age-old metric of population size as a register of military strength and contrasted the combined populations of the two German-speaking nations of 70 million and an annual increase of their male population of military age with that of France. That same year, Churchill backtracked on the advocacy of disarmament implicit in the ten-year rule that he himself had imposed on the British military.[2] In 1932, Churchill predicted to the House of Commons that Germany would soon demand the return of lost territories and colonies.[3]

History has not been kind to Stanley Baldwin, especially for some of the things that he said publicly. Some were instantly spotted as faux pas; others sound deeply unfortunate with the benefit of hindsight. Of the latter, the most damaging both to his reputation and in its malign influence on public thinking and policy was his declaration in November 1932 that 'the bomber will always get through'. It nourished the hopeless terror of an imaginary 'knock-out blow' against London by the German air force that hypnotised the public and policy-makers until the outbreak of war.

The fear of a knock-out blow is a remarkable instance of collective delusion. It fed off the shock and horror provoked by the German air raids of the First World War which exposed mainland Britain to the realities of warfare that Continental cities had long known. It wildly exaggerated the powers of modern air attack. Perhaps worst was that it arose from an entirely abstract assessment of the options available to German military planners: unable to sustain a war as long as the First World War had proved, Germany would need to eliminate Britain – its most dangerous adversary – rapidly and would thus resort to a sudden, devastating air attack. There was never a scrap of evidence that Germany planned this or had the means to do so, but it fitted neatly into the Royal Air Force's view of the world. As an independent air service, the RAF was committed to the prediction of Sir Hugh Trenchard, its founding father, that future wars would be bombing contests in which the nation capable of delivering the greatest weight of bombs would win. The only response that the British government's professional advisers on air warfare believed was to increase Britain's bomber force.

Mordantly complimenting Baldwin on his 'latent and often carefully concealed powers [of oratory]', Churchill recognised how dangerous and fallacious Baldwin's words were, tantamount to an admission that the government could not defend the country:

But that speech … led to no practical conclusion. It created anxiety, and it created also perplexity. There was a sense of, what shall I say, fatalism, and even perhaps helplessness about it, and I take this opportunity of saying that, as far as this island is concerned, the responsibility of Ministers to guarantee the safety of the country from day to day, and from hour to hour, is direct and inalienable. It has always been so, and I am sure they will not differ from their predecessors in accepting that responsibility. Their duty is not only to try, within the restricted limits which, I fear, are all that are open to them, to prevent war, but to make sure that we ourselves are not involved in one, and, above all, to make sure that if war should break out among other Powers, our country and the King's Dominions can be effectively defended.[4]

If Germany was rearming, Churchill was certain that the government had to do something active to protect Britain. This was his mantra for the rest of the decade. As the Nazis came closer to power, Churchill almost had the opportunity to meet the man who was to make European war practically inevitable when he rose to lead Germany on a platform of rebuilding the nation's strength. In 1932, Churchill, together with Randolph and Frederick Lindemann, passed through Munich on his way to visit the battlefield of Blenheim where his ancestor, 1st Duke of Marlborough, had defeated Louis XIV's attempt to make France the dominant power in Europe. Randolph was keen for his father to meet Hitler. He had been in Germany the previous year to cover the election campaign on his first journalistic assignment and been able to observe the Nazis at close hand; ominously, he had forecast that it would mean war if the Nazis came to power.[5] Randolph asked Hitler's friend and photographer Putzi Hanfstaengl to arrange a meeting. Both Hanfstaengl and Churchill were willing, but according to Hanfstaengl's memoirs, his chief was daunted by Churchill's political skills and put off by his affection for France. Despite Hanfstaengl's repeated attempts, nothing came of the idea and the Churchills left Munich.

Churchill did not need to meet Hitler to understand the danger that he posed. In a high-profile speech, Churchill called for rearmament the day that Franz von Papen resigned as Chancellor of Germany, opening the way for Hitler's appointment.[6] Within months of coming to office, Hitler made it plain that his goal was to rebuild Germany's military position and strength; Germany withdrew from both the disarmament conference and the League of Nations, in practice the guarantor of the Versailles settlement. The British Cabinet responded by trying to soften France's opposition to German rearmament. The policy of the British government remained to push for disarmament throughout Europe. Financial considerations played as great a part as idealism.

Even before Germany began to rearm, Churchill had been preoccupied by Britain's growing inferiority in the air. When he assailed a proposed cut in spending on the RAF of £0.34 million in March 1933, he pointed out that Britain had slipped to the fifth air power in terms of military aircraft owned.[7] The 1933 Budget marked the low of Britain's by then unilateral, voluntary and financially driven disarmament. The following year saw the first baby steps towards rearmament as the recommendation of the Defence Requirements Committee (DRC) – called in 1933 to assess how weak Britain's military had become in an ever-more threatening world – came under consideration. Even in advance of the DRC, the Budget for the RAF had been increased, albeit by the trivial figure of £0.13 million – a fraction of the reduction in 1933. Churchill had been provided with a perfect lead-in for his first direct attack on the government's defence policy. The increase was tiny and otiosely precise – perfect material for Churchill's technique of bludgeoning repetition.

*   *   *

On a personal level, Robert Boothby remained close to Churchill. Having suffered a severe car accident himself, he sympathised with Churchill's 1931 car accident in New York and wrote consolingly comparing their two experiences. He was also one of the main organisers of the collection amongst Churchill's friends to buy him an expensive motor car when he returned to the country.

Boothby did find an aspect of international affairs and policy that was to bring him back into a close relationship with Churchill. Since the late 1920s, he had visited Germany every year and had developed a strong affinity to the country. He was comfortable in its open and extensive gay and transvestite scene where he relished the attentions that he attracted as a young and attractive man. In late 1931, he went to Berlin and Hamburg to deliver lectures on the economic crisis billed as the former private secretary to Churchill during his time as Chancellor. Afterwards, he reported on his impressions to Churchill, pointing to the confused and fractured state of German politics, still suffering from the dislocation of the First World War, but he was not complacent: 'But as a people they are tremendously formidable still, and I don't blame the French for being frightened.'[8] On this visit, he met two politicians at the extreme ends of the country's political destiny. He judged Chancellor Brüning to be exhausted, pessimistic and overwhelmed by the challenges he faced. Brüning's government was the last gasp of the Weimar democratic experiment. Boothby also interviewed Hitler. He correctly read the power of Hitler's passion and warned: 'We should not underestimate the strength of the movement of which he is the living embodiment', predicting that the Nazis would 'profoundly influence German politics in the years that lie ahead'. He caught Hitler unprepared by asking him about Nazi policies towards the Jews and was told after guilty hesitation that there would be no pogroms. Inexplicably, Boothby expected that Hitler would not take power personally if the Nazis won. His later accounts of the conversation suppressed this feature of the interview. On his return to London, Boothby later claimed to have tried to alert people to his concerns but found even David Lloyd George and Winston Churchill unreceptive.

Curiously, in view of his anxiety to portray himself as an early opponent of Nazism, Boothby did not mention in his autobiography that he had raised the question in the House of Commons a month after Hitler came to power.[9] He used the time-honoured device of following up an innocuous question to the Foreign Secretary, Sir John Simon, with a supplementary, asking whether the government knew anything of Hitler's plans to purge his political opponents. Simon merely told Boothby that he was asking something not covered by the question he had tabled and was widely supported by other MPs, including the Conservative Michael Beaumont who expressed the widespread sentiment of the day that the Germans should be 'allowed to manage their own affairs'.

Churchill was less interested in German internal affairs but focused on the threat that a rearmed Germany under the Nazi regime might pose to Britain. He was particularly alert to Germany's growing strength in the air, and rearming the RAF to meet this danger became his new cause just as his campaign against the India Bill was fading. Boothby actively supported his call with speeches, albeit less persistently than Bracken. In his later account, Boothby claimed that he was in constant touch with Bracken through this period, but it is hard to verify this independently.[10]

Rearmament in the air was the keynote of Churchill's opposition to the policies of Baldwin's government. These are often classed as appeasement but, in reality, were no more than cautious, passive and pragmatic responses to developments which hindsight tells us demanded a far more aggressive and positive response. Baldwin did rearm, but the scale of his programmes was limited by electoral hostility to anything that smacked of accepting the risk of war and the fiscal conservativism championed by Chamberlain, who was terrified of compromising Britain's weak and faltering recovery from the ravages of the Great Slump. In Baldwin's rhetoric, rearmament was merely something forced on Britain by Germany's actions.

By some measures, Churchill's campaign against Baldwin over rearmament opened fully in November 1934. Until then, he had still played the card of party loyalty, but when Parliament reassembled, he tabled an amendment to the Loyal Address which openly stated Churchill's belief that Britain was no longer safe from air attack: 'But humbly represent to Your Majesty that, in the present circumstances of the world, the strength of our national defences, and especially of our air defences, is no longer adequate to secure the peace, safety and freedom of Your Majesty's faithful subjects.' Churchill delivered a picture of the nightmarish damage that an air attack could inflict on London every bit as horrific as the most dedicated Trenchardian could have come up with. He called for a committee to examine possible defences – a small nod to the analysis of Lindemann who had already written to *The Times* stating it was 'profoundly impossible' that one could not be found –

and also stated the Trenchardian doctrine that only counter-bombing provided a sure defence. Much of the debate evolved around the question of whether Germany had already achieved, as Hitler had boasted, 'parity' with Britain in the air or would soon achieve it. Baldwin had pledged that no country would be allowed to put Britain in a position of inferiority in the air and Churchill challenged Baldwin's parity pledge head on. Without giving any explanation for the source of his belief, Churchill claimed Germany's air force would very soon be equal to Britain's, half as big again by the end of 1936 and almost double the size in 1937. He insinuated that British aircraft were slower than foreign – and so, German – ones. Baldwin met Churchill's challenge directly and chose to nail the government's colours very firmly to the mast: in practice claiming that its policies had brought safety. Baldwin doubled down on his commitment to parity with the assertions that Britain was twice as strong as Germany and would keep an advantage of 50 per cent. Boothby vigorously supported Churchill's stance. The government had been sucked into an arms race with Germany and for the next four years, Churchill and his allies were able to hammer its lacklustre performance in the race.

Five other MPs had signed Churchill's amendment. They included his old sparring partner Leo Amery, a former India diehard Lord Winterton and Boothby. Baldwin had noted with alarm Boothby's rekindled closeness to Churchill and wrote to his father, warning him the Churchill was a 'bad guide for youth'.[11] Boothby senior duly passed the warning on, but his son took no notice.

In the main, Churchill confined his campaign for rearmament to Parliament and the newspapers, but he made an exception on a visit to Birmingham in July 1938 where he had been speaking in favour of the League of Nations at the town hall. Accompanied by Ronald Cartland, the anti-appeasement MP for a Birmingham constituency, he then visited the shadow aircraft factory operated by the Austin Motor Company as part of the programme to build up the strength of the RAF.[12] According to Cartland – admittedly a hardly unbiased observer – Churchill was rapturously received by the workers.

Churchill's disagreements with the government extended beyond rearmament and diplomacy. With the support of Bracken and Harold Macmillan, Churchill challenged Neville Chamberlain, then Chancellor of the Exchequer and advocate of tight money, over whether transport infrastructure such as railways should receive favourable local tax treatment.[13] Macmillan was a committed quasi-Keynesian, but nothing in Bracken's record suggests that he was moved by principle. For once, Churchill was reading the sentiment of his party's backbenchers correctly. The opinion of the Conservative whips and central office swung the debate in Churchill's favour against Chamberlain's fiscal conservatism.

* * *

Winston Churchill's son-in-law Duncan Sandys came closest to the stock image of an ambitious young Conservative MP amongst Churchill's parliamentary supporters. He had followed the traditional route from a brief career at the Foreign Office into politics after Eton and Oxford, but marrying into the Churchill clan set his career on a different path. Unlike Boothby who had hitched his star to Churchill when he was a front-rank Conservative politician, Sandys linked himself to a near pariah in the party. Opposing appeasement was a decidedly minority political cause in those days. He claimed to have objected to the Foreign Office's misreading of the dangers of Hitler. A good number of other professional diplomats shared this view, but almost no other Conservative MPs. Sandys also put himself ahead of the era's social mores in marrying a divorcee: Diana had divorced her husband, John Bailey, after barely two years of marriage on the grounds of his adultery in early 1935. The gap between her divorce and remarriage was unusually short. Even in wartime when Oliver Lyttelton was being parachuted into a safe Conservative seat to make him a minister, the first concern of the vice-chairman of the Conservative Party was whether he had, in the damning phrase, been 'through the Divorce Court lately'.[14]

In the words of one of Sandys's closest friends:

He was tall, broad-shouldered and, with his red hair, exceptionally good-looking. He was forceful and extremely able. He could be very persuasive but, if he thought he was being unreasonably thwarted, ruthless. He had little sense of danger, be it physical or of any other person. He had independent means. To his friends he was loyal and generous to a fault.[15]

Sandys was possibly the most readily accessible of the Churchill clan. He even won over the arch Chamberlainite 'Chips' Channon, admittedly assisted by his part in humiliating Randolph whom he detested in the Norwood by-election campaign.[16] Channon also thought that Sandys had a boyfriend, but this might have been no more than a projection of his own sexuality.[17] Churchill took swiftly to his daughter Diana's husband and the young couple accompanied him on holidays in Morocco. Clemmie, too, liked Sandys, albeit with reservations:

They are sweet together & his devotion to [Diana] makes me like him better – I think when he is in London he is so taken up with his 'Career' & the excitement of Parliament that he has no time to talk to her or play with her, & she is a lovely fragile little flower which droops when neglected.[18]

Sandys was a close enough colleague of Churchill to be admitted to the 'bathroom group', with whom Churchill would talk whilst he was in his bath.[19] Bracken, too, enjoyed the privilege, and traditional Conservatives mocked Churchill's 'Companions of the Bath'.[20]

Sandys's first contribution to the campaign against appeasement rather jumped the gun. In response to rumours that Britain would attempt to return African colonies stripped from Germany at Versailles, he and a number of other young, right-wing Conservative MPs wrote a letter to the *Morning Post* in 1936 deploring the possibility.[21] In fact, it was not until early 1938 that Chamberlain made a serious, albeit misconceived and futile, attempt to win over Hitler with a deal for African colonies.[22]

Sandys habitually sat next to another staunch anti-appeaser, Ronald Cartland, in the House of Commons. Their striking hair colour – Sandys's red and Cartland's black – prompted the nickname 'Black Beauty and Ginger'.[23]

12

INTO THE LABYRINTH
OF COMMITTEES

Frederick Lindemann was no stranger to high-level attempts to improve Britain's defences against air attack. Even whilst efforts to improve the armed forces were held back by the dead hand of the ten-year rule, the possibility that the nation might once again be attacked from the air attracted attention. The German air raids on London in 1917 and 1918 produced little short of a national trauma. The RAF had been created as an immediate military defence, but a wholly spurious war scare in 1922, inspired by France's supposedly massive preponderance in the air, had revived fears. Lindemann was at the heart of moves to address the problem.[1] He sat on a committee chaired by Lord Haldane, the lawyer, politician and philosopher famous for successfully reforming the British Army before the First World War, which worked from 1925 onwards to study the problem. Captain Stephen Roskill – who was the definitive historian of Whitehall's military committee world between the wars – believed that Churchill, then Chancellor of the Exchequer, was almost certainly responsible for the invitation to Lindemann.[2] Haldane had left office when Ramsay MacDonald's Labour government fell in 1924, but he was still a powerful figure. The heads of the three armed services were also members.

To say the least of it, Lindemann did not prove to be a good committee man. He attempted to hijack the committee by trying to set down its terms of reference in ways that implied that he alone of its members grasped the science of the issues.[3] He launched into a recondite debate over the mathematics behind the sound detection system that offered the only method of detecting incoming aircraft at long range and spawned the huge concrete sound mirrors that were to give warning of approaching French bombers which stood (and still stand) at Dungeness. He picked a fight with the First Lord of the Admiralty over the best defence for ships at sea. He tried to railroad through approval for the pet schemes that he conceived: detecting aircraft by electrical impulses from their engine ignition systems and a chain of kite balloons the length of the coastline to force attacking bombers to the then unimaginable altitude of 20,000ft. A special subcommittee of service scientists found the first proposal 'improbable'.[4] In parallel to this, he proposed an 'aerial minefield' of small balloons carrying explosive charges. This was an idea that was to recur.

Haldane's committee fell squarely into the realm of the Committee of Imperial Defence, Britain's supreme military planning body. The Committee of Imperial Defence was formally chaired *ex officio* by the Prime Minister and came only one step down from the Cabinet itself in the Westminster/Whitehall pecking order, but in practice, it was controlled by one of the era's master bureaucrats. Sir Maurice Hankey had practically invented modern Cabinet government by setting up the Cabinet Secretariat (today the Cabinet Office), which recorded, formalised and oversaw the implementation of ministers' decisions. Hankey was the ringmaster of a myriad of subcommittees which shaped military policy. The peak of Hankey's influence had been as trusted personal adviser to David Lloyd George, but he was a formidable force in the machinery of government until the end of the 1930s. Hankey was called in to observe the committee's discussion of the kite-balloon scheme, in practice to judge how the committee was functioning. He was not impressed by its make-up or deliberations. When Lord Haldane died in 1928, Hankey simply wound the committee up and replaced it with a lower-profile but more practical body of the service scientific directors. Nothing serious came of Haldane's committee and air defence was left in the unimaginative but safe hands of the Air Staff. This was not to be the first time that Whitehall made the problem of a committee in which Lindemann was an awkward participant go away by simply consigning the committee itself to oblivion.

The rise to power of the Nazis made the danger of air attack all the more acute in Lindemann's eyes. His German heritage gave him no sympathy with Germany; quite the reverse: he feared the nation's aggressive tendencies. In parallel to Churchill's efforts, he launched his own campaign. On 2 August 1934, Lindemann wrote a letter to *The Times*, triggered by a parliamentary debate in which Churchill had asserted that Britain ranked as only the sixth largest air force in the world and would probably drop even further down the ranks. Lindemann took issue with one of the key tenets of the knock-out blow doctrine that he observed had become accepted almost as a law of science, which stated that there was no possible defence against the bomber:

In the debate in the House of Commons on Monday on the proposed expansion of our Air Forces, it seemed to be taken for granted on all sides that there is, and can be, no defence against bombing aeroplanes and that we must rely entirely upon counter-attack and reprisals. That there is at present no means of preventing hostile bombers from depositing their loads of explosives, incendiary materials, gases, or bacteria upon their objectives I believe to be true; that no method can be devised to safeguard great centres of population from such a fate appears to me to be profoundly improbable.

If no protective contrivance can be found and we are reduced to a policy of reprisals, the temptation to be 'quickest on the draw' will be tremendous. It seems not too much to say that bombing aeroplanes in the hands of gangster Governments might jeopardize the whole future of our Western civilization.

To adopt a defeatist attitude in the face of such a threat is inexcusable until it has definitely been shown that all the resources of science and invention have been exhausted. The problem is far too important and too urgent to be left to the casual endeavours of individuals or departments. The whole weight and influence of the Government should be thrown into the scale to endeavour to find a solution. All decent men and all honourable Governments are equally concerned to obtain security against attacks from the air and to achieve it no effort and no sacrifice is too great.[5]

Lindemann had logic and experience on his side to assert that the 'bomber will always get through' doctrine was flawed: 'An antidote has always been found hitherto for every offensive weapon and I see no reason to suppose that aircraft are the only exception.'[6] Churchill and Lindemann were in alliance to push the government to take positive steps to ward off the menace of bombing.

A few weeks later, Churchill and Lindemann travelled up from the Côte d'Azur where they were staying to visit Stanley Baldwin at his customary holiday spot, Aix-les-Bains, and put their case to him directly. Baldwin received them courteously and suggested that Lindemann might attend a committee that was meeting under the chairmanship of one of the RAF's highest officers, Sir Robert Brooke-Popham, air officer commander-in-chief of the misleadingly named Air Defence of Great Britain, which controlled all of the RAF's home-based fighters and bombers. The invitation was a red rag to Lindemann, and his angry response revealed both his obsessions and the high-handedness that made him a singularly inept bureaucratic operator. He recognised that the greatest obstacle that had to be overcome was the Trenchardian dogma of the RAF and its Whitehall parent, the Air Ministry, but chose simply to denounce its incompetence. It takes long, patient and skilled campaigns of manoeuvre to overcome anything so well entrenched in a national power structure.

Lindemann wanted a committee but one that bypassed all existing machinery with top-level political authority. It was to have funding of its own to launch experiments. He was right that the Air Force bureaucracy was a dangerous opponent but entirely failed to see that it had to be isolated on its own battlefield. He imagined that identifying a counter to bombing attacks was merely a scientific problem, which could be solved through purely abstract research; questions of practical engineering and the military organisation needed were trivial. He protested that open-mindedness was vital but tipped his mitt that he had a solution: the successor to the kite-balloon barrage that he had promoted ten years before. Even if a means could be found to detect enemy bombers, he wanted to avoid having to rely on fighter interception.[7] He blithely assumed that the problem of intercepting day bombers was already well in hand and focused on the question of night bombers. Here he was prescient but well ahead of the game. The final proof that Lindemann was operating in a world of his own was his recommendation of Lord Weir as the chairman of his committee. Weir certainly had the standing as a former Air Minister and highly successful businessman necessary to make a success of such a venture – in fact, a couple of years later, he was briefly given a major role in coordinating Britain's rearmament efforts – but Lindemann seemed to be entirely unaware that Weir was a vehement advocate of the Trenchard doctrine of the primacy of the bomber. He was a long-standing patron of Trenchard and the last person on the planet who would have approached air defence with an open mind. Lindemann was similarly unwise trying to parlay what seems to have been a purely social acquaintanceship with Lord Londonderry, the grand aristocrat whom MacDonald had appointed as Air Minister as part of his programme to climb through society. Londonderry served as the political mouthpiece of Air Chief Marshal Sir Edward Ellington, the Chief of the Air Staff, one of Britain's worst service chiefs ever, who had firmly opposed rapid expansion of the Royal Air Force. The kindest assessment of Ellington's motives was that he wanted to hold his hand until a truly heavy bomber force was in prospect, but he might simply have been acting out of knee-jerk conservatism and discounted the threat of Nazism as well. Londonderry was also a cousin of Churchill.

Unbeknownst to Lindemann and his political cohorts, the wheels of bureaucracy had already been turning to apply science to air defence. The summer air exercises of 1934 featured night attacks on London and Coventry which the umpires held to have destroyed both the Air

Ministry and the Houses of Parliament.[8] This spurred A. P. Rowe, a mid-level official in the Air Ministry's scientific research department, to look through its fifty-three files on air defence and established that none of these featured any attempt to mobilise new scientific methods. The memorandum he wrote to his boss, Harry Wimperis, might almost have come from Lindemann's pen: 'Unless science evolved some new method of aiding air defence, we were likely to lose the next war if it started within ten years.' Like Lindemann, Wimperis was a scientist who had been brought into the First World War effort to lift military aviation from its rudimentary beginnings. In 1925, he had become the first head of the department. The committee was formed with three distinguished scientists as external members: Harry Tizard, assistant secretary to the government Department of Scientific and Industrial Research; Professor A. V. Hill, veteran of First World War military aviation development; and Professor Patrick Blackett, a distinguished physicist. A more reasonable man might have supported a move that was unarguably progress in the right direction, but Lindemann dismissed it almost out of hand.[9] He objected that Wimperis and Tizard drew salaries from the Air Ministry as though that automatically tainted their judgement. Moreover, Tizard was not in the Air Ministry, albeit a civil servant. Lindemann accused one member, presumably Blackett who was a Fabian socialist, of 'holding himself out to be a communist'. He ignored Hill's First World War work on anti-aircraft gunnery when he claimed that neither Hill nor Blackett 'ever had anything to do with aeroplanes'. The committee did not have the vaulting terms of reference to which Lindemann aspired. Perhaps reflecting his unhappy time on the Haldane committee, Lindemann held the established bureaucracy in contempt. The instinct to challenge existing structures chimes with Churchill's own approach.

Lindemann stepped up his assault on the value of the Tizard committee when he addressed the powerful Conservative backbench MPs' organisation, the 1922 Committee, to promote his own schemes for air defence and the mechanism that was needed to push these schemes through.[10] When the RAF was pooh-poohing high estimates of how fast the Luftwaffe had expanded, the Air Staff insisted on the length of time that was needed to train an air force. Lindemann sniffed that this might produce excellent formation flying, such as the RAF displayed at the Hendon air pageants, but insinuated that this had no military value. He labelled as a 'counsel of despair' the sacrosanct Trenchardian dogma that it was practically impossible to stop bombers so only counter-bombing offered a defence. He claimed quite falsely that Baldwin's statement that 'the bomber will always get through' applied to night bombers, which was in fact Lindemann's own hobby horse. He dwelt on the horrors of gas and incendiary bombing, offering to demon-strate to listeners the effect of thermite bombs in his own laboratory. The start of the solution that Lindemann proposed blended common sense with contempt for the lesser brains of service officers: 'History shows us that for every weapon there is a shield, but it also shows us that it is very difficult to get military authorities to realize that such a shield exists.' He doubted that traditional anti-aircraft guns gave pro-tection but 'something in the nature of an aerial minefield is required'. He proposed a mechanism to study defence methods that was a naked pitch for he and Churchill to be given quasi-dictatorial powers:

> In my view the best procedure would be to set up with the full au-thority of Parliament, and with the collaboration of the Committee of Imperial Defence, a small and powerful committee consisting of a few scientists and a few service members and presided over by a man of Cabinet rank though not necessarily a member of the Cabinet. This body should have the right to claim and secure priority for its research in the various experimental establishments of the Defence Ministries. It should be given means of supervising the work and assured of the full support of the Government.[11]

Until war arrived, Lindemann, with Churchill's support, tried to force this scheme on the government and brooked no alternative. In prac-tice, he wanted complete authority over air defence to be put into the hands of a committee which Churchill would lead politically and he would lead scientifically. He dismissed Tizard's efforts to Terence O'Connor, chair of the 1922 Committee, as 'merely [a] … blocking committee, likely to do more harm than good'.[12] Lindemann's quest for an effective aerial minefield lasted until well into the war and was to consume much resources and efforts.

Lindemann had better luck than with Londonderry when he and Churchill mobilised Tory grandee Sir Austen Chamberlain to join their push for a committee to look at new methods. Together they worked on Prime Minister MacDonald, who was unaware of Tizard's committee. The issue of air defence received a further fillip when Baldwin started to take an interest in the matter as he planned to reshape the government when he replaced MacDonald as Prime Minister. MacDonald was manifestly ailing and Baldwin had long held the serious power in the government. Lord Londonderry was marked for replacement as Air Minister and he was to be succeeded by one of Baldwin's close associates, Sir Philip Cunliffe-Lister, soon to be ennobled as Lord Swinton. Baldwin was counting on Cunliffe-Lister to bring some dynamism and competence to preparing Britain for a war in the air that had been conspicuously absent under the Londonderry–Ellington regime. Even before Londonderry was formally sacked, Cunliffe-Lister had been made chairman of two new high-profile committees, one that gave political dimension to Tizard's and the other to look at Britain's air strength relative to Germany. The political committee was formally an outgrowth of the Committee of Imperial Defence. At Cunliffe-Lister's suggestion, Baldwin asked Churchill to join the political committee. Churchill accepted; he was not going to repeat his refusal to join the parliamentary committee on the India Bill which had marked the start of open hostilities over the issue. Baldwin astutely granted Churchill's wish to remain free to criticise the government's policy unless this involved secret information he learned on the committee. He might not be muzzled, but he would struggle to dissociate himself entirely from government policy. In turn, Churchill insisted that Lindemann be put on Tizard's scientific committee. Lindemann overrode his doubts and accepted the move and joined 'the somewhat unimportant Tizard Committee'.[13]

From the outset, Lindemann had a quite different view of what the committee should be doing. He thought it should sign off and fund projects that 'enthusiastic believers' would drive forwards. Even more damagingly, he was already firmly convinced of one project that he believed needed this kind of treatment and so deserved the highest priority. He rejected a flak barrage as too wasteful and, presumably because he saw the difficulties of interception, was suspicious of fighters. Almost by default, he came on the idea of an 'aerial mine' which would somehow be suspended or dropped in the path of oncoming bombers as sea mines deterred warships. It was a lineal successor to the kite-balloon barrage that he had championed in the 1920s. Tizard's committee did undertake some work on aerial mines but with far less intensity than Lindemann demanded. There is no sign that Tizard himself had any great hopes for the scheme. At one point, the committee proposed a full-scale experiment of the destructive effect of aerial mines, but this would require the use of a high-speed pilotless Queen Bee drone that would not be available for another year. Lindemann riposted by offering to reprise his First World War aircraft spinning heroics by piloting a target plane himself to conduct the test. Tizard was hardly tactful in turning him down on the grounds that this would reflect badly on the courage of regular RAF pilots.[14] Lindemann's enthusiasm was so strong that he practically ceased to be a scientist and joined the legion of inventors who dreamed up war-winning devices. Tellingly, he was only ever to find a single 'enthusiastic believer' in aerial mines amongst either servicemen or scientists; only Churchill shared Lindemann's faith, such was his confidence in his judgement. In thrall to his faith in Lindemann's abilities, Churchill blindly swallowed his friend's conviction and began to treat it almost as a proven weapon of war. Ahead of his first attendance at the Swinton committee, Churchill submitted (risibly, he claimed, 'with much diffidence') his proposals for air defence. Presciently, he advocated that fighters should be vectored onto the attacking bombers, albeit by high-speed reconnaissance aircraft (he had yet to be briefed on the progress made on radar), but he also wanted high priority for research into Lindemann's 'aerial mine-curtain'. Lindemann constantly complained that Tizard was not giving aerial mines the priority and attention that they deserved.

Relations between Lindemann and Tizard descended into a personal feud. Lindemann drafted Churchill in to support his case, which only poisoned the atmosphere further. Lindemann's blind advocacy of aerial mines made him 'ruder, more objectionable and less co-operative'.[15] The crisis came in June 1936 with another paper from Churchill promoting Lindemann's aerial mines and complaining that he had encountered 'all sorts of difficulties'.[16] Tizard was a member of both committees and protested vigorously at the attempt to use political influence to override scientific judgement: 'I take the strongest exception to a member of the Committee who has not succeeded in convincing his colleagues on scientific and technical questions, endeavouring to force his views through a member of [Swinton's] Committee, however distinguished.'[17] Swinton was able to secure a brief truce, but a fortnight later, Lindemann told the committee that he was standing for Parliament and would be bringing the supposed inadequacy of air defence to public attention. His counterblast to Tizard's complaint opened by accusing the committee of dilatoriness: 'It will scarcely be contended that the investigation of all the Air Defence problems is proceeding at the maximum rate.'[18] He went on to accuse the other members of contriving specious grounds to restrict research into aerial mines. For good measure, he demanded that government scientist Robert Watson-Watt be put into research into aircraft communications as well as radio direction finding (RDF) for which he was already responsible.

The other scientists on the committee refused to work further with Lindemann and offered their resignations. Swinton side-stepped this initiative by simply dissolving the committee and setting up a new one with all the same members except for Lindemann.

*   *   *

Frederick Lindemann and Henry Tizard also disagreed on the question of whether infrared offered a practical method of detecting hostile aircraft. Here Tizard was openly sceptical, but Lindemann's support for the scheme might have been coloured by the fact that the scientist in charge of researching the technique was one of his proteges, Dr R. V. Jones, who was working from the Clarendon Laboratory. Jones was thorough and professional, but he by no means met Lindemann's requirement for an 'enthusiastic believer'. Jones recognised early that infrared might be useful at short ranges; indeed during the Second World War, the Germans did use the technique operationally in this role, but it was not a great success. Lindemann complained at the way Tizard's committee handled the research, but there is no truth in the story spread by C. P. Snow – a scientist and civil servant turned novelist – that Lindemann championed infrared against RDF (now known as radar). The only figure who seems to have believed that there was a direct competition between infrared and RDF was Watson-Watt, who was in charge of the development of RDF and soon all radio measures. Jones waspishly hypothesised that this was only because Watson-Watt was not a good enough physicist to understand the shortcomings of infrared and exaggerated the danger it posed for his area of research. Jones also saw Lindemann's bend towards infrared as another outgrowth of his long-running feud with Tizard.

In fact, Lindemann thoroughly approved of the work being done on RDF under the Tizard committee, although he had reservations about the ability of RDF to engage multiple aircraft simultaneously and its possible vulnerability to intentional disruption by spreading dummy oscillators to create return signals as made by aircraft (the principle was put into effective operational use by the British under the codename Windows during the war).[19] He found in Watson-Watt the kind of 'enthusiastic believer' on whom he pinned so much confidence. Watson-Watt recognised and heartily appreciated

Lindemann's support.[20] Watson-Watt was certainly a committed and effective advocate of RDF, but Lindemann did not appreciate how much else went into the successful development of the technology to make it a vital component of Britain's air defence in the Second World War.[21] Lindemann appears to have been more taken by Watson-Watt's drive than a scientific or military appraisal of the value of RDF. He viewed it as one of a number of projects, albeit the only one supported by suitable individuals.[22] Neither Churchill nor Lindemann seems to have been aware of the unstinting support given to RDF at the early stages by Air Marshal Sir Hugh Dowding, head of research and development in the RAF itself, who was soon to become the first commander of RAF Fighter Command, where he translated the scientific development into the practical military command and control system that gave the British a precious advantage in the Battle of Britain.

Churchill's pledge not to use military secrets that he gleaned by sitting on the committee and his eminence as a politician meant that he could be let into the work on RDF which was treated as immensely secret. He went to see the Bawdsey Manor experimental centre and responded enthusiastically to the potential of the technology, but he was not made privy to the full picture. In particular, he was kept out of the loop in 1937 when it was decided to build Chain Home, a full-scale line of operational radar stations protecting Britain's south coast. This was achieved after a well-concealed battle between the scientists and politicians on one side and the neanderthal Chief of the Air Staff Sir Edward Ellington, who did not believe RDF offered value for money despite the comparatively modest cost, on the other. The fight over Chain Home gave the lie to Churchill's and Lindemann's accusations that the government was slow to apply science to air defence, which created a political trap for Churchill. Hankey, who was now acting more like a political opponent of Churchill than a civil servant, advised Neville Chamberlain, now Prime Minister, that the news of something as 'epoch-making' as RDF could be held back to 'deliver a withering counter-blast' to Churchill's criticisms.[23]

* * *

Even before his de facto expulsion from the committee, Frederick Lindemann had been planning to broaden the political platform from which to broadcast his view on air defence. He had long coveted a seat in Parliament, although Lord Birkenhead had presciently and firmly advised him against trying.[24] But Birkenhead had died in 1930, leaving Lindemann free rein to pursue his ambitions. In 1935, he came close to securing the official Conservative nomination for the general election but lost out to a less contentious candidate, C. R. M. F. Cruttwell, a distinguished historian and principal of Hertford College, Oxford. It was some consolation to Lindemann when Cruttwell was defeated humiliatingly. In 1937, Lindemann had a second try. The parliamentary seat for Oxford University was falling vacant as its incumbent Lord Hugh Cecil took up the provostship of Eton. With his habitual high-handedness, Lindemann declared himself as the government candidate without troubling to secure the backing of the local Conservative organisation, the Caucus. The Caucus voted not to support Lindemann and to put up a candidate of its own, thus splitting the Conservative vote. The candidate was the magnificently named Sir Farquhar Buzzard, an elderly physician specialised in mental illnesses. He was also a student of Christ Church. Buzzard stood on a platform of unreflecting conservatism, but Lindemann's was dominated by air defence and he vehemently attacked the mantra that the bomber will always get through. He paraded his qualifications as former experimental pilot and scientist to drive the search for a means of defeating the bomber. Churchill travelled to Oxford to speak in Lindemann's favour in October 1936, but this might have been more hindrance than help. It was not customary to hold political meetings in support of candidates at university elections.[25] Churchill had not studied at Oxford (or any university) and the fact that he was a vocal critic of the government undermined Lindemann's claim that he backed Baldwin. Brendan Bracken provided cheery backing.[26] Lindemann was confronted by an extensive machine and he also disdained the process of cosying up to the socially insignificant dons of north Oxford who made up a large proportion of the electorate. Lindemann won slightly fewer votes than Buzzard. Their combined poll would have been just enough to defeat Sir Arthur Salter, the broadly left-wing independent candidate, who won easily against the split vote. As it had been a decision of the Conservative machine to divide their forces, Churchill's reputation suffered less than in his son's by-election ventures, but the incident confirmed his position as an internal opponent of the government. Lindemann's failure might have been a perverse salvation. It is difficult to imagine that his blunt arrogance would have won him any friends in Parliament, either for his vision of air defence or, more broadly, as a supporter of Churchill.

Churchill remained on Swinton's main committee, but his continuing criticism of the government tended to produce material which the government might turn against him. Even in 1938, he was berating Sir Kingsley Wood, who had just succeeded Lord Swinton as Air Minister, with the supposed failings of the 'slow-motion' work of the committee, essentially its failure to push Lindemann's ideas.[27] He promoted the supposed merits of aerial mines to Wood as the Munich crisis threatened to bring the country under imminent risk of German air attack.[28] He was so far under the spell of the idea that he even tamely trotted out Lindemann's ominous vision of German aircraft throwing out aerial mines into the path of attacking fighters: 'How easy to throw out aerial mines!'[29] This was not Churchill's only misjudgement on air defence technology. He had developed the entirely unfounded belief that fixed-gun fighters were obsolescent and shared the erroneous belief of the Chief of the Air Staff Sir Cyril Newall and many of his colleagues that turret fighters, such as the Boulton Paul Defiant, held the future of air combat; the Defiant was catastrophically ineffective and vulnerable when it faced combat.

In the wake of Munich, Churchill returned to the charge and attempted to foist Lindemann back onto the reconstituted Tizard committee.[30] This served to remind Downing Street of the disasters of Lindemann's first foray into the world of advising the government on air defence.[31] Tizard objected violently to the proposal, but the ministers concerned preferred to keep Churchill quiet politically and Lindemann was reinstated.[32] The possibility that the pair might dig themselves into further holes that the government might fill in at its leisure might also have played a part. The government was inclined to humour Churchill and Lindemann, who was briefed on the latest developments in Fighter Command at the behest of Sir Kingsley Wood.[33] Lindemann resumed his proselytisation on behalf of aerial mines that would now be launched into the path of bombers by rocket. He was behaving more like a huckster inventor than a scientist and was viewed with ever-less seriousness: 'The trouble about Lindemann is that he is getting so infernally unscientific. He takes no trouble to examine even his own proposals properly, let alone anyone else's.'[34] Lindemann's contempt for Tizard seems in part to have rested on the fact that in his own day as an experimental physicist, he had achieved more than him, but dismissing Tizard as a 'nobody' in the world of science as Lindemann did to his friend, the economist Roy Harrod, betrays the extent to which he reduced questions to personal judgement, with his own, naturally, as supreme.[35]

The whole episode of Lindemann's relationship with Tizard and his committees was unpleasant and futile. It rebounded against Churchill, who was still struggling against his reputation for poor judgement and high-handedness. The forceful support for Lindemann's dubious proposals helped dilute the impact of Churchill's far better founded and informed criticism of what was actually happening in air rearmament. It distracted the efforts of public servants and scientists from their true work. It provides an object lesson on how politicising questions of high policy can be a futile and damaging process. Perhaps worse, it distracted attention from genuine questions of science which might have contributed to Britain's war effort. Missed opportunities included Lindemann's perception that the effectiveness of flak could be improved if shell bursts could somehow be made lethal over a greater area. When proximity fusing for shells which detonated them near to aircraft rather than on making contact was developed in the course of the Second World War, it was a major advance. On his side, Tizard recognised that the crude navigational methods of the pre-war RAF would diminish the effectiveness of bombing. On his own, however, Tizard was unable to educate RAF Bomber Command that science could improve its potentiality.[36] It is an open question whether Tizard would have got any further in alliance with Lindemann and Churchill. Bombing inaccuracy was possibly the most important factor in making RAF Bomber Command a negligible force until well into the war when – admittedly under radically different circumstances – Lindemann took a hand with powerful support from Churchill.

With hindsight, it is easy to mock the proliferation of technological dead-ends that were treated seriously at the time, but these were almost inevitable outgrowths of the pace of technological development. Lindemann saw a theoretical possibility that aircraft engines could be made to malfunction by introducing nitrous oxide into their air intakes and distorting their ignition cycle. Remote sabotage of aircraft engines was a popular concept at the time. How the gas was to be delivered was never explained. In the event, both the Germans and, to a lesser extent, the RAF used nitrous-oxide injection as a means of giving brief bursts of improvement to engine performance. Open and untainted debate might also have headed the Tizard committee away from the blind alley of the 'silhouette' scheme of illuminating large areas of cloud to make aircraft visible at night. Much effort was devoted to 'silhouette' and a working scheme was planned and budgeted at a cost of millions of pounds. It came to nothing and its promoters may be thankful that the Lindemann controversies have more or less monopolised the historiography of the Tizard committee and 'silhouette' has disappeared from notice almost unobserved. The committee itself had outlived its usefulness and vanished when war broke out. Lindemann's second stint on the committee had sown one seed that germinated and grew under the care of Lindemann and Churchill but that lay some months in the future.

Parallel to sustaining Lindemann in his squabbles with the Tizard committee and his related campaign to invest in developing

Lindemann's pet system for air defence, Churchill kept up his far more valid pressure on the government on the question of the widening gap between the strength of Hitler's Luftwaffe and Britain's RAF. In addition to his limited goal of injecting his own input into developing the military technology of air defence, he pursued his campaign to push the government towards greater and more effective spending on the RAF. Here he could rely on insider leaks from the military establishment to feed his criticism of what was being achieved. He was not bound by his promise not to divulge information that he gleaned from his membership of the Committee of Imperial Defence; his ammunition came informally and, arguably, illicitly. His two greatest sources were Major Desmond Morton, head of the government's secret Industrial Intelligence Centre, and Wing Commander Tor Anderson, a serving officer. The information that they fed to Churchill fuelled his steady claims that rearmament was being conducted inefficiently and half-heartedly. Morton's data on intelligence estimates of German strength were especially valuable in supporting Churchill's argument that the goal of air parity with Germany was as far from being achieved as ever.

Churchill's assault on air rearmament reached its apogee in the parliamentary debate in May 1938, where the government put up such a poor showing that Chamberlain replaced the entire ministerial team, not just Lord Winterton directly responsible for the debacle in the Commons. There was considerable surprise that he sacked Lord Swinton, the Air Minister who sat in the Lords. Despite their political differences, Churchill respected Swinton, who was an energetic and efficient administrator. Unknown to the outside world, Swinton had clashed with the government's air rearmament czar, Sir Charles Bruce-Gardner, who promoted a quantity-before-quality approach so as to deliver politically attractive output figures.[37] Chamberlain replaced Swinton with Sir Kingsley Wood, a close ally who had made a name for himself on housing programmes and marketing household telephone lines. Wood paid little attention to the detail of policy and concentrated on his own publicity.

13

IN LEAGUE WITH THE LEAGUE

In early 1936, political isolation was near total. Winston Churchill had not been asked to contribute anything significant to the government's campaign in the 1935 general election. When Stanley Baldwin formed his government, there was no place in it for Churchill. Perfunctory efforts at hinting that he might be given a seat in Cabinet were deployed to keep him quiet, but he had ever more the air of yesterday's man. His standing had suffered further when Randolph had stood at yet another by-election in Ross and Cromarty with even less success than his previous forays. The local conservative association had taken umbrage when Ramsay MacDonald's son Malcolm was foisted on the constituency as the National government candidate, bringing him back into Parliament after losing his seat in the 1935 general election. This was in keeping with the dynastic tinge to politics of the era. Two of David Lloyd George's children were MPs and one had been a minister. Andrew Bonar Law's son was also an MP. Randolph was tempted into standing against MacDonald as the 'real' Conservative candidate. Partly on the advice of Brendan Bracken, Churchill did not support his son publicly but was still blamed for his move.[1] Frederick Lindemann was also cautious about the project and alerted Churchill to widespread suspicion that he was behind it.[2] Randolph was beaten decisively.

The 1935 election did, though, give Churchill a significant ally in his campaign for rearmament. The leader of the Liberals since their split from the National Government had been Herbert Samuel, who had savagely criticised Churchill's calls for rearmament which he described as the 'language of a Malay running amok'.[3] Samuel lost his seat and was replaced by Sir Archibald Sinclair, who was a long-standing friend of Churchill from the days of his initial affiliation to the Liberals and had served as his battalion adjutant on the Western Front. More important, Sinclair believed in a far more resolute stance towards the dictators, albeit via the League of Nations. The Liberals were burdened with none of Labour's commitment to unilateral disarmament.

At the start of 1936, Churchill was still a long way short of outright opposition to the government but was beginning to distance himself. Austen Chamberlain came to a weekend at Chartwell in late February, along with other malcontents including Robert Boothby and Lindemann. Chamberlain mused whether the gathering counted as 'a cave of Abullam', the traditional label for Conservative anti-leadership cabals.[4] Churchill held back from vocal dissent from the government and was broadly supportive of the passive line it took over the Nazi reoccupation of the Rhineland. It was known that Baldwin intended to appoint a minister to coordinate defence and Churchill unrealistically thought that he might be a serious candidate for the job, which might explain his quiescence. In the event, the low-key lawyer-politician Sir Thomas Inskip got the job, and Churchill could afford to distance himself again. In May 1936, Churchill and Boothby were guests along with other Conservative dissidents at a widely publicised meeting at Lord Winterton's house, which prompted Baldwin to remark publicly and scathingly that it was 'the time of year when midges come of dirty ditches'.[5] Churchill's gesture of dissent was almost perfunctory; Baldwin had nothing to fear. Churchill became attached to a number of groups broadly opposed to Nazism such as Eugen Spier's Focus, the New Commonwealth Society and the Anti-Nazi Council. Sinclair became a frequent guest at Chartwell. The Other Club became something of a focus for anti-appeasement sentiment, although of the five of Chamberlain's ministers who were members but opposed his diplomacy, only one (Duff Cooper) resigned.[6]

Churchill was isolated not just in the world of Westminster but also outside, as his warnings of the need to protect the country against the menace of Germany still fell on mainly deaf ears. His campaign to rearm had received spasmodic assistance in Parliament, but he had attracted no backing from heavyweight figures from any party. Pacifist sentiment was still strong in the country; Baldwin's promise of 'no great armaments' in the 1935 election platform struck a chord in tune with popular feeling. The new leader of the Labour Party, Clement Attlee, was a far more pragmatic figure than his predecessor George Lansbury, who was an unequivocal unilateral pacifist, but he still mounted a vigorous campaign against the limited rearmament measures that the government had undertaken. The early months of 1936, though, did see the start of glimmerings of hope that Churchill might be able to broaden the campaign, when an opening came from a perhaps unexpected quarter. The League of Nations still enjoyed enormous prestige in Britain; its public spin-off, the League of Nations Union, had reached a peak of no less than 400,000 members. The league was widely revered for its idealistic aim to settle international differences by negotiation; it was the incarnation of hopes for a new world order after 'the war to end all wars'. But its prestige had suffered a dent from its entirely ineffective attempts to deter Italy from invading Abyssinia at the end of 1935, and it needed to bolster its credibility. Lord Cecil, a former British delegate to the league and a high-profile advocate, sounded Churchill out about his speaking at a large meeting at London's Albert Hall that the League of Nations Union was planning for May to broadcast the dangers of Fascist Italy. By coincidence, Churchill had already been approached to address a meeting organised by the Anti-Nazi Council at the same venue against the dangers of Nazi Germany scheduled for ten days before. Churchill persuaded the council to defer the meeting, thus making the League of Nations event de facto against both dictators. Churchill was happy to don the cloak of an advocate of peaceable negotiation but did not soften his call for rearmament. He told Cecil, 'It seems a mad business to confront these dictators without weapons or military force.'[7] This did not stop the Foreign Office which had hopes of restoring the league's standing from encouraging Churchill semi-officially to help them with an initiative to mobilise public sentiment in favour of the league.

For a few months, the idea of a League of Nations-sponsored meeting went into abeyance, but by the autumn, it had resurfaced with a vengeance. A new set of allies had emerged for a firm line towards the dictatorships. The outbreak of the civil war in Spain that summer and the support given to General Franco by Hitler and Mussolini had brought home the fact that the extreme right was the enemy of the working class. At their annual conference in September, the leaders of the Trades Union Congress (TUC) had adopted a far more trenchant attitude than the political Labour Party, which was still essentially unilateralist pacifist. There was an unspoken acceptance that military force might need to be deployed against the dictators, in practice discarding the ideal of non-violence. The British trade unions saw more clearly than their political colleagues what might be needed to deal with this. The boost to employment of extensive rearmament was another motive. Churchill leapt on the idea of a broadly based movement in favour of the principle of rearmament. It would be launched with a mass meeting at the Albert Hall, chaired at Churchill's insistence by Sir Walter Citrine, the general secretary of the TUC. The date was fixed for 3 December and all looked well to create a formidable movement. It was to be held under the auspices of the League of Nations Union and Lord Lytton, who had been a delegate to the League of Nations in Geneva and was one of the Tory grandees most conspicuous in its support, attended. As well as Citrine, Ernest Bevin, another high-profile trade union leader, was there, as were figures from both the left and right of the Conservatives: Harold Macmillan and Lord Lloyd. The movement's slogan 'Arms and the Covenant [of the League of Nations]' combined pragmatism with idealism. Churchill was poised to transform his call for urgent measures against the Fascist dictators from a lone voice in the wilderness to an expression of a powerful national sentiment, supported by influential forces across politics, society and the bureaucracy. He was on the verge of riding a swing in national sentiment to restoring his political fortunes and perhaps taking him further. The fates decided otherwise and the blame falls heavily on Churchill himself.

Edward VIII had come to the throne in January 1936 surrounded by high hopes that, as a young, open and attractive figure, he would renew the monarchy and bring it away from the daunting conservatism of his father, George V. As Prince of Wales, he had been a golden boy, a glamorous, handsome and charming sportsman, happy to talk openly to all his subjects. These hopes were short-lived. Edward VIII proceeded to antagonise pointlessly much of the establishment and adopted a perfunctory approach to his royal duties. His attention was monopolised by his infatuation for Wallis Simpson, an American divorcee on the fringes of acceptable society whom he had met in the early 1930s and rapidly fallen in love with. The relationship was already scandalous, but when it became known that she was seeking a divorce from her second husband in October 1936 this sparked the horrible realisation that Edward intended to marry her and make her Queen. Churchill had long known and admired Edward VIII; as Home Secretary, he had organised his investiture as Prince of Wales in 1911. Churchill did not share the horrified rejection of Mrs Simpson in the government, but he had been sufficiently alert to the danger of scandal to advise against her second divorce and Edward VIII's plan to invite her in September to Balmoral, a place of near religious standing for the royal family. In Mrs Simpson's eyes, this transformed him into an enemy and relations cooled; the King was utterly under her command. Churchill did not abandon his affection for the King and mutely swung behind the conservative establishment. When the news that Mrs Simpson was seeking a divorce transformed scandal into a crisis, Churchill moved away from his earlier conservatism. He said at least once that he saw no difficulty in the King marrying 'his cutie'.[8] It entirely escaped him that the choice of a royal consort went far beyond a personal choice. A fellow guest at a dinner party reported:

Winston Churchill was one of the few people around the dinner table that night who found Mrs Simpson acceptable. Curiously enough, he considered that she just did not matter and had no great significance; he believed that, in the ultimate analysis of the Monarchy, she simply did not count one way or the other. Moral and social considerations apart, he considered her presence to be irrelevant to King Edward's performance as Sovereign.[9]

From early in the crisis, Churchill had attracted suspicion amongst the government by holding back from the consensus that the King's behaviour had to change. He had declined to join a delegation of senior privy counsellors organised by the arch-conservative grandee Lord Salisbury, which saw Baldwin on 17 November express their disquiet at the King's behaviour and, implicitly, at the failure of the government to do anything about it. His next step away from the common line was even more drastic. Baldwin foresaw the danger of an outright constitutional crisis and began to take precautionary steps against the risk that the government might have to give formal advice against marriage which the King might decline. This would oblige the government to resign under the rules of the constitution. Baldwin had set out to obtain 'the concurrence of the leaders of the Opposition' to issuing formal advice, in practice, to committing themselves not to form an alternative government if the advice were rejected. Clement Attlee, the recently chosen leader of the Labour Party, and Sir Archibald Sinclair of the opposition Liberals fell in practically unhesitatingly. Churchill appears to have stopped well short of giving such a promise: 'his outlook was rather different', although he would support the government.[10] He was more cooperative when Baldwin 'specifically and positively banned' him from seeing the King, from which he does not appear to have demurred.[11]

The burgeoning crisis revived the relationship between Churchill and Beaverbrook. They had drifted apart in the early 1930s: Beaverbrook was out of sympathy with Churchill's stance on India and rearmament; he was an enthusiastic imperialist but focused on the white dominions and promoted British isolationism from the troubles in Europe. Beaverbrook had even resigned from the Other Club in 1930, an unusual move that generally signalled a breach with Churchill on high policy.[12] Earlier that year, he had denounced Churchill and

Bracken as committed opponents of empire free trade.[13] The abdication crisis thrust them firmly, and for Churchill fatally, back together. From an early stage in the crisis, Beaverbrook had seen the matter as offering the kind of troubled waters in which he loved to fish. Edward VIII had originally sought Beaverbrook's help to suppress press discussion of Mrs Simpson's second divorce. She was terrified that it might make her a public figure subject to criticism for her relationship with the King. In the event, the press stuck to the law of silence it had maintained over the relationship for months, but the King was grateful for Beaverbrook's noisy show of helpfulness. As the confrontation with Baldwin intensified, Edward VIII increasingly saw Beaverbrook as a potential ally in an open battle with the government. His tentative attempts to obtain support from friendly politicians had fallen on deaf ears.

The one promising way out of the crisis that presented itself to the King was to marry Mrs Simpson morganatically, so she did not become Queen and any children would lose their place in the line of succession. This possibility had been mooted in a number of quarters for some time, but it became a real possibility when the press magnate Esmond Harmsworth persuaded Mrs Simpson of its merits. In turn, she overrode the King's doubts and the scheme was put to the government. Baldwin and his colleagues were unenthusiastic but went through the motions of consulting the dominion governments as required under the statute of Westminster. Underlying the government's handling of the crisis was a fear that unscrupulous figures might exploit it to their own ends, possibly as far as plotting to manoeuvre the government into resigning in a quasi-coup d'état. Their suspicion fell on Churchill and the press magnates – Beaverbrook, Harmsworth and his father Lord Rothermere – whom they labelled the 'King's Party' in a damning echo of the build up to the English Civil War. In the government's eyes, the morganatic scheme was the centrepiece of a plot by the King's Party. In reality, the government wildly exaggerated the extent to which the King and his allies were working together. The only member of the triumvirate of press barons and Churchill who had as his primary motive to topple Baldwin was Beaverbrook. He later admitted that his goal was to 'bugger Baldwin'.[14]

The King refused to authorise the all-out press campaign on his behalf that Beaverbrook wanted to launch, partly because he was responsible enough not to want to split the country but partly because Mrs Simpson feared the adverse publicity it would bring to her. Churchill may well have seen an opportunity, but he was also driven by a romantic notion of the status of monarchy and personal affection for Edward VIII. Churchill was not specially attached to the morganatic scheme and the strategy that he vainly recommended to the King was to be patient and leave the government to make active moves.

It was an outright lie by Beaverbrook that transformed Churchill from a somewhat suspect figure into an active opponent in the eyes of the government. He and Churchill had already discussed what they called the 'Cornwall plan' (after the idea of making Mrs Simpson Duchess of Cornwall) and Beaverbrook freely admitted to Churchill that he had told the King that the plan was his, although he went on to tell Churchill that the King was enthusiastic, which was certainly not the full truth.[15] Beaverbrook had little faith or sympathy with the morganatic scheme, but he wanted to use it as a lever to embroil Churchill deeply in the affair and he succeeded amply. The King believed Beaverbrook and the government's well-developed intelligence operation rapidly reported his conviction that the morganatic scheme was Churchill's own. It had been promoted by the US press baron W. R. Hearst, who was keen to make Mrs Simpson queen. MI5 admitted from the start that its operation against the King was driven by fears of a quasi-coup d'état. The key figure in organising the operation was a long-standing foe of Churchill, Sir Horace Wilson, a senior civil servant who acted as Baldwin's chief of staff.

The wall of silence that the British press had erected around, first, the affair with Mrs Simpson and, second, the burgeoning crisis finally collapsed on 2 December, when an obscure bishop publicly criticised the King for his weak religious faith. This opened the floodgates of public discussion, just as the 'Arms and the Covenant' meeting in favour of rearmament took place in the Albert Hall on the evening of Thursday 3 December. Whatever the ostensible purpose of the meeting, it was inevitable that listeners would detect some connection with the royal crisis. Walter Citrine had to threaten to withdraw from the meeting to prevent Churchill from using it as a platform to speak in favour of the King, although Churchill did manage to slip in one neutral mention of the King which provoked loud applause.

By then, the King had already almost decided that he had little choice but to abdicate, but the following evening, the King bounced Baldwin into acquiescing in him seeing Churchill. This piece of defiance offered the King an outlet for his fury at a statement by Baldwin to Parliament that afternoon which rejected flatly the possibility of a morganatic marriage and gave abdication or renunciation of Mrs Simpson as the only alternatives. This sparked a glimmer of resistance. Churchill responded with enthusiasm. He was enthralled by the idea of his King seeking his help in his hour of need and entirely failed to read either the King's true intentions or the politics of the affair. Over dinner on the Friday night, the King was momentarily taken by Churchill's passion and thoughts of resistance flickered into life, but this was only fleeting.[16] Churchill was far too wrapped up in his plans and the King did not disabuse him. He was happy for others to fight on his behalf but had no appetite to do anything himself. He showed no inclination to accept Churchill's advice to withdraw into Windsor Castle and lift the drawbridge. He was determined to bring the crisis to an end and to marry Mrs Simpson. The government saw the discussion between the King and Churchill as a manoeuvre of the King's Party.

Baulked of the opportunity to attack the government frontally, Beaverbrook changed tactics and tried to persuade Mrs Simpson to end the crisis by giving up the King, albeit only temporarily and hypocritically. Unwittingly, she and the King had opened themselves to this manoeuvre when the King picked Lord Brownlow to escort Mrs Simpson when she fled to France to escape the press on the Wednesday night. Brownlow was firmly in Beaverbrook's pocket, but he could not be sure that Mrs Simpson would yield to his blandishments. Moreover, Brownlow and Mrs Simpson were not to arrive at their destination on the Saturday morning, so Beaverbrook could not tell whether his plan was working or whether he might need a fallback. When he saw Churchill that morning, he did tell him his judgement on the King's lack of resolve: 'Our cock won't fight.' And the verdict: 'No dice.' What he failed to disclose was that he had just been visited by Sir John Simon, who was Baldwin's closest collaborator in the crisis, and told that the King had reached an agreement with the government and the practicalities of abdication were in hand. In reality, what Simon told Beaverbrook was well in advance of what had actually been decided. Holding this information back from Churchill shows that Beaverbrook, like the King, was happy to keep the light of battle in Churchill's eyes. Churchill spent the weekend in a ferment of passionate desire to prevent the King being hustled into what he saw as a premature and unnecessary abdication. He sent out an overwrought press statement calling for patience. He wrote a similarly passionate letter to the King, which shows how little grasp he had on what was happening. Churchill referred to Mrs Simpson as a 'minor inclination', which might have been calculated to infuriate the King given his obsessive passion for her.

14

ALLURING BUT FATEFUL

On the Sunday evening, two of Winston Churchill's friends came to Chartwell and tried to head him away from the folly of persisting in his support for the King. Sir Archibald Sinclair, like most serious politicians, knew that the King was doomed unless he abandoned Mrs Simpson and had already swung behind Stanley Baldwin's approach. Robert Boothby was personally sympathetic to the King but knew that his case was hopeless. They thought they had an escape route from the crisis. Together, they drafted a statement for the King to make, which Boothby could present to him through Sir Godfrey Thomas, the King's assistant private secretary, who was his personal friend. The King would promise publicly not to marry against the advice of his ministers. It is more than likely that the exercise was aimed solely at providing Churchill with an outlet for his enthusiasm that would be less damaging than siding with the King in an open battle with the government. The statement was not calculated to appeal to the King. The day after he abdicated, the newly named Duke of Windsor told Churchill that the proposal had been passed on to him but that even with the backing of Churchill and Sinclair, he was not willing to countenance it as the declaration would simply have been playing for time when his mind was actually made up.[1]

If Churchill took the draft declaration at all seriously on the Sunday night, he had entirely forgotten about it on the Monday afternoon when he performed one of the most dramatic pieces of unintentional self-immolation ever witnessed in the House of Commons. Boothby suspected that one of the ex-India diehards had egged him on to challenge Baldwin in the House of Commons.[2] Baldwin had just delivered a neutral holding statement which Clement Attlee, the leader of the opposition Labour Party, amply supported. Churchill rose to repeat his demand of the previous week that no 'irrevocable action' should be taken. Neither the King nor Beaverbrook had seen fit to tell him the truth and he was still wrapped up in some romantic vision of defending his sovereign to the last. And it proved to be almost the last for Churchill. Yet again he fell victim to his own headstrong and unreflecting approach. He persisted in the face of a hostile House and was shouted down when he tried to follow up his initial question. MPs from both sides of the House yelled 'twister' at him, a legacy of the distrust he had earned by crossing the floor twice. He was called to order by the Speaker for attempting to make a speech at Question Time, a poignant blow for a politician who respected Parliament and its traditions deeply. Bitterness and frustration overwhelmed him and he shouted at Baldwin, 'You won't be satisfied until you've broken him.'[3]

The King's Party was dead and buried, and with it, almost, Churchill's political career. Churchill had suffered many rebuffs at the hands of the House of Commons in the course of a long and bruising career, but this has a strong claim to having been his worst. Immediately afterwards, J. C. C. Davidson was reading the ticker tape in one of the corridors when Churchill joined him and said that his political career was finished. Days later, he was still profoundly depressed by what had happened.[4] He had utterly failed, confirming government suspicions that he was a dangerous plotter and alienating a large majority of the public which fully supported Baldwin's stance.

The vast bulk of MPs were happy to see Churchill humiliated, but even Bob Boothby, one of the tiny band who kept their loyalty to him through thick and thin, was struck by bitterness that Churchill had casually tossed aside the approach that he and Sinclair had agreed with him the day before. This touched his broader frustrations at working with Churchill. Boothby immediately poured out his anger into a furious letter:

Dear Winston,

I understood last night that we had *agreed* upon a formula, and a course designed to save the King from abdication, if that is possible. I thought you were going to use all your powers – decisive, as I believe, in the present circumstances – to secure a happy issue, on the lines that were suggested.

But this afternoon you have delivered a blow to the King, both in the House and in the country, far harder than Baldwin ever conceived of.

You have reduced the number of potential supporters to the minimum possible, I think seven in all.

And you have done it without consultation with your best friends and supporters. I have never said anything to you that I did not sincerely believe. And I never will.

What happened this afternoon makes me feel that it is almost impossible for those who are most devoted to you personally, to follow you blindly (as they [would] like to do) in politics. Because they cannot be sure where the hell they are going to be landed next.

I am afraid this letter will make you very angry. But not, I hope, irretrievably angry. I could not leave what I feel unsaid.

Yrs ever

Bob[5]

Two days later, he was still seething and gave a venomous but telling account to a fellow MP:

I knew that Winston was going to do something dreadful. I had been staying the weekend with him. He was silent and restless and glancing into corners. Now when a dog does that, you know that he is about to be sick on the carpet. It is the same with Winston. He managed to hold it for three days, and then comes to the House and is sick right across the floor.[6]

On 11 December, the day of the abdication itself, Boothby had calmed down sufficiently to write apologetically but still repeating the substance of his first letter. He also added a claim to be able to offer Churchill disinterested advice and argued that this was something he needed vitally:

> But this raises an old issue between us.
>
> I have made many mistakes in my life, and paid for them; but I still don't think my political judgement is altogether bad, although you have never attached any value to it.
>
> For ten years, as one of your most devoted followers, I have fought a losing battle against the die-hards, the Press Lords, and Brendan.
>
> Because I believe that the die-hards are not fundamentally loyal to you, that the Press Lords (and especially one of them) are your most dangerous enemies, and that Brendan is the best friend and the worst counsellor in the world ...
>
> All these people give you advice which is immediately the most alluring and ultimately the most fateful. I cannot help feeling that one of them got at you last Monday night.

How much Boothby deserved to class himself as a good adviser is uncertain, but it is hard to fault his analysis of the flaw in Churchill's relationship with Brendan Bracken and Lord Beaverbrook.

Churchill replied in a neutral tone, but he claimed that the substance of the Chartwell proposals of the Sunday night, together with the fact that he and Sinclair were involved in the initiative, had been passed to the King. The King had turned them down so no great opportunity had been lost. He responded to Boothby's fear that the letter would have annoyed him by writing that 'even if you had not written it, our old relations would have been unchanged'. Boothby was to soldier on Churchill's side through his continuing battles over appeasement, but when Churchill's loyalty was put to a test comparable to what Boothby's loyalty had faced, he flinched.

Churchill might have been insincere in consoling Boothby, but his pessimism as to his political future was overdone. Curiously, it was one of his most dedicated critics through the crisis, Nancy Dugdale, wife of

Baldwin's parliamentary private secretary, who saw through the immediate setback and recognised Churchill's resilience, observing shrewdly,
but not necessarily charitably, that he had received 'a rebuff from which
only a ferro-concrete man would recover' and that 'it is astounding you
cannot kill Winston with any known political axe'.[7]

By Thursday, Churchill knew that he was fighting for his political
survival. He sat hunched through Baldwin's speech setting out his
own version of the crisis and how the government had handled it,
anxious that the Prime Minister might take the chance to hammer the
final nail into his coffin as well.[8] Baldwin did refer to the abhorrence
of King's Party but went no further in castigating Churchill and his
associates. The speech was widely seen as a triumph and crowned the
resurrection of Baldwin's reputation. After the leaders of the other
major parties had delivered their pieces, endorsing Baldwin's words,
Churchill rose to speak to a House still seething with indignation and
hostility for what some in government saw as outright gangsterish
behaviour during the crisis. This time, Churchill judged the mood of
his fellow MPs correctly and, in the words of one of them who had
criticised him savagely a few days before, 'in an admirably phrased
little speech executed a strategical retreat'.[9] It was just enough, and another MP, who was better disposed towards Churchill, thought he had
'regained a good deal of the sympathy he had lost'.[10] But the strategic
damage had been done. Any hopes that he would soon lead a broadly
based movement which brought Britain round to robust opposition
to Hitler were fading.

But the abdication crisis doomed the 'Arms and the Covenant'
movement. Coverage of the events swamped reports of the Albert
Hall meeting. The union leaders' tolerance towards their old foe
Churchill had been sternly tested and their common front with him
was never resuscitated. All the effort that he had devoted to rebuilding
his credibility around the campaign to counter Nazi rearmament had
been destroyed. In the words of the anti-appeasement MP Harold
Nicolson, he had 'undone in five minutes the patient reconstruction
work of two years'.[11] The view was echoed by another opponent of

appeasement in the House of Commons, Harold Macmillan, who was probably unaware of the role played by his wife's lover in the attempt to rescue Churchill at the last moment:

> His personality, which was just emerging from a long period of shadow into the light of power, was once more shaken. All the effect of the Albert Hall meeting was destroyed – first by the Abdication and secondly by the catastrophic fall in Churchill's prestige. It was not possible to restore the situation.[12]

The six final 'precious' months of Baldwin's premiership were 'therefore wasted' in Macmillan's judgement. Baldwin's successor Neville Chamberlain was bent on an active policy of constructive dialogue with the dictators, but Baldwin might just have leaned in Churchill's direction. This pushed the bar even higher for Churchill to surmount. Conservatives were held back from supporting him by loyalty to government policy. The French embassy in London, ever alert for its national security and thus an objective but private ally of Churchill, confessed it was 'worried at his loss of ground'.[13]

Churchill had missed a golden opportunity to appear as a leader of a valid form of national sentiment and not merely as a maverick politician riding his own hobby horse. It took another six months for the leaders of the political Labour Party to follow their trade union colleagues and ditch unilateralist opposition to rearmament.

Later, Churchill did accept criticism of Beaverbrook's damaging influence on his reactions to the abdication crisis when he was challenged by the wartime Tory Chief Whip who was in open conflict with Beaverbrook: 'Yes. I was doing very well on the sidelines at the time and then this happened. My stock went right down and Baldwin's came up again.'[14] He accompanied this with an extravagant gesture illustrating the height to which Baldwin's reputation had rebounded. Beaverbrook had thought he could use the affairs of Edward VIII to ruin Baldwin; instead he gave his standing a huge fillip by showing to insiders what he had saved the country from.

15

A NEW WAY TO DEAL
WITH DICTATORS

Neville Chamberlain became Prime Minister in May 1937. He took a radically different approach to Britain's relationship with the dictator states to his predecessor's. He set out to reverse what he castigated as Stanley Baldwin's policy of 'drift' and to work proactively to remove the risk of war. The method he chose was to seek constructive dialogue with the dictators and to identify their grievances and, insofar as they were legitimate, to settle them by negotiation, thus avoiding the danger of war. His goal was to bring peace to Europe, literally appeasement before the word acquired its pejorative meaning. This conscious and radical change in British foreign policy has rather been forgotten as history places in the foreground the growing aggression of Hitler's moves to expand Germany. Chamberlain's foreign policy is often analysed as a response to the ramp-up in Hitler's programme of domination. Of course, it had to be executed against this background, but it was not a response. After the traumas of 1936, Europe looked as though it was entering calmer waters. The British public showed no inclination to challenge the fairness of Germany's rearmament or the reoccupation of the Rhineland in March 1936. Both steps reversed provisions of the Versailles Treaty which looked unjust and an unreasonable and excessive exploitation of military victory. Dialogue with Germany was anything but an unreasonable option. It was Chamberlain's tragedy that he pursued dialogue through his premiership as evidence piled up that dialogue was the wrong way to deal with dictators. Worse, he and his principal adviser Sir Horace

Wilson devoted great efforts to suppressing anything that might provoke the dictators. They knew just how much Hitler recognised Churchill as his implacable opponent, so distancing the government from anything that Churchill said or did became an integral part of appeasement.

At no point did Chamberlain admire Hitler or even think that he was a decent human being. Even in the depths of his delusion that he had formed a strong partnership with Hitler during the discussions of the Munich crisis, he did not succumb to the temptation of detecting any good in the Führer beyond, by implication, his wisdom in recognising in Chamberlain the ideal partner in a new duumvirate that would dominate the diplomacy of Europe. Chamberlain was not a naive man and his comments are larded with suspicion of the motives and goals of the French, Americans and Soviets. But his suspicions were uneven and he showed no such reservations about Hitler or Mussolini. Indeed, he fulminated against the Foreign Office's suspicions of Mussolini. Chamberlain failed to grasp that an eternal struggle against enemies, external and internal, was a central plank in the platform of fascist dictatorships. It is as though he accepted that they had demands and only wanted to find the cheapest way in which they could be satisfied.

Churchill had a far clearer understanding of Hitler's true nature. In 1935, he had written a profile of the Führer which focused on the fact that Hitler had risen by violence and the exploitation of hatred. It was a question not of reversing unfair clauses in the Versailles Treaty but of winning a struggle. He accused the Foreign Secretary of the time, Sir John Simon, of failing to grasp this:

[He] made no distinction between victors and vanquished. Such distinctions, indeed, still exist, but the vanquished are in process of becoming the victors, and the victors the vanquished. When Hitler began, Germany lay prostrate at the feet of the Allies. He may yet see the day when what is left of Europe will be prostrate at the feet of Germany.[1]

Reviewing Hitler's blood-spattered ascent to power, Churchill asked, 'Can we really believe that a hierarchy and society built upon such deeds can be entrusted with the possession of the most prodigious military machinery yet planned amongst men?' As a backbench MP, Churchill had the luxury of unrestrained comment, but when he was publishing this essay in his book *Great Contemporaries* in 1937 as Chamberlain's diplomatic evolution was building up steam, he sought the advice of the Foreign Office. An appeasement-minded official described the article as 'unpalatable' to the Germans and asked for its suppression. Churchill persisted but did bowdlerise the essay, omitting the passages just quoted. They lay at the heart of an unbridgeable gulf between the way in which he and Chamberlain approached diplomacy towards Nazi Germany.

Chamberlain did not idealistically trust diplomacy alone and wanted Britain to be militarily strong; he spoke frequently of his dual policy of appeasement and rearmament, but here again there was a profound difference in the way that he and Churchill approached the question. In 1936, as Chancellor of the Exchequer, Chamberlain had put a firm stamp on Britain's military policy by identifying Germany as the main potential enemy and giving the Royal Air Force the priority in meeting the threat. But after that, he left the detail of how the policy was executed to his Air Ministers and only changed them when he judged that they included political liabilities. Britain was thus saddled with an unquestioned and strictly Trenchardian approach to military strategy posited on the dogma that 'the bomber will always get through'. Chamberlain had doubled down on Baldwin's faith in the bomber, which Churchill and Frederick Lindemann emphatically rejected. The political and public debate over air rearmament was dominated by a crude numbers game in which the numerical strength of the Luftwaffe was set against the RAF's with almost no regard for whether the aircraft were fighters or bombers, modern or obsolete. Chamberlain was acutely aware of his vulnerability on this score. By contrast, Churchill immersed himself in the minutiae of RAF rearmament, not necessarily wisely.

Chamberlain had no qualms about micro-managing the work of his ministers, but again the instinct worked unevenly. He treated the professional diplomats of the Foreign Office with suspicion and contempt when he detected opposition or scepticism towards his policy of constructive dialogue. He conducted an increasingly personal and hidden diplomacy towards Mussolini and Hitler which bypassed Britain's professional diplomats. All he sought from the Air Ministry was the efficient execution of rearmament policy that did not leave him exposed to Churchill's criticism; otherwise he showed no inclination to doubt their judgements. Had the position been reversed and had he applied a fraction of the scepticism he directed at the diplomats to the air marshals, history might have been very different. The Air Staff strove for a fleet of large bombers capable of dropping a huge tonnage of bombs on Germany, but this was not going to be ready for years. In the meantime, the interim designs of bombers were put into service inefficiently.

In the early months of Chamberlain's premiership, Churchill had contented himself with continuing to hammer on about the need to rearm, especially in the air. His network of insider contacts continued to feed him with evidence of the difficulties and delays that the programme was encountering. Often these were not more than the inevitable difficulties of such a vast programme that was being implemented in a hurry, but they provided Churchill with ample ammunition to lambast the government, although he held back from direct criticism of the government's foreign policy. Pushing for rearmament was broadly uncontroversial as this was the government's official policy; only the scale and execution of the programme was at issue. Disagreeing with the direction of foreign policy would have marked an open breach.

Churchill had been tempted by the public outcry over the Hoare–Laval agreement in December 1935. The cynical deal between the Foreign Secretary and France's repellent Prime Minister to acquiesce in Mussolini's occupation of Abyssinia looked like a step too far in avoiding a direct confrontation with Fascist Italy. Baldwin disavowed

Samuel Hoare, in practice forcing him to resign, even though he was essentially carrying out the government's policy. Perhaps fortunately, Churchill was abroad at the time and not subject to the same level of acute temptation to intervene that was to lead him so badly astray over the abdication. Randolph, Brendan Bracken and Lindemann had all strongly advised him to remain abroad and to stay out of the fight. It was a rare instance of unanimity amongst the trio.

Two and a half years later, things had changed. The turning point was the *Anschluss* on 13 March 1938 by which Austria and Germany fused together and gave unarguable proof of Hitler's expansionist strategy. It was impossible to represent it as a reversal of some unfair clause of the Versailles Treaty, even if the majority of the Austrian population were as enthusiastic as the Germans. The general condemnation of 'the rape of Austria' was wide of the mark, although it found an echo in the later national self-exculpation that the country developed under the label 'the first victim of Nazism'.[2] The *Anschluss* prompted Churchill to renew his call for more rearmament in a debate on defence policy, but he now introduced a clear call for a change in the direction of foreign policy. He advocated an outright, open military alliance with France to face Germany down and appealed for some form of direct commitment to protect Czechoslovakia, which was widely expected to be Germany's next target. He assailed Chamberlain's complacent optimism supported by his journalistic lackey, Geoffrey Dawson, in the House of Commons:

> Now, after Austria has been struck down, we are all disturbed and alarmed, but in a little while there may be another pause. There may not – we cannot tell. But if there is a pause, then people will be saying, 'There now, see how the alarmists have been confuted; Europe has calmed down, it has all blown over, and the war scare has passed away.' My Right Hon. Friend the Prime Minister will perhaps repeat what he said a few weeks ago, that the tension in Europe is greatly relaxed. *The Times* will write a leading article to say how silly those people look who on the morrow of the Austrian incorporation raised a clamour for

exceptional action in foreign policy and home defence, and how wise the Government were not to let themselves be carried away by this passing incident.[3]

Churchill finished by echoing the same vision of Germany returning to a quest for mastery of Europe that had been a key plank in his analysis of Hitler: 'Now the victors are the vanquished, and those who threw down their arms in the field and sued for an armistice are striding on to world mastery.'

By an uncanny coincidence, on the same day as this speech, Churchill's uneven relationship with Lord Beaverbrook reached a turning point. Beaverbrook advocated a policy of avoiding war by shunning entanglements in the diplomacy of Continental Europe. He was a full-blown British isolationist. He was far too disreputable to become a full-blown press ally of Chamberlain in the same way as Geoffrey Dawson on *The Times*, but the support that the *Daily Express* gave to appeasement strengthened its popular appeal. Beaverbrook was at odds with Churchill on the question and also declined to help Churchill's work on *Great Contemporaries* with material that he held on Andrew Bonar Law, still Beaverbrook's idealised lost leader. He judged, probably correctly, that Churchill 'will not make the use of the material I would like you to'.[4] Beaverbrook was a great collector of documents and used access to them as a tool in his manipulation of history. Churchill had been upset by Beaverbrook's star cartoonist David Low who had savaged his campaign on India. In October 1937, Beaverbrook was given material on which to judge Churchill's current stance in the shape of a long report by one of his senior journalists, Frank Owen of the *Daily Express*, of a dinner at Chartwell. Owen was clearly taken with Churchill but tailored his comments to match the prejudices of his boss.[5] He told Beaverbrook that the invitation to Chartwell was 'primarily to pump his armaments propaganda into me' and referred to Lindemann who was also at the dinner as 'the air force rearmament agitator'. Churchill criticised the language of the *Daily Express*, but as his examples were 'unprintable', the full report had to be held over to an oral one. Owen described the evening coming to an end at 2.30 a.m. in Churchill's bedroom, with his host stripped to his underwear but still lecturing on history. With his trademark mischievousness, Beaverbrook sent Churchill a copy of Owen's memo under the pretence that it would amuse him. It did not.

In early 1938, Beaverbrook decided to crack the whip. His *Evening Standard* ran a fortnightly column by Churchill which gave him both a powerful public platform and a source of significant income; as well as the £50 basic fee, the article earned syndication royalties on which the newspaper advanced £70.[6] On the day of Churchill's *Anschluss* speech, the new editor, Reginald Thompson, informed Churchill that the contract was cancelled forthwith: 'As it is my duty to be completely frank it has been evident that your views on foreign affairs and the part which this country should play are entirely opposed to those held by us.' The 'us' places it almost beyond doubt that the decision was Beaverbrook's. Thompson was an insignificant figure in the Beaverbrook organisation. There was also a large element of hypocrisy in Thompson's justification: the *Evening Standard* continued to run David Low's cartoons which by then were chiefly known for their savage attacks on the Fascist dictators and on appeasement. In the wake of the acrimonious correspondence that the termination sparked, Beaverbrook meted out further punishment in the form of an article in the *Daily Express* about Churchill's financial problems, reporting that Chartwell was up for sale. If the judgement to terminate Churchill's contract was a purely commercial one, it was not shared by Beaverbrook's competitor Lord Camrose, the owner of the *Daily Telegraph* which signed Churchill up immediately on the same terms, albeit for only an initial six months. Lord Camrose was closer to Chamberlain than was Beaverbrook, so ideology can have played little part.

The *Evening Standard* featured in an obscure episode that risked bringing Churchill into discredit. It ran a story which could have been read as showing Churchill as the inspiration for a ministerial revolt over a guarantee for Czechoslovakia triggered by the *Anschluss*.

The article arose from a conversation between Bob Boothby and an extreme left-wing journalist, John Strachey. Boothby frantically attempted to persuade Churchill that the newspaper had more or less invented the material, but the suspicion lingers that he was the true author.

Bracken's more passive posture continued into the early phase of Chamberlain's appeasement. His most noticeable intervention in the House of Commons was to flay the National Defence Contribution levy on corporate profits which Chamberlain had devised to finance rearmament in his last weeks as Chancellor of the Exchequer. The plan was deeply unpopular in business and the City, so he was hardly going out on a limb. The opposition was so ferocious that Chamberlain backtracked and left his new Chancellor of the Exchequer, Sir John Simon, to scratch together the funds as best he could.

But for the help of Bracken, Churchill might indeed have been forced to sell Chartwell. This had also happened a few years before, when Bracken's contact Alexander Korda threw Churchill a financial lifeline. Through the good offices of Bracken, who knew him well through City circles, Churchill had also come to know the mining magnate Sir Henry Strakosch, who fed him with informed data on the state of the German economy and, far more important, rescued him financially. Strakosch took over Churchill's heavily loss-making holdings in US shares and underwrote the losses that he had incurred of £18,000 – worth around £2 million in today's money. Churchill told Bracken privately, 'This is only to tell you that as Hitler said to Mussolini on a recent and less worthy occasion, "I shall never forget" this inestimable service.' When Strakosch died in 1943, he left Churchill the then immense sum of £25,000 and £2,500 to Bracken. Robert Bruce Lockhart, who knew Strakosch well, believed the legacy to Bracken was a reward for having introduced Strakosch to Churchill.[7] He judged Strakosch to have been motivated partly by snobbery in his cultivation of Churchill.

16

BANDITS SNIPE AT THE
PRIME MINISTER

The first serious crack in the edifice of Conservative solidarity around Neville Chamberlain's policy of constructive dialogue with the dictators came in February 1938, when the Foreign Secretary Anthony Eden, along with his junior minister Lord Cranborne, resigned in protest. Eden, however, did not turn openly against the government and remained broadly loyal. His departure was a shock, but it did not create a homogenous anti-appeasement movement. Eden's followers were essentially a personal following, derided as the 'glamour boys' by the Chief Whip Captain David Margesson.[1] Ronald Cartland, Edward Louis Spears, Harold Nicolson and Harold Macmillan were on the fringes but far from fully committed. Vyvyan Adams ploughed a lonely furrow. Even Winston Churchill's handful of supporters were not entirely in harmony. In the debate on Eden's departure, Bob Boothby launched into furious criticism of almost every aspect of foreign policy since the end of the First World War. He flayed Churchill for his quiescence over the Rhineland two years before, to the fury of Brendan Bracken.[2] It is hard to guess what Boothby was trying to do; he even threw in some critical comments on David Lloyd George, which had practically no bearing on the question, and his guarded praise for Chamberlain was mixed with qualifications.[3]

Churchill's was generally a lonely voice speaking against Chamberlain's foreign policy, but on one occasion, he and his allies triggered something approaching a widespread revolt. Chamberlain was willing to run the risk of upsetting the right wing of the Conservative Party.

His plan to buy Hitler off with African colonies is ample proof of this. He was also willing to acquiesce in direct attacks on British people and property if protest might provoke the dictators. Italian ships and submarines attacked ships supplying Republican Spain, but they had spared British ships after Chamberlain forced Eden out of office as Foreign Secretary as part of his programme of appeasing Mussolini. Chamberlain's reward was short-lived and the attacks resumed in the early summer of 1938, providing very public proof of the aggression and bad faith of Fascist Italy. British ships were sunk and British sailors killed. The day after one bombing, Duncan Sandys tabled a question in Parliament asking whether the government was going to do anything about the attacks. Clem Attlee, the Labour leader, followed up with a demand for a full debate. The arch-appeaser 'Chips' Channon cursed Sandys for 'beginning to overreach himself' as he battled to organise the government's response in his capacity as parliamentary private secretary to 'Rab' Butler, the junior Foreign Office minister.[4] Channon moaned at Franco's inconsiderateness in making life so hard for his British backers.

In the debate itself, the government was savagely criticised over an affront that only the most committed appeasers in the Conservative ranks could accept. In the words of the head of the Foreign Office, Alec Cadogan, 'the House blew up about the bombing of ships'.[5] Chamberlain faced possibly the most difficult moment in the House of Commons of the entire appeasement process, which he described as facing 'a pack of wild beasts when you just had to fight for your life'.[6] Channon saw that the Prime Minister was firmly on the back foot:

> He was not at his best: he is better with a prepared brief than impromptu. Four long hours we sat listening to the howling opposite, the catcalls of the bellicose, the jeers of the innocent. Feeling ran very high and threatened to explode when people in the gallery made a demonstration and were bustled out by the attendants.[7]

Chamberlain began by attacking a British shipowner with the

conveniently Jewish-sounding name of Billmeir for supposedly profiteering and then brought out the feeble claim that his hands were tied by the non-intervention agreement, so resolute action would risk a European war.[8] Publicly and officially, Chamberlain had to maintain the pretence that this was purely a question for the Spanish Nationalists; the aircraft now carrying out the attacks carried Nationalist markings, but they were supplied by Mussolini with Italian crews based on Mallorca. Lloyd George had already stated openly that the aircraft were Italian and (inaccurately) German. Britain's well-connected and effective consul in Mallorca, Alan Hillgarth, was well aware of the true position: that they were Italian.[9]

The debate marked another step along Churchill's path to outright opposition. He had a field day, lambasting the government for the 'debasement of a currency … The British flag is not giving protection to persons proceeding about their lawful vocations.' He skewered Chamberlain with the suggestion that the 'prime minister should use his personal influence with Signor Mussolini' which he had devoted 'so much exertion' to cultivating. Chamberlain ruefully admitted that 'Winston was far more subtle and kept quiet except his *banditti** were sniping when they could'.[10] To Chamberlain, anyone who threatened to compromise his policy of constructive dialogue with the dictators was a danger to peace and could be classed as an outlaw. Archie Sinclair contributed a lengthy speech as well, nailing the feebleness in the government's case: it flinched from inspecting supplies to Francoist-held Mallorca whilst meekly accepting the bombing of British ships. Duncan Sandys pulled up Chamberlain on the distinction between reprisals and retaliation.

Soon afterwards, Sandys moved further into the limelight as an ally in his father-in-law's campaign for effective military spending. He triggered a series of events that led Churchill into possibly the most futile and wasteful initiatives of his campaign for rearmament. Sandys was a second lieutenant in a Territorial Army anti-aircraft unit,

---

* Bandits.

which gave him direct information on the state of preparations to protect Britain against the Luftwaffe, and he saw significant deficiencies. Along with his fellow officers, he was enraged at the bland and dishonest public assurance of War Minister Leslie Hore-Belisha that units were equipped with modern guns.[11] Sandys obtained further information well above his pay grade from a more senior officer, which he embodied in a draft parliamentary question which he submitted in advance to Hore-Belisha. The matter escalated. Chamberlain advised Hore-Belisha to consult the Attorney General on the legal position, as Sandys might have committed an offence against the Official Secrets Act by using confidential information which he had obtained from his military position. The Attorney General, in turn, summoned Sandys for a conversation which Chamberlain fondly hoped would set the matter at rest.[12] He was mistaken and Sandys, likely egged on by Churchill, placed the matter before the Privileges Committee of the House of Commons. Sandys claimed that he had been ordered to appear before a military tribunal in uniform and claimed that this was a breach of parliamentary privilege. The existence of the military tribunal soon proved to be imaginary, but Churchill and his son-in-law persisted. Soon, two separate Commons committees were at work, which dragged on for months. This occupied much time and effort on Chamberlain's part but singularly failed to score points against the government or arouse sympathy. In Chamberlain's words: 'I think the House is beginning to be aware that they have been humbugged by Winston & Sandys and they don't want to hear much more about it.'[13] The final inquiry produced majority and minority reports according to which there was error on both sides. Brendan Bracken had also pitched into the fight with an affront to bureaucratic proprieties when he erupted in the office of Colonel Ismay, who headed the military secretariat of the Committee of Imperial Defence, slapped him on the back and pumped him for information on anti-aircraft weapons.[14] Ismay saw through the 'idiot boy' pose Bracken adopted to try to catch him off guard. Churchill had fallen into the same trap as when he had succumbed to the temptation to bring the Privileges Committee into the India Bill debate, when he saw far greater prospect of securing a triumph over the government on a procedural point than actually existed. Churchill revered the standing of the House of Commons but tended to exaggerate the extent to which this could short-circuit normal considerations of political debate. He could have banked an easy tactical win on Hore-Belisha's dishonest optimism and opened a second front against the execution of the rearmament programme by bringing in anti-aircraft defences. Instead, Churchill preferred to fight a futile attritional campaign on a profitless issue whilst the burgeoning Czech crisis presented far more crucial issues.

After the *Anschluss*, it was widely expected that Hitler would move on to Czechoslovakia. He had a ready-made issue in the country's large German-speaking population, the *Sudetendeutsche*, which it inherited accidentally at its foundation under the Versailles Treaty. The ancient kingdom of Bohemia had been part of the Austro-Hungarian Empire and its population was made up of both Czech and German speakers but no one at Versailles had thought to redraw boundaries to accommodate them. Through the spring of 1938, agitation of Sudeten autonomy grew. Czech independence was sustained by a formal 'Treaty of Alliance and Friendship' with France, signed in 1924, which was designed further to strengthen the 'Little Entente' grouping of smaller Eastern European nations. Chamberlain feared that Germany might attack Czechoslovakia, triggering a war with France into which Britain would be sucked willy-nilly. True to his instincts for proactive measures, Chamberlain wanted to do something in advance to ward off the danger. In that crowded final week of June 1938, Chamberlain announced to the Cabinet that, 'in case conversations broke down, he proposed to have a wise British subject available to slip off quickly to Central Europe to try and get the parties together again'.[15] Here Chamberlain was also showing his faith in purely bilateral solutions. There does not appear to have been any prior discussion, certainly not with France which was the party directly engaged because of its treaty obligations. The 'wise British subject' who was bullied into acting as mediator was Lord Runciman, a former minister who had been chosen by Downing Street. The whole initiative was entirely gratuitous and shaped British involvement in the crisis. Privately, a senior diplomat understood immediately that 'it committed [His Majesty's Government] up to the hilt'.[16] Later, Chamberlain's parliamentary private secretary, Alec Dunglass, better known as Prime Minister Alec Douglas-Home, admitted in his memoirs that it was 'a mistake. It drew us in too much.'[17]

Churchill, too, wanted Britain to engage deeply in the affairs of Europe. His goal was a dual alliance between Britain and France that could face down Nazi Germany. This was exactly the opposite of what Beaverbrook wanted. He loathed the idea of British involvement on the Continent and saw no need to halt Hitler. It was from this perspective that Beaverbrook judged the Runciman mission. At the time, Beaverbrook was almost alone publicly in spotting the significance of the move. He wrote in the *Daily Express* after the Munich conference that 'Chamberlain put pussy in the well. It is quite true that we owe him gratitude for pulling pussy out again. But the original mistake should never have been made.'[18]

Beaverbrook failed to appreciate that the ultimate goal of the Runciman mission had been no more than to bully the Czechoslovakians into ceding the Sudetenland, which was finally achieved at the Munich conference. What he saw and deplored was the engagement of British prestige and moral authority that transformed the Sudeten problem from a central European imbroglio. The extent of British involvement in the Sudeten problem was a gratuitous choice by Chamberlain, but his legacy is judged on the outcome and not on the choice itself.

Runciman's efforts did not bring a resolution. Hitler ramped up his demands. On 13 September, Chamberlain implemented the self-consciously dramatic 'Plan Z' and sought a meeting with Hitler to ward off a German attack on Czechoslovakia. Chamberlain's flight to Munich for talks with Hitler at his mountain retreat, the Berghof at Berchtesgaden, initiated the series of negotiations in which the British sought a settlement of the Sudeten question that would be acceptable to Hitler. The Czechs played no part and Chamberlain left only a secondary role for the French. Chamberlain had transformed a dispute between Germany and Czechoslovakia, with France standing on the sidelines and Britain as a distantly interested party, into an Anglo-German crisis. Churchill and others who had been dubious about Chamberlain's diplomacy scented an imminent and shameful sacrifice of Czech interests to appease Hitler.

It is often said that Churchill's verdict on Munich was that 'Mr Chamberlain was given a choice between war and dishonour. He chose dishonour. He will have war.' Sadly, this seems to be one of the many Churchill quotations that prove to be apocryphal when anyone tries to find the original statement. It does, however, encapsulate the gulf in the contemporary judgements passed on the Munich agreement. For Chamberlain's supporters, the agreement genuinely meant 'peace for our time', the removal of tension from Europe; for Churchill's supporters, it simply put off an unavoidable confrontation.

Many recognised that war was inevitable after Munich, many of whom had hoped for better, but this was not a universal sentiment. The political reaction to Munich was uneven and it exposed the cracks in the opposition to appeasement. The contemporary critics of Munich ensured their place in history and their reputations, but they entirely failed to dislodge the forces of appeasement from the levers of power. The doubters made their voices heard, but they achieved nothing. Chamberlain never disowned the Munich agreements. Some form of negotiated settlement with Germany remained the true policy of the Chamberlain government until April 1940, when the German invasion of Scandinavia brought the Phoncy War to an end.

When the House of Commons debated the Munich treaty, it was absorbed by hysterical adulation for Chamberlain for saving the country from war. With five exceptions, the MPs rose to their feet to deliver a standing ovation when the Prime Minister entered the House. The MPs who remained on the benches were Winston Churchill, Duncan Sandys, Harold Nicolson, Robert Bower and Ronald Cartland. Given the unreasoning (and short-lived) wave of gratitude to Chamberlain for preventing a war, this called for reserves of moral courage. When it came to the vote, more government MPs were prepared to signal their displeasure. The roll call of MPs who did not support the government in the debate on Munich shows that there was substantial concern over the agreements in Parliament but fails to tell us how badly the critics were divided amongst themselves. It is still unknown how many Conservative MPs abstained in the vote at the end of the debate; thirty-nine is the figure most-often quoted. The most important distinct group was the 'glamour boys' around Anthony Eden. Churchill had lambasted the agreement as 'a disaster of the first magnitude' but only abstained in the vote. His immediate allies – Brendan Bracken, Bob Boothby and Duncan Sandys – also abstained. However, the vote produced confusion over whether Boothby had actually abstained, which led to Bracken accusing him angrily of supporting the government.[19] Churchill accepted that Bracken was in the wrong when Boothby protested but in notably tepid terms which angered Boothby further. Perhaps Churchill remembered Boothby's speech in the Eden resignation debate. Boothby remained an ally of Churchill, but the mutual trust and loyalty fell well short of the relationship between Churchill and Bracken. The Conservative diehards who had supported Churchill over India voted solidly with the government: Henry Page Croft, Patrick Donner, Alan Lennox-Boyd, Victor Raikes and Murray Sueter. The argument that Munich bought a vital 'year's breathing space' in which Britain was able to rearm and avoid abject defeat is a gloss made after the event. There is no contemporary source that puts a timescale on Chamberlain's 'our time'. The argument further ignores major points. The duration of the grace that was accorded to Britain was entirely Hitler's choice. It lasted two years, ending when Germany attacked France in May 1940. Germany never had the means, plan or intention to deliver a 'knock-out blow' against London, which was the shape of the defeat that the British were terrified of.

17

THE DARK AT THE END
OF THE RAINBOW

The vote on the Munich settlement shows the scale of shame at Neville Chamberlain's sacrifice of Czechoslovakia, but this fell well short of active support for Winston Churchill's stance on how to improve Britain's readiness for conflict. The formation of a Ministry of Supply had become a shibboleth of those who believed that the country should make itself ready for all-out war. It was practically a euphemism for a Ministry of Munitions which had directed war industry in the First World War, an element of Britain's first total war. It was anathema to the Chamberlain government's doctrine of preserving national finances intact, as well as potentially sending a clear signal to Germany that Britain did not believe that permanent peace had been achieved. Six weeks after Munich, the Liberals, under the leadership of Archibald Sinclair, tabled an amendment calling for a Ministry of Supply. The motion was backed by Labour, now finally weaned away from unilateral disarmament. Only three Conservative MPs voted in favour: Churchill, Brendan Bracken and Harold Macmillan, then very much a maverick and even further from the Tory mainstream. Even Duncan Sandys did not join his father-in-law in the Aye lobby and Bob Boothby appears to have abstained as well. Just as Anthony Eden's resignation had done, Munich failed to create a united bloc against Chamberlain. Macmillan noted that his opponents became more offensive in tone, adopting Bracken's nickname for him, 'the coroner', but this hardly counted as effective political organisation.[1]

At the beginning of 1939, Sandys and Randolph joined in an

initiative to mobilise public backing for greater preparations. They tried to promote a new grouping under the name the 'Hundred Thousand' for critics of government policy 'who are alarmed at what they regard as the weak state of our defences and at the course of British foreign policy'. The title was a grandiloquent echo of the name applied to the British Expeditionary Force in the First World War, which instantly exposed it to ridicule and a charge of wild over-optimism. Sandys and Randolph might even have entertained grander ideas for their project: a file jacket in Sandys's papers containing relevant press cuttings is marked 'New Party'.[2] According to Randolph's biographer, Churchill senior had given it no encouragement and had been openly doubtful that it was wise.[3] Bracken declined an invitation to attend, pleading a prior engagement, but he did give Sandys a crumb of support: 'The Muddled state of the Tory mind certainly requires a good deal of clarification.'[4] Only 300 people turned up for the inaugural meeting at Caxton Hall, Westminster, presided by Sandys, of whom a fair number were there to express their opposition. The MPs who attended in support included Macmillan and another well-established Conservative anti-appeaser: Vyvyan Adams. The scheme fared no better than any of Randolph's forays into politics and flopped. When Sandys suggested that those who were not prepared to support the movement might like to leave the hall, a considerable number walked out. Amongst these was the high-profile figure of Captain Basil Liddell Hart, *The Times* defence correspondent, who issued a statement dissociating himself from 'a new political group', hinting that the involvement of Randolph made it all too plain that he suspected that the group was merely a tool for Churchill to oppose Chamberlain. Sandys had claimed the support of Vernon Bartlett, who had just won the by-election at Bridgewater on an anti-appeasement platform in a stunning defeat for the government, but Bartlett publicly described this as premature and took no part. Macmillan was rather more sympathetic and saw Sandys's move as symptomatic of dwindling suspicion of Churchill.[5]

Churchill gained nothing from this episode and it cannot have improved his standing. It also put a damper on his son-in-law's scope for independent action. Soon afterwards, Chamberlain was exulting, 'Duncan Sandys is a reformed character & makes moving speeches in favour of the Govt.'[6] Lord Beaverbrook was publicly gleeful at Sandys's 'troubles'.

The revolt over Munich never remotely threatened the government, but Downing Street set out to punish the rebels. More or less orchestrated, and certainly condoned, by Conservative Central Office and the whips, led by the ruthless Captain David Margesson, a number of anti-appeasers found themselves challenged by their constituency organisations. The challenge to Churchill in his Epping constituency was led by Colin Thornton-Kemsley, who had previously been an enthusiastic supporter of his but now seemed to be working for Conservative Party Central Office to weaken Churchill. Thornton-Kemsley led the attack on Churchill at a special meeting of the West Essex Unionist Association held in the City of London on 4 November.[7] His speech read like a prospectus for appeasement in its purest form. Armed opposition to Germany had failed and there was no real conflict of interest between Germany and Britain. A 'policy of friendship' amongst the Munich powers would prevent war in Europe. Fortunately for Churchill, the chairman of the association, Sir James Hawkey, steadfastly supported him against this assault and an artfully worded resolution urging Churchill 'to continue his work for national unity and national defence' was carried by a healthy majority. Churchill had survived, but Thornton-Kemsley continued his campaign, trying to force Churchill to stand as an independent: 'We wanted to support the Conservative administration, not to discredit them.'[8] It received a shot in the arm from Beaverbrook on 5 February 1939 when the *Sunday Express* published an article over his signature quoting at length:

> Many of the Branch associations in the Division are in practically open revolt against the Member.
>
> They demand a candidate who will support the Prime Minister and

the National Government in place of a member who, while he does not hesitate to shelter under the goodwill attaching to the good name of a great party, constantly and almost, it seems, inevitably criticises the policy and actions of the Party's leader.

Beaverbrook renewed his call for Churchill to be deselected. Churchill immediately protested against what he saw as a personal attack. Tellingly enough, this episode does not appear in the laudatory biography of Beaverbrook by A. J. P. Taylor, who worshipped him. As well as demonstrating Beaverbrook's continuing commitment to appeasement, it suggests that he was viewing Churchill as a spent force in politics. It was in the same article that Beaverbrook had assailed the futile 'One Hundred Thousand' project by Sandys.

It is only with hindsight that Churchill's reaction to Munich appears prescient. Chamberlain was privately disappointed that Hitler's supposed admiration for him had not led to any concrete move to embody 'peace for our time', but otherwise he was still basking in the glow of self-satisfaction at having saved Europe from war. In early 1939, he was still congratulating himself that he was viewed as the 'Father of Peace', boasting that Hitler had missed the bus at Munich and that 'we have at last got on top of the dictators'.[9] His party was solidly behind him and practically the only serious dissent came from the clutch of abstainer MPs. By early March, Chamberlain was rejoicing to his most docile press constituency, the parliamentary lobby correspondents, that Franco's victory in the Spanish Civil War had removed the cause of tension between Italy and the democracies and that Germany's supposed economic problems opened the way for British economic cooperation to provide a springboard to a full peaceful agreement. This was done behind the back of Sir Alec Cadogan, head of the Foreign Office, who labelled it as a 'ridiculous rainbow story'.[10]

Chamberlain's glow of optimism was at least temporarily dispelled when Hitler tore up the Munich treaty and seized the remainder of Czechoslovakia in March 1939 to the extent that he admitted 'it was impossible to deal with Hitler, after he had thrown all his assurances to the winds'.[11] When Mussolini showed he would not be outdone by his German ally and seized Albania a few weeks later, Chamberlain confessed that 'such faith as I ever had in the assurances of dictators is rapidly being whittled away'.[12] Chamberlain's conversion to something like Churchill's understanding of the dictators did not mean that he had any intention of adopting Churchill's policies. Indeed, his immediate reaction to the seizure of what remained of Czechoslovakia was to say outright that his policy was not going to change because of this. To Cadogan's dismay, 'he would go with his "policy" (? "appeasement"). Fatal!'[13] Chamberlain came up with a legalistic excuse for doing nothing, fully worthy of Sir John Simon, the weasel lawyer of appeasement. According to this, the guarantee of Czechoslovakian independence, promised after the Munich agreement, had not become operative and that could now be ignored, as the state it was supposed to protect had just ceased to exist. He trivialised the military occupation of Bohemia as 'symbolic' and proposed to make a brief and anodyne statement in a debate in the House of Commons merely 'regretting' the military occupation.[14]

It took external pressure to persuade Chamberlain that this was not tenable and that he was not going to be able to pursue appeasement as wholeheartedly as before. Accordingly, he made a speech in Birmingham taking a more resolute line. He persuaded himself that the balance of popular opinion still supported appeasement, but he could not escape the pressure from Parliament. The most important of the slew of measures that he came up with to demonstrate resolve in dealing with Hitler was the guarantee to Poland (and Romania) against German aggression that forced Britain to go to war later that year. Next, Chamberlain practically reversed the unspoken but absolute refusal to send a large army to the Continent that had ruled British thinking since the end of the First World War. To sustain this, it was announced that the size of the Territorial Army would be doubled and then conscription was introduced. There was minimal serious military preparation for any of this, which suggests that the moves were intended firstly for public consumption. Chamberlain even went so far as to accept the creation of a Ministry of Supply, albeit one dedicated solely to the needs of the army. Churchill would have been willing to take on even this limited task, but there was a limit to the extent that Chamberlain was willing to take military preparation seriously and the job was given to a nonentity.

Amidst all this flurry of activity, the one red line that was drawn was against bringing Churchill back into government. Chamberlain was prepared to display firmness towards Hitler, but in his mind, making Churchill a minister would be a challenge too far, tantamount to an open declaration that war was inevitable. Chamberlain was also determined to defend his authority against the encroachment of either Churchill or the Eden group of supporters. Somehow, Chamberlain managed to ignore the implication of his misjudgement of the dictators:

> That does not show that I have been wrong as my partisan critics declare. The fruits can be seen in the consolidation of world opinion and in the improvement of the military position of ourselves & France. But it does enable my enemies to mock me publicly and to weaken my authority in this country.[15]

Parallel to the parade of firmness, as Harold Nicolson detected, 'there is a very widespread belief that [Chamberlain] is running a dual policy – one, the overt one policy of rearming, and the other the *secret de l'Empereur*, namely appeasement plus Horace Wilson'.[16] He was correct; the prospect of friendly dialogue between Britain and Germany was held open through a variety of hidden back channels orchestrated by Wilson. There was no place for Churchillian resolve.

18

THE MOST SQUALID FORM
OF APPEASEMENT

Most of the City supported appeasement and the *Financial News* fell in with the general sentiment in its editorial line, as did its larger rival the *Financial Times*.[1] In the judgement of Lord Beaverbrook, Brendan Bracken 'never challenged directly the powerful interests of the City, preferring to fall in with them', and 'he refused to quarrel with the banks'. Bracken fell under the influence of Beaverbrook, who brought him round to his own isolationist and naively optimistic view that conflict with Germany could be avoided.[2] Bracken, though, was immediately hostile to Neville Chamberlain's proposed National Defence Contribution to finance rearmament and amended the proposed description from the socialist-sounding 'soak the rich' to the more business-friendly 'soak the enterprising'.[3]

Tearing up the Munich agreements and seizing the remainder of Czechoslovakia had exposed Hitler in his true colours as a ruler bent on expansion whose word could not be trusted. With hindsight, it appears to be the moment that Britain as a whole became aware that war was inevitable. But this was far from the case at the highest reaches of the British government machine. Germany had not become some kind of outlaw state; the norms of international relations would continue unimpeded. The tone was set by Downing Street, where the Prime Minister still hoped fervently that some kind of peaceful accommodation could be achieved. The measures reached in the panicky aftermath of Prague – national service, doubling the Territorial Army in size and the guarantees to Poland and Romania – were as far as Chamberlain was willing to go. Once these were in place, the old imperative to do nothing that might provoke Hitler was restored.

Even though it was legally a private and self-governing entity, the Bank of England subscribed fully to this policy. Almost from the start, it had been a serious backer of the policy of appeasement. Its autocratic governor, Montagu Norman, was a close ally of Sir Horace Wilson, the joint architect of appeasement. Norman was a friend and supporter of his German opposite number, Hjalmar Horace Greeley Schacht. As the last representative of fiscal – and probably any kind of conservatism – in the Nazi state, Schacht appeared to the optimists of Downing Street to be a voice of reason in Berlin who would respond positively to Chamberlain's persistent search for a rational composure of the differences between the countries. Even though Norman shared the hostility towards Jews which was widespread in financial circles, he approved of Schacht's moves to obtain 'decent treatment' for Jews in Germany. Norman had been the key figure in Downing Street's short-lived attempts to secure 'economic appeasement' of Germany in the months following Munich, until his involvement was firmly squashed by the Foreign Office, which was starting to resist the appeasers' use of back channels to Germany. Supposedly, the Nazis would leap at the prospect of bringing the country's finances back to an even keel now that 'peace for our time' meant they would no longer have to spend massive sums on armaments; Britain was going to offer its full assistance in achieving this goal. Norman had a ready-made international platform from which to launch his efforts. He had been a pivotal figure in the creation of the Bank for International Settlements (BIS), the bank for central banks in Basel founded in 1930. He was an almost invariable attender at the BIS's board meetings, where he could meet Schacht. The strength of the informal relationship between the BIS and the British state was manifest in the person of Sir Otto Niemeyer, one of the British directors and chairman of the board from May 1937. Niemeyer had been a senior Treasury civil servant until he was recruited to the Bank of England by Norman in 1927.

The illusion of economic appeasement vanished overnight when

Hitler tore up the Munich agreements and seized the remainder of Czechoslovakia on 16 March 1939. The Germans lost no opportunity to take full advantage of their control of the Czechoslovakian state. Barely a week after the seizure of Prague, the National Bank of Czechoslovakia was prevailed upon to instruct the BIS to transfer its reserve holdings of gold to the Reichsbank. The gold was physically held in the deep underground vaults of the Bank of England on Threadneedle Street in the heart of the City of London. Dr Johan Beyen, the Dutch vice-president of the BIS, tried to resist executing the instructions. The bank's legal officers gave him no help as they pointed out that there was no evidence that the Czechs were acting under duress; common sense is a weak principle in law. Beyen next tried to recruit the BIS's British and French directors; the French were more receptive, but after consultation with London, Paris told Beyen that he was not to delay the transfer. The Bank of England did actually consult the British Treasury, which advised it to continue with the transfer; this rather made a mockery of the bank's supposed independent status. The BIS thus instructed the Bank of England, which acted as the depository for most of the central banks' gold reserves, to transfer some £5.6 million worth of gold from the BIS's 'No. 2' account, known to be an account of the National Bank of Czechoslovakia, to the BIS's 'No. 17' account, which was believed to be a Reichsbank account. As was (and is) perfectly common, the BIS maintained a number of different sub-accounts at the Bank of England which mirrored the direct accounts that the various central banks held with it. Just as the BIS had no legal grounds to resist the instructions to transfer the gold, the Bank of England had no legal grounds for refusing to obey the instructions of its client, the BIS. Over the next ten days, this gold was disposed of, mostly to the Dutch and Belgium central banks with the remainder sold on the open bullion market.

From the bankers' point of view, that should have concluded the affair, but a few weeks later, the fate of the Czech gold began to attract hostile public attention and the Bank of England moved to cover its own tracks in the affair. It proposed to the BIS that it should change the structure of its gold deposit accounts and move to one single account, abolishing the sub-accounts which had made internal movements within the BIS's account visible to the Bank of England. The Bank of England was acting legally but furtively for very good reason. The central bankers' business-as-usual approach was about to be subjected to critical examination. The actions of the BIS and the Bank of England had been unimpeachable at law, but in the court of public opinion and politics, they were anything but.

On 18 May 1939, two months after the occupation of Prague, two prominent London journalists were tipped off about the removal of the Czech gold. One wrote for the *Daily Telegraph* and produced a garbled account of the story, but the other was Paul Einzig, possibly the star in the firmament of Bracken's journalistic empire and one of the best financial journalists of the day. Originally from Hungary, he had settled in London in 1919 to pursue his career as a financial journalist. By a process of mutual attraction, he had come into Bracken's orbit and their relationship was to become the driving factor in Einzig's career. He was hired as foreign editor of Bracken's *The Banker* and their relationship became even more extensive when Bracken bought the *Financial News*, which was Einzig's London alma mater. There were the usual tensions in the relationship between a driven and effective journalist and an editor, who had to take larger issues into consideration, but the Bracken–Einzig partnership was harmonious and powerful. As a Jew from central Europe, Einzig was more acutely aware than most of the threat posed by Nazi expansionism, but in the normal course of business, he had little professional scope to do anything about it. Bracken might have been Winston Churchill's ally in his fight against appeasement, but he could not deploy his press empire on their side in the campaign. Bracken's operation was first and foremost a money-making business. Its readers wanted to be informed about developments in financial markets and policy; they did not require reinforcement for their preconceptions about diplomacy. Many would, anyway, have been more inclined to take the view of Norman and Downing Street that ethical judgements on Hitler's regimes were out of place in the financial press. Bracken had to be constantly alert to behave as an ordinary pressman would. Bracken, moreover, was no more than an influential shareholder and executive at his publications, beholden to others with a larger financial stake. He did not enjoy either Beaverbrook's undisputed control over his papers or the immense financial resources that meant he could use them as tools in his political ploys.

The Czech gold affair, however, played to Bracken's strengths. The top-flight journalism that he nurtured could work on an influential and informed readership in the financial world. He could subject Neville Chamberlain's government to one of the most bruising passages of arms that the opponents of appeasement were able to inflict on it. It was a perfect subject for him to mount an attack where his skills complemented those of Churchill. Bracken's grasp of financial affairs allowed him to identify the weak points in the government stance and construct a case that was hard to dismiss. It called for forensic skills, rather than vaulting Churchillian rhetoric.

It was David Lloyd George who first took up the Czech gold story in the House of Commons and Chamberlain opened a flank by pooh-poohing it as a 'mare's nest', something entirely imaginary, so they just needed to prove the facts. By the time his opponents forced a full debate, Chamberlain adroitly pulled himself out of the firing line and left the Chancellor of the Exchequer, Sir John Simon, to deploy his legal skills and capacity to distort reality to put up what defence the government could. Bracken rose to the challenge of constructing a case that addressed the government's moral as distinct from legal responsibility and here his knowledge of financial markets was a trump card. He made full use of the Bank of England's ambiguous status: Britain's central bank was a private company over which the government had no control. The Bank of England represented Britain internationally on the BIS, but Britain had formally disclaimed any control over the BIS. The government's weakness vis-à-vis the Bank of England and the BIS was cruelly exposed by the Czech gold affair, which was a legitimate and important question for public interest.

Simon was trying to defend in Parliament something he claimed to be unable to influence. The Bank of England pursued a policy of 'sealed lips', true to its hallowed dictum 'never explain, never apologise', so Simon's was the only voice available to speak in its defence.

From the outset, Bracken could acknowledge that the BIS was a 'peculiar', an organisation with a unique legal status almost above the law. He showcased the failure of the British directors of the BIS to do anything to stop a blatant seizure by force; they could not but have been aware of government legislation designed to prevent the Germans seizing Czech-owned assets in London. Norman and Niemeyer had condoned a transfer by the BIS that breached the spirit of this legislation, even though the law did not cover directly the BIS accounts. Bracken could accuse the government of outright connivance in the disposal of stolen goods in the pursuit of a surreptitious form of appeasement. Norman and Niemeyer had not failed in their legal duty but their moral one and, in practice, the government endorsed their decision. With pointed sarcasm, Bracken commiserated with the Chancellor on his weakness vis-à-vis the bankers:

> I must say again that the point at issue is this, that the two British directors on the Bank for International Settlements were perfectly aware that the British Government had passed an Act, called the Czecho-Slovakia (Restrictions on Banking Accounts, etc.) Act, and that the British Government would not recognise the Government of Czechoslovakia. They are two of the most influential directors of the bank and are regarded as its co-founders, and it was their duty to go to Basle and protest against this surrender of Czech assets and, if their colleagues would not take notice of them, they should have resigned.
>
> The Nazis have got control of Czech bank balances by violence and we have to hand over the money to the gangsters who have broken into Czecho-Slovakia and seized the title deeds of the property of the Czechs. The directors of the Bank for International Settlements simply said, in effect, to the gangsters, 'We realise that you are right.' I think of these directors, it must be said that they came, they saw and they capitulated.[4]

The feebleness of the British directors led them to immoral conclusions, but Bracken skewered the embarrassing fact that conciliating Germany still fitted Downing Street's requirements. The weakness of Chamberlain's commitment to resisting Hitler was also painfully obvious in the half-hearted negotiations with the Soviet Union for some kind of common stance.

Bracken continued:

> Really, this is the most squalid form of appeasement. Political appeasement at the present time is, of course, out of the question. The by-elections and the various political developments in the last few months show that that policy at any rate is dead and damned, but some form of appeasement is still, apparently, dear to the heart of the Government, so they go in for financial appeasement.

Simon's attempt at defence was especially unconvincing, combining a wholly artificial claim that he was unsure if he was able to find anything out from the Bank of England and the statement that he only knew anything at all about the matter because of a chance mention by a third party. Practically, the only backbencher to support Simon was the dependable pro-appeasement hack Sir John Wardlaw-Milne. The government's floundering performance gave Churchill the perfect opportunity to deliver the *coup de grâce* with the contrast between the government's 'butter-fingered' failure to prevent £6 million slipping into Nazi hands and the financial and personal sacrifices that were now being imposed on the British people. Boothby and Sandys weighed in by pointing out that handing Germany the Czechs' gold implied de facto diplomatic recognition of the annexation of their territory.

The Czech gold debate attracted great public attention, although it has faded from memory. It was important enough to be the subject of a cartoon by David Low, arguably the highest profile cartoonist of the day, in Beaverbrook's *Evening Standard* that, as so often, caught the essential of the story pungently. Captioned 'Mind yer back!', Low's cartoon depicted Montagu Norman as a railway porter hurrying through a crowded station pushing a luggage trolley, laden high with boxes marked 'Czech gold' carrying labels saying 'To Germany', followed by the owners of the baggage, two strutting uniformed Nazi officials. Norman is manifestly determined to bring his precious consignment to the train that will take it to its new owner before the train has to leave the station. The British holidaymakers are an inconvenient obstacle.

Simon must have been aware of just how weak his position was, and the British government side put together a quite different line of defence which should get them out of the trouble they had put themselves into: the termination of the system under which the BIS held different sub-accounts at the Bank of England which made it possible to detect what the Nazis were up to. Here Simon failed to take into account the extent of Einzig's network of City contacts and his own indiscretion. One of Einzig's best contacts was the financier Sir Henry Strakosch, whom he knew was in the habit of playing golf with Simon at Walton Heath at weekends. A few days later, Einzig made a point of calling on Strakosch and conversation inevitably turned to the gold. Strakosch had indeed played golf with Simon and, unwittingly, had served as a guinea pig for the government's new line of defence, when the Chancellor of the Exchequer claimed that the Bank of England was simply not in a position to tell whether the transfer had been made. Einzig spotted immediately that he had been gifted an extra scoop, which made doubly plain the government's dubious position in the whole affair. Einzig then had to overcome Bracken's reluctance to pursue the story. Over tea after the debate, Simon had privately repeated what he had said in the House: that he doubted he was entitled to question the fate of the Czech gold. Einzig knew that it was only afterwards that Simon could have spoken to Norman and arranged for the smokescreen, so he was able to insert a firm forecast in his next column in *The Banker* that Simon would indeed shift his ground. The forecast proved entirely accurate and Simon was soon telling Parliament that the initial assumption that he would be able to tell them anything useful had been incorrect. The government's duplicity and moral complacency was beyond argument. Bracken spotted an open flank when Simon claimed that he was anxious to keep the gold in London and challenged Simon to use what influence he had over the British BIS directors to reverse the transfer. This forced Simon into a lame admission that he was unable to sway the BIS. Once again, Bracken could hammer home the moral bankruptcy of the stance taken by the British BIS directors and the failure of the government to remedy this.

Einzig accumulated further detail to pursue the story, but Bracken knew that it had been milked to the full, in both parliamentary and journalistic terms. Failing the emergence of some entirely new angle, he knew that the time had come to move on. Even though war lay only a few weeks away, the government's attempts to pursue appeasement had further to go, exploding into the scandal of a back-channel offer of a huge loan to Nazi Germany.

Long afterwards Bracken acknowledged the value of Einzig's work over the affair: 'I think your scoop about the Czech gold did more damage to the appeasement policy than dozens of fine parliamentary speeches.'

Of course, Bracken's compliment to his employee left open the door for recognition that it had taken the contributions by Churchill and Bracken himself to the Commons debate to wring the maximum advantage from Einzig's scoops to the discomfiture of the government.

As well as undermining the Chamberlain government's pursuit of appeasement long after the policy had failed, the Czech gold affair played its part in ending the Bank of England's centuries-long status as a privately owned organisation, independent of the government. When the bill to nationalise the bank tabled by the post-war Labour government was going through Parliament, the 'disgraceful episode' was quoted as a reason for bringing the Bank of England under government control. Hugh Gaitskell, then a rising star of the Labour Party, reminded the House of Sir John Simon's endorsement of the bank's freedom from state influence as an example of something that should not be allowed to recur.

*   *   *

A couple of months after the appeasers had been pitilessly exposed for using gold stolen from the Czech state to appease Nazi Germany, Bob Boothby was becoming involved in a scheme to compensate others who had lost out financially from the German seizure of the remainder of the Czech state but by chance found himself handing on a plate a golden opportunity to Neville Chamberlain's supporters a near perfect opportunity to even the score. One of Boothby's business partners, who had become a close personal friend, was a Czech Jewish businessman called Richard Weininger, who had been an officer in the Hapsburg Army during the First World War. Weininger had moved to Britain in 1938, but he and his family had left considerable assets in Czechoslovakia, which they hoped to get out of the country. After Prague, this became immensely more difficult. Boothby and another MP, Colonel Nathan, formed a committee to try to help Czech refugees claim compensation for assets frozen in the now Nazi-controlled territory. These naturally included Weininger's family. Boothby began to lobby on behalf of holders of Czech assets who signed up to the committee. This was all in the public eye and perfectly above board. Boothby was not paid for his work on the committee. His committee worked in parallel to a far more prestigious committee. A well-established City of London organisation – the Council of Foreign Bondholders, which had represented British investors in securities issued by defaulting entities abroad since the late nineteenth century – had established a committee to advise the Treasury on Czech assets. It featured luminaries such as Sir Edward Reid, a partner in Baring Brothers, the prestigious merchant bank. They viewed Boothby's upstart operation with 'some misgivings'.[5]

What was not disclosed was a private arrangement under which Weininger agreed to pay Boothby 10 per cent of anything recovered for him. Weininger put the family assets involved at £242,000 (worth perhaps £25 million today), so Boothby's share would have been £24,200. This would have been enough to pay off some very pressing debts with which he was faced, including £6,000 to another MP, the sinister figure of Alfred Butt, who doubled as a theatrical impresario and moneylender. Even more dubiously, Boothby had helped transfer the legal ownership of the Weininger assets to a British company, Zota Limited, and antedated this transaction to a week before the occupation of Prague. At a point when it was unclear whether British holders of Czech assets would be treated more favourably than Czech émigrés, this looked like an attempt to paint a Union Jack on the Weininger claim using forged documents.

All this was to remain hidden for over a year, but Boothby overreached himself fatally in the summer of 1939 by trying to recruit some more wealthy Czechs to his committee. The Petschek family of bankers and industrialists might have claimed to be the Rothschilds of Czechoslovakia and, being Jewish, had fled their homeland. They had even greater assets frozen in Czechoslovakia than Weininger, approximately £900,000. They had heard of Boothby's committee but had no interest in it and preferred to deal directly with the Bank of England. Colonel Nathan attempted to blackmail the Petscheks and Louis Infield, a junior civil servant, was also recruited to attempt to apply pressure.

Paul Petschek was prompted to protest all this and sent a copy of Nathan's blackmailing letter to Sir Edward Reid of Barings, who in turn passed it on to a senior civil servant at the Treasury, Sigismund Waley. Petschek might have been a refugee, but he could operate in far more rarified spheres of power and influence than Boothby. The correspondence worked its way up the system and landed on the desk of Sir Horace Wilson, Chamberlain's right-hand man and a firm opponent of Churchill and his allies, together with a covering letter from Waley giving the background to the two committees. Waley suspected predatory intentions on Boothby's part: 'Mr Boothby expects a rake-off.' He also made the welcome suggestion that Boothby's pretensions might be disposed of by way of a parliamentary question, for which he had attached a draft. This gave Wilson the opportunity to bring the political heavy artillery to bear on Boothby. He forwarded the papers to Sir John Simon, together with the recommendation that the parliamentary question route be used. The very next day, Simon told the House of Commons that Boothby's committee did not have official standing and that all holders of Czech assets who filed their claims with the Bank of England would be treated equally. Boothby's claim to being able to do anything useful on behalf of Weininger, the Petscheks or anyone else had been very publicly flattened.

Merely squashing Boothby's scheme was not enough for Wilson. He had struck a rich vein of material deeply discreditable to Church-ill's parliamentary acolyte, and he set out to mine it to the full with minimum delay. Wilson called Paul Petschek in for a conversation that same Friday. Wilson opened by telling Petschek that Infield's sug-gestion that the Petscheks would be at a disadvantage if they did not place their claim via Boothby was 'one which we in this country could not tolerate'. Wilson did not say so outright but he clearly implied that Infield had behaved quite wrongly and asked Petschek to 'help him get a full and clear picture of the whole incident'.[6] He was begin-ning to prepare the indictment of Boothby. Petschek was desperate to avoid getting involved in any controversial issues given his and his family's status but bowed to the inevitable and reluctantly agreed to send Wilson copies of all the correspondence involved. Wilson prom-ised that he would be discreet about their involvement.

The following Tuesday, Wilson moved on to the next potential source of dirt on Boothby. Infield was a far softer target than Pet-schek. He was petrified at being called in by the head of the civil service at very short notice. He did not admit to having intentionally pressurised Petschek but otherwise sang like a canary. He described in detail how Boothby had recruited him and provided crucial testimony to the damning fact that Boothby had personally asked him to call Petschek in. Wilson accepted Infield's claim that he had been naïf and that he had not been given any financial incentive to do what he had done.[7] Infield agreed happily to provide a full written account of what had gone on. Wilson had no reason to punish Infield; he was far more useful as a junior civil servant terrified for his job and correspondingly willing to cooperate. The chief civil servant of the Ministry of Health agreed with Wilson that Infield had been 'indiscreet & foolish' but no more and that a severe reprimand would 'meet the case'.[8] Given the gravity of what Infield had done, he had got off lightly, but he was more valuable on tap on the government payroll for future operations against Boothby.

Boothby himself had to be left to the politicians and Sir John Simon called him in for the final scene in the first act of the drama. Simon warned Boothby that the ground was about to be cut from under the feet of his committee by the parliamentary question. In what was to prove a near suicidal move, Boothby repeatedly assured Simon on his honour that he had no financial stake in the affair. This was true in the narrow sense that he was not being paid anything but expenses by his committee and that he had no direct financial motive to persuade the Petscheks to join; he made no mention of the 'rake-off' from Weininger's claim that had already been agreed. Boothby's economy with the truth of this point would come back to haunt him the following year, but for the time being, Wilson and his allies could be content with having hobbled Boothby's committee. His forgery of the antedated share transfer was another ticking time bomb.

19

EVERY CRIME IN THE CALENDAR

In the wake of Prague, Conservative discontent with Neville Chamberlain's diplomacy began to spread beyond the small cohort of committed anti-appeasers who had signalled their unhappiness at Munich. They found an unexpected outlet in the form of urging the government towards some form of alliance with the Soviet Union, ideological enemy of Nazism but anathema to traditional Conservatives.

In Chamberlain's eyes, Winston Churchill condemned himself by being amongst the first to push for a Soviet alliance to hold Germany back. Chamberlain was deeply suspicious of the motives and military capacity of the Soviet Union. (Curiously, few on either side of the debate recognised the extent and evil of Stalin's personal dictatorship.) Chamberlain had no positive sympathy or affection for the dictators, but one of the greatest flaws in his diplomacy was that whilst he was racked by distrust of potential allies – France, the USA or the USSR – he never applied the same scepticism to Hitler or Mussolini. On a more practical level, he was well aware of the huge diplomatic and geographical problem that lay in the existence of Poland lying between Germany and the Soviet Union. Poland quite correctly hated the Soviet Union as much as Germany, seeing it as being as great a threat.

Chamberlain's views were positively objective and balanced compared to the traditional loathing of Bolshevism amongst some members of his government and mainstream MPs. Ivan Maisky, the Soviet ambassador, was a particular hate object for 'Chips' Channon, who observed Churchill and his allies talking to him at the House of Commons at the end of the debate on the seizure of Czechoslovakia: 'I saw [Churchill] with Lloyd George, Boothby and Randolph, in a triumphant huddle surrounding Maisky. Maisky, the Ambassador of torture, murder and every crime in the calendar. To these depths have the Churchill–Eden group descended.'[1]

Chamberlain succumbed to the pressure, notably from his Foreign Secretary Lord Halifax, who was viewed by 10 Downing Street as unsound. A delegation under a superannuated admiral was sent to the Soviet Union by a slow boat. Talks with the Soviets were conducted with no obvious sign of urgency or enthusiasm on the British side. They dragged on for weeks in an atmosphere of growing distrust and suspicion without producing a glimmer of agreement until finally Stalin cut the Gordian knot and agreed a deal with Germany which partitioned Poland, triggering the Second World War.

Throughout the negotiations, Chamberlain saw Churchill as a helpmeet of the Soviets. It can be assumed that the Soviet embassy was targeted by British intelligence and that Downing Street was alerted of its contacts with Churchill. Sir Joseph Ball, Chamberlain's thuggish henchman, a former MI5 officer, boasted that he had dissident MPs under surveillance. Downing Street suspicions grew when the *Daily Mail* and the *Daily Telegraph* mounted a concerted drive to bring Churchill into the government in July 1939. Chamberlain blamed Randolph for the articles which advocated Churchill's elevation and he went further when contacts between Maisky and Randolph were reported. Chamberlain dreamed up a sinister Soviet plot, detecting a '"drive" to put Winston into the Govt. It has been a regular conspiracy in which Mr Maisky has been involved as he keeps in very close touch with Randolph.'[2] Even if Maisky actually participated in the manoeuvre, he confessed to his diary that he doubted it would go any further than similar tales of a pending government reshuffle of which he had heard many.[3] Chamberlain's suspicion that Randolph was involved in this episode are all that connect him to it.

Churchill's final major attempt to head the government away from its business-as-usual approach to dealings with Hitler came as Parliament approached its normal summer break in August. Churchill believed that holding the normal long recess would appear to be a retreat, which would allow the forces of appeasement to hold sway untroubled by parliamentary criticism. He suspected that it would leave the field open for another surrender to Hitler. The public revelation of one very high-profile set of back-channel contacts with Germany can only have strengthened this fear. It had leaked out that the possibility of a massive British loan to Nazi Germany had been discussed with Helmuth Wohlthat, Hermann Goering's economic adviser. The spirit of positive engagement with Hitler lived on in Downing Street, but Churchill knew better and understood how this had sent entirely the wrong message together with darker forebodings for Chamberlain's intentions:

> Evidently a great 'crunch' is coming and all preparations in Germany are moving forward ceaselessly to some date in August. Whether H[itler] will call it off or not is a psychological problem which you can judge as well as any living man. I fear he despises Chamberlain and is convinced that the reason he does not broaden his Government is because he means to give in once Parliament has risen.[4]

With Churchill's support, the Labour Party formally proposed that the holiday be limited to a couple of weeks. Chamberlain was enraged and put the move down to a manoeuvre by Churchill against him personally: 'The real protagonists of a change are Winston (backed by L. G.!) and Archie [Sinclair] and their real object is of course to attack and weaken the PM.'[5] Fuelled by the twaddle that had been fed to him by another of his back channels, Chamberlain was smugly complacent that Hitler was backing down. The historian Arthur Bryant passed on to Chamberlain the outright lie that Hitler was in no hurry to settle the question of Danzig, the German city left as an island in Polish territory by the Versailles Treaty which was the likely flashpoint of a new conflict.

By that stage, Chamberlain was not averse to sending signals to the Germans of British military preparedness, but he still bridled at anything that looked like he was paying any attention to Churchill.

Obstinacy and suspicion of Churchill played as much a part as any rational diplomatic calculation. Chamberlain thought that military moves showed strength but that a domestic political move to prepare for war would show weakness:

> Whether I shall be able to carry out my plans remains to be seen. All my information indicates that Hitler now realises that he can't grab anything else without a major war and has decided to put Danzig into cold storage. On the other hand he would feel that with all these demonstrations here, mobilisation of the fleet, territorials & militia-men training, bombers flying up and down France, he must do some-thing to show that he is not frightened. I should not be at all surprised therefore to hear of ... large bodies of troops near the Polish frontier, great flights of bombers, and a crop of stories of ominous preparations ... That is part of the war of nerves and no doubt will send Winston into hysterics. But to summon Parliament to ask questions & demand counter measures is to play straight into Hitler's hands and give the world the impression that we are in a panic.[6]

Just to ram home his belief that genuine foreign policy considera-tions had far less to do with the motion than partisan self-interest, Chamberlain told the House that the vote was one of confidence in the government, even though the whips had not issued a formal three-line whip. Even allowing for the risk of some Tory defections, this upped the ante greatly, as there was no serious risk that the gov-ernment would be defeated. Chamberlain had goaded Churchill in a brief conversation before the debate which fed a bitter exchange during the debate itself.[7] The debate was the last set-piece discussion of how Germany was to be handled and it was notably acrimoni-ous. Churchill and his supporters were present in force. The extreme Conservative right-winger Victor Raikes accused Brendan Bracken and Bob Boothby of indifferent voting records and labelled them 'the heavenly twins who sit at [Churchill's] feet'. Bracken retaliated by claiming that government supporters did not even deserve to be called 'yes-men'; they were merely 'nodders'. Duncan Sandys contributed a more measured set-piece speech in support of his father-in-law, which touched on the nub of the issue: a long holiday for Parliament was fine in normal times, but these were anything but normal times. None of the rebels went so far as to vote against the government, but Churchill, Bracken, Boothby and Sandys together with Ronald Cartland defied Chamberlain and abstained. The government inevitably won the vote with a healthy majority, leaving Chamberlain to relish Churchill's annoyance. He could depart for his summer holiday fishing with the Duke of Westminster at his luxurious house at Lochmore in the Scottish Highlands. Churchill and his allies were right to have feared the worst. When war did break out a few weeks later, Chamberlain claimed that 'up to the very last it would have been quite possible to have arranged a peaceful and honourable settlement between Germany and Poland', which suggests that he had foreseen bullying the Poles into accepting German demands, just as he had done to the Czechs the previous year.[8]

The military exercises that Chamberlain deluded himself were frightening Hitler had no effect whatever. Nor should they; RAF bombers might have demonstrated that they had the flying range to attack Germany, but the Air Staff were hiding from the politicians the fact that the head of Bomber Command had so little confidence in his force's state of preparation that he was close to declaring it unfit for combat. Churchill was entirely correct in thinking that Hitler had a low opinion of Chamberlain. When Chamberlain was briefing his commanders for the attack on Poland, he brushed aside any reason to fear intervention. Hitler had seen his opponents at Munich and they were 'pathetic little worms' (*armseligen Würmchen*).

20

A REAL WAR IN WHITEHALL

Just as Neville Chamberlain's rainbow delusions had been obliterated by the occupation of Prague in March, his delusions that Hitler had been put on the back foot were shattered by the news of the Molotov–Ribbentrop pact which gave Germany a free hand to attack Poland. Hitler invaded Poland on 1 September 1939. Britain was bound to try to help stop the Germans. That day, Chamberlain summoned Winston Churchill to Downing Street and, according to Churchill's later account, offered him a place in a small war Cabinet, the step that he had fought so long to avoid.[1] When Chamberlain had sounded out Maurice Hankey, now Lord Hankey, the previous week about arrangements for a Cabinet in wartime, he raised the question of Churchill joining, apparently acknowledging that public opinion would leave him no alternative.[2] Neither Chamberlain nor the French had any appetite for fighting a serious war against Germany, but Chamberlain could scarcely advertise the fact by leaving his Cabinet of appeasers unchanged. Churchill accepted but heard nothing the following day, although Chamberlain did discuss his position with Hankey, to whom he had certainly offered a seat in the Cabinet. Chamberlain's invitation to Churchill to join the Cabinet did not mean that his suspicions of him had abated. A week later, when the appointment had been confirmed, Hankey wrote to his wife that his 'main job is to keep an eye on Winston!'[3]

But the fact that Churchill had heard nothing the day after his conversation with Chamberlain fed the suspicion that Chamberlain was dragging his feet over declaring war. The suspicion was deepened on the evening of that day when Chamberlain spoke to the House of

Commons and failed to make any mention of an immediate ultimatum to Germany. Instead, he raised the possibility of further discussions if German troops were withdrawn. Downing Street appears to have entertained serious hopes that this fantasy would be realised. Churchill did not speak in the House – according to his later account because he felt himself to be a member of the government already. It might have been with precisely this kind of muzzle in mind that Chamberlain had dangled a seat in Cabinet in front of Churchill the previous day. The question that faced Churchill was whether to maintain his silence and this was the subject of conversation when he and his MP allies – Bracken, Boothby and Sandys – together with the most important Conservative dissidents, Anthony Eden and Duff Cooper, gathered at his flat in Morpeth Mansions. They debated through the night as a colossal thunderstorm raged outside. All were in a state of rage at the prospect of Britain trying to wriggle out of its commitments. The tone for the conversation was set by Clemmie, who was present at the start and was even more critical of Chamberlain than Churchill himself. The most hawkish of those present was Boothby, who 'was convinced that Chamberlain had lost the Conservative Party forever and that it was in Winston's power to go to the House of Commons tomorrow and break him and take his place. He felt strongly that in no circumstances now should Winston serve under him.'4

Everyone urged Churchill not to join the Cabinet unless Eden were included. Eden had been told that he would be given only a minor role in the government: Dominions Secretary, outside the Cabinet. All the other proposed members of the War Cabinet were appeasers and established supporters of the government – Chamberlain, Lord Halifax, Sir John Simon, Hankey and Admiral Lord Chatfield, the Minister for Defence Coordination. Churchill would have been in a minority of one. Bracken went even further and told Churchill to insist that Duff Cooper together with other ministers who had resigned over Munich should be included in the government. Churchill stopped short of agreeing to lead a rebellion against Chamberlain, but he did draft a letter to Chamberlain asking him not to say anything publicly about the composition of the War Cabinet until he had spoken to Churchill, thus practically withdrawing his agreement to serve. In the event, it did not take Churchill's actions to jolt Chamberlain out of his dream of avoiding war. Leslie Hore-Belisha, the war minister, tipped Churchill off that a Cabinet revolt led by Sir John Simon had forced Chamberlain's hand and an ultimatum was to be sent to Germany the following morning.

The War Cabinet that was actually formed differed from what had been discussed between Chamberlain and Churchill. The ministers for the fighting services had insisted on being included. Two were first-rank politicians and Chamberlain loyalists – Leslie Hore-Belisha and Sir Kingsley Wood, the Air Minister – but the First Lord of the Admiralty, Lord Stanhope, was a marginal figure who had not been especially successful and was expendable. Churchill was given Stanhope's job and he returned to the Admiralty twenty-five years after his questionable handling of the Gallipoli campaign had forced him out of office. Bracken became officially his parliamentary private secretary, continuing in practice the work he had been doing for Churchill unofficially and without title. Otherwise, the anti-appeasers were left in the cold, except Eden in his tokenistic job as Dominions Secretary.

The Royal Navy was the only one of the fighting services to be heavily in action during the Phoney War, partly by default. The government deliberately restrained the army from offensive action in France, and the RAF was kept on a tight leash as well but was incapable of a serious attack on Germany anyway. At the Admiralty, Churchill's aggressive instincts had free rein. Churchill knew that he was once again politically responsible for a service where conspicuous defeat was an ever-present possibility and how this could rebound on him. Within days of his appointment, he visited the great fleet base in Scapa Flow together with Bracken and Sinclair, his new and his old companions in arms. He mused presciently about 'how First Lords are treated when great ships are sunk and things go wrong'. The memory of Gallipoli hung heavy. Within days, Churchill's strategy led to just such a loss. The aircraft carrier HMS *Courageous* was following his orders in conducting a futile hunt for U-boats when one found and sank it in the English Channel. Weeks later, the old battleship HMS *Royal Oak* was sunk by a U-boat in the supposed safety of Scapa Flow itself. Fortunately for Churchill's reputation, the Royal Navy's two other high-profile engagements in 1939 added to the service's lustre. The sinking of the antique armed merchant cruiser *Rawalpindi* by the modern German battlecruisers *Scharnhorst* and *Gneisenau* showcased the service's capacity for, in this case literally, suicidal (and sadly futile) bravery. The sinking of the pocket battleship *Graf Spee* after the battle of the River Plate against inferior British warships offered the only conspicuous military success of the Phoney War.

Rawalpindi's captain was a relative of Bob Boothby, who took up the cause of his widow who was left destitute by his death. Brendan Bracken responded by displaying his instinctive kindness and energy on behalf of Mrs Kennedy: 'Within days Mrs Kennedy was installed, with a pension, in a grace-and-favour home at Hampton Court Palace. Brendan's skill as a fixer was not unknown to me already, but certainly not for the last time did he earn my admiration for the bigness of his heart.'[5]

From his privileged position, Bracken could observe the dilatory and inefficient conduct of Britain's Phoney War effort. He wrote to Garret Moore, his chief assistant in his journalistic empire, then briefly serving in France:

> The real war seems to be raging in Whitehall. If our service departments and the Ministry of Supply would stop fighting each other and concentrate on Mr Hitler one might hope for a short war. As it is, Mr Hitler is looked upon as an interloper in the struggles between the services, their politicians and the bureaucrats who control all.[6]

With his insider's awareness, he saw the weakness and incompetence of the Ministry of Information, Britain's wartime propaganda machine. He observed its failure to cultivate American journalists and tried to recruit Beaverbrook for a campaign to remove its 'ossific' influence.

A particular bugbear for Bracken was the Minister of Home Security, Sir John Anderson, civil servant turned politician, revered throughout Whitehall as one of the great administrators of his generation, but he took himself immensely seriously, earning Bracken's nicknames 'God's butler' or 'Maestro Pomposo'.

As he had during the Munich crisis, Bracken served as a channel of communication with the Labour leadership. Chamberlain had perfunctorily and insincerely offered Labour a minor place in the wartime government which they refused, so full-scale party politics continued through the Phoney War. Bracken talked to Labour leaders such as Sir Stafford Cripps on the possible structure of a coalition government, but this fell well short of a serious plot against Chamberlain. By April 1940, Downing Street was riddled with suspicion of Churchill's ambitions and intentions. Sinclair featured in Chamberlain's demonology too.[7]

Bracken's unhappiness at the conduct of the war was rooted in his dislike of Chamberlain. He saw the continuing Conservative domination of politics enforced by their Chief Whip, Captain David Margesson, as the root of the problem. With practically the same team in power, the Phoney War looked little better than a form of armed appeasement. Bracken feared that Churchill would be tarred by this brush. The main thrust of his efforts was journalistic. He gave two long, off-the-record interviews to W. P. Crozier, editor of the *Manchester Guardian*.[8] He urged his star journalist Paul Einzig, now a parliamentary lobby correspondent for the *Financial News*, to publicise the ineffectiveness of the economic blockade against Germany, which the government deluded itself would bring down the Hitler regime in a bloodless defeat. He told Einzig that government appeasers were using the supposed success of the blockade, which featured routinely in government press releases, to mask genuine failures in the conduct of the British war economy, especially aircraft production.[9] Churchill repeatedly tried to challenge the Air Minister, Sir Kingsley Wood on what he saw as a failure to increase the size of the RAF. Einzig obliged with articles assailing the loopholes in the blockade which recalled the doggedness of his articles against Nazi economic encroachments in the

Balkans, provoking merriment on the part of some of his colleagues. The lobby correspondents were the most loyal and best disciplined of Chamberlain's press claque. Einzig's efforts began to draw blood, notably on the day in April 1940 when no fewer than sixteen parliamentary questions were tabled on how easy it was to evade the blockade. This drew the fury of Sir John Simon and Margesson, whose language against Einzig was unprintable.

Frederick Lindemann, too, benefited from Churchill's elevation. The Tizard committee was quietly put to sleep, but Lindemann was brought into the Admiralty to set up a private office for Churchill and to act as his scientific adviser. With Churchill's determined support, Lindemann used his position as a platform to launch full-scale research and development of his pet weapon, the aerial mine. Ostensibly, this would be used to defend the ships of the Royal Navy from German bombers, but its potential for application to wider air defence requirements was inescapable. By this stage, the weapon had taken the definite shape of a system in which the aerial mines or strips of wire that served the same purpose would be fired by rocket into the path of oncoming bombers and descend on parachutes. From the start, Lindemann and Churchill worked on the assumption that this was a viable weapons system that merely needed to be refined to become fully operational.

As Territorial Army officers, Duncan Sandys and Randolph were immediately called up for service and joined their units – Sandys in the Royal Artillery, Randolph in his father's old regiment, the 4th Hussars. Sandys devoted almost no time to politics for the following months and eventually saw action in the ill-fated Norwegian campaign of April 1940. Before he joined his unit, Randolph undertook a personal mission for his father. Under the command of Lord Louis Mountbatten, the destroyer HMS *Kelly* was despatched to bring the Duke of Windsor back to Britain from France for the first time since his abdication. An aircraft would have been quicker, but the Duchess was terrified of flying, so with a certain symmetry, the Duke returned by the same transport as he had left under the authority of his one unconditional ally in the abdication crisis. The day after his abdication, the Duke had sailed to Boulogne on the destroyer HMS *Fury*, selected by Churchill's predecessor as the First Lord of the Admiralty, Sir Samuel Hoare. Hoare had spotted that it would have invited dubious comment if he had sailed on the Admiralty yacht *Enchantress*. Randolph had also attended the Duke's wedding to Mrs Simpson (or Warfield, as she had briefly been rebaptised) in 1937, in the ambiguous status of guest and journalist. With his unerring instinct for catastrophe, Randolph proceeded to inject an element of abject farce into the proceedings. He decided that the proletarian British Army battledress was inappropriate and changed into full-dress uniform of the 4th Hussars, complete with an excessively long cavalry sabre. Even worse, as the Duke hastened to alert him with a splutter of laughter, 'Randolph your spurs are not merely inside out but upside down! Haven't you ever been on a horse?'[10] Mountbatten was vastly entertained and confessed to Randolph that he had not warned him of his faux pas so as to leave the pleasure of doing so to the Duke.

On the eve of war, Randolph did not forget the Churchill family interests. After a brief and perfunctory courtship, Randolph married the nineteen-year-old Pamela Digby, who had been taken up and schooled, if not crudely as a courtesan, as a woman dedicated to keeping a man happy, by the American socialite, Lady Baillie, at her luxuriously modernised home, Leeds Castle in Kent. Part, and possibly chief, in Randolph's motivation was dynastic considerations. Hitherto, he had been a carefree womaniser, but with the likelihood of being in combat soon, he wanted to guarantee the furtherance of the Churchill line. He paraded his fiancée unabashedly as a 'brood mare'.[11] He succeeded in this goal and Pamela was soon pregnant. Their son Winston, named in line with tradition, was born in 1940. Lindemann and Bracken were the godfathers, suggesting that Bracken's relationship with Randolph was at one of its calmer patches. In the event, Randolph would not see action for many months.

The appeasers around Chamberlain were going through the motions of conducting – fighting would be too much of a word – the

Phoney War, but no such consideration applied to Beaverbrook. His isolationist appeasement segued into outright defeatism with the goal of forcing a negotiated peace with Germany. In January 1940, he tried to recruit the Duke of Windsor as the figurehead of a peace drive that would begin by appealing to financial interests of the City. The Duke was supposed to abandon the job he had been given as a major-general liaising with the French Army and return to Britain. Mercifully, the Duke's adviser Sir Walter Monckton was present at the meeting and pointed out that coming back to Britain would make him liable for British tax. Monckton had chosen wisely to appeal to the Duke's avarice rather than family loyalty or even basic decency and the Duke lost interest in this borderline treasonous scheme. Bizarrely, Beaverbrook was simultaneously hankering after a job in government, but when Chamberlain got wind of his plot with the Duke, any thought of indulging him vanished.[12]

Beaverbrook conducted a campaign for a negotiated peace with Hitler on a broad front. The *Sunday Express* published an article by David Lloyd George that was so defeatist in tone that Churchill was deputed to protest to Beaverbrook. The US ambassador to Britain, Joseph Kennedy, held strongly defeatist and anti-war opinions. He and Beaverbrook were reported as conducting a joint campaign; the *Evening Standard* was under orders to promote Kennedy's views.[13] The Duke and Kennedy opposed the war from a right-wing standpoint, but the Independent Labour Party (ILP) on the extreme left held to the ethical pacifism that had led it to oppose the First World War. The ILP was a fading force, but in March 1940, Beaverbrook invited James Maxton and other leaders to dinner to discuss their efforts to oppose the war. The ILP later claimed that he had offered to finance these, but Beaverbrook denied this.

Beaverbrook's *Evening Standard* also sniped at Churchill's work habits, insinuating that his late nights working left him over-tired.[14] Unwisely, the journalist gave as his source an entirely imaginary conversation with Lindemann in the Savoy Grill at midnight. Lindemann detested any such publicity at the best of times and complained to

Beaverbrook and asked for his name to be kept out of his newspapers.[15] In keeping with his usual habit, Beaverbrook wrote back as though the article had come as a surprise to him and outfaced Lindemann by challenging him to ask for the journalist's dismissal and a formal ban on mentioning him.[16] It was not a promising start to their wartime relationship.

*　　*　　*

During the Phoney War, Bob Boothby began to fall from Winston Churchill's graces. Some of the details rather beg the question of how firmly Boothby was ever there. Certainly, there is no sign that Boothby offered the same unconditional loyalty that Brendan Bracken and Frederick Lindemann extended. The winds of chance and genuine concern over Germany had blown Boothby back into Churchill's camp after the India Bill had divided them, but there is no sign that his relationship with Churchill had returned to the happy state it had reached when he was parliamentary private secretary to Churchill as Chancellor of the Exchequer. Boothby had, after all, gone into politics as a professional before he was ever a friend of Churchill.

As a backbencher, Boothby was entirely free to lambast the government's indifferent performance through the Phoney War. Here his view was in line with the private opinions of Churchill and Bracken, but on other points, his platform began to take a more conspicuously independent line. He adopted a notably egalitarian if not downright redistributionist approach to the wealth of the upper classes in his column in the populist *Picture Post*.[17] Along with Leo Amery and Harold Macmillan, Boothby called publicly for the conduct of the war to be put into the hands of a genuine war Cabinet on the pattern of Lloyd George's during the First World War. But Boothby's vision was not simply one of what he thought would make the best machinery of government. Lloyd George was a friend of long-standing. For Boothby to promote his claims combined genuine admiration with hedging his own bets.

On 29 September 1939, Boothby wrote a letter to Lloyd George which he subsequently erased from his version of history.[18] Talk of peace initiatives had swirled around, inspired by the Duke of Westminster. They found a degree of interest, notably on the right, but Chamberlain's personal pique against Hitler was an obstacle. Days later, Lloyd George did call in the House of Commons for Britain to 'seriously consider any proposals for peace which were specific, detailed, broad, which excluded nothing, but reviewed all the subjects that had been the cause of all the troubles of the last few years'. The need for full restitution of Czechoslovakia or Poland did not feature and there was an implicit acquiescence in the justice of German claims, including the gratuitous addition of colonies. Duff Cooper tore the speech to shreds as a manifesto for surrender, with Churchill nodding vigorously.

Boothby's advocacy of Lloyd George was not limited to discreet private communications and found public expression in a *Picture Post* profile in April 1940 marking fifty years since Lloyd George was elected as an MP. The article contained the breathless claim that 'a hundred years hence the historians will write that the greatest man produced by this country was unquestionably David Lloyd George'. Soon afterwards, as the Norway campaign degenerated into abject failure, Boothby was in the throes of deep indiscretion and at a lunch with journalists and other MPs, 'used big words and built new Cabinets with Lloyd George as PM'.[19]

* * *

In the last days of the Phoney War, Bob Boothby became involved in an outlandish and mysterious episode which has never been fully elucidated. Boothby and his friend and business partner, the Czech émigré Richard Weininger, travelled to Belgium and the Netherlands on a mission to buy small arms, mainly rifles. Both men left accounts of the affair soon after the war and these have not been contradicted by anyone else involved; Boothby's gives anything but the full story.

Boothby had been the director of a Belgian arms company called Induscobel which featured in the project. It was part of the web of nebulous and largely insubstantial businesses in which they were involved. Weininger had deputised for Boothby on a mission which ended up with a deal to buy railway sleepers in November 1939.

According to Boothby, the intelligence division of the Admiralty was instructed by Churchill to sound out whether Boothby would go to Belgium and the Netherlands on a 'private and secret' mission to obtain arms, particularly rifles. In reality, his cousin Captain Carney R. N., who worked in the Naval Intelligence Division, merely signed off the visit; journeys outside Britain were strictly controlled in wartime and required approval. When MI5 later tried to get to the bottom of what had happened, Boothby and Carney each claimed that it was the other who had vouched for Weininger's bona fides. In Boothby's version, he asked Weininger to accompany him as an interpreter; it is not clear if Weininger spoke any Dutch and he depended on Boothby for French.

Boothby negotiated a contract to buy 9,000 rifles in Belgium and 200,000 to 400,000 new Krupp rifles in the Netherlands. As MI5 later established, one of the intermediaries was an arms dealer David Wulf, who had strong contacts with German intelligence. How substantial any of this was, in fact, is unsure, but there was enough in it for Weininger – according to his own account – to be allowed to speak directly to Sir John Simon, the Chancellor of the Exchequer, when the Treasury refused to release dollars to conclude the deal. However, Simon declined to discuss the rifles. The kindest interpretation is that the whole episode was no more than one of the many Boothby–Weininger fly-by-night money-making schemes which came to nothing.

21

MUDDLE AND SCANDAL

When Winston Churchill joined the War Cabinet as First Lord of the Admiralty on the outbreak of war in September 1939, he had no intention of giving up his interest in building up the RAF. The urge to increase British aircraft production to match the expansion of Hitler's Luftwaffe had been a central plank in the platform on which Churchill had rebuilt his political career. He had called for the government to face the reality of the German threat and to spend the money needed on the RAF. He then harried the government and the RAF itself to spend the money well and effectively when he found their efforts wanting. Their failure to rearm successfully was a key part of the narrative that he composed sedulously to establish his credentials as a far-sighted statesman. As a minister, he switched from being a vocal external critic to being a vocal internal critic. Britain's air position during the Phoney War provided him with ample material for criticism and probing. The struggle to achieve air parity with Germany was continuing, but now as part of a war.

To begin with, Neville Chamberlain's decision to put the weight of British spending onto the RAF had failed in the objective of deterring Germany from war. The RAF did more than the army during the Phoney War but not much. It had launched a handful of completely ineffective and sometimes calamitous attacks on coastal targets in Germany and bombarded the country with propaganda leaflets, which the future head of Bomber Command Sir Arthur Harris later claimed did nothing but meet all of Germany's imaginable needs for toilet paper. The RAF had been banned from bombing German land so as not to risk provoking the Germans into bombing Britain. The Air

Staff had been only too happy to accept this ruling because it was fully aware of just how slowly and inefficiently Bomber Command had put in place its massive rearmament programme. Sir Edgar Ludlow-Hewitt, who led Bomber Command into the war, came close to declaring formally that his command was unfit for battle which led to a ferocious squabble with the Air Staff. This reached the ears of the Air Minister, Sir Kingsley Wood, to his shock and surprise in the spring of 1939, but there is no sign that he gave his Cabinet colleagues any indication of the weakness this revealed in the service for which he had been responsible for over a year.[1] For their part, the Germans had been equally passive; fewer people were killed by Luftwaffe bombs than by road accidents caused by the blackout in Britain rigorously enforced to frustrate air raids that only came in the summer of 1940.

Eleven days after the declaration of war, the Cabinet began to ask Wood for detailed information on how the RAF stood in relation to the Luftwaffe and the outlook for aircraft production.[2] The Cabinet minutes do not state which minister or ministers proposed this, but Churchill was to make the question his own over the remaining months of the Phoney War. Here he was confronted with a combination of furtiveness, complacency, cheerless news and bland optimism from Wood. It is an intriguing speculation as to whether Churchill would have had a better relationship with Wood's predecessor, Lord Swinton, who had been a collateral victim of Churchill's campaign against the government's air rearmament in peacetime. Wood insisted that the documents with hard figures that he gave to ministers should be returned after they had been discussed, which betrays a fear of public leakage of embarrassing data.[3] At the end of September 1939, Wood admitted to the Cabinet that the Germans still had more aircraft than the British, notably heavy bombers, but claimed that the speed with which the Luftwaffe had expanded meant that it was weaker than the RAF in terms of leadership and quality of aircraft. He advanced the dubious proposition that German fighters were less efficient than British ones because they only had four guns compared to eight (two of the German guns were 20mm cannon, vastly more destructive than British 0.303-inch machine guns). Churchill challenged him on a point which was to become his mantra: the British were producing large numbers of aircraft, but this never seemed to translate to a rise in the RAF's operational strength.

Worse was to follow at the end of October when Wood admitted that it would not be possible to reach again the figure of 892 aircraft manufactured in September 1939 for the next six months, because factory staff had been called up and because of the effect of the blackout, together with the fact that the production of some types were run down. Unless regular wastage of aircraft were held at peacetime level, the frontline strength of the RAF would actually decline as a result. Wood followed up his misguided comments on fighter armament with the outright fiction that Bristol Blenheims, which were originally designed as bombers, were giving valuable service as fighters. When discussion turned to what had become of all the new aircraft manufactured, Churchill had the benefit of work by Frederick Lindemann's Statistical Section which identified a discrepancy between the statistics for aircraft output and the rise in the combat strength of the RAF. Lindemann estimated that the 4,500 new aircraft delivered since April 1939 should have translated to seventy-three new squadrons.[4] His first contribution shows all the hallmarks of his method: an attempt to reconcile different sets of statistics with the implication that some jiggery-pokery was being created.[5] Lindemann's estimates suggested that the 4,500 aircraft produced since April 1939 should have allowed forty-seven new bomber squadrons and twenty-five new fighter squadrons to be formed, far in advance of what had taken place. Lindemann also questioned how a fall in output could have been both unexpected and attributable to the introduction of heavy bombers, as this move had been foreseen and allowed for in an earlier paper.[6]

At the beginning of 1940, Wood still had to confess that Germany was making almost double the number of aircraft: 2,050 per month whilst British output would reach only 869 in March 1940 and France's barely 400.[7] He offered some comfort with a rosy prediction that production would finally rise from the plateau where it had been stuck since the outbreak of war and would jump 31 per cent to 1,139 in the three months to June 1940, including a 56 per cent increase in fighter production. Less happily, he disclosed that obsolete Fairey Battles accounted for almost one third of total bomber production. The Deputy Chief of the Air Staff pointed out that eight squadrons in France were still equipped with the type and needed replacement aircraft, thereby admitting unintentionally that much of the RAF striking force in France was worthless.[8] Churchill nailed the fallacy of Wood's claims for the technical superiority of the new generation of heavy bombers by saying that what mattered here was how many of them could be produced. He pointed out that the strength of the RAF had actually shrunk from 1,700 in April 1939 to 1,456 at the end of September, despite the production of 2,711 aircraft during the period.[9] He complained that things were not set to improve much as the slightly higher production of 2,886 aircraft in the six months to March 1940 would only increase strength by 588; a 'poor return' in his eyes. The picture on current strengths was if anything bleaker. At the turn of the year, the British fielded 1,745 first-line combat aircraft compared to Germany's 4,330. France had 1,625, so the Luftwaffe enjoyed near 30 per cent superiority despite severe attrition during the Polish campaign.[10] It was as though the efforts to rebuild the RAF had never been. Wood trotted out the old Air Staff mantra that the Germans were concentrating on numbers whilst the British were producing 'a somewhat higher quality'.[11] Wood's 'somewhat' sounds painfully defensive, but the RAF genuinely believed that its four-motor Short Stirling bombers were immensely superior to German aircraft. The catch was that they were only just entering production and would not be combat-ready in strength for some months. The promise of heavy bombers was one aspect of the jam tomorrow that Wood kept promising his colleagues. Churchill followed with a questionnaire probing how the manufacture of over 5,000 operational aircraft types was only going to yield between twenty and thirty new squadrons by the beginning of April 1940.[12] Churchill reminded his colleagues that it had been taken as certain that the British lag on the Germans would have been narrowed.[13]

Political control of the RAF stayed securely in the hands of Chamberlain loyalists when Chamberlain reshuffled the Cabinet in a despairing bid to maintain his credibility as (phoney) war leader in the face of Admiral Lord Chatfield's resignation in March 1940. He gave Wood's job to Sir Samuel Hoare. Churchill was as convinced as ever that air warfare was vital and would possibly decide the outcome of the war. According to Anthony Eden's diary, Churchill was 'saddened and disgusted'. He had simply been informed of the appointment which had not been discussed with him despite his interest in the topic. He told Eden that he had much wanted him to have the job and that Admiral Sir Dudley Pound, the First Sea Lord, 'had been unable to conceal his consternation'. Churchill wrote to Chamberlain, with a faint note of menace, that 'it is a very good thing that Sam has come up to scratch in good form. He has a stiff job and difficult start before him.' Hoare was anything but Churchill's true choice for the work and he was not included in the government that Churchill formed a few weeks later, the only senior appeaser to be left out, although Cadogan suspected that he was afraid and wanted to escape from Britain.[14]

Hoare was able to report a rather but far from decisively happier picture on the industrial front, with the estimate that the Germans had produced 12,400 aircraft in the previous twelve months compared to 9,000 in Britain and 4,900 in France.[15] Here again, though, as Churchill observed, German production had produced a far sharper improvement in operational strength than British. He 'found it difficult to accept' (even in the usually understated language of Cabinet office minutes) that five-eighths of British output had been devoted to reserves and training or swallowed by wastage. Churchill had come to see what was going on as an outright 'muddle and scandal' emerged which had to be cleaned up.[16]

22

AN ENTHUSIASTIC BELIEVER

Frederick Lindemann's second stint on the Tizard committee took Winston Churchill and Lindemann a major step forwards for their pet project of aerial mines. Along with many other countries, Britain was beginning to research potential military applications of rockets. This was being conducted by the Projectile Research Department that had been spun out of the Royal Arsenal at Woolwich under the leadership of Dr Alwyn Crow, who had been in charge of ballistics research since 1917. All three services had potential applications for rocket weapons, so the Projectile Research Department acquired an autonomous existence of its own. It also examined the possibilities for rockets as anti-aircraft weapons, although no country succeeded in making a worthwhile unguided weapon for this application. When Lindemann visited Crow in early 1939, they agreed that the three-inch rocket (or Unrotated Projectile in the coded designation for rockets) might be used to carry aerial mines into the sky and released into the path of German bombers.[1] After years of butting against caution or outright scepticism towards aerial mines in the defence establishment, Lindemann and Churchill had found an ally who was in direct control of a significant part of weapons research and willing to take them seriously: an 'enthusiastic believer' to match Robert Watson-Watt on radar. Lindemann was seized by enthusiasm for Unrotated Projectiles as a vector for his aerial mines, but the established bureaucracy was not going to let itself be stampeded that easily.[2] It was declared that 'the stowage of aerial mines in, and their ejection from [three-inch Unrotated Projectiles], might be possible but that considerable research work would be necessary to solve the technical problems involved. In consequence these weapons, if found practicable, could not be made available for some time.' Moreover, as the supply of cordite propellant for rockets was limited, there was a straight choice between developing Unrotated Projectiles as missiles to aim at aircraft or as vectors for aerial mines. Crow would have to demonstrate that the latter was more effective than the former to devote resources in that direction. He was being offered a choice between backing the defence establishment's *bête noire* with the support of a maverick backbench MP or sticking to his existing work. Unsurprisingly, he chose the lower risk option and aerial mines remained as no more than a concept. In the discussions between Lindemann and Crow, the scheme for aerial mines had evolved from its original concept of explosive charges descending on parachutes. Rather than a simple charge, it was now intended to lay a curtain of wire strips that would damage aircraft in a so-called wire barrage. These might carry charges as well.

Roughly in parallel to his enthusiasm for aerial mines, Lindemann had become a passionate advocate of proximity fuses which would detonate the charge when it was near an aircraft without the need to score a direct hit. In 1938, he had opened discussions with a businessman and inventor who had devised a rudimentary form of the fuse which he put into production by early 1940.[3] Churchill saw immediately that an effective proximity fuse would increase the lethal effectiveness of anti-aircraft weapons and he became as enthusiastic about this as he had been about the original aerial mine scheme. The proximity fuse could also be fitted to a standard anti-aircraft artillery shell, but a combination of military hardware politics and science meant that it became closely tied to Unrotated Projectiles. Conventional artillery was the province of the established military bureaucrats, whilst Unrotated Projectiles were under the sympathetic control of Dr Crow. Artillery shells experienced much greater acceleration than rockets, so the comparatively fragile early attempts at proximity fuses had a much better chance of surviving in rockets. At this stage, proximity fuses were only at a preliminary experimental stage; the British never succeeded in developing a working version. No one seems to have understood the value of the sample of a German valve for a proximity fuse that accompanied the Oslo report – an unsolicited package of documents gifted to the British by an unknown dissident scientist in 1939. The Americans did develop an efficient proximity fuse which was to prove invaluable in shooting down V-1s in 1944. Aerial mines, Unrotated Projectiles, wire barrages and proximity fuses became intertwined and it is sometimes hard to disentangle which combination of them might be under discussion at any one point. This did not interfere with the passionate enthusiasm with which Churchill and Lindemann drove development work on.

Things changed overnight when Churchill was appointed as First Lord of the Admiralty on the outbreak of war. This gave him full control of the weapons budget and development work of one of the armed services. The Royal Navy had no general remit to research or procure anti-aircraft weapons, but this was a trivial obstacle; anti-aircraft defence for Royal Navy ships was unarguably its affair. Crow and his team were set to work and, within ten or so weeks, Churchill was confident that Unrotated Projectile-launched aerial mines were ready for action. Mistakenly, Churchill thought that Crow was under his formal authority, but in practice, Crow was the executive arm of Churchill and Lindemann's joint dream.[4] Churchill ordered launchers to be fitted to four battleships and six cruisers.[5] In Churchill's enthusiastic vision, the system would lay a series of four minefields each as large as Horse Guards Parade in the way of attacking dive bombers. It was of the 'utmost urgency' and Lindemann was to brief the relevant Sea Lord. Churchill was rather running ahead of what had actually been developed and some weeks after the order had gone out, Lindemann was not quite sure of the form that the mines should take.[6] By March 1940, a note of caution about the extent to which the aerial mines system was ready was allowed to creep into Churchill's orders. The abandonment of Operation Catherine, Churchill's plan to sail the fleet into the Baltic where it would have been exposed to attack by shore-based aircraft, provided a pretext for delaying the deployment of the launchers: 'Teething problems would bring [the system] into discredit.'[7] The pause was only temporary and very soon the launchers were fitted to capital ships as intended, where they proved almost entirely ineffective. Some Royal Navy officers even blamed the launchers for the loss of HMS *Hood* in May 1941, but this is more likely to reflect prejudice generated by foisting an unproven weapon on the service.[8]

Churchill was aware of the hostility towards the wire barrage weapons. One misfired when he was aboard HMS *Nelson*, during one of his visits to the fleet at Scapa Flow, and came alarmingly close to him; he joked that the admirals were showing their anger at having these weapons foisted on them.[9] He even proposed at one stage including this anecdote in his history of the Second World War.[10]

23

THE SCUM SURROUNDING WINSTON

It was not Winston Churchill or his cohorts who changed the shape of the war and, with it, British politics. In April 1940, Hitler put an end to the Phoney War by launching a German invasion of Denmark and then Norway. The British military response was confused and ineffective with inadequate forces sent to Norway to try to block the Germans with little by way of a clear, definite plan. Churchill bore much of the responsibility for these failures, as he involved himself deeply in the operational planning of the Royal Navy, the service which did most of the work. Perversely, it was Churchill who benefited when the House of Commons debated the episode on 7 and 8 May. Neville Chamberlain faced ferocious criticism from the Conservative benches and previous supporters, although Churchill loyally spoke in his favour. One of the most lethal interventions came from Leo Amery, who had loyally supported the government through appeasement. He repeated the words with which Oliver Cromwell ended the Long Parliament of the Civil War: 'You have sat too long here for any good you have been doing. Depart, I say, and let us have done with you. In the name of God, go.'

Just as the roll call of the dissident Conservative MPs after the Munich debate shaped careers, the choices taken at the Norway vote put down permanent markers. Brendan Bracken voted with the government – any revolt would have compromised Churchill – but Bob Boothby voted with the opposition. It is unsure whether Duncan Sandys was present; he may well still have been in service in Norway. The government's strength was sufficient to secure a healthy majority in the ensuing vote, but forty-one Conservative MPs voted against and perhaps sixty abstained. The scale of the rebellion made it inescapable that Chamberlain's time had run out. The final and fatal blow was delivered by Sir Kingsley Wood, hitherto his staunch supporter, who told him that he would have to resign.

Chamberlain resigned, but the choice of his successor was far from a foregone conclusion. The preferred choice of Chamberlain (and the King) to take over as Prime Minister was Lord Halifax, the Foreign Secretary who had overseen the official aspects of the appeasement policy. The idea was floated that Halifax would be Prime Minister with Churchill as his second-in-command. Word reached Bracken that Churchill was willing to accept this arrangement and he objected violently.[1] Bracken's doubtless romanticised account has him finally tracking Churchill down at 1 a.m. and telling him that this arrangement would cost Britain the war. Bracken claimed that Churchill refused to go back on his word but after much argument did promise to follow Bracken's advice and to hold his tongue when he discussed the future at Downing Street with Chamberlain and Halifax.

Even if only in retrospect, Bracken had read correctly the dynamics of the three-way conversation that was to take place to decide who would be the next Prime Minister. Chamberlain may have preferred Halifax to succeed him but could not pressurise him to do so. Had Halifax asked for the job, Chamberlain would have supported him and Churchill would have been left in the cold. Halifax, though, had his doubts. He certainly knew that Churchill would be an uncomfortable subordinate and Halifax probably knew that he was not cut out to be a war leader. Churchill needed only to remain silent for the premiership to fall to him practically by default. There was certainly no other remotely viable alternative candidate. Churchill remained silent and he became Prime Minister. He was proved right to have resisted the advice of Bracken, Boothby and the others on the outbreak of war; he had not been compromised by his formal association with the last gasps of appeasement in the guise of the Phoney War.

Churchill was faced with the immense responsibility of leading

Britain through a military crisis of the first order. This demanded a truly national government which would have to be built at speed from bitterly hostile parties and factions. The man to whom Churchill turned in this hour of crisis was Lord Beaverbrook. They lunched and dined alone on 10 May. The following day, they had lunch and the day after, Beaverbrook spent the afternoon with Churchill followed by dinner.[2] At its simplest, Churchill needed a high-level ally in government with whom he felt personally comfortable. He needed someone with no affiliation other than himself as a counterweight to the heavyweight figures of the established parties. It was as though Beaverbrook's appeasement, defeatism and opposition to the war had never been. Churchill was alone at the top and there was no one else he felt able to turn to. There was no other surviving politician with Cabinet-level experience who could fill the place: Lord Birkenhead was long dead and David Lloyd George was not only a defeatist but, probably more important, would seek once again to dominate the younger man.

A true national government was necessary and inevitable, but Churchill was at home with neither of its chief components. He had no friends amongst their leaders. The traditional established Conservatives were not going to slough off two decades' worth of suspicion which had only deepened as the years wore on and Churchill had paraded his loathing of socialism too long for Labour to take him to its breast. He could not afford a full-scale purge of his old foes. Apart from Sir Samuel Hoare, whom he despatched to Madrid as ambassador, Churchill kept practically all the senior ministers of the old regime in government. Hoare might even have welcomed the move. Sir Alec Cadogan describes him as desperate to accept the job in Spain out of an anxiety to leave Britain.[3]

Beaverbrook was no more palatable to the traditional Conservatives than Churchill himself. According to Beaverbrook's account, Churchill still had to perform an adroit manoeuvre to defang Conservative opposition to his inclusion: flushing out complaints from the Conservatives that including Labour's Herbert Morrison in the Cabinet would upset the balance of parties and then putting up Beaverbrook as a counterweight.[4] Churchill wanted Beaverbrook for more than support in party politics. He had earmarked Beaverbrook for what he saw as a vital task in the war effort: taking charge of the production of aircraft for the Royal Air Force, which he felt still to be lagging badly even after eight months of war. Sir Kingsley Wood's weak defence of his performance as Air Minister had left a poor impression.

Churchill had to assemble a new government at speed as the German invasion of the Low Countries and France, which coincided with his accession to power, transformed the conflict into a full-scale shooting war in which the vital interests of Britain and France came under threat. It became a fight for Britain's survival when France collapsed. Churchill, Beaverbrook and Bracken made most of the decisions in close consultation with the Chief Whip, David Margesson. Bracken did not improve his reputation by the equivocal way he handled some of the appointments. He told a journalist that Leo Amery was to be Dominions Secretary and to act as Churchill's deputy in contacts with the chiefs of staff. When Amery spoke to Churchill, he discovered that he was to be offered the India Office and that Bracken 'must have been romancing for that particular idea had never entered Winston's mind'. In the event, Amery did go to the Dominions but neither job was particularly crucial. Amery would not be at the front rank of Churchill's government and Bracken may just have been trying to sugar the pill. Further down the pecking order, the treatment was even more abrupt. Sir John Reith learned he had been dismissed as Minister of Information from the editor of *The Times*. He was not mollified by Bracken's explanation that Reith gave no address in *Who's Who*. Even though he was lucky to be kept on in government as Minister of Transport despite his long-standing hostility to Churchill, Reith was not appeased and muttered that it was a 'dirty business every way'. Boothby, too, did not make the top cut and was minimally rewarded with a junior ministry in the food department. Bracken apologised to him that this was part of a 'stop-gap formed during a whizzing crisis', but it was another sign of the extent to which Boothby had lost ground since he was Churchill's 'blue-eyed boy'.

Nothing better illustrates Churchill's mercy towards former enemies than Margesson's involvement, given the extent to which he had enforced ruthless discipline amongst Conservative backbench MPs under appeasement. Admittedly, Margesson transferred his allegiance with a completeness worthy of the Vicar of Bray and former Chamberlainites sniffed at his ability to serve 'God & Mammon with equal ease'[5]. Bracken, too, had his suspicions of Margesson, whom he christened 'the parachutist'.[6] He asked Bernard Sendall, Churchill's civil service private secretary at the Admiralty and later Bracken's own private secretary when he became a minister, to keep an eye on Margesson. Sir Kingsley Wood was another Chamberlain loyalist kept on, but he clearly knew where the true power was and crawled to Beaverbrook and Bracken, who in turn 'treated him as an inferior being'.[7] Bracken christened him 'Little Joe' and derided him as the 'arch time-server'.[8]

Churchill made one large exception to the merciful treatment of his previous opponents. The civil service would do as it was told at the change of any government and there was no need to conciliate them, so Churchill could take full revenge on Sir Horace Wilson, head of the civil service and personal adviser to Chamberlain, who had been his implacable enemy through the appeasement years. Since Wilson had arrived at Downing Street in 1935, he had become a one-man Whitehall institution, surrounded by an aura of omnipotence and permanence. Churchill would gladly have sacked him entirely and sent him to some unpleasant corner of the globe, but this would have appeared too much of a concession to Labour, who detested Wilson almost as much as he did. But Wilson's days as the mighty personal adviser to the Prime Minister were numbered and he was ejected from the office adjacent to the Cabinet Room from where he had dominated Whitehall and Westminster, first as Stanley Baldwin's civil service adviser and then as Chamberlain's mighty lieutenant. The room's location makes it one of the most powerful places at the heart of government and generations of new arrivals at Downing Street have fought to occupy it.[9] The tale of Wilson's expulsion is the subject of differing anecdotes, but it certainly occurred the day after Churchill's appointment. Wilson infuriated Churchill by asking for extra time to clear his room but did not appreciate the extent of his disgrace. The stories of precisely how this occurred are all equally colourful and all equally proof of the relish with which his fall from grace was received outside the narrow world of Chamberlain and his supporters.[10]

> One more incident, symbolic of the Great Change, may be recorded. In Chamberlain's time Sir Horace Wilson occupied the small room opening out of the Cabinet Room at No. 10 Downing Street, facing towards the Horse Guards Parade. There every morning he reported for duty. But when he came, as usual, in good time on the morning of May 11th, he found that the paratroopers had arrived before him. On the couch, opposite the door through which he entered, sat Brendan Bracken, the new Prime Minister's Parliamentary Private Secretary, and Randolph Churchill, the new Prime Minister's son, the latter in uniform. They stared at Sir Horace, but no one spoke or smiled. Then he withdrew, never to return to that seat most proximate to power.[11]

In a symbol of the transfer of power, Bracken took possession of the room, although the departure from structured, peacetime Cabinet government deprived it of its tactical value. Bracken's standing with Churchill meant that this hardly mattered. Almost in imitation of Wilson, who had no job title when he advised Prime Ministers, Bracken hesitated to become Churchill's formal parliamentary private secretary, which would simply have continued his position at the Admiralty and implied that his tasks were restricted to liaison with the back benches. Bracken's remit ran far further. Just as Wilson's authority had flowed from his closeness to Chamberlain, Bracken's standing as fixer and confidant came from his friendship with Churchill. When an American visitor wanted access to Britain's most sensitive data on military industrial resources for a report to the US President, the natural channel to funnel the request was Bracken (and the head of the military Cabinet secretariat, Hastings 'Pug' Ismay).[12] Churchill also took care to signal Bracken's standing by a conspicuous public signal and he was made a privy counsellor, which is usually a badge of Cabinet rank. At the age of thirty-nine, Bracken was one of the youngest privy counsellors; he had never held public office of any kind. Alert to his master's moods, he could judge whether he should be told particularly depressing news.[13] Bracken maintained his prewar direct familiarity with Churchill and could tease him out of a grumpy mood.[14]

Bracken never became wholly deferential to Churchill as Prime Minister and displayed the easy familiarity of their early days. They continued to have violent arguments. Harold Macmillan thought that this 'helped keep [Churchill] on the rails … They quarrelled like husband and wife, but WSC expected that – and it never lasted or affected their true harmony. Few others had the entrée or privilege to do it with impunity.'[15] When he was asked to give his view on whether a particular job should be given to an old Harrovian (like Churchill) or the Etonian preferred by the Chief Whip James Stuart (himself an Etonian), Bracken supported Stuart: 'I agree with the Chief Whip. You only want X because he was at that bloody old Borstal of yours.'[16]

Ensconced in the Prime Minister's private office, Bracken developed an unexpected enthusiasm for ecclesiastical patronage.[17] He never forsook the Catholicism of his childhood but developed an intimate knowledge of the personalities in the Church of England and devoted close attention to the appointment of bishops. Theological discussion was one of his relaxations, even if he could become heated in his arguments.

Even before it was installed, the old establishment was braced for dramatic and unwelcome changes in the machinery of government. Bracken featured high in the demonology and one observer wrote: 'I'm afraid Winston will build up a "Garden City"* at No. 10, of the most awful people – including Brendan Bracken.'[18] Chamberlain insiders also lamented that their calm ordered world had gone. Whilst Chamberlain and Wilson discussed affairs after hours alone together,

---

* Like Lloyd George's 'garden suburb'.

Churchill's late-night conversations were more raucous affairs almost invariably featuring Beaverbrook and Bracken. Tellingly, the absence of Boothby from these conclaves was noted; his fall had already begun. Hostility to the new regime went further than simple nostalgia and jealousy. The old guard objected violently to not just personalities but what they perceived as ethical flaws in the newcomers. Alec Dunglass, later Douglas-Home, ranted: 'since W. came in the H. of C. has stunk in the nostrils of the decent people. The kind of people surrounding W. are the scum, & the peak came when Brendan was made a P. C.! For what services heaven knows.'[19]

The contrast between Dunglass, Chamberlain's aristocratic and urbane parliamentary private secretary and Bracken appalled John Colville, the Downing Street civil servant who had yet to transfer his allegiance to the new regime.[20] Buckingham Palace, too, had deep reservations about the new men. Tommy Lascelles, King George VI's assistant private secretary and confidant, had fully absorbed the hatred of Beaverbrook amongst the Canadian establishment when he was working in the governor general's office in Ottawa during the 1920s. Beaverbrook had never been forgiven for worsting the local grandee Sir Sandford Fleming in the deal that formed the Canada Cement Company, one of the cornerstones of Beaverbrook's wealth:

> For fifty years I've been learning more about Max Aitken than I ever wanted to – and learnt it both in this country and Canada where I lived for four years. So far as I know, he never did me any personal harm, but I've always been 100 per cent antipathetic to the man and all his works. He was, in my opinion, always ready to sacrifice truth to his personal likes or dislikes – the latter being always irrationally virulent.[21]

The King might also have been influenced by the neanderthal conservatism of Lascelles's chief, Sir Alec Hardinge, who was critical of the behaviour of Churchill and Beaverbrook over the abdication crisis.[22] The King asked Churchill to reconsider the appointment of Beaverbrook as a minister in an unprecedented handwritten letter. He warned of 'repercussions ... especially in Canada ... The Canadians do not appreciate him.'[23]

The King was possibly even more doubtful about making Bracken a privy counsellor; the proposal left him 'surprised and not a little disturbed'.[24] Bracken's lack of the traditional qualifications for the office doubtless played a part in provoking royal reticence. Once again, Churchill braved royal displeasure with a heartfelt letter that made a joint plea for recognition of their combined efforts during Churchill's wilderness years:

> Mr Bracken is a member of Parliament of distinguished standing and exceptional ability. He has sometimes been almost my sole supporter in the years when I have been striving to get this country properly defended, especially from the air. He has suffered, as I have done, every form of official hostility. Had he joined the ranks of the time-servers and careerists who were assuring the public that our air force was larger than that of Germany, I have no doubt that he would long ago have attained high office.[25]

Bracken's nomination was not withdrawn and he was duly sworn in as a member of the Privy Council. He gave the conservative establishment a crumb of consolation by displaying his lack of *savoir faire* at his swearing-in ceremony when he tried to shake hands with the wrong people.[26]

Churchill had much ground to make up with George VI, who still nursed bitter memories of how Churchill had supported his brother Edward VIII during the abdication crisis. The King had been an enthusiastic appeaser and supporter of Chamberlain, whom he had invited onto the balcony of Buckingham Palace on his return from Munich in 1938 in an unprecedented display of royal approval. Churchill was willing to face down the King over the positions of his two confidants, but he also knew that creating national unity would be a hollow affair unless it enjoyed the monarch's endorsement. Churchill set out to invest considerable charm, effort and ingenuity into establishing what proved to be a highly successful partnership with the monarch that did much to cement national unity through the war. The key feature was a private weekly lunch at Buckingham Palace, where Churchill took the King fully into his confidence.

*　　*　　*

The new regime at Downing Street was Churchill's own and his friends featured in it largely, but he was wise enough to see the limits that were needed. In particular, he had to impose some discipline on Beaverbrook's peculiar concept of how government should be conducted. In the words of John Colville, who was there as a humble staffer in the Prime Minister's office but went on to become one of Churchill's closest allies:

> A man who had been so assiduously, and happily, involved in political intrigue at the highest level between 1916 and 1925 could not be expected to renounce all pretensions to it when his friend became Prime Minister in 1940. He was unsuccessful for the most part because Churchill was too independently minded to be influenced in his decisions by Beaverbrook, Bracken or any other close friends. The importance of maintaining an acceptable balance between the parties forming his Coalition Government was never far from the Prime Minister's thought, so that he paid more attention to the promptings of Attlee for the Labour Party and successive Chief Whips, David Margesson and James Stuart, for the Conservatives than he did to those of his more intimate friends and dining companions.[27]

Colville initially shared common prejudice against Churchill's friends. Like most people, he was quite soon converted by Bracken's charm and transparent good-heartedness but admitted that the acerbic Lindemann, whom he first thought 'supremely unattractive', remained an 'acquired taste', even though it was one that he came to share. [28] Even the Chamberlainite diehard 'Chips' Channon was won over to Bracken.[29]

24

CONTROLLING FIGURES

Winston Churchill did not face royal hostility or political revulsion at promoting Frederick Lindemann in May 1940, but the move was no less important in shaping the machinery of government through which he wanted to operate as Prime Minister. By default, incoming Prime Ministers in that era had huge scope to choose the tools for the job. As the British civil service evolved into a vast machine through the nineteenth century, the resources available to the Prime Minister had lagged hugely. The regular staff of a handful of private secretaries was little bigger than those of a provincial bishop. The Cabinet Secretariat was firmly installed at the heart of the administration, but between the wars, it was the private empire of Sir Maurice Hankey, the first Cabinet Secretary, who had only a distant relationship with all the Prime Ministers who succeeded David Lloyd George. In common with many, if not most Prime Ministers, Churchill needed the support of individuals close to him whom he could trust entirely and whose advice was untainted by entrenched interests or prejudices. They could be relied on to handle established bureaucracies in the way that their masters would have done so themselves. Lloyd George had built a powerful partnership with Hankey, who was instrumental in outflanking the Admiralty's fanatical resistance to convoys as a counter to the U-boat threat and who acted as Lloyd George's right-hand man in the succession of international conferences that followed the First World War. Lloyd George had also built the 'garden suburb' of policy advisers which did not outlast Lloyd George's premiership. Neither Ramsay MacDonald nor Stanley Baldwin felt the need of such help and ministries were left on their own. Churchill's predecessor Chamberlain had depended on his personal civil service adviser Sir Horace Wilson as a soulmate in his commitment to appeasement and an ally in his battle to prevent Foreign Office diplomats who were hostile to Germany from derailing the policy. With an insider's mastery of bureaucracy, Wilson dominated Whitehall effortlessly. When Churchill became Prime Minister in May 1940, no formal autonomous structure was in place to support him.

Lindemann's Statistical Section moved en bloc in the organisational chart of Whitehall from the Admiralty to 10 Downing Street. It was to serve as Churchill's personal office in the top job. All that changed was that the Statistical Section now had the full authority of the Prime Minister behind it when it grilled and harried the ministries; from being an irritant, it became the visible face of Churchill's control in Whitehall. And it was not entirely popular. The Statistical Section fed its information to the Prime Minister in brief memos, usually covering about three-quarters of a page. Churchill detested prolixity. He often read direct from Lindemann's briefs at Cabinet meetings.[1] This allowed Lindemann to spring proposals on the Cabinet unheralded, whilst normal Cabinet ministers had to go through the set procedure.

It was Lindemann who was tasked with creating a personal unit to serve Churchill at the heart of the administration.[2] This had been put in hand whilst Churchill was First Lord of the Admiralty at the outbreak of the war. Perhaps with the benefit of hindsight, one of the unit's most distinguished members, the economist Roy Harrod, believed that it had been established with a view to the day when Churchill moved to the top.[3] Certainly, the Statistical Section that came into being in September 1939 never restricted its interests to narrowly naval topics. The navy naturally did not exist in isolation and Churchill wanted to be well informed of the broader context of its operations, most especially seaborne trade which was a key mission of the navy to protect. Shipping requirements were to become a topic of major interests to the Statistical Section. Moreover, the War Cabinet was responsible for the overall direction of the war and Churchill had no intention of being constrained by his departmental remit.

Lindemann continued to advise Churchill on scientific subjects which inevitably led to some overlap with the Statistical Section, but the Statistical Section was a distinct organisation with no particular scientific remit. Moreover, the Statistical Section lived up to its name and its chief immediate function was to provide Churchill with the analysis of internal government figures. It was made up of six or seven economists led by Lindemann's colleague from Christ Church, Roy Harrod, and also included G. D. A. MacDougall. Both these economists were to have glittering careers. Other members such as David Bensusan-Butt and Thomas Wilson also went on to reach the heights of academia. By some standards, it was the most distinguished team that Lindemann had ever headed. Lindemann's relationship with economists was less fraught than his relationship with fellow scientists, perhaps because the difference in fields of professional expertise meant that Lindemann felt that his own judgement was not being held at stake.[4] It was not, though, entirely smooth. Harrod found his relationship with Lindemann strained and in 1942 left the Statistical Section.

The task of the Statistical Section was apparently innocuous and uncontentious: the collection and interpretation of numerical data from the Admiralty itself and other departments which might be relevant. They were to be Churchill's personal scouts through the dense jungles of material that Whitehall departments accumulated and used to define problems according to their taste, often deliberately impenetrable to outsiders. From the outset, the Statistical Section's broader task was made clear: 'To make special enquiries analysing for 1. L. [First Lord i.e. Churchill] Cabinet Papers and papers from other departments which have a statistical character, as requested by 1. L.'

Many years before ministers inveighed against 'the blob', the Statistical Section was Churchill's tool to fight bureaucrats on their own ground, not so much smashing their weapons as dismantling them. As a member of the Cabinet, Churchill was entitled to involve himself in matters outside the narrow responsibilities of his department and Chamberlain was soon complaining of 'the barrage of letters from

Winston, arriving every day & increasingly devoted to matters outside his sphere at the Admiralty'.[5] Much of the necessary follow-up became a thorn in the flesh of Sir Horace Wilson, Chamberlain's mighty personal civil service adviser and de facto chief of staff, whom Churchill harried for information on a slew of aspects of government.

From the start, the Statistical Section was destined to be far more than simply a branch of one Whitehall department. Churchill and Lindemann held a fundamentally different view of how to pursue the war from the Chamberlainites – Sir John Simon, the Chancellor of the Exchequer, and his ally in fiscal conservatism Lord Stamp, an admirer of Nazi Germany who was the government's chief financial planner. They called for as gentle a build-up as possible of the war economy, so as to minimise disruption to peacetime structures. Churchill and Lindemann knew that Britain could not afford to delay, that Chamberlain's vision of Germany ultimately being forced out of the war by its economic weakness was unfounded. Lindemann and his colleagues challenged the papers issued which embodied this view and pushed for a rapid transfer of resources from civilian to military use.[6]

It took some weeks for the Statistical Section firmly to establish its standing in Whitehall. With Churchill firmly installed as Prime Minister, Lindemann could bring out the big stick and seek formal recognition via the Cabinet Secretary from the service and supply departments that Statistical Section could have access to 'any of their statistical material'.[7] The move was triggered by a two-month delay in obtaining figures from the Air Ministry showing the impact of different factors on the frontline strength of the RAF, which were incomplete and obscure when they finally appeared.[8] Harrod could report that most of the departments from which Statistical Section sought information were cooperative, although the Air Ministry and the War Office still required persuasion.

The Statistical Section's briefs were a routine part of Churchill's contacts with departments. Often, ministers and civil servants would have nothing more than the usual printed formal proposals to go, whilst Statistical Section would already have gone through them and via Lindemann provided the Prime Minister with a verdict. The supporting data could also be sprung as a surprise. This did not make Lindemann popular in the individual departments.[9] He was a particular bugbear of General Hastings Ismay, who had inherited the military part of Hankey's empire and whose job as the interface between the government (in practice, Churchill alone) and the armed services was undercut by Lindemann's activities:

> Churchill used to say that the Prof's brain was a beautiful piece of mechanism, and the Prof did not dissent from that judgement. He seemed to have a poor opinion of the intellect of everyone with the exception of Lord Birkenhead, Mr Churchill and Professor Lindemann; and he had a special contempt for the bureaucrat and all his ways. The Ministry of Supply and the Ordnance board were two of his pet aversions, and he derived a great deal of pleasure from forestalling them with new inventions. In his appointment as Personal Assistant to the Prime Minister no field was closed to him. He was as obstinate as a mule, and unwilling to admit that there was any problem under the sun which he was not qualified to solve. He would write a memorandum on high strategy on one day, and a thesis on egg production on the next. He seemed to try to give the impression of wanting to quarrel with everybody.[10]

Ismay complained to Lindemann's biographer that Lindemann pontificated about subjects which he did not understand and issued memoranda on topics that had already been covered by Ismay's own memoranda which made Churchill (who would have received Ismay's papers) appear foolish in the eyes of the military.[11] Whatever Ismay's true opinion might have been of Lindemann at the time, there is no sign that they clashed. Given Lindemann's prickliness, this is likely due to Ismay's tact. Ismay had a far happier relationship with Bracken: 'B. was very sympathetic and, in spite of all his blarney, understood the difficulties of routine office work.'[12]

Lindemann was abrasive, but he could also be effective. He shared Churchill's ability to focus on big issues which mattered.[13] With the backing of the Prime Minister, he could also follow the instinct to attack entrenched positions directly: a poor strategy when he and Churchill were outsiders in peacetime but potent when he had wartime urgency and insider status on his side. He also developed a workable technique of bureaucratic haggling and impressed one of his economists – who wanted to save shipping capacity for the invasion of North Africa in November 1942 by cutting sailings further eastward from 120 per month to sixty – by asking Churchill for a cut to forty to fifty sailings in the expectation of being argued back to the true goal of sixty; in fact Churchill forced through a cut to forty sailings.[14] Lindemann combined his habitual high-handedness with scepticism in dismissing military 'requirements' as just arbitrary figures put on paper by a junior staff officer.

The Statistical Section took time to gain credibility in Whitehall. Lindemann's statistical advice in departments other than the Admiralty had a poor start when the civil service head of the Ministry of Shipping detected elementary statistical errors behind criticism of supposed under-loading of shipping, which he pointed out forthrightly at a meeting with Churchill and Lindemann present.[15] Lindemann's iron self-confidence together with the persistence and integrity of his staff gradually ensured that it became a regular feature of the Whitehall world, with a recognised place in the order of things. In part, this was due to the tactfulness of its chief economist Donald MacDougall, which was far more effective than Lindemann's arrogant and confrontational style.[16] When he was confronted by one of Lindemann's misguided prejudices, MacDougall was willing to wear him down.[17] MacDougall later went on to become a fixture in Whitehall in his own right. The steady improvements in Britain's war prospects from the autumn of 1942 onwards took the edge off many internal debates. Churchill was acutely attuned to markers of status and he had a fine sense of what the political market would bear in advancing his personal followers up the chess board with marks of conspicuous favour. Just as he had placed Brendan Bracken on the Privy Council in May 1940, Churchill gave Lindemann a peerage in the false dawn of 1941 when the Soviet entry into the war gave a fillip to British prospects. Even so, elevating Lindemann to the peerage was denounced as a scandal by the arch-Chamberlainite 'Chip' Channon, who called him 'Baron Berlin'.[18] Lindemann compounded the aggravation by taking the title Lord Cherwell, which might have been expressly chosen to annoy other Oxford dons. The distinction was not the start of a broader political career; Lindemann barely ever spoke in the House of Lords.

Part of Ismay's aversion to Lindemann stemmed from the fact that Churchill had directly turned down Ismay's proposal that the Cabinet Secretariat should have a monopoly of servicing the Prime Minister.[19] Ismay was opening his mouth rather too wide; he was already a major beneficiary of the Churchillian revolution. His operation might have been tailor-made for Churchill. When Churchill created the job of Minister of Defence for himself, he had first envisioned a 'defence office' to back him, but the existing military wing of the Cabinet Secretariat did the job perfectly well. As Secretary to the Committee of Imperial Defence, Ismay had inherited the intricate network of subcommittees that Hankey had built up and the secretariat that administered it constituted a virtual ministry of defence already. Churchill was more than happy to use Ismay's operation to support him, but he wanted something that was entirely his own, such as the Statistical Section, as a complement. Churchill had no qualms about working with conservative establishment figures that he inherited as well as his long-standing maverick cohorts. Ismay became one of the most important figures in Churchill's government, working as a link to the military chiefs of staff, acting as a buffer to dampen Churchill's high-handedness as well as diluting his more impetuous and ill-founded military schemes. By the same token, Sir John Anderson, the former civil servant who had been brought into government by Chamberlain, operated as Churchill's executive on domestic policy.

Brigadier Ian Jacob was a senior member of Ismay's team and echoed his chief's view. Lindemann was a 'licensed gadfly' who occasionally 'hit a winner'.[20] Jacob did recognise that Lindemann was influential but far from all-powerful:

[Churchill] has his own familiar spirits, such as Professor Lindemann and Morton; but the activities of these are closely circumscribed, and can only take effect in the form of advice to the Prime Minister personally. The machine is strong enough to keep on the rails, and ensure that the decisive say is in the hands of those who hold responsibility.[21]

The Tizard committee had vanished, but the pre-war establishment managed one last gasp of an attempt to shape science policy. Almost Chamberlain's last act as an active politician was to set up the Scientific Advisory Council (SAC) in October 1940 under the chairmanship of Maurice Hankey.[22] It included Lindemann's old adversary A. V. Hill but also two distinguished physicists. Lindemann was not a member and complained that 'it is a pity that this committee had ever been appointed, that it had been called into existence only to appease the *amour propre* of the scientific establishment, and that he himself did not think it worth a minute of his worry'.[23] There is no sign that Lindemann actively undermined the SAC, but, by the same token, it never achieved great influence on Whitehall. Churchill did not look far beyond Lindemann for advice on science and Hill accused him of having 'monopolized the grace and favour of the Prime Minister'.[24]

25

SHORT-FUSED

Frederick Lindemann's acolyte in developing weapons systems naturally benefited from their common patron's elevation, too. Dr Alwyn Crow's apotheosis followed Winston Churchill's premiership within a fortnight. Churchill was no longer restricted to mandating weapons for navy vessels and he ordered that the use of Unrotated Projectiles and proximity fuses was to be extended from the protection of ships to land targets, 'aircraft factories and other exceptionally important points'.[1] In Churchill's mind, rocket weapons were already a revolutionary improvement in surface-to-air defence. They were to be put into full-scale production as soon as possible. He admitted that individual designs might fail, but his confidence in the concept did not waver.[2] When a land battery of rockets at Dover fired on German aircraft in July, Crow was despatched to report with full authority to obtain details.[3] Churchill circulated Crow's formal report of one bomber certainly brought down, one probable and one damaged to the Cabinet with the optimistic gloss that it 'may well inaugurate a decisive change in the relations of ground and Air'.[4] The miserable days of battling unavailingly the cautious sceptics of Tizard's committee were now in the past. The Prime Minister and his visionary adviser were poised to transform the technology of anti-aircraft defence.

Just as Robert Watson-Watt had proved to be the 'enthusiastic believer' required to drive RDF, Alwyn Crow was the man to do the same for Unrotated Projectiles. Crow was to be given carte blanche in an unprecedented delegation to a single, named individual:

(a) That the whole responsibility for the future work on this scheme should be vested in Dr Crow;

(b) That for this purpose Dr Crow should be given absolute authority to place contracts to any necessary amount and to lay down the priority necessary to ensure that the work shall be given immediate attention by the firms selected to undertake the manufacture of the projectors, the projectiles and the fuses.[5]

Nominally, Crow was under the wing of the Ministry of Supply, but in practice, he answered to no one but the Prime Minister via Lindemann. Lindemann imagined that Unrotated Projectiles together with proximity fuses could make aircraft obsolete as weapons of war.[6] Churchill clearly flagged that Crow was working for him personally.[7] Crow's position was never seriously challenged. When Harold Macmillan became a junior minister at the Ministry of Supply, he remembered that there was 'perpetual worry about unconventional weapons, especially the P. F. (proximity fuse) and the U. P. (unrotated projectile). There was constant pressure from No. 10 about the development of these arms. Dr Crow's activities were a mingled source of excitement and anxiety in our Ministry.'[8]

Crow was responsible for all types of military rockets, but there is no sign that Churchill or Lindemann took much interest in such mundane things. At that stage in the war, anti-aircraft defence was one of Britain's top priorities. The Luftwaffe's daylight assault had only just been repelled in the Battle of Britain, the night-time blitz was getting under way and if the Germans renewed their plans to invade in the spring of 1941, Britain would again face an all-out assault from the air.

*   *   *

Once Churchill had become Prime Minister, Lindemann's ideas on air defence moved to the top of the agenda. Even whilst he was still First Lord of the Admiralty, he had urged that the surge of work on Unrotated Projectiles as a vector for aerial mines should not lead to the concept of aerial mines being released from aircraft being neglected.[9] With Churchill in charge, something not too different from this was put in hand. Here wires bearing explosive charges were to be towed across the path of oncoming bombers by British aircraft. The project was baptised the long aerial mine (LAM), which was perhaps inevitably changed to mutton by the RAF personnel involved. An RAF flight was formed which succeeded in destroying a handful of German bombers.[10] The project marked the start of an open feud between Lindemann and Lord Beaverbrook. Beaverbrook had been sceptical from the start of the value of diverting resources to the scheme.[11] He gleefully castigated Archie Sinclair and the Air Ministry for having diverted eight Lockheed aircraft away from being used to tow LAMs – for which they were 'urgently desired' – to 'civilian flying expeditions'.[12] Beaverbrook was possibly unaware that Churchill had dismissed the plan to assign three obsolete Harrow bombers to the task as 'paltry'.[13] At one stage, he was reluctant to manufacture any more aerial mines until they had been put to the test of battle.[14] Churchill came down firmly on Lindemann's side and ordered preparations to be made for a tenfold massive increase in the number of mines to be produced.[15] At this point, Lindemann drew in his horns somewhat and conceded that the project was still at an experimental stage. Lindemann was also seized with enthusiasm for the idea of mounting searchlights on aircraft. Churchill was also taken with this and threatened dire punishment for anyone who obstructed the scheme.[16] This appears as one of the rare instances in which Lindemann and Beaverbrook agreed on anything; the promoter of the scheme praised Beaverbrook effusively for his support.[17] A number of American-built A-20 Havoc aircraft were diverted from their intended use as ground support aircraft – of which the RAF was cripplingly short – modified to carry the Helmore Turbinlites and operated with Hurricane fighters. They are recorded as having shot down a single German bomber.

Lindemann's pet schemes for air defence gradually faded from view. None was especially effective and the mounting of airborne radar in fighter aircraft, which took time to bring to maturity, provided a much more efficient method of dealing with night attack. The scale of German air attack on Britain dwindled greatly after Hitler attacked the Soviet Union, which became a serious drain on air resources. The British anti-aircraft rocket fell well short of the expectations of Churchill and Lindemann, but Crow's department did develop some widely used rocket weapons, of which the best-known and most effective are the 60lb air-to-surface missile used against sea and land targets, most famously the German armies trapped in the Falaise pocket after D-Day in 1944, and the 'Mattress' rocket, salvo-fired from converted landing craft against coast defences. After the war, Crow shared an award of £5,000 from the Royal Commission on Awards to Inventors on the strength of this work.

* * *

By September 1940, twenty-five batteries with an establishment of 8,000 men and 1,600 rockets launchers had been formed, with a further twenty-two batteries to come. These 'Z Batteries' were integrated into the local formations of the air defence of Great Britain command, along with conventional anti-aircraft guns. As the island of Malta came under attack from Italian aircraft, the British planned to send a battery there to improve the defences. The launchers themselves were simple to make, but it was the supply of rockets that acted as a limiting factor. A dedicated factory to manufacture the necessary cordite propellant had to be brought on stream. An experimental operation was set up at Aberporth in Wales to develop tactics and new features.

Churchill's son-in-law Duncan Sandys soon became heavily involved in the rocket anti-aircraft weapons project, confirming the family interest in Lindemann's pet project. Sandys had acquired practical experience of anti-aircraft artillery the hard way when he was posted to Norway as part of the chaotic British attempt to repel the German invasion of the country in April 1940. German air superiority had made an immense contribution to their victory. Sandys had commanded a battery at Narvik which was in daily action from the day it arrived.[18] It twice came under heavy attack from German aircraft. He was amongst the last of the British troops to be withdrawn from Norway when the collapse of France made their position futile and untenable. On his return to Britain, he did not return to routine soldiering and was attached to Hastings Ismay's Committee of Imperial Defence Secretariat that Churchill had taken over to support him in the job of Minister of Defence – to the horror of John Colville, who saw this as nepotism.[19] This put Sandys at the heart of planning Britain's war effort, but he wanted to return to active service, in particular the nascent glider-borne air assault force. His wife disliked this and through her father's influence, Sandys was shortly given command of the rocket battery that was to be sent to Malta. In the event, it was never despatched. Rocket ammunition was still short, the Italians bombed from high altitudes whilst the rocket was better suited to defending against dive bombers and, perhaps most important, Churchill knew that the proximity fuses had yet to be fully developed. Churchill wanted further development work to be done under the reliable and watchful eye of Crow. Just as he had put a brake on the deployment of the early naval systems fitted to battleships when he saw that the reputation of the system might be hurt, he was willing to pull back.[20] Making doubly sure that the development work was in good hands, Sandys's battery was sent to Wales to be near the scientists and to serve as an experimental unit to test equipment and techniques.

Sandys soon found himself in a rather uncomfortable position. He spotted how faith in Lindemann's weapon concepts had far outrun their development as a practical system. Churchill wanted to visit Aberporth for a demonstration of the weapon, but Sandys was aware that it was not yet ready for a triumphant display of its powers.[21] He had already been briefed on delays and problems with the fuses amongst other things.[22] He was not able to wriggle out of the appointment, but the event proved to be less of a disappointment than he had feared. Exceptionally bad weather provided cover for any shortfall. Lindemann was at hand to provide an optimistic gloss on the proceedings.

Sandys doubted that the proximity fuses so far developed were up to the job.[23] They used photoelectric cells to detect changes in light caused by passing aircraft. As well as the normal difficulties in refining any device, these fuses were subject to variations in the strength of sunlight and could not be used at night. Nonetheless, 100,000 had been made. Sandys believed that a simple timer fuse would be more effective. Rockets flew far more slowly than artillery shells, so the potential for range error was less. Lindemann was annoyed that his system was being put into question and Sandys, together with his second-in-command, were summoned to Downing Street. It was the kind of gladiatorial debate that Churchill relished. Lindemann failed to present an effective case against the timed fuse. Churchill's enthusiasm was undimmed and he moved on to agitating for the rocket to be developed for use against high-flying aircraft.

With further topics for investigation and experiment in view, Sandys lobbied him personally and via Ismay for an upgrade in his unit to an experimental regiment with a large expansion of its operation.[24] It went unmentioned that this proposal would have brought a promotion for Sandys. It is inconceivable that a normal temporary major, even an MP, would have had direct access to Britain's top military bureaucrat without the kind of high-level personal support that Sandys enjoyed and even less so that his wish list should have been passed unaltered to the military hierarchy.

Sandys was promoted to lieutenant-colonel, but his work at Aberporth was cut short soon after he tried to expand the operation by a car crash which permanently damaged both his feet and forced him out of active service. He returned to politics full time. His father-in-law accepted the risk of being accused of nepotism and made him a minister in a reshuffle that saw Brendan Bracken made Minister of Information in July 1941. To begin with, Churchill wanted to give Sandys the job of the junior Foreign Office minister, the most senior of all junior ministerial posts, but Foreign Secretary Anthony Eden demurred, and he had to settle for the financial secretaryship to the War Office.[25] Sandys's first appearance as a minister in the House of Commons was indeed greeted with derisive cries of 'What about Vic

Oliver?'[26]* Churchill's personal followers were rising up the ranks of power. Sandys was both relatively young at the age of thirty-three and had little political qualification except for his opposition to appeasement. The appointment was criticised by both the 1922 Committee and Chamberlainite diehards, notably 'Chips' Channon.[27] Sandys was not popular amongst his colleagues; his naked ambition and ruthlessness were too obvious. Even for a former government whip to whom such things were unexceptional, Sandys was noted for his 'tremendous lust for power'.[28]

He kept up his involvement in anti-aircraft rockets, first at the War Office and then at the Ministry of Supply. Sandys was not above abusing family invitations to the Churchill household to sneak readings of papers that he was not meant to see.[29] He was unabashed to join conversations far more sensitive than his regular pay grade would have entitled him to hear.[30]

---

* Churchill's other son-in-law. An Austrian-born singer and actor.

26

AN INSPIRED BRIGAND

When Churchill became Prime Minister, one of his priorities was to address what he saw as the poisoned legacy from the Chamberlain government of the failure to build up the RAF rapidly. He appointed Lord Beaverbrook as Minister of Aircraft Production, a complete innovation. In his usual style, Beaverbrook made the new Prime Minister sweat for a few days before accepting.[1] Over the next few weeks, Beaverbrook's task became acute as the Allied defeat in the Battle of France exposed the RAF's inability to stem or even delay the German advance. The Fairey Battles of the Advanced Air Striking Force, which had been sent to France to wreck the Ruhr when the political signal was given, were being massacred over Maastricht and Sedan but this was rather lost in the welter of disastrous news of the ground war. Bomber Command was finally unleashed to attack Germany proper and its purported successes were reported to the Cabinet, providing a fillip to British morale even amongst informed and rational commentators such as the professional head of the Foreign Office, Sir Alexander Cadogan, who was unduly impressed by the Royal Air Force's performance generally, although its impact on Germany was negligible.[2] Only after Germany's total victory over France expressed in the Armistice of 22 June was it clear that Britain needed fighters above all to repel the German assault.

Before he became Prime Minister, there is no sign that Churchill believed that a separate ministry was needed for aircraft production. According to his memoirs, he made the decision on the basis of experience from the First World War with little elaboration.[3] The creation of the Ministry of Munitions in 1915 is probably what he had in mind. Its formation marked the recognition that Britain was fighting a total war and needed to mobilise all national economic resources. It was the brainchild of David Lloyd George and provided the springboard from which he displaced the government of Herbert Asquith, a languid relic of peacetime unable to provide the leadership required. Its first and most important mission was to bypass the War Office's established activities in arms procurement. The Ministry of Munitions lay close to Churchill's heart; it had been Churchill's route out of the political wilderness when Lloyd George brought him back into government in July 1917 and the platform from which he could influence military policy. The other strand to Churchill's thinking lay in his experience of the peacetime Air Ministry, as he pushed for the RAF to be rearmed through the 1930s, when he came to perceive the Air Ministry as a negative force. The Chief of the Air Staff, Sir Edward Ellington, had certainly tried to impose a brake on the expansion of the service, partly because he feared that quality would be diluted and partly because he thought the German threat was exaggerated. The paper-shuffling bureaucracy of the Air Ministry did not create an impression of dynamism or urgency. Churchill seems to have viewed the existing structure as such a drag on realising war potential that he was prepared to risk the ill-effects of a major structural change at a crucial moment.

Beaverbrook was given the title of Minister of Aircraft Production and the job with the power to act. Questions of structure and organisation followed. In the first few weeks, he operated the ministry from his London home, Stornoway House. Its top-level personnel were a mixture of personal hires by Beaverbrook, often from his newspaper empire, and established businessmen and administrators. The former included Sir Charles Craven, head of Vickers, and Patrick Hennessy of Ford UK; the latter and possibly most important, Air Marshal Sir Wilfrid Freeman. Freeman had been in charge of the RAF's research and development; he holds a claim to have been the service's most clear-sighted and effective leader of the war. He had been transferred to the Ministry of Aircraft Production along with his entire function at the Air Ministry; he fought a constant rearguard action against Beaverbrook's capricious and damaging notions.[4] The Ministry of Aircraft Production functioned as anything but a traditional government department. Beaverbrook vastly preferred conversation to paper and was on the telephone to his subordinates or industry figures at all hours of the day. Two slogans decorated his office: 'Committees take the punch out of war' and 'Organization is the enemy of improvisation'.[5] One of his watchwords was 'urgency'; it signalled that something had to be dealt with immediately without consideration of longer-term effects and, still less, who might be offended. Beaverbrook's constant harrying of one and all in the quest for greater effort and results recurs routinely in accounts of the Ministry of Aircraft Production's early days. He described himself to Churchill as the 'cat that walks alone'* and detailed how his reputation had evolved during his time at the Ministry of Aircraft Production: 'In fact when the reservoir was empty, I was a genius. Now that the reservoir has some water in it, I am an inspired brigand. If ever the water slops over, I will be a bloody anarchist.'[6]

Churchill tolerated and possibly encouraged Beaverbrook's abrasiveness, albeit in the context of his broader philosophy of how the war should be fought. He set this out in his response to one of Beaverbrook's resignations from the Ministry of Aircraft Production:

The reason why there is this crabbing is of course the warfare that proceeds between the Air Ministry and the Ministry of Aircraft Production. They regard you as a merciless critic and even enemy. They resent having had the Ministry of Aircraft Production functions carved out of their show, and I have no doubt they pour out their detraction by every channel open. I am definitely of the opinion that it is more in the public interest that there should be sharp criticism and counter-criticism between two departments than that they should be handing each other ceremonious bouquet. One must therefore accept the stimulating but disagreeable conditions of war.[7]

---

* A common misquotation of Rudyard Kipling.

Churchill was fully aware of the potential damage that bureaucratic complacency could inflict unless it were exposed to crucial examination, but it is hard not to catch the echo of Lord Copper's ideal of 'strong mutually antagonistic governments everywhere'.[8] The catch was that, in any dispute, Churchill would almost always come down on Beaverbrook's side. Insiders knew that challenging Beaverbrook was tantamount to challenging the Prime Minister.

Beaverbrook's offices had the flavour of a chaotic mediaeval court with a series of supplicants obliged to wait in successive anterooms at the ministry's permanent home in Imperial Chemical House for the great man to favour them with his time.[9] Air marshals were treated peremptorily as flunkeys or irrelevant bores. He complained, 'It's the curse of my life having to talk to these Air Marshals for an hour or two hours every morning. I have to do it to keep the machine running smoothly but I can't bear having to sit and listen to them talking, talking, talking.'

Beaverbrook's confidence that he could get away with treating the RAF officers at the Air Ministry roughly might owe something to the exaggerated belief that he had gathered from Churchill that their actions during the Phoney War were so suspect that they merited a judicial inquiry.[10] Some of the tales of Beaverbrook's domineering habits doubtless grew in the telling, albeit from authentic foundations. In one instance, he tried to contact Lord Nuffield, then still heavily engaged in aircraft work, on a Friday when he had already left for the country.[11] When Beaverbrook was told that Nuffield would not return until the Tuesday, he threatened to send the Prime Minister's car with a police escort to fetch him. Sholto Douglas, who succeeded Hugh Dowding as commander-in-chief of Fighter Command, complained of the performance of British fighters to the Air Ministry.[12] He was summoned to the Ministry of Aircraft Production where Beaverbrook subjected him to a tirade of abuse. Only when Douglas lost his temper and shouted back did Beaverbrook back down and accept the need to improve designs. Beaverbrook failed to grasp that progressive aircraft design was an elementary and vital factor in air warfare.

The early weeks at the Ministry of Aircraft Production were

Beaverbrook's hour. The priority required for aircraft was almost beyond argument and the relics of peacetime complacency were easy and necessary targets. Thereafter, Beaverbrook's style and tactics became ever less suitable. He had gone straight from being a pure financier in Canada to running a single-product organisation as an autocratic proprietor. His claim to be qualified to run aircraft production as an experienced businessman was decidedly shaky. Beaverbrook's judgement was spoiled by the forgiving economics of the newspaper industry when it was by far the dominant medium. All that mattered in business terms was circulation. The only major organisations that required deference were a handful of major advertisers; newspaper readers and small advertisers were inchoate masses. In practice, Beaverbrook was a law unto himself. Like all the press proprietors of that era, Beaverbrook was complicit in breeding the nightmarish and fantastically expensive and inefficient world of the newspaper print sector that was finally and brutally destroyed by Rupert Murdoch in the 1980s. The counterpart of Beaverbrook's method was the Soviet system of 'storming', in which everything was sacrificed to meet a particular target. The management of Britain's war effort in the Second World War, like any sizeable enterprise, required decisions to be taken on priorities and active continuous management. Beaverbrook was not a man for rational process and here he was utterly in his element. One MP left a telling picture of him at the height of the Battle of Britain:

> Lord Beaverbrook was essentially a dramatist who preferred life to move at the fastest possible pressure, but on this occasion he had no need for any contrived theatre to accelerate the pace. Secretaries came and went, as did officials of his ministry. Telephones rang continuously on the lunch-table and in the sitting-room, and he snapped out staccato orders with immense speed and forcefulness. His assessment of the situation was as depressing as it was undoubtedly true. We left him sitting on a curiously ugly basket-chair in the garden of Stornoway House, a Panama hat on his head, his shirt off, enjoying to the full his newly acquired power.[13]

The Ministry of Aircraft Production first operated from Beaverbrook's London home, Stornoway House, but then moved to permanent quarters at Imperial Chemical House, the opulent headquarters of chemical giant ICI, on the Thames embankment Millbank, today converted into super-luxury apartments. Beaverbrook had first wanted to requisition the imposing Shell Mex House on the Strand, but he had been baulked by Sir Andrew Agnew, a former Shell director who headed the government's petroleum board and could point out that Shell Mex House's dedicated teleprinter communication network was indispensable to organising Britain's oil supply. Beaverbrook then conducted a vendetta against Agnew in which he sent two journalists at government expense on a world tour of Shell sites in a fruitless attempt to dig up material discreditable to him.[14]

The legend of Beaverbrook at the Ministry of Aircraft Production features above all his achievements in pushing fighter production and he is ranked as one of the victors in the Battle of Britain.[15] But providing fighter defence was certainly not the sole reason why Beaverbrook was appointed, assuming it figured at all. Soon after he took office, Churchill was emphasising his hopes that the RAF would be able to bomb German airfields in France and the Low Countries.[16] Churchill even used Beaverbrook's work in an initiative that would have gravely weakened Fighter Command in the Battle of Britain. He relied on Beaverbrook's data for improved production in his pitch to Cabinet to persuade his colleagues to accede to French requests for more British fighters to be sent to France to try to stem the German advance.[17] Fortunately for Britain, the resolute opposition of the RAF Chief of Air Staff, Sir Cyril Newall, and Dowding, the head of Fighter Command, saw off the proposal. Even as the Battle of Britain was getting fully under way, Churchill accepted that fighters were the 'prime consideration' but hammered home to Beaverbrook the importance that he attached to a bombing offensive against Germany. 'But there is only one thing that will bring [Hitler] down, and that is an absolutely devastating, exterminating attack by very heavy bombers from this country up on the Nazi homeland.'[18] The five types to which Ministry of Aircraft Production awarded super priority status included three – admittedly medium – bombers.

Even on Air Ministry figures included in a paper hostile to Beaverbrook, production figures do show a powerful uptrend, but here lies a reason to question how much of this was due to Beaverbrook's efforts. The Air Ministry projections that Wood had set out to the Cabinet in January 1940 were already showing strong growth in output, albeit more modest in what was actually achieved in the weeks before Beaverbrook arrived. The repeated promises to the Cabinet of jam tomorrow which had so irked Churchill during the Phoney War proved to have been accurate. Two air marshals later vehemently and publicly rejected Churchill's claim that there had been a scandal: 'a grotesque travesty' to one; his 'most unjust accusation' to another.[19] Output was already on a strongly rising trend before Chamberlain fell. Fighter production in April was almost double that of January. It rose by another 30 per cent in May, beating the Air Ministry's projections from January 1940 by 25 per cent. As Beaverbrook came into office halfway through the month, at least a good part of this improvement must reflect the positive factors operating earlier in the year. The figure rose further by about one third in June but then stayed at around that level for the remaining months. Overall output in the three months from June beat the January projection by 54 per cent, but the overshoot then began to shrink. In the words of historian John Terraine, who examined the question closely, 'the turning-point of production came in April, before Beaverbrook's appointment'.[20]

Beaverbrook had inherited a favourable starting point which included two vital fighter factories that had been given the go-ahead in 1938. What proved to be the crucial decision to switch the new Hawker shadow factory at Hucclecote in Gloucestershire from making Wellington bombers, as originally planned, to Hurricanes had been taken at the height of the Munich crisis. The heroes of this episode do not rank amongst the public list of Battle of Britain victors: Sir Warren Fisher, head of the civil service and the Treasury, more usually an organisation that comes high in the demonology of those who opposed rearmament sceptics; and Sir Wilfrid Freeman, the air marshal in charge of aircraft production, who was willing to risk the wrath of his boss, Chief of the Air Staff Sir Cyril Newall, who was obsessively devoted to the Trenchardian strategy of the supreme importance of the bomber. Hucclecote had entered production in the summer of 1939 and like any new plant did not begin at full capacity immediately and was only reaching peak output as Beaverbrook entered office. The other fighter factory had proved a severe disappointment. The contract to build Spitfires at a new factory at Castle Bromwich had been awarded to Lord Nuffield's motor car business in May 1938. Nuffield was chosen as a nationally known figure, patriarch of British mass production, by Sir Kingsley Wood, who was highly sensitive to questions of public perception, over Vickers-Armstrong, whose Supermarine subsidiary had designed the Spitfire and would have been the more rational choice. The factory had been built and equipped with expensive machine tools but only a handful of aircraft had been produced. Nuffield attempted to apply the utterly different norms of car making to an already complex and state-of-the-art aircraft design. The workforce was accustomed to a gentle world in which labour was short and the balance of power in negotiation lay with them. Here Beaverbrook was in a position to act decisively and removed Castle Bromwich from Nuffield and gave responsibility to Vickers. Improvement came swiftly and strongly: Castle Bromwich built ten Spitfires in June, twenty-three in July, thirty-seven in August and fifty-six in September, almost the initial target of sixty aircraft.

The rise in aircraft output under the new Ministry of Aircraft Production was fed by simple decisions of national resource allocation. After the fall of France in June 1940, the government gave absolute priority to making aircraft. Working hours in factories lengthened dramatically. Double shift working had become the norm and seven-day working weeks became common.[21] Output of new aircraft was boosted in the short term by sacrificing longer-term considerations. The Ministry of Aircraft Production instructed factories to draw on spare parts held further down the logistics chain as part of aircraft maintenance in the field to be used on aircraft being newly built. This might have served to pull production forwards without increasing capacity in the long term. Output of Hurricanes actually fell in July and August, which probably shows this effect unwinding. Spitfire production showed a similar pattern, albeit influenced by the ramp of output at Castle Bromwich. It jumped in July, rose gently in August and fell in September and October.

Beaverbrook's sphere of responsibility when he was appointed had been defined only vaguely. The only existing administrative body that the Ministry of Aircraft Production absorbed was the Air Ministry's existing production division, which had been moved up to the northern spa town of Harrogate as part of a long-established plan to evacuate government offices from London at the outbreak of war. Over the first months of his ministry's existence, Beaverbrook staged a series of power grabs to take over identifiable organisations for the Ministry of Aircraft Production. Just as he had given Lord Nuffield responsibility for the Castle Bromwich shadow factory, Wood had put him in charge of a new Civilian Repair Organisation (CRO) in 1939 to coordinate private sector firms' work on bringing damaged aircraft back into service, but this had degenerated into a state of chaos.[22] CRO was taken from Nuffield's control and given to the Ministry of Aircraft Production in the first week of its existence.[23] Beaverbrook faced more of a challenge with the body controlling the pilots tasked with ferrying completed or repaired aircraft to operational units and, most important, the equipment depots, storage units and repair and salvage depots under direct RAF control as operational units: 40 Group, 42 Group and 44 Group. At the end of July, the Air Ministry conceded everything that Beaverbrook wanted but only as a personal concession. The letter conceding defeat concluded with the same plea that recurred in almost every other intra-Whitehall battle during wartime: 'The division of responsibility is by no means ideal and I would not recommend it except that it meets the wishes of the minister of Aircraft Production and will, I trust, enable us to fight the Germans instead of each other.'[24]

Beaverbrook applied his approach in managing newspapers to the ministry.[25] What counted was raw production figures, as though these had the same importance as daily circulation figures. He imposed a strategy of concentrating all resources on five 'super priority' types: two fighters, the Hurricane and the Spitfire, and three bombers, the Wellington, the Whitley and the Hampden. Only projects that would produce results within three months were to be permitted. The chief victim were the heavy bombers not yet in service on which the Air Staff counted to attack Germany. Even more invidious, Beaverbrook opposed the use of resources on trainer aircraft, which threatened to cut off the supply of new aircrew. The Air Staff fought back and were backed by the combined chiefs of staff in calling for the three-month rule to be softened.[26]

Beaverbrook treated his work as a permanent battle against anyone he believed to be difficult or obstructive – in reality, anyone he could not sack out of hand. In his eyes, the Air Ministry was the principal source of all the problems of aircraft production. His contempt embraced both the civil servants and the RAF officers involved. He maintained a superficially cordial relationship with Archie Sinclair, whom Churchill had made Air Minister, but in reality, viewed him with similar contempt to the air marshals.[27] Beaverbrook's cavalier approach extended to the way he treated the professional staff of the Ministry of Aircraft Production, including the civil servant Sir Archibald Rowlands who was the ministry's Permanent Secretary. At one point, Beaverbrook gave him such perfunctory instructions on a point on which Rowlands disagreed fundamentally enough for Rowlands to tender his resignation.[28]

In Beaverbrook's turf fights with other ministries, Churchill almost invariably backed Beaverbrook. When he and Churchill's other old friend Archie Sinclair were fighting for control of the transatlantic air ferry operation bringing US-made aircraft to Britain, the Prime Minister decided in favour of the Ministry of Aircraft Production. He also pressured Sinclair to hand control of RAF equipment depots from the Air Ministry to the Ministry of Aircraft Production.

Winston Churchill's wife Clementine was a distinct and forceful personality who was not afraid to try to influence her husband. Frederick Lindemann was the only one of the bandits of whom she wholeheartedly approved. She came to recognise Brendan Bracken's merits but never lost her suspicion of Lord Beaverbrook. SOURCE: WIKIMEDIA COMMONS

Beaverbrook was devious and manipulative, but Churchill drew strength from their relationship. SOURCE: WIKIMEDIA COMMONS

Churchill and Lindemann (*left*) were convinced of each other's genius. Dr Alwyn Crow (*right*) was an 'enthusiastic believer' in Lindemann's anti-aircraft weaponry schemes.
SOURCE: WIKIMEDIA COMMONS

Bracken (*centre*) was doggedly loyal to Churchill, though they argued furiously and often. He knew the importance of Harry Hopkins (*left*) in Franklin D. Roosevelt's government better than the Foreign Office.
© FREMANTLE / ALAMY STOCK PHOTO

ABOVE Chartwell was the centre of Churchill's family and his political life. His son Randolph inherited his mother's good looks. His daughter Diana ('PK' or 'Puppy Kitten') was the eldest.
SOURCE: WIKIMEDIA COMMONS

LEFT Bob Boothby was parliamentary private secretary to Churchill from 1926 to 1929 when he was Chancellor of the Exchequer (seen here on Budget Day in 1928). The fight against appeasement brought them back together, but the relationship became increasingly ambiguous. SOURCE: WIKIMEDIA COMMONS

March 1, 1935

PRINCES' DEFENCE LEAGUE

BY-ELECTION SUPPORT FOR THE CHURCHILL PARTY.

ABOVE Beaverbrook's star cartoonist at the *Evening Standard* was David Low. He depicted the India Defence League, backed by the Churchills, as a front for the wealthy and unpopular Indian princes. © PHOTO 12 / ALAMY STOCK PHOTO

LEFT Duncan Sandys was an ambitious young Conservative, and marrying Churchill's daughter Diana shaped his career. SOURCE: WIKIMEDIA COMMONS

"MIND YER BACK!"

Low castigated the governor of the Bank of England, Montagu Norman, for his subservience to the Germans in the Czech gold affair, in which the bank transferred gold held for Czechoslovakia to the Nazis after they invaded the country.
© ESTATE OF SIR DAVID LOW

Churchill shared Lindemann's blind confidence in his concept of aerial minefields as a defence against aircraft. All the variants of the system, such as this one mounted on a Royal Navy capital ship, proved a disappointment.
SOURCE: WIKIMEDIA COMMONS

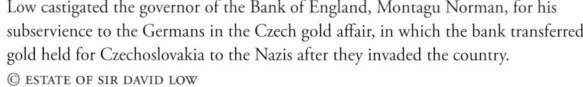

Randolph married Pamela Digby in 1939 to maintain the Churchill dynasty.
© CHURCHILL ARCHIVES CENTRE, CHURCHILL COLLEGE, CAMBRIDGE

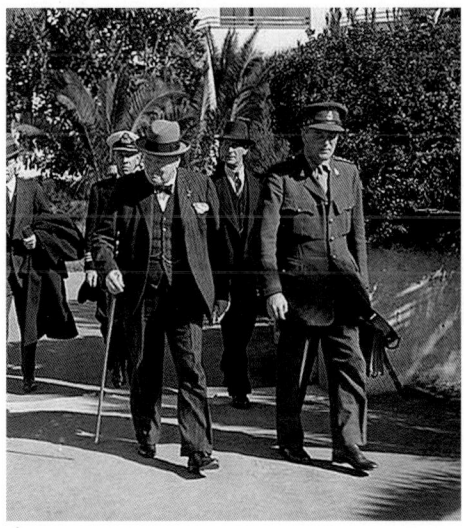

By the time of the Casablanca conference in 1943, where Churchill and Roosevelt met to discuss the Allies' continuing military strategy, the years had not been kind to Randolph.
SOURCE: WIKIMEDIA COMMONS

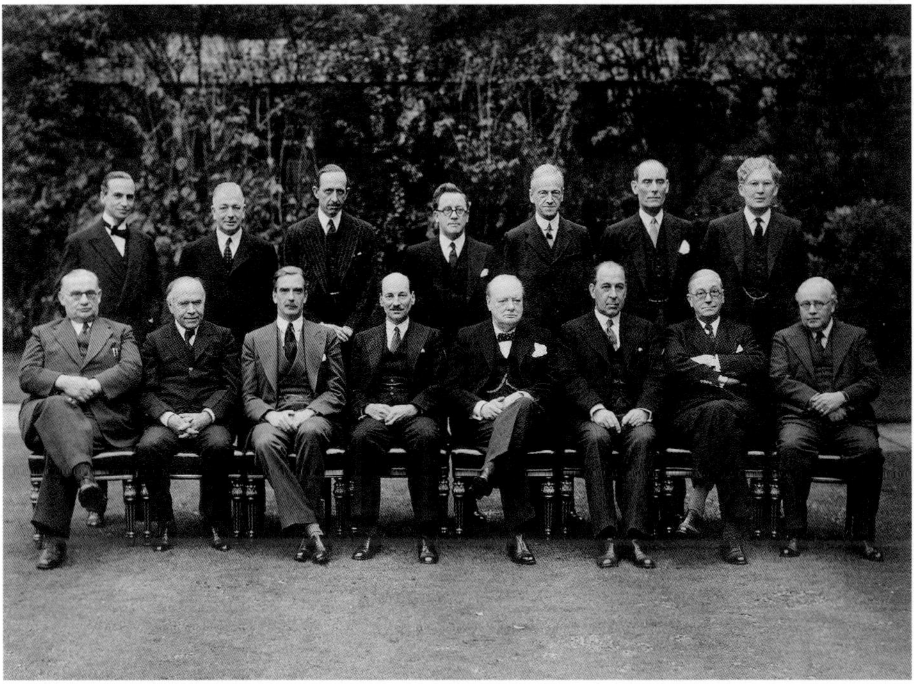

The coalition War Cabinet: (*standing, from left to right*) Sir Archibald Sinclair (friend and ally of Churchill but Beaverbrook's punchbag as Air Minister), A. V. Alexander, Lord Cranborne, Herbert Morrison (one of Labour's rival big beasts), Lord Moyne, Captain Margesson (renegade arch-appeaser) and Brendan Bracken. And (*seated, from left to right*) Ernest Bevin (his supreme authority over labour matters was a thorn in Beaverbrook's flesh), Lord Beaverbrook, Anthony Eden, Clement Attlee, Winston Churchill, Sir John Anderson (civil servant turned politician and the master of wartime committees), Arthur Greenwood and Sir Kingsley Wood (Churchill was deeply suspicious of his handling of the Royal Air Force's expansion during the Phoney War).
SOURCE: WIKIMEDIA COMMONS

ABOVE Beaverbrook ruled the Ministry of Aircraft Production (*left*) like a chaotic mediaeval court from its plush headquarters in Imperial Chemical House. Bracken inherited the Ministry of Information (*right*) and transformed it into a viable element of government after shambolic beginnings. Its home in the University of London's Senate House inspired the Ministry of Truth in George Orwell's *Nineteen Eighty-Four*.
© ADRIAN PHILLIPS

LEFT Churchill inherited General Hastings Ismay from Maurice Hankey's Whitehall, but Ismay became a vital cog in the wartime machine. He despised Lindemann but adroitly avoided a fight. SOURCE: WIKIMEDIA COMMONS

Churchill had an ambiguous relationship with his alma mater, Harrow, which Bracken called 'that bloody old Borstal of yours'. Churchill once threw Leo Amery (*centre*) into the swimming pool there. John Colville (*fourth right*) worked his way up from a lowly position to join the inner circle. John Moore-Brabazon (*third right*) ended the warfare between the Air Ministry and the Ministry of Aircraft Production, which Beaverbrook had fostered. Geoffrey Lloyd (*second right*) may well have been the Harrovian preferred by Churchill for a job that Bracken made him give to an Etonian. © CHURCHILL ARCHIVES CENTRE, CHURCHILL COLLEGE, CAMBRIDGE

Sir Charles 'Peter' Portal was Churchill's favourite amongst his chiefs of staff and he stood up to Beaverbrook. SOURCE: WIKIMEDIA COMMONS

W. Averell Harriman was President Roosevelt's trusted emissary to both Churchill and Stalin. His affair with Pamela Churchill stayed on the right side of scandal. SOURCE: WIKIMEDIA COMMONS

Beaverbrook supported giving aid to Stalin unconditionally. The Valentine was one of Britain's better tank designs (albeit against weak competition), but half of the combat vehicles were shipped to the Soviet Union rather than being used by British forces.
SOURCE: WIKIMEDIA COMMONS

The British had little hard evidence about the V-2 rocket on which to work; this aerial photograph of the Peenemünde research centre was decisive. Lindemann's dogmatic insistence that the V-2, also pictured above, was a scientific impossibility transformed an intelligence debate into an acrimonious squabble. SOURCE: WIKIMEDIA COMMONS

Sandys championed the winning side in the argument over the V-2 and garnered much praise for his handling of countermeasures. Here he announces (prematurely) the end of the threat. SOURCE: WIKIMEDIA COMMONS

Churchill had pragmatically accepted a coalition with Labour during wartime but reverted to his visceral anti-socialism in the 1945 election campaign, egged on by Beaverbrook and Bracken.

Within weeks, Churchill was trumpeting the success of creating the Ministry of Aircraft Production to the Cabinet.[29] He presented figures showing 'large' increases in fighters at operational units and aircraft ready for service. The actual figures that the Prime Minister presented do not seem to have survived. Churchill described this as 'a remarkable achievement on the part of the Minister for Aircraft Production' and called on his colleagues to place on record their appreciation. They complied. Churchill believed that Beaverbrook had already gone a long way to clearing up the 'scandal'.

Almost as soon as Beaverbrook had been appointed, the sceptical and perceptive head of the Foreign Office had detected his priority in favour of presenting success: 'I got a bad impression that he was trying to rush things into the shop window.'[30] Soon afterwards, Beaverbrook was broadcasting his work to the Cabinet with the claim that new aircraft production over the previous week had risen to 363 from 249.[31] New engine production was up from 411 to 620. In October 1940, Beaverbrook reported again to the Cabinet. This time he had no great strides in output to report. He began with a litany of bomb damage to aircraft factories, with five listed as having been hurt severely as an implicit explanation for the output figures. He could only claim a 'dignified' level of production. Notwithstanding, he boasted that the strength of the RAF had grown during his period in office. He claimed that there were now 107.5 fighter and bomber squadrons compared to 88.25 when he began, with 1,222 aircraft compared to 884. Of these aircraft, 780 were the six most modern and useful types in full service: Hurricane, Spitfire, Blenheim, Wellington, Whitley and Hampden. A week and a half later, Beaverbrook's figure for operational aircraft was 1,045, but this was contrasted against the preposterously low number of forty-five that Beaverbrook claimed when Churchill became Prime Minister.[32] But this was not the limit of Beaverbrook's capacity to make myths when he wanted to trumpet his achievements. By early 1941, he claimed to Churchill, apparently in all seriousness, that 'when your Government came in, Kingsley Wood had left you one Hurricane and not many more Spitfires'.[33] This was a fiction that he repeated with slightly different numbers three months later when he was challenged on the Ministry of Aircraft Production's performance.[34] In reality, the RAF fighter squadrons in Britain had 247 Spitfires available for operations and ninety-nine Hurricanes in May 1940, just after Beaverbrook had been appointed, and there were even more Hurricanes still in France, but Beaverbrook's parallel universe had become history and Churchill was not going to challenge this.[35] Beaverbrook was only slightly less ambitious in the fictions that he had spread to the public through his secretary and amanuensis David Farrer, who claimed that production of new fighters was doubled within a month of Beaverbrook's appointment, with a further improvement in July compared to June.[36]

Beaverbrook's paper provoked an outburst of fury in the Air Staff.[37] He did not trouble to disguise his contempt for 'the air marshals' who resented being stripped of responsibility for production anyway. Beaverbrook had also left open a bureaucratic flank by setting high production targets for the Ministry of Aircraft Production, more as motivational tools than aids to planning, but which could be turned against him. The Air Staff riposted with a paper of its own which pointed out that whilst output to October 1940 was 1,139 aircraft higher than the Air Ministry's programme of January 1940, it was 426 lower than the Ministry of Aircraft Production's own projection from June 1940.[38] Given the absolute priority given to aircraft production in raw materials and labour after the Battle of France, the Air Staff contended that the Ministry of Aircraft Production's June 1940 projection gave a truer yardstick to measure its performance.[39] Moreover, the excess production was concentrated in established types of aircraft, but there was a shortfall of 303 units in more modern types. The paper observed that the Ministry of Aircraft Production figures showing a 38 per cent rise in the numbers of operational aircraft referred purely to the strength of fully equipped frontline units. If the figure for all units including those in formation and not operational were included, the improvement fell to 15 per cent. Beaverbrook's claim that German bombing of aircraft factories had severely hurt production was not borne out by records of physical damage. The Air Staff chided the Ministry of Aircraft Production with boasting that 671 US-made aircraft had arrived in Britain without mentioning that only seventy-eight had been completed and issued to the RAF.

In his account of the Second World War, Churchill praises Beaverbrook for his work at the Ministry of Aircraft Production and 'his personal force and genius'. He endorses Beaverbrook's exaggerated claims for boosting output immensely: 'New or repaired aeroplanes streamed to the delighted squadrons in numbers they had never known before.' But he also focuses on the psychological fillip that Beaverbrook gave him: 'His personal buoyancy and vigour were a tonic. I was glad to be able sometimes to lean on him.'[40] Given the generally impersonal tone of Churchill's history, it is striking that Churchill singles out the emotional side to the relationship.

Air Marshal Tedder, director-general of research and development at the Air Ministry, was also swallowed by the Ministry of Aircraft Production. He delivered the verdict that, 'for the first four weeks or more, Beaverbrook did a fine job in keying everybody up to a higher pitch of energy. As for the remainder of the Beaverbrook regime, that is a very different story.'[41] When Tedder left the Ministry of Aircraft Production in November 1940, he wrote to the Air Minister who was now his boss again: 'The present organisation and working of the Ministry [of Aircraft Production] are such as to gravely threaten the efficiency of the Service and consequently the safety of the country.' This was echoed by Sir Maurice Dean, Air Ministry civil servant, who pointed to the sheer impossibility of accelerating dramatically and almost overnight the complex industrial process of manufacturing aircraft:

Fighters available in the battle [of Britain] were there because of groundwork done by the Air Ministry over the previous three years or more. Beaverbrook's part must not be overstated or understated. Had the groundwork not been done Beaverbrook's efforts would have been without avail. Fortunately, the groundwork had been done.

Beaverbrook, in his own phrase, provided 'a stimulus'. The presence of a man possessed of such drive with direct access to Churchill at an hour of desperate danger was of incalculable value. Fighters poured out, not because of him, but 'stimulated' by him. Of course a price had to be paid ... Spares were used up, corners were cut ... In the long run, of course, Beaverbrook's effect on aircraft production would have been disastrous. He was all for the problems of the hour and for a few months this was the right policy. But if continued ... it would have stultified the production of new designs of aircraft and denied to Britain the new types which were in the end the agents of victory. We should in fact have fallen into the same blunders that Goering and his staff brought about.[42]

Beaverbrook's practice of treating the commanders of the Royal Air Force as a hostile force who had to be fought rather than equipped was anything but constructive, as his successor, Colonel Moore-Brabazon, spotted immediately: 'The Air Ministry and the [Ministry of Aircraft Production] were scarcely on speaking terms, so to speak, and as our sole reason for existing was to supply the Royal Air Force with planes, this struck me as rather ridiculous.'[43]

Moore-Brabazon appreciated that Beaverbrook's practice of running the ministry in a state of permanent crisis was not good for aircraft production.[44] He swiftly reinstated the ministry's planning operation.

Beaverbrook's self-promotion was skewered by the Labour politician Ernest Bevin, to whom Churchill was lauding him: 'Max saved the country – owe everything to him. A wonderful man – don't know how he did it – a living magician.' Bevin replied: 'Yes magic is nine-tenths illusion.'[45]

27

DEFENDING A PRIVATE EMPIRE

Some of Lord Beaverbrook's initiatives were flawed, capricious or both. He developed a fixation that every single aircraft had to be kept in Britain to defend the country. He proposed that deliveries of Fairey Battles to Canada should be switched to British-based bomber units. It was pointed out to him at a Cabinet meeting that these aircraft were equipped as non-combat target towers for training purposes and it would have involved significant effort to convert them to the bomber role. Worse, the Fairey Battle was obsolete and practically useless for combat anyway.

At first, Winston Churchill weighed in heavily on Beaverbrook's side in a venomous and pointless dispute over the Empire Air Training Scheme (EATS) in Canada. This had been set up largely through the efforts of Harold Balfour, the junior minister at the Air Ministry since May 1938, and proved to be a highly effective method of providing the RAF with aircrew. The dispute threatened to poison relations with Canada and even to compromise the existence of the EATS. Beaverbrook was generally hostile to the idea of training aircrew in Canada and had already over-ridden the concern of the Air Ministry and temporarily blocked the export of Avro Anson and Fairey Battle aircraft to Canada to be used in the training scheme after the fall of the Low Countries. Beaverbrook was straying far beyond his remit in meddling in an operational matter.

The flashpoint came when it was reported that Billy Bishop, a distinguished Canadian airman, had broadcast remarks that he had made which were hostile to the scheme – supposedly saying it had produced 'nothing of value'.[1] This provoked Beaverbrook into trying to block the export to Canada of 105 US-made Harvard advanced trainers, which came under the authority of the Ministry of Aircraft Production until they were delivered to RAF units. He managed to work in the pretext that as the Air Ministry was not providing adequate protection to 'his' factories, no aircraft should be diverted. From there, the whole affair escalated, with Beaverbrook demanding that the British High Commissioner to Canada be sacked. Churchill threated dire punishments and supported Beaverbrook's version of the facts.[2] Churchill's letter to Anthony Eden complaining of the attitude of the Canadian Prime Minister Mackenzie King hints at an underlying feud between Beaverbrook and the Canadian establishment. Churchill was unconcerned that Beaverbrook had admitted to having told the defeatist US ambassador to Britain, Joe Kennedy, that he was against training pilots outside Britain, on the feeble grounds that 'this was the battleground', thus setting aside the entire logic of the EATS.[3] By the end of the squabble, Beaverbrook had shown himself to be so far in the wrong on the question of RAF training requirements that this was one of the rare topics on which Churchill confronted his hunger for power without responsibility: 'I attach the greatest importance to your opinion, but you must either face the facts and answer them effectively and with a positive plan, or allow the opinion of those who are responsible to prevail.'[4]

Beaverbrook's obsession with keeping military resources in Britain might have pointed to a darker aspect of his thinking. For all his bullish approach at the Ministry of Aircraft Production, Beaverbrook did not share Churchill's confidence in ultimate victory. In the autumn after the Battle of Britain, he showed signs of reverting to his earlier defeatism when the excitement of the early days at the Ministry of Aircraft Production cooled. The combination of successful German bombing of two aircraft factories with the fiasco of the attack on Dakar sent his spirits down and he sent the Cabinet a memorandum which had the overblown tone of a newspaper leading article urging that all resources be kept in Britain even at the expense of any future programme.[5] He did not understand that the postponement of Sealion, the planned

German invasion of Britain, gave Britain a few months' breathing space to look further ahead. Churchill ignored Beaverbrook's advice and reinforced the British Army in Egypt with tanks, taking the risk that they would not be needed to combat an invasion. Churchill's gamble paid off and these tanks helped inflict a massive defeat on the Italians in Libya.

The protection of aircraft factories from German attack became a near obsession for Beaverbrook. He had been briefed on Churchill's concern that German paratroopers might attack aircraft factories and transformed this into a personal crusade.[6] The immediate trigger seems to have been the raids on two aircraft plants within a relatively easy range of German aircraft flying over the Channel: Vickers's Brooklands and Supermarine at Southampton, the vital centre of Spitfire production. Beaverbrook lost whatever sense of proportion he might ever have had and viewed German bombing of Britain as aimed solely at aircraft factories.[7] In one of his occasional flashes of religiosity that betrayed him as a son of the manse, when a Luftwaffe raid failed to hit an important aircraft factory with a single bomb, he declared: 'In fact God is the Minister of Aircraft Production and I am his deputy.'[8]

Beaverbrook concluded that this mission required military structures parallel to the established armed forces tasked with defending the rest of Britain. Beaverbrook also came up with the notion of 'goalkeeper' fighters, which were to be kept at the aerodromes which were an integral part of aircraft factories in those days.[9] They would be flown by the test pilots based at the factories and scrambled at the approach of German bombers. This implied that RAF Fighter Command, with its highly sophisticated command and control organisation, was inadequate for the task. Moreover, half of the test pilots were familiar with bomber aircraft and all had different skill sets to combat fighter pilots'. Losing test pilots in battle would have been wasteful. It is barely surprising that Sir Hugh Dowding, the head of Fighter Command, opposed the scheme which seems to have gone no further.[10] Beaverbrook expected aircraft factories to be priority objectives if the

Germans invaded. His most extreme plan was to form special ground forces solely to protect his factories. The whole effort was put in the hands of Commander Stephen King-Hall, a former naval officer who had become a successful publicist between the wars. They would be equipped with armoured lorries built on commercial chassis. These so-called Beaverettes actually entered production and were issued to units in the post-Dunkirk dearth of equipment, but it is doubtful that they would have been anything other than deathtraps in combat. Beaverbrook also wanted the RAF to send him fifty officers to serve as factory rooftop spotters.[11] For once, he overreached himself with this preposterous idea and Sinclair turned him down flat.[12]

The true solution to prevent German bombing from disrupting British aircraft manufacturing was to disperse the production sites, reducing the importance of individual plants. It was a far more practical and effective response to German bombing of factories than Beaverbrook's goalkeeper fighter fantasy. Beaverbrook claimed that his three major personal contributions to winning the war were making fighters for the Battle of Britain, driving aid to the Soviet Union and saving the aircraft industry from the Blitz by dispersing production.[13] The first two are debatable, but the value of dispersal is beyond argument. The Germans adopted the practice from 1943 onwards to protect their own arms industries from the ravages of the massive Allied air assault. The first steps were semi-spontaneous local initiatives, but Beaverbrook adopted it enthusiastically.[14] Dispersal was also a programme which brought Beaverbrook's political and managerial strengths to the fore. When the Bishop and Mayor of Salisbury objected to sites being opened at their historic city with the attendant risk of air raids, Beaverbrook informed them bluntly that there was no point in their supporting the fundraising drive if they prevented the aircraft being built. The Ministry of Aircraft Production was also competing with other ministries for real estate and Beaverbrook's political clout was a major trump card. Beaverbrook requisitioned unused premises which, in the words of his assistant, 'secured him aircraft for the duration and enemies for life'.[15] It is perhaps telling that in another list of his greatest achievements that Beaverbrook gave, he also cited saving Merlin aircraft engines that might have been left behind in France.[16] Like this dispersal, the rescue of the Merlins involved Beaverbrook getting the upper hand of another minister. Victory in the internal fight validated the achievement more than the practical outcome.

The work of the Ministry of Aircraft Production did not transform Beaverbrook into a rational industrial manager. He kept his taste for the large-scale publicity stunts that the press barons used to promote their newspapers. Most famously, he launched the 'pots and pans' appeal, under which aluminium cooking utensils would be transformed into Hurricanes and Spitfires. Saucepans poured in from the public and immense publicity was generated. The amount of usable aluminium actually recuperated was derisory – a single days' supply – and it required energy and effort to harvest it.

*   *   *

It is one of the striking ironies of the historiography of Beaverbrook's tenure at the Ministry of Aircraft Production that one of his achievements which brought the greatest benefit to the Allied war effort is rarely mentioned. Since before the war, the British had been looking for a partner to produce Rolls-Royce Merlin engines in the USA and had negotiated a contract with Edsel Ford, under which the Ford Motor Company would make the engines. Soon after he became Minister of Aircraft Production, Beaverbrook suffered a setback when Henry Ford took umbrage at a speech that Beaverbrook gave trumpeting the contribution the deal would make to Britain's war effort, which offended his isolationist instincts, and he blocked his son's deal at the last moment. The British switched their attentions to the Packard Motor Car Company. Beaverbrook's agent in North America was his long-standing banker at the Royal Bank of Canada, Morris Wilson. This time, the British got their deal and Wilson personally went to the docks to take receipt of the technical drawings needed to start manufacture. Unfortunately, Wilson knew finance and business but not engineering. He had brought a normal briefcase to carry the plans away and was non-plussed when he was shown the packing case full of material that was actually involved. Against an order for 9,000 engines, Packard built a new factory. Production got under way in the last quarter of 1941. Applying US automotive industry mass-production techniques to the Merlin allowed Packard to produce very large volumes and, ultimately, its factory made almost double what any other single plant did. Packard made some 55,000 of the total 168,000 Merlins manufactured. They were exported to Britain to equip one mark of the Lancaster bomber and they were used on Canadian-built Hurricanes, Mosquitos and Lancasters.

It was, though, in an American airframe that the Packard Merlins made a war-winning contribution to the Allied effort. They were used to power the North American P-51 fighter, which had been built to meet an RAF requirement but whose performance with its original Allison engine proved disappointing. The Merlin gave the P-51 competitive performance to German fighters and its long range allowed it to escort US bombers deep into Germany and, from early 1944, put an end to the massacres wrought on the Eighth Air Force's daylight raids. More important, the attrition inflicted on the Luftwaffe in the resulting air battles was a – if not the – decisive element in winning air superiority over Europe for the Allies, without which the liberation of western Europe would have been far harder, if not impossible. But this all took place long after Beaverbrook had left the ministry. For once, Beaverbrook had backed a project with a payback period far longer than the three months on which he usually insisted. Wilson had actually spotted the prospect of using Merlins in US designs at the outset, but this went no further.[17]

Beaverbrook's employee David Farrer claimed him the credit of the Packard deal in his laudatory account of his master's time at the ministry, *The Sky's the Limit*, which was published in 1943 well before the full benefits flowed through.[18] In fact, Beaverbrook left the deal to Wilson and was only interested in its financial aspects.[19]

The British grasp on what was happening was anyway weak at best.

Even the Chief of the Air Staff thought that it was superior British piloting skills that gave the P-51 the extra range. In reality, the vast bulk of the escort missions were flown by American pilots. Beaverbrook inhabited a world of instant results; the fruits of his labours had to be visible within days or hours – the timescales of any normal industrial investment were alien to him. The notion that something that he undertook in 1940 should deliver a spectacular result in 1944 was outside his mental compass. The episode does not feature in A. J. P. Taylor's near-adulatory biography of Beaverbrook. The Anglocentric approach taken towards the Ministry of Aircraft Production has helped draw attention from what, by some standards, could be treated as a collateral result of his efforts. By some quirk, the fact that the P-51 airframe arose from a British requirement appears in most British accounts of the type's history, as does the transformation achieved by fitting a Packard Merlin engine, but the Ministry of Aircraft Production's role in bringing Packard Merlins into being passes unremarked.

28

INTRIGUING AGAINST
THE AIR MARSHALS

The weightiest testimony to Lord Beaverbrook's achievements must be that of Sir Hugh Dowding, head of Fighter Command. In his despatch on the Battle of Britain, Dowding gave Beaverbrook much of the credit.[1] As well as supplying Fighter Command with aircraft, Beaverbrook showed to Dowding a courtesy and attention that was singularly absent from the way in which he was treated by his professional colleagues. The Air Staff was deeply in thrall to the Trenchardian dogma that fighters were an ineffective counter to the German attack and that only bombing Germany provided a real defence. When Dowding retired, the RAF did not promote him to the rank of Marshal of the RAF, an extraordinary slight to the commander of the unit that won the service's most celebrated victory. Dowding was a frequent visitor to the Ministry of Aircraft Production and Beaverbrook would personally escort him down the two flights of stairs to his waiting car; only Winston Churchill rated the same treatment.[2] A. J. P. Taylor said Beaverbrook praised Dowding to visitors, but when he became the collateral target of one of Beaverbrook's manoeuvres, Beaverbrook had no instinct to spare him.

Beaverbrook did not merely fume about the air marshals. He indulged his predilection for management by intrigue. He waged his war against the air marshals by conspiracy as well as confrontation. He found a useful tool in Wing Commander Edgar Kingston McCloughry, a highly decorated First World War fighter ace passed over for further promotion who had found himself assigned to the Ministry of Aircraft

Production. Beaverbrook took McCloughry up and he became, briefly, a regular guest at Stornoway House. McCloughry composed three
venomous and anonymous papers savagely critical of senior officers of
the Air Staff, the first entitled 'A Weak Link in the Nation's Defences'.
He and another Air Ministry official, Squadron Leader J. A. Norris,
also personally briefed Clement Attlee, the Labour leader and member
of the War Cabinet as Lord Privy Seal on their concerns.[3] These were
distributed to targeted members of the establishment and found their
way to the Prime Minister. They were manifestly written with inside
information which gave them some authority. McCloughry's papers
made waves and spread the word that there were serious concerns
over the leadership of the RAF. McCloughry seems genuinely to have
held the view that the Chief of the Air Staff, Sir Cyril Newall, had
misled the Cabinet about aircraft numbers for some time, but it is
an open question as to how much the rest of his papers were honest.[4]
A. J. P. Taylor's favourable biography of Beaverbrook does not mention anything about the removal of Newall – his usual way of dealing
with potentially embarrassing episodes – but he is reported as believing that Beaverbrook even wrote part of the report.[5]

The principal target was Newall in an unremittingly ad hominem
attack:

> He is a real weakness to the RAF and to the nation's defence …
>
> His mental ability is inadequate for his appointment. Moreover, he
> is not a master of strategy [*sic*] or tactics.
>
> Lacks character and personality. For example, until March 1940 he
> was deceiving the Cabinet as to the strength of the RAF in aircraft …
>
> He is reluctant to stand up to a strong personality such as Air Chief
> Marshal Dowding.

Newall's supposed failure to govern Dowding was a major weakness
to McCloughry:

> Indeed, HQ Fighter Command is substantially a one man show and is

ruled by Air Chief Marshal Dowding who has definite personality, but unfortunately he has inadequate mental ability and a very slow brain. He is also a classic example of a complete non-co-operator either with the Air Ministry or any other authority. His treatment of his staff is deplorable and he tolerates only 'yes' men.[6]

McCloughry assailed Dowding's staff officers but made no mention of his subordinate Group commanders, Keith Park and Trafford Leigh-Mallory, who were anything but 'yes' men.

The papers came at a moment when Dowding's future hung in the balance. He would have left and gone into retirement before the war, but his intended successor, Air Marshal Christopher Courtney, had been seriously injured in an air accident. But for this, Dowding's immense achievement in building up Fighter Command's defence system centred on radar would be far less well known. His retirement had already been postponed a number of times before the Battle of Britain and Archie Sinclair had some reason for wanting him to go. Dowding was difficult and querulous, entirely lacking in the political adroitness necessary at the top of a service. Churchill had been impressed by Dowding's performance during the Battle of Britain and seriously contemplated promoting him to be Chief of the Air Staff.[7] Churchill strongly opposed removing Dowding from Fighter Command. Sinclair had openly pushed for Dowding to be retired, but Churchill wanted him to be left in place for the duration. Churchill had something of a blind spot about elderly military commanders, mapping his own resilience and energy in his mid-sixties across to men who had carried the burden of high office through their fifties. He had just appointed Admiral Sir Roger Keyes to command Combined Operations at the age of sixty-seven. McCloughry's paper hit the debate squarely. One of the people who was sent the paper was the outspoken maverick Conservative MP Irene Ward. She forwarded it to Churchill with the rider that 'the RAF would consider it a disaster if the Commander-in-Chief of Fighter Command [Dowding] were given the supreme office'.[8]

McCloughry also turned his fire on another widely respected figure in the RAF's leadership, Sir Wilfrid Freeman, in a way calculated to boost Beaverbrook's standing:

> For the past five years the technical direction of the RAF has been vested in Air Marshal Sir Wilfrid Freeman, who has filled the post of Air Member for Development and Production. In this capacity he has been responsible for the production of aircraft, and it is largely due to his lack of drive, coupled with his scanty technical knowledge, that our output has not approached that of Germany.[9]

Freeman had a notably tense relationship with Beaverbrook when he found himself absorbed into the Ministry of Aircraft Production. Beaverbrook's work was praised by McCloughry: 'The formation of the Ministry of Aircraft Production under Lord Beaverbrook has cleared up much of the fog and general lassitude on the subject of provisioning. Bottlenecks have been blasted open, and the supply of materials is developing into something like a smooth flow.'[10]

McCloughry's activities came to the attention of Newall and Freeman. Over the protests of Beaverbrook, McCloughry was posted to South Africa.[11] McCloughry believed his efforts to unseat Newall had all but ruined his own career.[12]

The next phase of Beaverbrook's intrigue against the RAF's leadership brought him into alliance with the clique of founding fathers of the RAF. Lord Trenchard and his acolytes still enjoyed an exaggerated status as arbiters on the service's future, despite the immense technological advances that had occurred since they had been actively involved in operations. All four of the men who succeeded Trenchard as Chief of the Air Staff had been helped to their positions by his endorsement. There is a fascinating indication that Trenchard might have been involved in the McCloughry phase of the intrigue. Trenchard's name was handwritten onto the list of referees in the CV that McCloughry's henchman Norris circulated in early August 1940 to support his application for a safe job in Canada with the Ministry of Information.[13]

Newall had been helped in his rise to the top by Trenchard's support, but he disappointed his patron. When Hitler attacked Denmark and Norway, Trenchard had expected that Newall would launch a devastating air assault on Germany. He did not, but Trenchard was unaware of how ill-equipped Bomber Command was to perform any such task. Even when Phoney War restrictions were lifted, Newall preferred to attack targets such as the invasion fleet and air bases. Trenchard shared the delusion that became the keystone of Air Chief Marshal Arthur 'Bert' Harris's strategy for Bomber Command that attacking Germany's cities could win the war on its own. He told the man who succeeded Newall, Sir Charles 'Peter' Portal, who advocated such an attack, 'I am sorry that you could not use [Bomber Command] where I and others think it would probably have ended the war by now.'[14]

The drive against the RAF's current leadership was fronted by Sir John Salmond, who had succeeded Trenchard as Chief of the Air Staff. Beaverbrook and Salmond appear to have been in regular direct contact, discussing the tactics in their campaign. Salmond so detested Dowding that he even contemplated the extreme and unconstitutional move of trying to lobby King George VI personally to have him removed.[15] Trenchard fully supported Salmond but preferred to mask their alliance.[16] The primary target of the manoeuvre that Beaverbrook set in place was Dowding. The old guard's horror at Newall's offence against the Trenchardian doctrine is beyond argument, but there is nothing firm in the record to explain its dislike of Dowding. Of course, his triumph in the Battle of Britain was living proof that Trenchard's dogma that the only effective defence against bombing was counter-bombing was not true.

Whatever might have triggered Beaverbrook's initial doubts about Dowding, his tepid reaction to Beaverbrook's scheme to devote air defence resources essentially to the protection of aircraft factories was an error of judgement. In particular, he scorned Beaverbrook's plan to use single-fighter squadrons exclusively to protect individual factories: 'I do not think that the "goal-keeping" method of using fighter squadrons is sound. They would protect their own vicinity very inefficiently, and if this policy had been adopted we should already have been beaten, through not being strong enough to hold off the mass attacks of the Germans.'[17]

The first step in the elimination of Dowding was to set up a committee in early September 1940, chaired by Salmond under the authority of the Ministry of Aircraft Production. Supposedly, it was to investigate what equipment the RAF needed to fight German bombers at night and thus within the remit of the ministry, but in practice, it was to serve as a kangaroo court to condemn Dowding's handling of the night-time Blitz which was just getting under way. Tactics and operational control lay outside Beaverbrook's area of responsibility, but this was no obstacle and Sinclair knew he was powerless to hold back this encroachment on his area. The old guard knew that Newall was in the firing line as well as Dowding and warmly supported this aspect. Salmond wrote to Trenchard:

> When I saw Beaverbrook he said to me, 'If Dowding is to go, why not Newall, as Newall, must be responsible too.' Personally, of course, I have no objection to coupling them as I think that Newall's strategic judgement completely at fault ... as you and I know [Dowding] has not got the qualifications of a commander in the field, as he lacks humanity and imagination ... If you go and see Beaverbrook I would very much like you to bring up the matter of Dowding, and also of Newall, because I believe that with these two in the saddle, we are not getting the best we should expect.[18]

Salmond clearly knew little of Dowding, who mourned the loss of his 'chicks' in battle and who had devised a defence system melding the new technologies of RDF, direction finding and VHF radio with a network of fighter control rooms.

Wittingly or otherwise, Newall linked his own fate to Dowding's by inviting Beaverbrook to broaden Salmond's inquiry to cover his own work.[19] After minimal, if any, research, Salmond's committee came up with a shopping list of inadequacies that Fighter Command was supposed to address. The Air Ministry also found another issue calculated to appeal to Churchill and Frederick Lindemann when they exhorted Dowding to support the deployment of an experimental long aerial mine (LAM) unit.

Dowding did not fall into the trap of expressing scepticism about the LAM, but his curt statement that development was 'progressing satisfactorily' cannot have been calculated to nurture Churchill's support.[20] Otherwise, though, Dowding made plain his low opinion of the committee's work, bluntly pointing out errors of fact and aggressive statements such as 'I have no idea what is meant by "dense lanes" of searchlights' or 'I do not know what is meant by this.'[21] He was especially scathing about the proposal that the performance of the Blenheim as a night-fighter could be improved by removing its redundant gun turret as the aircraft was already almost obsolete. It was poorly armed and slower than new German bombers. Major modifications like the one proposed would 'always take longer than is expected, divert attention from other channels'. The Blenheim had already been wished upon him as a fighter before the war when its low value as a bomber was becoming all too apparent in a nakedly political move. The project's backers had cheerfully described the work of converting Blenheims to be fighters as 'simple blacksmith's work' before months of delay.[22] Dowding saw clearly that practically the only weapons systems that would be effective against German night bombing was the new Beaufighter aircraft fitted with airborne interception radar (AI), but he could not promise that this would be available soon. Production of the Beaufighter was only just ramping up and AI was at an early stage.

Newall had borne up to the stress of the Battle of Britain poorly. One colleague described him as a bag of nerves. The need to find a new governor general for New Zealand provided a dignified exit for him. The head of the army, the Chief of the Imperial General Staff, had already been changed in May, so even insiders could be made to believe that this was part of a purge of 'Chiefs of Staff, who are sound but old and slow'.[23] Beaverbrook's intrigue stayed well hidden. Dowding survived only a few more weeks. No record of the events leading immediately to his removal has emerged, but it took place and it is inconceivable that it happened without Churchill's endorsement. It occurred nine days after the devastating bombing of Coventry, which made painfully apparent how Britain was nearly defenceless against night bombing. Salmond's inquiry had failed to reveal any remediable flaws in Dowding's preparation for night defence, but it had put him squarely in the frame as the man most responsible. Beaverbrook provided a fig leaf of consolation by creating a place for Dowding on an aircraft procurement mission to the US. The mission was important, but Dowding was ill-suited. It is one of the great ironies of the Battle of Britain legend that Dowding, along with Churchill and Beaverbrook himself, were the most potent advocates of the myth of Beaverbrook's achievement. Dowding never discovered Beaverbrook's part in his removal. Beaverbrook's show of support and courtesies towards Dowding that had won his heart were hypocritical ploys that someone who knew him better would have seen as merely a cloak for his true intentions. Dowding later recognised the dishonesty with which Beaverbrook handled the Spitfire Fund, but by then, it was too late. The fund was immensely successful, bringing in millions of pounds, but it had little direct effect on fighter production and served mainly as a means to promote Beaverbrook's public image.[24] Beaverbrook later attempted to mask his part in the elimination of Dowding by claiming entirely falsely that Churchill had seen Dowding as an enemy and thus removed him; this was almost the exact opposite of the truth, concealing that Churchill had defended Dowding to the last.[25]

The intrigue against Newall had succeeded, but Beaverbrook might soon have felt that he had exchanged King Stork for King Log. The new Chief of the Air Staff Sir Charles 'Peter' Portal was a formidable figure, whom Churchill ranked above all the other chiefs of staff who served him. Portal was an adroit politician and his judgements were unlikely to be swayed by the kind of blandishment that had worked on Dowding. Portal was also a full disciple of Trenchard, to whom the RAF's strength in bombers was the vital measure of the service's strength. The Air Staff had decided to convert the entire bomber force to heavy bombers in 1936 and in the midst of post-Munich panic two years later, the politicians had, largely unwittingly, acquiesced. The Air Staff never deviated from this goal. In the context of the emergency of the invasion scare in the summer of 1940, they had had to swallow Beaverbrook's strategy of classing fighters and light or medium bombers as 'super priority' types, but now Beaverbrook was to be held to his job of supplying the RAF with the aircraft that it really wanted. Portal quickly spotted that Beaverbrook was also keen to meddle in the decisions of the Air Staff by supporting the First Lord of the Admiralty, A. V. Alexander, in his attempt to take over RAF Coastal Command for the navy.[26]

The strategy and priority behind the RAF's 1938 post-Munich expansion, Scheme 'M', with its goal of 1,280 heavy bombers in mid-1941, was officially revived. Here the Ministry of Aircraft Production was conspicuously failing to deliver and production was well behind schedule. Portal opened the onslaught with a direct appeal to Churchill. Beaverbrook deflected the charge by accusing the RAF of low serviceability rates which made inadequate use of the aircraft that had been delivered, but Portal tackled Beaverbrook directly with hard statistics. Even applying the Ministry of Aircraft Production's own allowance of 20 per cent margin for caution (or recognition of the unrealistic but motivational dimension to Ministry of Aircraft Production targets), 108 of the three new types of heavy bomber should have been delivered in the three months to January 1941. Only forty-three had arrived and there was no sign of improvement in the monthly numbers. Only the ultimately disastrous Manchester came anywhere close to meeting its target production and Portal told Beaverbrook, 'How eagerly we await a larger output of Stirlings and Halifaxes, and how grateful we would be for anything you can do to hasten this.'[27] Beaverbrook pleaded once again that output was hampered by bomb damage to factories – fairly, in the case of the Stirling factory at Rochester – and tried to wriggle out of even the 80 per cent of target figure benchmark. Beaverbrook had opened a flank and Portal lunged with a request for similar data on other types; the Air Ministry was asserting its rights as the client department. Moreover, Churchill fully backed the strategy of bombing Germany to which Portal was committed. Churchill had explicitly endorsed the heavy bomber as the tool for this work. Beaverbrook responded with a mixture of hard data and another surge of weird religiosity:

> These are my estimates. May God forgive me if those figures are misleading and if our realisations fall short of them.
>
> I ask God's forgiveness because I know that it is a sin which God may forgive but man will not. There may be mercy in heaven. There will be none on earth. That applies to my colleagues and to myself.[28]

As well as insinuating that more junior employees at the Ministry of Aircraft Production were just as responsible for failures, Beaverbrook made the ludicrous claim that he would not give even Churchill the same production estimates that he was passing on to the Chief of Air Staff. Beaverbrook fell back on the old gambit of comparing his ministry's work with the Air Ministry's programme of January 1940. In late April, Beaverbrook was still having to defend the quality of the heavy bombers that the Ministry of Aircraft Production was supplying, which suffered numerous maintenance and serviceability problems. He blamed the original aircraft designs without stopping to consider that the ministry responsible for supplying the RAF with aircraft might fairly have been expected to ensure that flaws were remedied.

Beaverbrook's defensive, if not downright deferential, attitude to Portal contrasts with his high-handedness towards Portal's political superior, Air Minister Archie Sinclair, when he had the temerity to complain that the Ministry of Aircraft Production was supplying the Royal Air Force with an unbalanced mix of aircraft types: too few trainers, too many fighters and serious shortages in heavy bombers and flying boats.[29] Beaverbrook peremptorily repeated to Sinclair what had become his mantra, that 'production is still based on what we can get and not on what we should like', telling Sinclair bluntly that he would not get the bombers that he needed.[30] Churchill, too, used Sinclair as a punchbag: a poor reward for having swung the Liberal Party in favour of rearmament and supported the fight against appeasement.

The methods that Beaverbrook had applied in the early weeks of the Ministry of Aircraft Production had served their purpose. What was now needed was the detailed organisation and planning that was required to manufacture the 4,000 heavy bombers that the RAF wanted. Beaverbrook knew that he was trapped in a position for which he was radically unsuited. He continually resigned or threatened to resign to pressurise Churchill. His first resignation from the Ministry of Aircraft Production had come within weeks of his taking office. In April 1941, he composed two long papers which were in practice an ultimatum to the Air Ministry.[31] As well as being exposed by the failure of his ministry to meet the RAF's needs, Beaverbrook had a positive reason to move on when Churchill proposed to give him a vague overlordship of all war production.[32] He frequently gave his health as a reason for standing down and it is more than likely that the stress of the job worsened the asthma which was a lifelong complaint. When Beaverbrook finally resigned as Minister of Aircraft Production in May 1941, he used his health as the pretext.

*   *   *

In a neat mirror image of the past, Lord Beaverbrook acted as Winston Churchill's messenger in a potentially sensitive piece of ministerial selection that echoed his role as David Lloyd George's go-between with Churchill during the First World War. In 1940, it was a case of eliminating a minister and not bringing one in. The established Conservative hierarchy had not lost its historical distrust of Churchill when he became Prime Minister and he was alert to the risk of provoking his one-time sworn enemies into revolt. He had conciliated his displaced predecessor Neville Chamberlain, who still enjoyed immense standing in the ranks of both Tory MPs and activists. He was kept in Cabinet as Lord Privy Seal with a broad but vague remit to manage civilian affairs. Other Chamberlainite figures such as Sir John Anderson, Sir Kingsley Wood and Captain David Margesson also remained in government. In Anderson's case, Churchill had been impressed by encountering him as a young civil servant when he was Home Secretary before the First World War.[33]* Even Brendan Bracken was not allowed to detract from Anderson.[34] When terminal stomach cancer took Chamberlain out of the picture in November, the moment had come to consolidate Churchill's position further. Lord Halifax had remained as Foreign Secretary; he presented little threat amongst the Tory rank and file, but he had been Chamberlain's strongly favoured candidate to become Prime Minister. Another death created an opportunity to move against him when Lord Lothian, all-purpose grandee and the British ambassador to Washington, paid the penalty of his Christian Science beliefs and succumbed to an otherwise treatable uraemic infection. Churchill knew full well that representing Britain in the US was a crucial task with considerable status, so it was a role worthy of Halifax. Beaverbrook was delegated to win Halifax over to the scheme and was also present at Downing Street when Churchill overcame Lady Halifax's objections by the simple expedient of giving in to all her onerous financial demands.[35]

Beaverbrook had no hesitation in advising Churchill to take over Chamberlain's leadership of the Conservatives, about which he had some doubts.

---

*   In this respect, Anderson is a mirror image of Sir Horace Wilson, whom Churchill had treated very roughly before the First World War when he was a comparatively junior civil servant.

29

CZECH ASSETS

Bob Boothby was less than happy with the minimal recognition for his services and advance to his career when he became no more than a junior minister at the Ministry of Food. His job had already been offered to Labour extreme left-winger Manny Shinwell, who rejected it as a 'bloody insult'.[1] Boothby seems to have made his discontent sufficiently plain to Winston Churchill that he wrote apologising to him for having appeared 'ungracious'.[2] The choice of a ministry intimately connected to personal consumption provided Boothby with a dangerously tempting outlet for his new egalitarian instincts. He visited Edinburgh and Glasgow to launch an official 'Kitchen Front Campaign' in which he doubled up on the implicit call for moderation in widely reported speeches attacking 'luxury eating', notably in London's hotels and restaurants, a barely veiled criticism of upper-class habits.[3] Churchill, a complete stranger to personal austerity, complained of this 'indiscretion'. There was a decidedly defensive ring to Boothby's reply that he had stuck to a brief from his minister. Boothby's instincts did translate to a rule imposing a single main course in restaurants, which was a success with public opinion, albeit of only trivial value as a food-saving measure.

Boothby's flirtation – largely one-sided – with David Lloyd George as a candidate to become war leader touched its nadir in what came to be called the 'undersecretaries' plot'. The chief driver of the initiative was discontent at the distasteful but politically necessary inclusion of the Chamberlainite old guard in Churchill's government, but the belief that Lloyd George could play a helpful role in government came into the equation. Boothby might even have thought that he was helping Churchill after Brendan Bracken wrote to him saying that 'W has been making great efforts to enlist the aid of L. G.' and admitted to great sympathy for Lloyd George's views on the unfitness of some of the men in government. If Boothby thought this, he was brutally disabused when he lunched with Lloyd George at London's most prestigious men's club, White's, ostensibly in response to Lloyd George's request to discuss food supplies. Lloyd George had been discussed as a possible Minister for Agriculture. Word of this reached Churchill almost immediately, as a tale that Boothby was plotting to replace him as Prime Minister with Lloyd George spread through Westminster. Worse was to follow when Lloyd George was taken to a meeting at Leo Amery's house of other also-rans and left-outs from the government, including Boothby and Harold Macmillan. The conversation featured nothing more than generalised mutterings and led to nothing but reached the ears of Downing Street. Boothby hammered the final nails into the coffin of his previous relationship with Churchill in a long rambling letter which can only be described as unhinged. It proposed that the Cabinet should be replaced by a 'Committee of Public Safety' with truly dictatorial powers. A self-justificatory whine about not being to blame for the shortage of rifles to arm what was to become the Home Guard throws an intriguing sidelight on the Belgian rifles episode and suggests deeper ramifications, real or imagined. In Boothby's account, Churchill remarkably spared the time to call Boothby in and 'scorch' the letter 'sentence by sentence', although his description of a red ink minute from the Prime Minister telling him 'it would be very much better if you confined yourself to the work you have undertaken to do' has more of an authentic ring.[4] The letter's hint that Lloyd George, as a 'phenomenal exception', be taken into government despite a rant against the old men in charge was possibly one of its less objectionable features. Churchill invited Lloyd George to join the Cabinet, but there is no record that they discussed this in person. Boothby continued to act as an emissary between Churchill via Bracken and Lloyd George. The story of Churchill's attempts to bring Lloyd George into his government are analysed with clarity and detail in Richard Toye's magnificent study of the relationship between the two men.[5] Boothby was no more than a go-between, albeit one inspired by conviction and affection for Lloyd George. To what extent his personal ambitions tainted his involvement, especially when the larger aspects of the 'undersecretaries' plot' is factored in, is open to question. At all events, he displayed fatally poor judgement.

Whilst Lord Beaverbrook was building his legend as a hero of the Battle of Britain and Bracken relished his influence as consigliere to the Prime Minister, Boothby ploughed his minor ministerial furrow. Under other circumstances, he might have disappeared from view as just another second- or third-tier professional politician with a great future behind him, but the old enemies that Churchill and he had made through appeasement still had accounts to settle.

The first step in the denouement came in September 1940, when his friend and business partner Richard Weininger was arrested at Boothby's flat under an 'aliens detention' order. Both Boothby and his naval intelligence cousin were there at the time. MI5 later claimed that the arrest was unconnected to Boothby, but the actual grounds that it gave for the arrest were feeble: Weininger was an 'unscrupulous' businessman – this was distasteful but hardly a threat to national security; he had many influential contacts, so if he had been a spy, he could have been a dangerous one; the 'international element' (euphemism for Jewish) was strong in his make, so the French were correct to say that he would 'sell himself to the highest bidder'; he had contact with two German agents (one sentenced to death by the French), but 'evidence that he has [carried out espionage for the Germans] is not very definite'.[6] The Treasury Solicitor gathered 'in casual conversation that MI5 have imprisoned Weininger because he is a crook financier. They hardly seem to be the best judges of this.'[7] Control of 'aliens' fell to the newly established Security Executive and one of its leading figures was Sir Joseph Ball, Neville Chamberlain's ally in manipulating the press and a ferocious hater of Jews.

Weininger's papers, which were found at Boothby's flat, did provide Boothby's enemies with one priceless item: clear proof that Boothby had forged the document that supported his claim to compensation for Czech assets. When they were shown to a criminal barrister, he pronounced that they were 'conceived in fraud and brought forth in iniquity'.[8] The papers made their way up to the head of the Treasury and thus the entire civil service, because they concerned the Czech claims which were being handled by the Treasury. Sir Horace Wilson had been Chamberlain's right-hand man and a ferocious enemy of anyone who opposed appeasement; he had worked with Ball to manipulate the press. He began to draw the net around Boothby, briefing a former subordinate still at Downing Street of the investigation.[9] The moment had arrived to spring the trap and Wilson called together the government's highest law officers. Together, they concluded that the affair was too serious for Boothby simply to be offered the opportunity to resign quietly.[10] Wilson homed in on the 'forgery & intent to deceive' aspects.[11] He insisted that the papers be referred to the Director of Public Prosecutions 'as to the apparent forgery', ostensibly for their own protection (presumably from accusations of leniency) and because it would be difficult to decide on whether to pay the claim otherwise.[12] More likely, Wilson hoped that Boothby might be prosecuted. The letter to Boothby that they drafted for the Prime Minister to sign focused on his false claim in August 1939 that he had no financial interest in the Weiningers' claim. They stated that the letter was concerned only with the 'ministerial and Parliamentary aspects' but referred darkly to 'other matters' that were 'being inquired into'.[13]

When Boothby was confronted with the evidence suggesting that he had misled Sir John Simon and then Parliament in 1939, he responded with a series of panicked letters to Churchill. These Churchill passed to Sir Kingsley Wood, who had replaced Simon as Chancellor of the Exchequer and thus was the relevant minister, and the long-standing Attorney General Sir Donald Somervell. Their conclusion was damning:

We are agreed that these letters do not dispose of the case; on the contrary, we think they tend to confirm it. The contents of the letters are a little difficult to follow ... It is difficult to reconcile the different statements with one another or with the assurance ... that Mr Boothby had no financial interest whatever in the success of the claims.[14]

They held back from recommending that Boothby resign but knew that an inquiry would be needed.

Churchill's immediate reaction was to appoint a judicial committee, which would have forced Boothby to resign as a minister, but this did not happen.[15] Churchill had sought Beaverbrook's opinion, and he may have pushed for a softer line.[16] Instead, a parliamentary committee was set up to examine the case. The choice of committee members gave Boothby a tough fight. It was chaired by Sir John Gretton, a Conservative traditionalist and right-winger. Gretton had been an active India diehard but since then had lapsed into near senility. The committee was reckoned to be 'a hangman's committee' which allowed Chamberlain's 'henchmen [to] enjoy getting their own back, if they can, on one who never loved him'.[17] Another member was Patrick Spens, whom Boothby rated as 'no friend' and who questioned him bluntly.[18] According to Duncan Sandys, Churchill was deeply concerned about the potential damage to the government from a minister being accused of corruption.[19] Churchill's distaste for Boothby being the target of a 'man hunt' was doubtless heartfelt at a human level, but political calculation held sway.[20] At that stage, Churchill's political authority was by no means as secure as it was later to become and the Chamberlainite wing of the Conservative Party was reserving its judgement on him. Boothby's antics over the summer had depleted whatever fund of political goodwill he still held with Churchill and he was now expendable.

Whilst Boothby's dealings in Czech assets were under examination behind closed doors, another aspect of his business dealings was the object of decidedly unfriendly public comment. Sir Joseph Ball secretly controlled the weekly *Truth*, which had already been used to undermine the Jewish War Minister Leslie Hore-Belisha. *Truth*'s attention now turned to Boothby. Under Boothby's guidance, the Ministry of

Food had mandated the inclusion of synthetic vitamin B1 in bread flour. *Truth* pointed out that Boothby was a director of the only producer of vitamin B1 in the country, the subsidiary of F. Hoffmann-La Roche of Switzerland.[21] The regulation was of debatable nutritional value but very lucrative to F. Hoffmann-La Roche as the monopoly supplier. One of the MPs who criticised the Ministry of Food over the issue was Ernest Graham-Little, a distinguished medical doctor, who was convinced that B1 was medically valueless. MI5 had also discovered that Boothby had been gifted 5,000 shares in the subsidiary, so he would have benefited financially from the huge extra business that the Ministry of Food mandate brought its way. The picture of Boothby's probity was darkening. One wit observed that Boothby's 'trouble is that his public life is too private and his private life is too public'.[22]

Harsh words about Weininger and his supposed dislike of Britain had also reached Churchill through Clemmie. A lady called Janetta Oppenheimer was moved by news of Weininger's arrest to send Clemmie an account of a lunch party in Berlin at which Weininger had also been a guest before the war – they had been introduced by the respectable scion of an ancient banking family, the Fuggers. At the lunch, Weininger had shown himself to be

> a fanatical enemy of England and a very dangerous, cool, and cynical adversary ... There was nothing about England that he did not denounce – politically, socially, morally, intellectually – he denounced everything. Particularly I remember every word he said about English women – he said they were all 'sluts' – using that word – that they were 'unmoral, cheap, without beauty, without charm, intelligence, or culture. French women at least had charm and grace and immense chic, but English women had nothing whatever to recommend them, except their cheapness, for those who liked to get things cheap.'[23]

The Churchills treated this seriously enough to forward the letter to MI5 via Major Desmond Morton, Churchill's personal intelligence service adviser, and it was brought into Weininger's appeal against internment.

Whilst Gretton's committee deliberated, Graham-Little returned to the charge over the F. Hoffmann-La Roche B1 rule scandal.[24] Here, though, Churchill practically exonerated Boothby in the House. When the committee reported early in 1941, its conclusions were deeply critical of Boothby on the Czech assets affair, practically endorsing the claim that he had lied. He was compelled to resign as a minister. These conclusions were considered at the time (and still are) to have been severely biased against him, but Boothby was not compelled to stand down as an MP.

Harold Macmillan, admittedly hardly an unbiased commentator, thought that even the most loyal Chamberlainites were disturbed by the combination of 'legalism and cynicism'.[25] The sums involved were tiny compared to the value of the Czech gold handed over to the Nazis in 1939, but the two affairs became vaguely confused in the public mind. The spectacular and public denouement to the Boothby affair probably helped the Czech gold scandal to fade into near oblivion.

30

CHURCHILL'S GESTAPO

Frederick Lindemann swiftly became an omnipresent feature of both the government machine and Winston Churchill's immediate circle. His remit ran across the Prime Minister's personal needs to the higher management of national affairs. Almost nothing was too trivial. When the offer of a gift of cigars from abroad provoked fears that they might be used to poison Churchill, the Prof was the natural person from whom to ask advice.[1] To the dismay of Churchill's parliamentary private secretary who loved cigars, his attempt to hijack the consignment for himself was frustrated by the lingering fear that they might indeed be harmful.

When Churchill was seized by a desire to know how big a swimming pool would be if it were filled with all the champagne he had drunk in his life, he set Lindemann to undertake (laboriously) the calculation.[2] Churchill was disappointed that his consumption would fill no more than a railway carriage.[3] As Lindemann was a scientist of European heritage, it was inevitable that Churchill should ask him personally to provide a conversion chart between imperial and metric measurements, then a mystery to most British people.[4]

The writ of Lindemann's Statistical Section ran almost untrammelled through Whitehall. It ranged over a broad and varied scope of topics: 30 per cent of its minutes were about the armed forces, 20 per cent shipping, 15 per cent food, agriculture and raw materials, 10 per cent post-war questions and the remaining 25 per cent with a miscellany of topics both at home (e.g. a shortage of doctors) and abroad (e.g. conditions in the Soviet Union or India).[5] The Statistical Section was in advance of its time in producing coloured charts to present important information vividly and comprehensibly.[6] Lindemann used these to explain to Churchill statistical data which he would have struggled to grasp in a conventional document.[7] These featured in presentations sent to prominent US figures, above all President Roosevelt.[8]

There was one major gap in Lindemann's influence. Even when the Statistical Section had established itself as a powerful force, Lord Beaverbrook enjoyed a protected status. Lindemann was the only man high in government with the courage and standing with Churchill to challenge Beaverbrook's approach of administration by aggression and imaginary statistics, but the scope to correct him was decidedly finite. Perversely, it might have helped the Statistical Section's standing with the Whitehall establishment that they had found a shared goal in trying to impose some kind of quantifiable measure on whether Beaverbrook's empire was delivering the marvels it claimed. When Lindemann's friend and helper Roy Harrod was amicably reviewing the Statistical Section's position in Whitehall with the Cabinet Secretary Sir Edward Bridges, they were on common ground addressing the issue: '[The Ministry of Aircraft Production] is a rather thorny problem and I expect you will agree that it should be dealt with in a special way!'[9] Beaverbrook preserved and even increased his protected status when he moved on to an ostensibly wider remit. The Statistical Section confessed – probably via Harrod – directly that once Beaverbrook had become Minister of War Production, 'it has not seemed feasible to refer criticisms to the Prime Minister with anything like the former frequency'.[10] Against this, Lindemann was able to relay to Churchill figures for the Ministry of Aircraft Production's poor showing in the critical area of making heavy bombers once Beaverbrook was no longer minister.[11] Lindemann was also chosen as a conduit to bypass Beaverbrook's territoriality and report to the Prime Minister severe weaknesses in the way female labour was handled at the Royal Ordnance Factories.[12]

Lindemann might not have held the upper hand over Beaverbrook, but he could act as a significant counterweight. He tried to use Churchill's authority to badger Beaverbrook into producing worthwhile statistical information.[13] The Statistical Section had complained that Beaverbrook avoided discussion of specific difficulties that were holding up aircraft output and Lindemann tried to persuade Churchill to force him to do so.[14] Lindemann exploited Beaverbrook's plan of October 1940, which was in reality more of a goad on the industry than a serious projection of output, as a tool against the Ministry of Aircraft Production when, inevitably, the reality proved to be disappointing.[15] January 1941 was especially disappointing, with a shortfall over 50 per cent.[16] Even when Beaverbrook admitted that his programme of 1941 was optimistic, Lindemann pointed out that he had already reduced his own projections compared to the October 1940 scheme. Worse, he observed that the shortfall in production was concentrated in the heavy bombers that were crucial to the RAF's offensive against Germany. He took Beaverbrook to task on the detail of his reports, practically holding him personally responsible for a drop in man hours worked in the industry despite a rise in worker numbers. Predictably, Beaverbrook did not like Lindemann. He left Lindemann's biographer with a sketch of 'an uneasy and far from popular figure' who was in the habit of entering other ministers' offices uninvited.[17] It is unlikely that Beaverbrook was being solicitous of the interests of any minister other than himself.

As has already been mentioned, air power statistics were of particular interest to the Statistical Section and they featured in a major passage of arms between Downing Street and Whitehall in the autumn of 1940. Victory in the Battle of Britain prevented Hitler from launching an invasion of Britain in 1940, but the government had to reckon with a strong possibility that Germany would try again in 1941. Only in the spring of 1941 did it become clear that Germany was bent on attacking the Soviet Union; until then, a repeated assault on Britain looked like the most likely possibility. Churchill was acutely aware that the balance of air forces was a crucial element in planning for this. The Air Ministry had a long track record of exaggerating estimates of the strength of the German air force that went back to the late 1930s. In the run-up to the Battle of Britain, Lindemann had succeeded in forcing the Air Ministry to scale back its estimates to a more realistic level.[18] He returned to the charge in the winter of 1940/41. One of the tools that was brought into the calculation was to apply actual British figures for aircraft production and wastage as a yardstick to estimate how the strength of the German air force might have changed. A blizzard of papers, including some from Lindemann, and a four-hour meeting failed to yield a satisfactory answer agreeable to everyone, and Churchill set up an inquiry under a judge, John Singleton, to 'ascertain the facts'.[19] Lindemann found that he had stirred up a hornet's nest by introducing the Prime Minister to the pleasures of probing statistics. Churchill seized on a puzzled comment by Singleton that 3,000 RAF aircraft were unaccounted for. He decided that the evidence presented to Singleton left a gap of 3,500 between its starting strength, the aircraft delivered to the RAF and a current strength of 5,000. Churchill was so infuriated that he was on the point of threatening the Air Ministry and the Air Staff that chartered accountants would have to be commissioned to find the relevant data unless they could produce it themselves. Lindemann headed the Prime Minister off by persuading him that he himself had been able to explain the discrepancy by asking the Air Ministry. Supposedly, the missing aircraft were previously operational machines transferred to training commands, but the figure given for transfers to training commands had covered only newly delivered aircraft.

The Statistical Section scored at least one major success in changing military policy. Shipping capacity was a permanent factor in almost every aspect of the war. Apart from a handful of items in which Britain was entirely self-sufficient, materials had to be imported, the population had to be fed and the fighting in distant theatres supported. With the Mediterranean route blocked, supplies to the fighting in North Africa had to travel round the Cape of Good Hope so shipping space was precious. Economist Donald MacDougall of the Statistical Section calculated that shipping vehicles manufactured in Britain to North Africa in a complete state demanded far more shipping space than would have been needed if they were shipped as 'knocked-down kits'. Naturally, this consumed resources to reassemble them in North Africa. Lindemann leapt on this perception and indulged in one of his rare ventures into red ink to emphasise its importance to the Prime Minister. The balance of economic calculation was in favour of the Statistical Section and it had its way. MacDougall's tact doubtless helped. This became one of Lindemann's favourite anecdotes of his contribution to victory.[20]

It is hard to tell whether the Statistical Section's interventions were decisive, but in a number of instances, its views, notably on weapons, were to be implemented and borne out as having been correct. The Statistical Section was against the import to Britain of bulky commodities and argued that finished steel and not the iron ore raw material should be imported. By the same token, it argued against imports of building materials, notably timber. It was the first to advocate switching effort from production of the Stirling to the Lancaster bomber.[21] Output is inevitably lost when switching between different types, so the skill of the calculation lies in balancing the value of units lost to the gain from later having superior equipment. The Stirling, which the RAF had once seen as the war-winner, had proved disappointing and the Lancaster was the only aircraft that 'Bert' Harris thought was worth producing. The Statistical Section then had to overcome the intentions of the Air Staff and the Ministry of Aircraft Production, which wanted to produce the Vickers Windsor bomber, which was intended to replace the Lancaster but would have taken far too long to make any worthwhile contribution at all and nothing that would have justified the necessary loss in Lancaster output. Similarly, the Statistical Section advocated using a former Stirling factory to manufacture Mosquito multi-role aircraft. According to one of its calculations, the Mosquito delivered the best military value for unit of effort spent building it.[22] Lindemann spotted early that the army's anti-tank artillery was lagging behind the needs of the battlefield, with the arrival of more thickly armoured German tanks. Both the two-pounder and its successor the six-pounder were obsolescent from their introduction. Only with the seventeen-pounder did British troops have a weapon fully adequate for the task.

Gradually, the Statistical Section became fluent in the figures that Whitehall departments generated, but it never became completely house-trained. It had been set up to challenge data and not to accept it meekly at its authors' valuation. Sometimes the Statistical Section was able to spot ways in which existing statistics fell well short of giving useful data. The section detected that the army inflated its requirement for shells by loading its formula: it always applied rates of fire in intense combat rather than using the average level and treated all ammunition delivered to forward depots as fired. Sometimes it did not. The risk of this was magnified when Lindemann was arguing a case on which he had already made up his mind. Even as late as 1944, he could confuse the total number of depth charges manufactured with the number used in attacks on U-boats.[23] He used this to create a falsely pessimistic picture of their effectiveness when he was pursuing one of his favourite arguments: that the RAF was much better employed bombing German cities than in patrolling the high seas against U-boats. The argument that he provoked was furious enough for the War Office – which was not directly involved in the argument – to impose strict restrictions on his access to raw data.

It is sometimes hard to disentangle objective judgements that Lindemann made as a scientist from things on which he detected Churchill's instinctive prejudices and trimmed his advice accordingly. Harrod was alert to any loss of integrity and paid close attention to Churchill's red ink annotations on Cabinet papers for any sign of manipulation, but he concluded that Churchill and Lindemann genuinely thought alike on many topics.[24] Against this, Nobel Prize winner A. V. Hill, who had locked horns with Lindemann on the Tizard committee, dismissed him as a 'scientific courtier' who had exercised a malign influence on the contribution of science to the war effort.[25] Lindemann was also prone to mood swings between 'startling optimism and querulous pessimism'.[26]

Lindemann's approach to personal consumption in the war economy was at odds with the austerity of his own lifestyle. The generous host held the upper hand over the ascetic man. Lindemann was highly attuned to how important the small indulgences of life were to individuals and how their morale counted for much in the war effort. Early in the war, he opposed rationing tea on morale grounds.[27] When it was proposed to cut the jam ration, he declared that using mangelwurzels would sustain normal consumption.[28] He found an ally in Lord Woolton, the Food Minister, in opposing the rationing of beer. He broadened his willingness to direct manpower away from the war effort in the narrow sense to providing people with the 'normal amenities'.[29] He positively relished the fact that this view was not universally shared. He could also enjoy a battle in 1941 when it was proposed to ration non-staple foods such as canned meat, rice, dried fruit, chocolates, biscuits and breakfast food.[30] He detected an enthusiasm amongst the civil servants for a system of imposing definite rations for each type of food. Against this, Lindemann's economist Roy Harrod had put up flexible points systems such as the one used to ration clothing which he presented to Woolton, who as a former clothes retailer could appreciate the point. Leaving consumers with some element of choice and free will compensated for the restriction and Lindemann's basic grasp of statistics informed him that across the whole population, variations in individual tastes would balance things out.

When Sir Stafford Cripps entered the government, he set himself up as the apostle of austerity. He had caught a moment when the success of the U-boat campaign threatened to cut Britain off entirely, which pushed the question of domestic consumption up the agenda. Churchill's solicitude for the interests of the common man had a new, political dimension and Lindemann was at hand to help. They shared a common outlook.[31] Here again, he found himself battling bureaucratic instinct, as captured by one of his subordinates in the Statistical Section:

> Unfortunately, it would appear that when a Whitehall committee is in search of economies, the *length* of the list of items is sometimes taken to be a clear sign of success, scarcely less important than the *total amount* that has thus been saved. Yet it is not really very sensible to save a few more pence, of a few man-hours, at the cost of extending more widely the inconvenience and annoyance.[32]

Lindemann set out his philosophy, which verged on the positively

Churchillian but concluded with an elementary observation on how a democracy can fight a total war:

> All the cuts of the last few months, taken together, have not saved more than 2 per cent of our imports or given us even 1 per cent in extra manpower. Is it for such small profits that we should expose the nation's will to Death by a Thousand Cuts?
>
> The arguments for and against prohibiting each small individual item may, of course, be nicely balanced. But it is wrong to consider them separately. Obvious savings are apt to be offset by less obvious losses. A cut in one commodity, e.g. coal, may increase the consumption of another, such as bread. Curtailment of bus services may reduce the married woman's readiness to work in factories; excessive clothes rationing may mean more mending; restriction of retail deliveries means more time spent in shopping, and so on. It is difficult to say in every case whether gains exceed losses, but we can be sure that none of these restrictions increases the comfort of the working classes. And if we prohibit the poor pleasures on which they can spend their money, how can we induce them to work overtime and increase output?[33]

Lindemann's capacity to draw striking, counter-instinctive conclusions from statistics could verge on the perverse. He believed that only 3 per cent of British people were housed in slum conditions compared to more than one third of Americans.[34]

The Statistical Section was no more popular amongst politicians than civil servants. Labour's Arthur Greenwood complained to Sir John Reith that 'Beaverbrook was public enemy No. 1 and Churchill's Gestapo No. 2'.[35] The Churchill–Reith feud went back to the days of the India Bill, when Reith required minimal bidding from the government to keep Churchill off the airwaves.[36] Reith was smarting after an incursion into his Ministry of Works of one 'of Churchill's women snoopers'. Even later in war, when he had joined the staff of the Admiralty, he was ranting in his diary: 'The swine Churchill sent one of the Cherwell Gestapo notes to the First Lord about repairs to [landing craft tanks] – an utterly ridiculous affair ... Spy work and grossly inaccurate information.'[37]

* * *

Operating under Lindemann's benign aegis was MD1, a freelance organisation tasked with the urgent development of innovative weapons. It was commanded by Millis Jefferis, who began as a major and rose to be a general. Jefferis had caught the eye of Churchill, then still First Lord of the Admiralty, and Lindemann when they were promoting Operation Royal Marine, under which mines would be air-dropped onto the Rhine to sink German barges. No suitable mine existed and the clandestine warfare department Section D under Colonel Lawrence Grand was set to the task of developing one. Jefferis responded vigorously, although nothing came of Royal Marine, but when Churchill became Prime Minister, MD1 was set up to develop weapons independently of any of the established service organisations, almost as a military hardware counterpart to the Statistical Section.[38] Grand and his Section D had fallen victim to the reshuffle of secret organisations that took place when Labour's Hugh Dalton was appointed Minister of Economic Warfare with overall control of clandestine warfare.[39] Lindemann tried but failed to find Grand a senior slot in the higher reaches of military bureaucracy, but MD1 thrived under Jefferis.[40] At one stage, Lindemann and his brother were financing MD1 from their personal funds.[41] It was inspired by Churchill's belief that officialdom had obstructed the development of tanks which he had initiated whilst he was at the Admiralty in the First World War.[42] In reality, his efforts had been hampered because he tried to develop tanks in secret as a way of establishing himself on the army's turf.

MD1 scored a major triumph over the established ordnance bureaucracy when it developed the 'sticky bomb', an anti-tank grenade. With Britain under threat of invasion, this caught Churchill's eye as a weapon that British infantrymen could use to counter German strength in tanks. The military authorities demurred, but Churchill peremptorily instructed them: 'Sticky bomb. Make one million.' He envisaged the grenade as practically a suicide weapon. It only saw limited battlefield use, apparently with some success. MD1's next infantry anti-tank weapon was adopted with less fuss. The Projector Infantry Anti-Tank (PIAT) did the same job as the US bazooka or German *Panzerfaust* but fired its munitions with a powerful spring rather than a rocket. The PIAT was adopted as standard issue for British infantry and was reasonably effective in combat.

Lindemann's influence over weapons development attracted the unfavourable attention of a Conservative MP, Waldron Smithers, who asked a hostile question in the House.[43] Smithers followed this provocation up the same day with a near-suicidal attempt to query Lindemann's presence in the party for Churchill's summit meeting with Roosevelt, with an insinuation that he was not truly British. Churchill bridled at the personal criticism, muttering to his parliamentary private secretary, 'Love me, love my dog, and if you don't love my dog, you damn well can't love me.'[44] Afterwards he found Smithers in the Smoking Room and, shaking with fury, yelled at him, 'Why the hell did you ask that question? Don't you know that "he" … is one of my oldest and closest friends?'[45] Churchill snubbed Smithers's attempt to make a grovelling apology in exceptionally blunt terms, although a few weeks after he consoled him with an insincere 'let bygones be bygones'.[46]

In the autumn of 1941, MD1 attracted the covetous eyes of Beaverbrook, by this time Minister of Supply, who proposed putting it under his ministry.[47] Jefferis was willing to fall in with this, as he saw the move in terms of exchanging his original fairy godmother for a better one. Lindemann does not seem to have been aware of Jefferis's defection and was still trying to shelter him from outside control a few months later when he contemplated stepping down.[48] Perhaps fortunately for Jefferis, Beaverbrook's annexation of MD1 came to an abrupt end when Beaverbrook left government in February 1942 and Churchill allowed MD1 to remain under his personal wing for the rest of the war.

31

A DELIBERATE ACT OF PROMOTION

Lord Beaverbrook's resignation as Minister of Aircraft Production in May 1941 opened a year of deep instability in the relationship between him and Winston Churchill, as they struggled to work out a mutually acceptable role for him in government. Churchill believed that Beaverbrook might still make a huge contribution to the war effort, but Beaverbrook wanted this to be on his own terms. This was also a critical phase in the war for Britain. As Churchill and Beaverbrook wrangled over Beaverbrook's role in governing Britain, the Axis powers inflicted vast defeats on British forces in the Balkans, North Africa and the Far East. Germany appeared poised to conquer the USSR. Even if Beaverbrook had been able to replicate his supposed miracles in boosting aircraft production in other spheres of the war economy, it is hard to imagine that the effect would have been decisive. Everything suggests that Beaverbrook's chief contribution was his personal boost to Churchill's spirits and the Prime Minister paid a high price for this. Beaverbrook deployed all his manipulative skills trying to get what he wanted from Churchill. Churchill did resist, but he never sought fundamentally to reform an abusive relationship.

Churchill was not blind to Beaverbrook's flaws and later in the war remarked on the resemblance between him and Edward G. Robinson, the movie actor, famous for portraying twisted criminals.[1] But in 1941, Churchill had little scope for detached observation. He confessed that he had become 'heartily sick' of Beaverbrook's unceasing struggles with the Air Ministry.[2] Soon after Beaverbrook's move from the Ministry of Aircraft Production, Brendan Bracken observed that Beaverbrook took up more of Churchill's time than the Germans.[3] Later in the year, at one of his low moments, Churchill complained to Randolph that 'Max fights everybody and resigns every day'.[4] Resignation and threats of resignation were Beaverbrook's favourite weapon against Churchill. During the twenty or so months that he was in Churchill's government, Beaverbrook was constantly telling Churchill that he wanted to resign or was actually resigning. His secretaries counted fifteen separate incidents.[5] He himself put the figure at a minimum of twenty, with five of them over a single issue.[6] His first resignation from the Ministry of Aircraft Production came after a few weeks. This established a pattern for their routine, part of his dialogue with Churchill. Beaverbrook openly admitted that the resignations were tactical:

> For twenty-one months that I was a member of your government I made a practice of submitting my resignation. It became a deliberate act of promotion. The object was 'urgency and speed'.
>
> It was in the storm over delays, protests on account of procrastinations, hostility and opposition to government by committee, fortified and strengthened by threats of resignation, that I tried to accomplish all the many tasks that you entrusted to me.
>
> I was always under the impression that, in your support for my methods, you wished me to stay in office, to storm, to threaten resignation and to withdraw again.[7]

Beaverbrook's reading of Churchill was correct. He did not want to lose him. Churchill did not want him to leave the War Cabinet or the government when he finally slammed the door to the Ministry of Aircraft Production. He still needed the infusion of dynamism and hope that Beaverbrook gave him. A grand title, Minister of State, was invented for him and he was given the prestigious accommodation of 12 Downing Street with a communicating door to the Prime Minister's own residence. Churchill offered the trappings of high office, but he did not offer Beaverbrook the quasi-dictatorial powers he had enjoyed at the Ministry of Aircraft Production. His remit was a vague one, to coordinate supply and production, and he recognised that the actual power of the job would depend on Churchill's whim: 'I do not know whether this new job will work or not. It will in large measure depend on how much authority the Prime Minister is prepared to delegate.'[8]

Beaverbrook hesitated but finally accepted that, as he had feared, there was little solid work for him to do. He was made deputy chairman of the Cabinet Defence Committee of Supply, but Churchill left him little scope. He soon repented of his move and was reported (doubtless with a degree of exaggeration) as telling journalists, 'in a broken voice and wiping tears from his eyes', that he had been dismissed:

> I never wanted to leave the Ministry of Aircraft Production. I loved that job. Don't believe anyone who tells you that I left it of my own free will. I never wanted to be made Minister of State. I wanted to have a department that would help to win the war.[9]

The Labour minister Hugh Dalton hastened to spread this story along with Beaverbrook's adverse comments on Labour ministers as proof of his disloyalty to the coalition.[10] Beaverbrook was shaken.[11] Churchill still valued highly Beaverbrook's advice on a range of topics and Beaverbrook was one of the handful of people whom he consulted when Hitler's deputy, Rudolf Hess, made his astonishing flight to Britain.[12]

At the start of June 1941, Beaverbrook wrote a long letter with sixteen points complaining of the specific restrictions on his power as Minister of State.[13] Churchill responded by – as far as can be seen – simply telling Beaverbrook that he was to become Minister of Supply. There was a vague hope that giving Beaverbrook specific responsibilities might make him less demanding.[14] Churchill dangled the prospect of repeating the public acclamation that Beaverbrook had garnered as the Minister of Aircraft Production, but the job was quite different. The Ministry of Supply had been running as part of the Whitehall landscape for two years, under the stewardship of Sir Andrew Duncan, businessman turned minister, who was perfectly comfortable in the atmosphere of quiet committees which was anathema to Beaverbrook, who was not going to be able to recreate something in his own image. The Ministry of Supply was a less comfortable billet than the Ministry of Aircraft Production and Beaverbrook put his finger on what made it unattractive to him: 'More responsibility, less power.'[15] No one complained about the quality of the aircraft that the Ministry of Aircraft Production had produced, but the Ministry of Supply was a different case. The quality of British tanks which were manufactured under its auspices was notoriously erratic and led to a parliamentary inquiry. Beaverbrook had no personal responsibility for their flaws, but it was a testing introduction to the realities of ministerial responsibility to which he was deeply sensitive. British tank quality had been publicly attacked by Alan Moorehead, the distinguished war correspondent who reported on the Desert War for Beaverbrook's own *Daily Express*. When Moorehead was in London, Beaverbrook pled with him unavailingly to stop his criticism.[16]

Just as Beaverbrook had done at the Ministry of Aircraft Production, expanding the empire was a goal in itself, with the added attraction in this case of coming at the expense of a rival for Churchill's favour. Beaverbrook was able to use the Ministry of Supply as the jumping-off point for an attack on Frederick Lindemann. His sights fixed on Lindemann's personal fiefdoms in developing military hardware: Alwyn Crow's rocket (Unrotated Projectile) and Millis Jefferis's MD1. In September 1941, Beaverbrook launched a determined drive to take control of both Crow's operation and MD1.[17] He claimed quite falsely that he already had parliamentary and budgetary responsibility for them and evoked his relationship with Churchill as the foundation of his control: 'Under the Constitution I am also responsible to the Prime Minister for their activities, and no person may stand between him and me.'[18] Lindemann appealed to Churchill and got his backing to keep things for Crow and Jefferis as they were under his personal umbrella as Minister of Defence, but this left the higher bureaucrats with the task of setting up a more formal and transparent structure than the loose arrangement that had prevailed up till then.[19] No other ministry was willing to step into the breach and the Cabinet Secretary Sir Edward Bridges was left to hammer out an agreement with Lindemann and Crow, under which Beaverbrook's Ministry of Supply would have formal responsibility for Crow and Jefferis but Crow would have freedom to pursue research with access to Lindemann.[20] Jefferis would enjoy similar freedom.

Here Beaverbrook received unheralded support for his assault on Lindemann's empire. Duncan Sandys, as the newly minted Financial Secretary to the War Office, visited Aberporth which as an army establishment came under his political oversight. He was to have witnessed trials of multi-barrel launchers, but they were abandoned when a design fault appeared. He did speak to the 'principal scientists'. His report made dire reading; it is unlikely that anyone without the shield of his personal connections would have had the temerity to deliver as formidable an indictment of the rocket anti-aircraft weapons project. He set out a litany of technical defects, beginning with the blank statement that the proximity fuse 'could not at present be regarded as an effective weapon. Furthermore, [the Aberporth staff] were able to hold no prospect that any substantial improvement would be made within any reasonable period.'[21] Even more controversially, he laid into the management of the project, backed by his own experiences as commander, concluding with an outright call for Crow to be replaced:

> In general, I found the officers and scientists at the Establishment despondent and disheartened. Without exception they are still firmly convinced of the potentialities of the rocket, but they mostly made no attempt to conceal their opinion that time and opportunity were being frittered away and that, for lack of effective direction and co-ordination from above, negligible progress was being made.
>
> These misgivings are fully borne out by my own experience last Winter, and now that I have had the opportunity of studying the activities of the Directorate of Projectile Development from another angle, I have no hesitation in saying that I consider it to be an unhappy,

unhealthy and inefficient organisation. Moreover, I am bound to add that, in my opinion (which is widely shared by those in touch with this development), unless the present Controller is replaced by a man of greater administrative ability and the Department thoroughly reorganised the money and effort already expended upon this project and immense opportunities which it offers may be entirely wasted.[22]

Lindemann leapt to the defence of his ally, sneering at the 'principal scientists' who he insinuated were moved by 'ancient prejudices'.[23] He did not hold back from a savage counterattack on Sandys in an area where the loyalties amongst Churchill's inner circle were tested to the limit:

> Finally, I consider the attack on Crow – alleged to be widely supported – grossly unfair. By his energy and initiative in a very few years Crow, almost single-handed, has converted the rocket from little more than a toy into a weapon which the Services are demanding in hundreds of thousands. If he were removed all development would in my view be ham-strung. I am surprised that Sandys, who must realise that he has not the faintest comprehension of the scientific and technical difficulties Crow has met and overcome, should in his privileged position, make such an attack.[24]

Churchill knew what was at stake and did not take sides immediately. Bridges was set the task of mediation. He interviewed Crow and seems to have come down more on his side than Sandys's. Bridges gently suggested to Churchill that some of his son-in-law's criticisms reflected 'mis-apprehension or misunderstanding'.[25] He expressed his preference for some informal solution rather than a formal inquiry by the Minister of Supply and spotted that personal grudges might indeed be playing a part. Here Churchill used the transfer of responsibility for Crow as a pretext for declaring that the case was closed, hinting strongly that he would frown on any attempt to fan the flames: 'There is only a situation which has to be retrieved. Leave it alone.'[26]

Bridges was heartily sick of trying to referee the squabble and was just as happy to close down the affair.[27] When Lindemann was presented with evidence that the Ministry of Supply had little intention of respecting Jefferis's autonomy and complained, Churchill bluntly turned him down, marking his minute 'no. The new arrangement will be tried.'[28] There the matter rested. The feud between Sandys and Lindemann, though, was far from over.

* * *

Lord Beaverbrook's stint as Minister of Supply exposed one of his deepest weaknesses which had been masked at the Ministry of Aircraft Production. He did not really grasp how politics operated and had no sympathy with the process; his natural habitat was the world of a dictatorial business leader in an unchallenging and lucrative industry. At the Ministry of Aircraft Production, he so clearly came ahead of Sir Archibald Sinclair in the pecking order that he could brutalise him to his heart's content; the Air Staff could be undermined by intrigue until, crucially, Beaverbrook found that he had bitten off more than he could chew in Sir Charles 'Peter' Portal. As Minister of Aircraft Production, Beaverbrook had already confronted the Labour Party's Ernest Bevin, who held the Ministry of Labour throughout the wartime coalition government. He was a tough-minded and pragmatic politician. Churchill admired his talents and his position in the Labour Party's elite made him indispensable to the coalition as well. Beaverbrook had no prospect whatever of imposing his will on Bevin. Beaverbrook's early, clumsy attempt to win him over by flattery fell flat.[29] From then on, Bevin became an enemy of Beaverbrook's work (in Beaverbrook's eyes), laying obstacles to production through his solicitude for the workers' conditions. Beaverbrook was also deeply irritated by Bevin's habit of constantly telling stories of his impoverished boyhood in Bristol.[30] Beaverbrook had entertained hopes that Churchill would have left the home front to him. The Prime Minister was chiefly interested in military affairs; the home front did not engage him, but he was still unwilling to delegate.[31] Beaverbrook christened him 'Old Bottleneck' for this. Bevin responded to Beaverbrook's challenge with a determination to curb his influence.[32]

The task of improving British military production was all the more urgent as the shape of the war changed. The Axis invasion of the Balkans had inflicted a significant military defeat on Britain, leaving Germany master of all of western Europe. The arrival of German forces in North Africa, which reversed the easy victories the British had gained there over the Italians, had revealed further weaknesses in Britain's military. The US President, Franklin D. Roosevelt, had opened informal and preliminary discussions of providing assistance to Britain by sending two close associates, Harry Hopkins and W. Averell Harriman, to London. Churchill did not know of Hopkins, but Brendan Bracken had instantly spotted the importance of the mission through his knowledge of US politics and arranged a suitably flattering reception.[33] Hardly had Beaverbrook moved into his new office as Minister of Supply when Hitler's invasion of the USSR transformed the war radically.

Beaverbrook was deeply involved in Churchill's management of Britain's relationship with the US. Along with Frederick Lindemann, he was one of the British party which sailed to America for the first of the wartime summit meetings between Churchill and Roosevelt. Harriman also attended as did Lindemann looking, for once, risible, wearing a yachting cap as he boarded the battleship HMS *Prince of Wales*.[34] The meeting produced the Atlantic Charter, a high-minded statement of the two nations' commitment to a common goal of democracy and liberty. Beaverbrook succeeded in persuading the British to obtain a small but significant change to early drafts. The charter included an aspiration to free trade, but Beaverbrook was conscious of the USA's economic expansionary goals and was ever alert to anything which might compromise his dream of the British Empire as a powerful trading bloc.[35] He insisted that a qualification be inserted into the clause calling for equal access to trade and commodities, 'with due respect to their existing obligations'. It is unlikely that Churchill was misled, but provided his pride was saved, he could bear the political sacrifice and he invested immense efforts in promoting the relationship with the US.

Beaverbrook was utterly different to President Roosevelt's trusted go-betweens to Britain. Harry Hopkins and Averell Harriman were controlled and polished performers, capable and willing of deploying the same inscrutability as to ultimate goals that their master practised. Beaverbrook made a large contribution to one of the less avowable components in Churchill's strategy of accommodating Harriman. Beaverbrook had rapidly befriended Randolph's new wife Pamela née Digby and the couple were frequent guests at his country home, Cherkley. Randolph was an atrocious husband and the marriage swiftly went onto the rocks, but his parents' affection for Pamela went well beyond what they might have given to their grandson's mother. Beaverbrook also kept up his contact to Pamela. She was exactly the kind of woman he liked; despite her youth, she was poised, clever, charming, amusing and deferential – an ornament to any dinner table. When she caught Harriman's eye and they began an affair, Beaverbrook recognised that this provided a perfect way to strengthen the Anglo-American relationship, albeit firmly across the wrong side of the blanket to Harriman. She passed on high-level gossip from her lover to both Churchill and Beaverbrook. After Randolph and Pamela separated, Beaverbrook acted as a financial conduit for Harriman to pay for her expensive flat in Grosvenor Square.[36] He also appears to have persuaded Pamela and Randolph to keep silent about their differences which might have caused scandal.[37]

Immediately after Hitler's attack on the USSR in June 1941, Churchill recognised that Soviet survival was a vital goal in itself. Britain was in no position to provide direct military assistance, so economic help was the next best thing. Beaverbrook took up the call enthusiastically and in September designated one week as 'Tanks for Russia Week'; supposedly, the entire output of tanks that week would be exported to the USSR. As with all of Beaverbrook's stunts, it is impossible to establish whether this had any true effect. The Soviet

Union did receive almost half of the 8,275 Vickers Valentine tanks manufactured.[38] The Valentine was one of Britain's better tank designs and popular with the Red Army, but this contribution to the Soviet war effort was far from decisive. The Soviets themselves built 35,000 of the contemporary (and superior) T-34/76 medium tanks. Beaverbrook set down his marker as the true representative of the left and won a small victory over his successor at the Ministry of Aircraft Production, Moore-Brabazon, who visited an aircraft factory where he was shouted down with cries of 'We want Beaverbrook!'[39]

The USA – then still not a belligerent – recognised the same logic. It was thus an Anglo-American mission that was despatched to Moscow in October 1941 to discuss how the two democracies could assist Stalin. It was led by Beaverbrook and Harriman. Here Beaverbrook discovered his vocation for the remainder of the war: the most highly placed of Stalin's 'useful idiots' – westerners who supported him blindly, usually for ideological motives, unaware of his nationalist agenda or blood-soaked tyranny. All Beaverbrook saw in Stalin was a leader committed to victory, driven by the same sense of urgency that he valued so highly. Stalin happily played up to Beaverbrook and left him with the delusion that they had established a rapport of trust and confidence. Many thought that Beaverbrook had impressed Stalin.[40] One observer remarked that they 'did everything two lovers can do except sleep together, and that only because [they were] too busy'.[41] The Permanent Secretary of the Foreign Office Sir Alexander Cadogan had a rather more sober view: 'Max gave light-hearted account of his Moscow mission which, as I know from my sources was a complete newspaper Stunt.'[42] In reality, Beaverbrook's fantasy of a partnership with Stalin was as fatuous and deluded as Neville Chamberlain's belief that he had established a strong and trusting relationship with Hitler at the Berghof during the Sudeten crisis of 1938.

Beaverbrook's central pitch to Stalin was that military aid promised by Britain would be despatched to the Soviet Union and shipments would be monitored closely, pressurising any minister whom he detected falling behind to improve their performance.[43] Harriman,

Beaverbrook's US counterpart on the mission to Stalin, estimated that deliveries would have fallen 25 per cent short of promises but for Beaverbrook's efforts.[44] Stalin's ambassador to London, Ivan Maisky, sang Beaverbrook's praises: 'He had seen to it that other departments kept their deliveries up to the promised schedule. He was like a hornet. He stung people into action. It seems that we had very few Beaverbrooks.'[45] Maisky compared this favourably to a legion of people he considered 'soft' on Germany, which included the House of Lords, the City, the church and the Labour Party (whose recognition of the dangers of the Stalinist dictatorship were labelled as sympathy with Nazism). For good measure, Maisky threw in eccentric relics of appeasement such as Kenneth de Courcy's Imperial Policy Group and Lord Londonderry. Beaverbrook's enthusiasm for the Soviet Union gave him an extra reason to be suspicious of the Labour Party, whose leaders, Bevin in particular, had long been alert to the dangers of Stalinist Communism and had fought communist attempts to seize control of the Labour movement through the 1930s.

From a quite different perspective, Lindemann endorsed giving the Soviet Union priority for supplies.[46] He calculated that the Red Army killed as many Germans in a day as RAF Bomber Command did in two months: 'To keep Russia fighting is the most economical way to kill Germans.'

When the Japanese attack on Pearl Harbor brought the USA into the war in December 1941, Beaverbrook's leading role in Churchill's government was again brought home. He was the only Cabinet minister to be on the delegation that Churchill took to meet Franklin D. Roosevelt for their second, and first wartime, summit meeting in Washington. Here, with the backing of Harriman and Harry Hopkins, he persuaded the Americans to increase drastically their goals for the production of military hardware. He also found time for a squabble over a trivial question of allocation of raw rubber, which he felt betrayed American ungenerosity. He threatened Churchill to resign over this. This semi-routine display of aggression did not imperil the friendship and Beaverbrook accompanied Churchill all the way home.

For the first time, a British Prime Minister crossed the Atlantic by air in a British-operated but American-built Boeing Clipper flying boat. Under close supervision, Churchill was allowed to take the controls before retiring to sleep in a private cabin. Beaverbrook spent the flight reading.

* * *

The Ministry of Supply did not give Beaverbrook a second run of his glories at the Ministry of Aircraft Production, but it did give him the means to score points against his old nemesis Stanley Baldwin. Beaverbrook had mounted an even more extensive successor to the 'pots and pans' appeal in the shape of a nationwide requisition of iron railings to be transformed into steel. It made just as little worthwhile contribution to the war effort and served to vandalise many treasures. These included the ornamental gates of Baldwin's house, Astley Hall, which had been presented by the Worcestershire Conservatives. Unwisely, Baldwin appealed the requisition that was upheld by the ministry. The decision was taken whilst Beaverbrook was still minister, although it was only announced afterwards. Baldwin was targeted in a venomous press campaign led by a non-Beaverbrook journalist, William Connor writing as 'Cassandra'. Churchill was reported as telling Beaverbrook to 'lay off Baldwin's gates', but according to one of his journalists, William Barkley, he did his utmost to have the gates taken down.[47]

32

FILIAL IMPIETY

Randolph Churchill's units were not deployed to either Norway or France, so he saw no military action in 1940. He, together with Brendan Bracken, did play a small part in eradicating the worst relic of the Chamberlainite regime when they staged the peremptory expulsion of Sir Horace Wilson, who had been Neville Chamberlain's civil service adviser and *éminence grise*, from the office next to the Cabinet Room at 10 Downing Street, which had been the symbol and seat of his power.

There was a wartime coalition deal in place between Conservative, Labour and Liberal parties under which the party which held a seat before the sitting MP resigned or died would not be opposed. Thus, Randolph's next step in the political world was an easy one. After being rejected by the electors in three pre-war elections, Randolph simply needed to find a sufficiently docile Conservative association in a constituency which needed a new MP to be adopted as a candidate. This was not a foregone conclusion, as more traditionalist Conservatives might still shy away from Churchill or the imputation that a prospective candidate was being parachuted in by the Prime Minister.[1] The association at Preston obliged, but this was a two-member constituency and the other sitting member, Captain E. C. Cobb, was not happy about the arrangement.[2] He threatened to resign at the next election if Randolph were adopted as a candidate. Some other constituency members supported him, believing that Randolph would be 'difficult to work with'. But the Prime Minister's reputation stood high after the Battle of Britain and it was said that 'the Churchill name would guarantee his election after the war'. It did not, but much water had flowed under the bridge by then. The dissidents were over-ruled and Randolph was selected 'unanimously'. Cobb lived up to his promise and stood as a candidate at another constituency in 1945.

Arch-Chamberlainite 'Chips' Channon moaned that 'we are soon to have that cad, coarse libertine Randolph in the House. With such a serpent in the House, Westminster will lose much of its attractions for me.'³ Randolph was very sensitive to any imputation that his elec-tion at Preston had been somehow disreputable; he felt that he had worked his passage by fighting three contested elections before the war.⁴ Randolph was elected on 29 September 1940 and took his seat two weeks later. Two days afterwards, Pamela gave birth to their son, named, in keeping with family tradition, Winston. Brendan Bracken and Lord Beaverbrook stood godfather. Randolph made his maiden speech on 26 November, an appropriate interval in the presence of a visibly proud father. His speech was humorous and well received, but he permitted himself swipes at the Chamberlain regime with a particular dig at its mighty Chief Whip who had transferred his alle-giance to Churchill.

> He had noticed recently that despite the repressive activities of Captain Margesson (laughter) some hon. members had been indulging in a great deal of criticism of the Government. He hoped it would not be thought too inappropriate if he answered some of it. There was a good precedent for that. Mr Gladstone was not deterred from defending slavery in his maiden speech in the House merely because his father owned a large slave plantation in Demerara … But perhaps there was rather more comprehension among the Armed Forces of the Crown how slender had been our resources in the past and more understand-ing of the folly of going off at half-cock. Looking round the House he could see a number of hon. members who, in greater or less degree, bore some measure of responsibility for the state of our affairs.⁵

John Colville observed Randolph hovering around Downing Street in the early weeks of his father's premiership, treating listeners to his own vaulting analyses and dislike of the previous political generation: 'Randolph is a most unattractive combination of the bombastic, the cantankerous and the unwise; yet at times he makes shrewd and penetrating comments and at times he can be pleasant. He has none of Winston's reasonableness.'[6]

Having done his bit for his father's political project, Randolph moved on to support one of his military projects. Churchill had driven the creation of commando units which would take the war to the German forces by staging 'butcher and bolt' raids on the occupying forces on the Continent. They were made up of a combination of professional soldiers, who were confronted by the prospect of a long period of inaction until a land battle against Germany resumed, and members of the upper reaches of London society; the two often overlapped as in the person of Colonel Robert Laycock, the overall commander of the commando forces. Randolph had many friends amongst the smart set, including the novelist Evelyn Waugh, who was especially close. Many of the characteristics for Waugh's ultra-cad Basil Seal could have been drawn from Randolph. After training in Scotland, which only mildly interfered with the social lives of the smart set, 8 Commando set sail for Egypt on the long route round the Cape. The smart officers amused themselves by high-stakes gambling and the more astute, including David Stirling, future founder of the Special Air Service (SAS), took full advantage of Randolph's compulsive chatter, which meant 'he could never concentrate on his cards long enough to win. I really did stock up the sporran at his expense.'[7] Randolph ended the voyage £500 the poorer.

When Randolph arrived in Cairo, he was treated in practice as an envoy from his father rather than a junior officer entering a combat zone. He was put up at the British embassy (Egypt was notionally an independent country) where he met Anthony Eden, the Foreign Secretary who was passing through the region.[8] Randolph was twice invited to meet General Archibald Wavell, the army commander-in-chief. He also had leisure time for tourism and judged the sphinx to be a 'pet', although he fancied that its face resembled Mussolini. Randolph's military career went less well. Like Waugh, he had not been judged as suitable to lead troops in battle and he held two non-command posts, in charge of stores and as unit intelligence officer. After a few weeks, Wavell sent 8 Commando in a last-ditch attempt to defeat the German paratroop attack, but Randolph was left behind. Even Waugh, who was as incompetent an officer as Randolph and similarly loathed by his men, was taken on the expedition to Crete. Randolph was left behind with the army rear echelons in Cairo. If he was intentionally kept out of combat, it was not by his own wish. He attempted to promote a number of raiding operations, none of which came to anything.[9]

In the early years of the war, Cairo combined the headquarters of armed services fighting serious battles sometimes only a few dozen miles away with sections of high society transplanted from Mayfair. Socialite MP 'Chips' Channon, who was passionately in love with Wavell's aide-de-camp Captain Peter Coats, adored the atmosphere – it was 'easy, even elegant, corrupt, luxurious, trivial, worldly, me, in fact'.[10] One of its most prominent figures was Maud 'Momo' Marriott, wife of a brigadier in the desert, with whom Randolph was soon on very close terms. They were believed to be lovers, but marital infidelity was not a one-way street here which adds a certain piquancy to one of Randolph's more serious tasks, which he was given at his father's prompting and which he relished.[11] He escorted Averell Harriman on a tour of the region to prepare a report for the President on British performance and prospects just as he was doing from London. Randolph was probably unaware of Harriman's growing intimacy with his wife, Pamela, but he did appeal to his father to ask her to make contact.[12] He acknowledged the financial help that his father provided for her as well as bailing himself out with large cheques.[13] Randolph was openly unfaithful to her with easily available local girls.[14]

Randolph was established as a feature of the higher reaches of the military and political world of Cairo. He behaved with his customary rudeness and aggression. Everywhere he hurt feelings and Freya Stark, the distinguished Arabist, reported: 'They say he is doing as much harm as any two Germans, just by being himself.'[15] At one dinner hosted by the ambassador, Randolph ranted drunkenly against the performance of the British military leadership in the failed campaign to hold back the German invasion of Greece.[16] He made no secret of his contempt for 'Muddle East' with its 'second-rate people', which he reported to his father.[17]

Randolph's activities were not confined to gossip and abuse. He was drawn into his father's bitter relationship with Wavell. Wavell had an almost impossible job of trying unsuccessfully to fight the German invasion of Greece and then Crete, next battling an uprising by nationalists in Iraq and active Vichy French assistance to the Germans, as well as the land campaign in the western desert, all with minimal resources. According to Boothby, Churchill was determined not to repeat the experience of the First World War when the politicians were unable to stop General Haig pursuing his offensive strategy on the Western Front at vast cost in lives and saw Wavell in the same light.[18] Moreover, Wavell had made no attempt to cultivate Churchill when he was a guest at Chequers, where his taciturnity made a poor impression.[19] Beaverbrook was another enemy of Wavell and had criticised the British foray into Greece and Crete.[20] When Randolph asked Wavell's aide Peter Coats to send his letters to Churchill in the commander-in-chief's confidential bag, Coats was afraid that he was harming his chief by facilitating the transmission of hostile comments.[21] Coats suspected that Randolph disliked Wavell; he had been surprised when Coats confirmed to him that the general wrote humorous verse and could thus be classed as 'literary'. The breaking point came in May 1941. Churchill had superintended the despatch of tank reinforcements for Wavell through the dangerous Mediterranean route by the 'Tiger' convoy. He invested great hopes in his 'Tiger cubs', but Operation Battleaxe, in which they were deployed, failed. Wavell was dismissed by Churchill and Randolph heartily approved the move, claiming that Wavell's 'extreme inability to discuss matters with any one, and his apparent lack of capacity to transmit drive to his subordinates were fatal handicaps'.[22] He had already complained of Wavell's uncommunicativeness which was one of the characteristics that most irked his father.

Randolph was more complimentary of Wavell's replacement, Claude Auchinleck, although he proved no more successful against the Germans.[23] Auchinleck was more enthusiastic about irregular soldiery and thus an improvement on Wavell who had used the Layforce commandos as ordinary infantry, albeit in an extreme crisis. Randolph lambasted a number of staff officers, in particular General Arthur Smith, whom he depicted as the epitome of 'military boobydom' and an obstacle to his father's ambitions for commando units. He tried to help relations with the Free French by decrying the work that General Edward Louis Spears was doing after a single conversation with General de Gaulle. Randolph claimed to be speaking for the majority opinion on Spears, who was a trusted friend of his father. Sadly, de Gaulle left no record of his conversation with Randolph.

One of Randolph's interventions had a happier and more productive outcome. He added his voice – according to one account, decisively – to a chorus of calls for a senior politician to be appointed to arbitrate between the conflicting agendas of military and civil authorities in the region.[24] The man Churchill chose for the job was Oliver Lyttelton, one of his personal allies from before the war. Lyttelton was a highly successful businessman who had first met Churchill in the trenches. He had also crossed paths with Bracken, who approved of his operations to resist German domination of international metals trading through the establishment of the British Metal Corporation. Lyttelton believed that Bracken had lobbied in his favour.[25] The appointment was a happy choice and set the pattern for British organisation in the Mediterranean. Unhappily for Randolph, he failed to get the reward he hoped for in sponsoring Lyttelton's advancement. Randolph was continually insisting that Cairo required a 'dictator of propaganda' and may well have seen himself in this role.[26] Churchill backed his son's ambition to be given some kind of role managing British propaganda activities, but Lyttelton firmly turned this down, although he did propose that Randolph serve as a liaison between himself and the Prime

Minister.[27] Lyttelton certainly approved of Bracken's appointment as Minister of Information, but he had a rather more limited vision than Randolph, whom he told that the man chosen to head propaganda in Cairo would be there to 'enlighten the darkies'.[28] Randolph thought that 'lots of poor whites' needed enlightenment too.

Randolph was probably better in the niche that he did carve out for himself. Promoted direct from the rank of lieutenant to major, he found a billet in public relations at General Headquarters. He soon established his popularity with the local press corps and the troops in the field. He was far better attuned to the needs and instincts of journalists than the cautious, security-driven bureaucrats who inevitably dominated army headquarters and established good individual relationships with reporters. His voice soon became so powerful that his father had to take steps to suppress any story that he was the army's official spokesman.[29] He worked to relax the previously draconian censorship practices. One of his innovations was to produce the *World's Press Review*, a selection of articles from British and American journalists, including some that criticised the army or advanced left-wing views; it was distributed to all officers.[30] The review was popular with its readers, although one brigadier was so enraged by it that he had a copy burned in front of his men in the desert. Another officer believed that soldiers needed reading material such as *Country Life* rather than Randolph's production. Randolph helped Ève Curie, daughter of the French scientists, visit the front as a war correspondent in defiance of a military ban.[31]

The outbreak of the war with Japan and America's formal entry to the war in December 1941 drastically shrank the importance of Cairo. They also ushered in a series of unparalleled disasters for the British Empire. The two battleships of Force Z, *Prince of Wales* and *Repulse*, which had been despatched to shore up the British position in the Far East were sunk by Japanese aircraft; Hong Kong had fallen; British forces were flung into precipitate retreat in Burma; and the Japanese established a secure lodgement on the island of Singapore, Britain's main base in the region and of vital strategic importance. Britain's Crusader attack on the Erwin Rommel's Axis forces had been only partially successful and the latest stage in the western desert battle had seen the British driven back once again. For the first time since he became Prime Minister, Churchill was facing open discontent with his handling of the war. He moved to pre-empt any challenge and let it be known when he returned from conferring with President Roosevelt on 15 January 1942 that he would make a comprehensive statement on the progress of the war which would be followed by a debate in the House of Commons.

The political stakes were rising as the return of the extreme left-winger Sir Stafford Cripps from his time as ambassador to Moscow ushered in the prospect of a ministerial reshuffle. Cripps wanted to convert the largely spurious kudos he had gained for the Soviet Union's war efforts into solid political coin. It was a near certainty that he would have to be accommodated, but it was not simply a question of finding an appropriate ministry; Cripps was still *persona non grata* in Labour circles and the Labour leaders would have to be appeased just as much as their Conservative colleagues. Initially, Churchill proposed that the parliamentary rules would be waived and a recording made of his speech for broadcast. This provoked concerns that he would use this to appeal to the public over the head of Parliament and it became far from certain that he would have won a majority of the House in favour. He swiftly withdrew and, ostensibly on medical grounds, dropped the idea of any broadcast. His next choice was whether to attach a vote of confidence in the government to the debate or, as Conservative backbenchers urged, allow a fully open debate. The magnitude of the political risk that Churchill faced was infinitely smaller than Chamberlain had faced in the Norway debate which had put him into power, but discontent was most acute in Conservative ranks. The leaders of his coalition partners were solidly behind the government, but any significant revolt would weaken Churchill's standing. Chamberlain's humiliation in the Norway debate had surprised many. Even if they did not translate into adverse votes, effective speeches questioning the government might make an impact, just as Leo Amery's speech had done in the Norway debate. Moreover, Chamberlain's own speech in his defence had contained the fatally ill-judged claim still 'to have friends in this House'; Churchill's speech on his behalf was no more than a display of routine ministerial loyalty. Dissident voices were threatening to table amendments to whatever motion was debated, so Churchill confronted the challenge head on by making the debate one of confidence, setting the scene for a major parliamentary event when the support shown to Churchill might be crucial.

Walter Monckton had provided Randolph with a thin pretext to return to London in December 1941.[32] He seemed to think that his activities in Cairo PR merited high-level personal discussions, but there might have been a more personal reason for his visit. He used his spell back in Britain to attempt to re-establish his position with Pamela. Pamela was young but a forceful personality and firmly spurned his attempts to behave 'like a pasha'.[33] When he told her that he wanted her to be with 'my son', she told him that young Winston was also *her* son. Randolph seemed to think this biological fact to be irrelevant: 'No, my son. I'm a Churchill.'

Churchill had already pushed up the stakes in the debate, but Randolph turned the screw further and his contribution was anything but statesmanlike and balanced. His praise of the government's actions was overshadowed by his vigorous personal abuse of its opponents, often delivered with some wit and humour. He described the House as 'the Parliament of Munich' which failed to rearm. To Channon, his speech was striking but counterproductive: 'The most colourful moment was an excursion by Randolph Churchill. He was quick, witty and amusing and made the House laugh, although he added fuel to the fires of bitterness ... He insulted everybody, men old enough to be his father.'[34] The House paid Randolph back in his own coin, pointing out that he had been elected unopposed and, when he expounded on questions of military detail, had never seen combat. To a more reflective listener, it was the attacks on Churchill which made a greater impact. Amery recorded

a very effective and really eloquent criticism by Wardlaw Milne. There was real passion in it and it deeply impressed the House ... [Later] Dick Bonar Law told me that Herbert Williams' speech with its direct attack on Winston had been quite well received by the House in spite of the fact that Williams is usually an unpopular speaker. It does look as if Winston's speech, admirable as it was within its limits, had not allayed the general sense of disquiet.[35]

Only one MP, the extreme left-wing James Maxton, voted against the government, but discontent with it was palpable at a meeting of the 1922 Committee described by Channon as a 'bear-garden'. Churchill seemed more concerned at the rough handling that his son had received there than at his own political travails.

The debate was at best a qualified win for Churchill, but his timing in moving aggressively to flush out critics early proved to be correct. Britain's military fortunes continued to ebb. In the days following the debate, the rout in the Far East worsened when Singapore with 85,000 troops surrendered to half the number of Japanese fighters. Worse came in June in the western desert when Rommel's next offensive took him to the border with Egypt and he overran the fortress of Tobruk, capturing 33,000 British and South African prisoners in the second largest military surrender ever after Singapore. The humiliation was compounded because the news reached Churchill at the White House where he was conferring with Roosevelt.

The debate after Tobruk was an altogether more menacing proposition for Churchill, although the practical threat to the government was remote. It was triggered by a censure motion table by Sir John Wardlaw-Milne, whose opening speech began very effectively in the same measured tone as January's debate. He proceeded to commit parliamentary suicide by suggesting that the King's brother, the notoriously stupid Duke of Gloucester, be appointed as military commander-in-chief. After that, Churchill had little effort to make, although he did prevail upon Bob Boothby to make one of his rare interventions in favour of the government. It is testimony to Boothby's residual devotion to Churchill that he obeyed the call despite having been consigned to the outer darkness a year and a half before. He was not unprepared and rose to the task willingly and with pride in his result:

Next year to my amazement, he beckoned me over to his table in the
House of Commons where he was lunching alone on the day of the
censure debate after the fall of Tobruk. He asked me whether I still
supported the Government. I said I did. He then asked whether I supported him. 'I have no reason to, but there is no one else.' Finally he
asked me whether I would speak in the debate. I said I had brought
some notes. Whereupon he marched me to the speaker and told him
he wished me to be called fifth in the debate. He himself listened to my
speech. It was not one of my worst. I managed to change the atmosphere from one of tension to one of relaxation. I made them laugh. In
this I was much helped by Wardlaw-Milne's suggestion in his opening
speech that the Duke of Gloucester should be made Commander-in-
Chief.[36]

Randolph was not on hand to repeat the support that he had given his
father in the January debate. He had returned to Cairo and a dramatic
decline in his fortunes. The powers that be had taken advantage of
his absence to give his PR job to another officer without notifying
him.[37] He was no longer his father's private informant on Cairo and
military gossip. In a huff, he joined David Stirling's SAS which partially recreated the Mayfair-in-khaki world of 8 Commando, albeit
with an admixture of far more serious soldiers. Randolph took part in
one inconclusive SAS operation and was then severely injured in an
accidental car crash. His political life fared little better; he was sucked
into a futile argument over the future of a discredited former, short-
lived Prime Minister of France who had been a friend of the family
and an even messier set-to with his fellow Conservative member for
the Preston constituency. After an acrimonious reunion, he separated
definitively from Pamela, who remained in high family favour and
a star in the de facto court surrounding Churchill, forming close
friendships with influential visiting Americans as well as Harriman.
She appears to have found her way into the hearts of senior air commanders: General Anderson of the US and Sir 'Peter' Portal, the head
of the RAF and Churchill's preferred amongst the chiefs of staff. One

of her biographers claims she received love letters from the two airmen and Harriman when they were all attending the Yalta Conference in 1945.[38] It barely matters whether she had physical affairs with these men; whatever happened provoked no or minimal scandal and helped create the atmosphere of an intimate and rather louche court around Churchill. It was understood that Randolph might cite her adultery with Harriman as grounds for divorce but that this would cause a scandal which could compromise relations with the US.[39] In practice, Churchill's daughter-in-law counted for more than her estranged husband. Randolph's behaviour did not improve and Clemmie was concerned that he was causing Churchill much trouble.[40] He had been so drunk and aggressive at a dinner with his father, sister Sarah and some chiefs of staff that his father had had to threaten him with being forcibly removed by Royal Marine guards. Randolph was duly despatched on an essentially symbolic liaison mission to Tito, the leader of the communist resistance to the Axis in Yugoslavia and a British client.

33

BEAVERBROOK'S
USEFUL IDIOCY

Winston Churchill and Lord Beaverbrook returned from the mission to Washington to find a desperate military position in January 1942. The Japanese had swept all before them and were on the verge of taking Singapore, Britain's crucial base in the region. The Eighth Army was firmly on the back foot in North Africa. The political picture was correspondingly awkward. For the first time, serious doubts in Churchill's war leadership were coming out. He met the challenge head on with a Commons debate on a motion of confidence, but more would be required. Since the summer of 1941, there had been calls for a Minister of Production to coordinate British industry fully to meet the needs of total war. The job had been offered to the Labour extreme left-winger Sir Stafford Cripps, who had returned from Moscow where he had been ambassador. Cripps had acquired a spurious lustre as the man who had brought Stalin into the war, which he hoped to convert into a strong position in domestic politics. Cripps turned the job down and Churchill offered it to Beaverbrook. Beaverbrook demanded unquestioned overlordship over domestic production, but Churchill bounced him into accepting a severely diluted job specification, set out in a government White Paper which would have left Beaverbrook little or no authority over Ernest Bevin or, indeed, the other production departments.

Rapidly, Beaverbrook began to have second thoughts about having accepted. He told Averell Harriman that he was going to resign (after only a few days in the job). Harriman reported to President Roosevelt:

Beaverbrook has quibbled and quarrelled with the PM to the point where the PM will not tolerate it any longer. He feels Beaverbrook has been unjust and disloyal to seize this moment of all moments to make an issue. I believe Beaverbrook over-emphasises the adverse effect on the government of his resignation. The PM is confident it will not be serious and, even if it were, there is nothing he can do about it.[1]

The stakes were pushed up again by the Channel Dash, in which the German battleships *Scharnhorst* and *Gneisenau* took British watchers by surprise and sailed up the Channel in daylight, beating off ill-organised attempts to stop them. *The Times*, which had never swung behind Churchill fully, thundered that the German Admiral Otto Ciliax had succeeded where the Duke of Medina Sidonia, the commander of the Spanish Armada defeated in 1588, had failed. In reality, the German ships were far more of a threat to the British in Brest and Hitler wanted them in the north to defend against a British attack on Norway that existed in the dreams of Churchill but was a military fantasy. The German ships were also severely damaged by hitting mines laid in their path, but the British knew this from Enigma and did not disclose it so as not to compromise security.[2] But in political terms, the Channel Dash was a major humiliation.

Beaverbrook wrote to Churchill proposing the elimination of underperforming ministers and various permutations for the reconstruction of the government, none of which included himself. He had played the resignation card so often that he seemed to have failed to appreciate that it was not a risk-free strategy. Beaverbrook was now facing a formidable combination of opponents. Clemmie saw the prospect of freeing her husband from the incubus. She had spotted that Beaverbrook feared losing ground to Cripps:

I do beg of you to reflect, whether it would not be best to leave Lord B entirely out of your Reconstruction.

It is true that if you do he may (& will) work against you – at first covertly & then openly. But is not hostility without, better than

intrigue & treachery & rattledom* within? You should have peace
inside your Government – for a few months at any rate – & you must
have that with what you have to face and do for us all – Now that you
have (as I understand) invited Sir Stafford, why not put your money
on him?

The temper & behaviour you describe (in Lord B) is caused I think
by the prospect of a new personality equal perhaps in power to him &
certainly in intellect.

My Darling – Try ridding yourself of this microbe which some
people fear is in your blood. Exorcise this bottle Imp & see if the air is
not clearer & purer – You will miss his drive & genius, but in Cripps
you may have new accessions of strength.[3]

Bracken brought Beaverbrook's letter to Churchill but urged him
against its suggestions: 'I told him that his advice was unsound. And I
beg you to make a thorough reconstruction of the government.'[4] The
mood in the House was running firmly against Beaverbrook; Labour
would be 'delighted' and a 'great many Conservatives will be equally
pleased', as Churchill's parliamentary private secretary reported.[5]

Frederick Lindemann opened another front against Beaverbrook
in payback for his seizure of – at least formal control – over Alwyn
Crow and Millis Jefferis. He used his adversary's favourite weapon, the
threat of resignation:

Now that all the production departments are to be under the control
of the Minister of War Production, it will be his task to see that output
priorities etc. are in proper balance and to keep you informed about the
position. He would be justified in resenting continuous investigation
and criticism on my part.[6]

He proposed to wind down the operations of his Statistical Section to
the production of graphics for the Prime Minister. The threat struck

---

* Presumably rattlesnake behaviour.

home. Churchill assured Lindemann that the services of his branch would still be required.[7] The Prime Minister had, though, been put on warning that, if he was going to allow Beaverbrook to mark his own homework as war production supremo, Lindemann was having no part of it. Churchill temporised: 'It is not possible to take a final decision on these matters until the Office of Minister of Production has been fully defined.'

Beaverbrook was summoned to attend a night-time Cabinet meeting on 18 February. Before the meeting, Churchill showed him two different lists for the proposed new government. Both had Clement Attlee as Deputy Prime Minister and one did not feature either Beaverbrook or Bevin.[8] Beaverbrook told Churchill that he wanted to resign but argued against Attlee on the grounds of his supposed lack of ability. Beaverbrook was not satisfied at the prospect of eliminating his direct nemesis, Bevin, but wanted to curb his boss as well. In practice, he was asking for Labour to be practically removed from government. They moved to the next room where Clem Attlee, Anthony Eden, Brendan Bracken and the Conservative Chief Whip James Stuart were waiting. Churchill stirred Beaverbrook to restate his objections to Attlee, which provoked a furious argument. Beaverbrook walked out. He seems to have spotted rather late in the day that he had burned his bridges and wrote to Churchill begging four months' leave of absence to handle newspaper publicity and then to return to government, implicitly outside the Cabinet.[9] It was too late; his departure was announced along with the names of the new Cabinet.

The announcement made a point of saying that Beaverbrook had been invited to join but his health had prevented this and that he would undertake a journey to Washington to continue his work co-ordinating the war effort, together with any specific task the Cabinet found. Afterwards, Beaverbrook recognised that the explanation was an error in seeming to disqualify him from major responsibilities.

The other pieces in the reconstruction jigsaw strengthened Churchill's position. Attlee was awarded the title of Deputy Prime Minister and Bevin joined the Cabinet, outflanking Cripps who had to content himself with the rank of Lord Privy Seal and the leadership of the House of Commons. Production questions were put into the hands of two technocrat temporary ministers: former civil servant turned minister Sir John Anderson and Oliver Lyttelton, metals market financier and friend of Bracken. Lyttelton was to take over Beaverbrook's duties as Minister of Production, but in a further concession to his predecessor's face, he was entitled merely Minister of State. For the rest of the war, economic and industrial management slipped back into the calmer waters of rational, albeit often heated, debate. The days for Beaverbrook's heroic permanent crisis had passed.

Churchill had been irked by Beaverbrook's persistent blackmail by resignation but instantly mourned losing him as a colleague.[10] He felt that his hand had been forced. To a friendly journalist, he laid open his personal loss, albeit not making any mention of Beaverbrook's supposed abilities as a minister, but also throwing the onus on Beaverbrook, hinting at his sense of disloyalty and ingratitude:

> So I am indeed [sorry that Beaverbrook has gone]. He needn't have gone.
> He could have had any one of three or four offices if he had liked to
> stop. He could have gone back to the Ministry of Aircraft Production
> if he had chosen. I didn't want him to go. He was good for me! Any
> number of times, if things were going badly, he would encourage me
> saying, 'Look at all the things on your side. Look what you've accomplished. Be of good courage!' And he put courage and pep into me.[11]

The version of his departure that Beaverbrook put out was to complain of having been bounced into accepting the White Paper specification for the Ministry of Production.[12] He did not hide his jealousy and distrust of Cripps, in particular Cripps's unwillingness to acquiesce unconditionally in Soviet demands for their 1940 frontiers which Beaverbrook treated as natural and a vital component in keeping Soviet friendship. Revealingly, he tried to parade his closeness to Labour's Herbert Morrison in an attempt to show that he had it in his power to launch a serious intrigue against the government.

Beaverbrook's exit from government freed him to mount a raucous public campaign to make supporting the Soviet Union Britain's chief war aim. This was far more to his taste than the minutiae and responsibility of an executive task. The centrepiece of Beaverbrook's campaign was to echo the Soviet call for an immediate cross-Channel invasion of Europe under the slogan 'Second Front Now'. Beaverbrook believed that a Second Front was vital in the same way that he had believed that aircraft production was vital in 1940.

Churchill had unintentionally given Beaverbrook a perfect platform from which to launch the campaign. As a further sop to Beaverbrook for his departure, he was despatched on an ill-defined mission to the USA. Beaverbrook let it be known that the true purpose of his visit was to promote the idea of a three-way alliance between Britain, the Soviet Union and the US.[13] At that stage, Roosevelt briefly favoured an early Second Front and Beaverbrook planned to take full advantage. Most of Beaverbrook's time was devoted to preparing a high-profile speech pleading for a Second Front. He was under no illusion that Churchill would not approve.[14] Beaverbrook's speech was approved by Roosevelt beforehand. Delivered to the annual dinner of the Newspaper Proprietors Association of America in New York, it might have been written by Stalin's speechwriter:

> Communism under Stalin has won the applause and admiration of all the western nations.
>
> Communism under Stalin has provided us with examples of patriotism equal to the finest in the annals of history ...
>
> Strike out to help the Soviet Union. Strike out violently. Strike even recklessly ... Britain should imitate the Soviet Union's spirit of attack by establishing somewhere along the two thousand miles of occupied coastline a Second Front.

Beaverbrook trumpeted the cause through his newspapers, public meetings and numerous speeches. When he made his New York speech, the Soviet Union was still under severe pressure from the

Germans and many saw a real risk that it would be defeated. Beaver-brook was obsessed that without a Second Front, the Soviet Union would collapse.[15] He naively imagined that Stalin would not make a separate peace with Hitler.[16] But he was a military illiterate. He entire-ly ignored the vast military challenge that a full-scale cross-Channel invasion would have involved. He claimed that the British Army was entirely ready for such an operation. Invading France was utterly un-realistic in 1942 and only marginally feasible in 1943. Churchill accept-ed the British military veto on the scheme, although this had as much to do with his preference for unsound ideas like an attack on Norway or a Mediterranean strategy against the supposedly 'soft under-belly' of the Axis powers. Beaverbrook was hostile to Churchill's predilec-tion for a Mediterranean strategy, recognising that he preferred it to a cross-Channel invasion.[17] He never understood Churchill's fear of the military risks of Operation Overlord. Instead, he raked up Church-ill's long-standing hatred of Bolshevism to explain his opposition to a Second Front as something that would assist a Communist regime.[18] He went on to imagine that Churchill preferred a long war rather than a speedy Soviet victory as a tool to secure a fourth term for Roosevelt as President. He accused Bracken of being Churchill's mouthpiece for a long war.[19]

Beaverbrook also wove the shadowy world of conspiracies against the Second Front into another of his great hatreds. In August 1942, Admiral Lord Louis Mountbatten had been the main driving force in the catastrophic Dieppe raid for which the Canadian Army provided the bulk of the troops, most of whom became casualties. Beaverbrook loathed Mountbatten for supposedly sacrificing his countrymen; in reality, the Canadian Army commander had been keen to use his men in battle. Beaverbrook fantasised that the operation had been mount-ed to discredit the Second Front proposal, rather than being, in part, a weak excuse to Stalin for not mounting a more significant opera-tion. The vendetta was arguably the greatest of the many that Beaver-brook pursued and lasted almost until the end of his life, fuelled by a string of personal and public complaints, including the possibility that Mountbatten had had an affair with Jean Norton, Beaverbrook's long-term mistress.[20] The wartime movie *In Which We Serve*, inspired by Mountbatten, features a scene in which the survivors of a destroyer that has just been sunk see a copy of the *Daily Express* with the infamous headline 'No War This Year'. Even A. J. P. Taylor admitted Beaverbrook's hostility to Mountbatten but tried to pass the affair off as an 'alleged feud'.[21]

The Second Front stood at the centre of Beaverbrook's vision of Britain and the US helping the Soviet Union defeat Germany. Maximum provisions of military supplies also counted, but Beaverbrook was willing to throw his weight onto Stalin's side on a purely political issue. His shibboleth for true support of the Soviet Union was to accept unconditionally its pre-Barbarossa boundaries, in particular the Baltic states which Stalin had seized in June 1940 under the cover of the Molotov–Ribbentrop pact whilst the western democracies were otherwise occupied. He refused to attend the signature of the Anglo-Russian treaty of friendship in July 1941 because it made no mention of frontiers. In his mind, this was also part of a battle against the Labour leadership, whose doubts over Stalin's claims to surrounding territories he labelled as quasi-fascist. Labour actively opposed unconditional support for Soviet war aims.

*　　*　　*

Even whilst he was nerving himself for his resignation as Minister of War Production, Lord Beaverbrook had been alert to the avenues that this might open in domestic politics. He believed that the shift in the war situation put Winston Churchill's position into serious jeopardy. He egged Churchill on to the idea of a snap general election to allow him to remove his critics instead of a government reconstruction.[22] Averell Harriman judged that Beaverbrook thought Churchill would fall and that he would be called upon to succeed. Beaverbrook had picked a good platform. The British public enthusiastically adopted the cause of support for Stalin. Almost overnight, it became publicly unacceptable to mention the fact that he conducted a blood-soaked tyranny. Beaverbrook was tempted to parlay his endorsement of the Soviet Union into wider political advantage. Churchill remained under political pressure after the dire days of February and March. The defeats of the British Army in North Africa, above all the fall of Tobruk in June 1942, followed on from the failures in the Far East. Political doubts culminated in a House of Commons vote of confidence debate in July. Partly through the ineptitude of his opponents, Churchill rode this out far better than might have been hoped, but concerns persisted.

Beaverbrook continued to muse vaguely that Churchill might be damaged irreparably and that he might be able to step into his place, but he gave little or no assistance to Churchill's detractors. His long-standing confidant Bruce Lockhart had long believed that Beaverbrook wanted to become Prime Minister. He saw behind Beaverbrook's analyses of the political situation which led to Churchill's fall as creating an opportunity for him to take over on the back of his public support for the Second Front.[23] Beaverbrook had invented for himself a scenario in which Churchill's survival as Prime Minister depended on the Soviets continuing to resist the Germans, with the implication that he was making a stronger domestic political call by his all-out support for Stalin.[24] In parallel to his pro-Sovietism, Beaverbrook even returned to the defeatist isolationism which he had championed before the war and during the Phoney War. He told one of his employees, 'Churchill has been a great Prime Minister. He saved the country. But now he should go, he's outlived his usefulness. What we want now is a Prime Minister who can make peace.'[25]

Beaverbrook's vision of himself as Prime Minister almost certainly went no further than a pipe dream. Beaverbrook had no support and the active hostility of almost every serious politician. The only figure of any standing that Beaverbrook sounded out about a serious political move was Sir Arthur Salter, who was barely second tier. It is more likely that Beaverbrook dreamed of a rerun of the crisis in 1916 which put David Lloyd George into 10 Downing Street when he had persuaded himself that he had been instrumental in swinging Andrew Bonar Law and the Conservatives against Herbert Asquith. Beaverbrook lionised and cultivated Labour politician Herbert Morrison, who might have played the Bonar Law role and brought Labour in against Churchill, but for all its internal divisions, Labour never seriously contemplated breaking the wartime coalition until the very end. The fatal flaw in Beaverbrook's plots was that there was simply no credible alternative to Churchill. The best candidate that Beaverbrook could come up with was Anthony Eden.[26] Making up to Morrison had the attraction for Beaverbrook of building up a rival to Clement Attlee and Ernest Bevin, whom he despised. Beaverbrook's taste for disruption easily trumped his distaste for socialism. Beaverbrook also cultivated left-wing Labour figures such as R. R. Stokes and his own employee Michael Foot.[27]

*   *   *

There is no sign that Lord Beaverbrook's efforts affected the military decision-making of the British and Americans one iota. The US tacitly accepted the British Mediterranean strategy by opening their first major commitment to the war against Germany with the Torch landings in North Africa in November 1942, which pushed any prospect of a landing in France into 1943. This was repeated in 1943, when they accepted the invasions of Sicily then Italy.

In public, Beaverbrook kept up his commitment to a speedy attack on France and he told the House of Lords in February 1943 that there was an 'urgent need' for a Second Front. In private, the emphasis shifted and the following month he appears to have passed up an opportunity to lobby for an attack on France that year, instead focusing on propaganda for what Averell Harriman labelled as an 'appeasement policy toward the Soviet Union', conceding all their territorial ambitions.[28] 'He doesn't give a hoot in hell for the small nations. He would turn over Eastern Europe to the Soviet Union without regard for future consequences.' Beaverbrook willingly accepted the Soviet lies about their massacre of Polish officers and rulers at Katyn, which had just come to light. Churchill allowed him to draft a telegram criticising the Polish government in exile on this issue.

Beaverbrook was also broadening his assault on the government and set himself up as a persistent critic on a range of other issues. The House of Lords, where he had barely set foot until then, became his favourite pulpit. He developed a sudden interest in rural affairs, calling for 30,000 farmworkers' cottages to be built. He tried to block an extension of central government control over food production and pushed for arrangements for milk distribution to be made fairer to small producers. He opposed a Bill to regulate town and country planning because it would create a new ministry and distract from the war effort. In private, he treated Bruce Lockhart to a litany of complaints at Churchill's doings which he forecast fondly would work against the Prime Minister politically:

> He predicts a slump in the PM's popularity; thinks it will come rapidly – in fifth winter [of war] people become more critical. Reasons for criticism are: (1) clothes coupons [i.e. rationing]; (2) blackout [still needlessly severe]; (3) TUC dispute; (4) unbusinesslike methods of government – travelling circus to USA because PM likes to travel, Eden as Foreign Secretary *and* Leader of the House and no plan for Europe; (5) family nepotism – taking his wife and daughter to Quebec; (6) his mania for taking decisions in the early hours of the morning, 1 a.m. to 3 a.m., and the effect of his late hours and alcoholism on the men who have to do the work [Beaverbrook was speaking from his own bitter experience as well as solicitude for others].[29]

Beaverbrook could re-excavate his old grievances against the air marshals which could also be woven into his pro-Soviet campaign. When Lord Trenchard opposed Beaverbrook's call for a Second Front, Beaverbrook turned the thrust round into an assault on the policy of bombing Germany:

Long ago [Trenchard] was proved wrong. Before the war he gloried publicly in our air arm, and that was at a time when, as he knows, we did not possess an air arm … Nonetheless he continues to give advice on strategy, but he does not at all approve of others doing the same thing. When newspapers are advising the bombing of Germany by land in the form of a Second Front he calls it criminal … So we get the noble Lord, Lord Trenchard, advising the Government to bomb Germany from the air and deploring suggestions to the Government to bomb Germany from the land. He has two programmes, has the noble Lord; one is to bomb Germany from the air, and the other is to get after the Admirals.[30]

Beaverbrook was not just content with attacking the Air Staff's bombing policy. He took up the cudgels on behalf of the other services in their differences with the RAF. This brought him into a head-on clash with Frederick Lindemann, who took on the unfamiliar guise of a minister defending the government's performance to Parliament. Beaverbrook demanded that the army be provided with dive bombers for close support, in practice its own air arm. He took up the case of the Royal Navy's Fleet Air Arm, which he claimed was fobbed off with poor-quality aircraft, which was debated in the House of Lords. Here he had a ferocious passage of arms with Lindemann. Lindemann was a leading advocate of the bomber offensive against Germany and opponent of using air power resources to help the navy. He insinuated that Beaverbrook's habitual rant against committees verged on supporting anarchy. This provoked an ill-judged protest from Beaverbrook, which he found himself trying to explain away by blaming a tirade against Lindemann as being due to 'mishearing' him.[31]

*   *   *

The breach between Winston Churchill and Lord Beaverbrook was serious, but it was anything but irrevocable. There was a fair degree of shadowboxing in their relationship over the following year. To begin with, Churchill's tolerance towards his old friend was stretched by Beaverbrook's pro-Soviet antics. He was glad when he was out of the country and even mused that it would be better if he went back to the Soviet Union (permanently?).[32] He was a 'menace' and his speech in the US in favour of a Second Front had been a 'great embarrassment'.[33] Churchill also suspected Beaverbrook of running candidates against the government in by-elections. There is no evidence for this, but the government did lose five by-elections in 1942 and it was a sore point.

Brendan Bracken helped dampen any talk of an open breach between Churchill and Beaverbrook. In January 1943, Bracken was reporting that Beaverbrook regretted having resigned from the government.[34] In April, he denied emphatically to the lobby correspondents that Churchill was at all critical of Beaverbrook's interventions and claimed that he actually enjoyed them as the kind of things that he himself had done before the war.[35] Bracken also urged patience on Beaverbrook, 'to bear with the barking of a number of old Edwardian frumps who have never forgiven you for offending the squirearchy by making Bonar Law leader of the Tory Party'.[36]

As ever, Churchill showed immense tolerance towards Beaverbrook. There is no sign that he spotted, or resented, Beaverbrook's nascent political intrigue against him. He appealed to Beaverbrook to speak in his favour in the House of Lords at Churchill's next military low point when Tobruk fell to the Germans.[37] Had Beaverbrook aspired seriously to hurt Churchill, this would have been the moment, but he chose to support his friend. Within weeks of this, at least according to Beaverbrook, Churchill was trying to lure him back into government.[38] In April 1943, Beaverbrook had proposed to follow up his speech urging an early Second Front with a formal motion in the House of Lords calling for one. Again he was urged to desist and accepted. His reward this time was supposedly the offer of the leadership of the House of Lords and the job of Lord Privy Seal.[39] Nothing came of any invitation to Beaverbrook to rejoin the government, but he was included in the British party for the next summit meeting with Roosevelt even though he had no official position in the government. Once in America, an intricate dance played out in which Roosevelt tried to enlist Beaverbrook as an ally to push for a Second Front that autumn. Beaverbrook did not yield but was still offended when Churchill forbad him to engage in military discussions with the Americans. They had an open quarrel.

* * *

Whilst he was still outside government, Lord Beaverbrook did not neglect his own legend and arranged a debate on the work of the Ministry of Aircraft Production, presumably to defend his own record and to lambast the work of his successors; the government forced it to be held in secret. Beaverbrook was not going to be denied a public platform to broadcast his record at the Ministry of Aircraft Production and he instructed his secretary David Farrer to write an account of his time there, which was written in 1942 and published the next year.[40] With apparent seriousness, he told Farrer that he wanted a 'warts-and-all' production, but when another of his subordinates read a draft of the book and suggested including examples of errors by Beaverbrook, he replied, 'My dear fellow, this is not a work of fiction.'[41] Farrer was forced to include an account of Beaverbrook witnessing personally the massive air raids on London of 14 September 1940, when in fact he had already left for the safety of Cherkley before the German bombers appeared.[42]

34

THE UNASSAILABLE WEAPON

The fear that Nazi Germany had developed some devastating secret weapon to use against Britain was almost as old as the war itself. It went back to a speech that Hitler gave on 19 September 1939, when he spoke in newly conquered Danzig. He castigated the British use of sea power, accusing them of exploiting their supposed unassailability in this area to attack German women and children through the blockade, but he warned them against a complacent belief in their own invulnerability: 'The moment could come very soon when we bring into use a weapon in which we cannot be attacked.'[1]*

Britain was still in thrall to the terror that the Luftwaffe would deliver a 'knock-out blow' to London, so Hitler hit a nerve here. He topped up the effect with similarly vague utterances over the next few days. Neville Chamberlain tasked the Secret Intelligence Service (SIS) with investigating whether anything concrete might lie behind this. This gave an unexpected career fillip to a young scientist, Dr R. V. Jones, who had been taken on by the SIS for just such tasks. He was summoned back from far distant and uninfluential Harrogate, to which his air intelligence section had been moved as part of the grand national evacuation plan. He was transferred to the service's central London headquarters and then to the heart of its codebreaking operation at Bletchley Park. He examined the evidence and concluded that the Foreign Office had been misled by the fact that the German word *Waffe* can mean both weapon and armed service and had caused an unnecessary panic.[2] This was Jones's first step on the way to becoming an authority

---

* The German original is unclear: '*Es könnte sehr schnell der Augenblick kommen, da wir eine Waffe zur Anwendung bringen, in der wir nicht angegriffen werden können.*'

on German secret weapons with a suitably high-level access to raw intelligence data. Within days, he was given a copy of the Oslo report, a unique intelligence gift which gave details of a number of advanced weapons systems under development, which had literally dropped into the letter box of the British embassy. It alerted Jones to the existence of a major German weapons research establishment at Peenemünde on the Baltic, where work was being carried out on remote-controlled rocket-steered anti-ship missiles. The package also contained an electric valve designed for use in proximity fuses for anti-aircraft shells, which was technically far in advance of anything that the British had. Jones seems to have been unaware that proximity fuses were one of Frederick Lindemann's pet projects (and one of his more sensible ideas), so the opportunity was missed to develop a viable system.

German secret terror weapons rather faded into the background as Britain fought for its survival from mid-1940 onwards against more conventional German weapons, albeit innovative, baffling and dangerous systems such as navigational radio beams which led bombers to their targets, but more than two and a half years later, the question once more surfaced. This time it triggered a confused and often acrimonious hunt by the British authorities for what are now called the V-weapons, in which difficulties of personality compounded with straightforward difficulties in obtaining and understanding intelligence on something completely unknown. From the end of 1942, a dribble of reports from the Continent had pointed to German development of rockets.[3] The turning point came with the report of a bugged conversation in March 1943 between two German generals at a specialist prisoner-of-war (PoW) camp for high-value detainees. The intelligence was now strong enough to persuade the British authorities that something serious was afoot. The German generals knew they were being held near London and because they were not hearing very large explosions, they believed that development of the rockets had been delayed:

> But no progress whatsoever can have been made in this rocket business.
> I saw it once with Feldmarschall Brauchitsch … They've got these huge

things which they've brought up here … They've always said that they would go 15kms into the stratosphere … The Major there was full of hope – he said 'Wait until next year and then the fun will start!' There's no limit.[4]

The first practical consequence of Whitehall's new inclination to take the secret weapon threat seriously came from the chiefs of staff who appointed an individual to 'establish the facts'. They were correct to treat the danger as a grave one, deserving top-level treatment, but their decision served to divide the responsibility for finding out what the Germans were up to with malign effects that were to become evident. The individual picked for the task was Duncan Sandys, who had left the army following his injuries and had returned to politics full-time. He had become a junior minister first in the War Office and then in the Ministry of Supply. Sandys's experience with Unrotated Projectiles had given him some grounding in rocket weaponry, but it is hard to believe that this is the full explanation for his selection. The choice of Sandys certainly gives a very strong indication that the matter deserved handling at a very high level. The written record states blandly that Sandys had been chosen by the chiefs of staff but does not refer to his connection to the Prime Minister. The chiefs of staff added another layer of complexity to the debate when they assessed the danger from the rockets to be great enough for a warning to be passed to the Minister of Home Security, who would be responsible for the civil defence measures to respond to a rocket attack.

Sandys's appointment opened the first front in a bureaucratic battle over the V-weapons intelligence that was still being fought (as history) thirty years later. R. V. Jones, who had been handling the flow of intelligence on rockets at SIS, was put out to be bypassed when Lindemann told him that Sandys had been appointed. Neither Lindemann nor Jones were happy: Jones from bureaucratic territoriality, compounded by a belief that it was premature to adopt radical measures; Lindemann because he had decided in advance that there was nothing in the story. He told Jones outright that he was sceptical of the rocket tale, in terms that made it obvious that he disliked Sandys;

a legacy of their squabble over proximity fused Unrotated Projectiles.[5] Once again, Lindemann muddled personalities with facts.

Inevitably, the British knew very little for certain about the German secret weapons programmes and major gaps in their knowledge created a fruitful environment for discussion and argument. One severe disadvantage was that they thought – quite forgivably – that the Germans were only developing one weapon. The British started by believing that the Germans were developing only long-range rockets; these were the A-4 missiles in German classification, later better known as V-2s. The British were unaware that the Germans were also developing pilotless, ramjet-powered precursors to cruise missiles, FZG 76 or Fieseler Fi103, in German terminology later better known as V-1s. Thus, the usual imprecision and uncertainty over agent and PoW intelligence was magnified because the analysts did not know that any piece of information might relate to quite different weapons. The British were further limited in their understanding of German rocket development because their own rocket technology was entirely solid fuel based, whilst the German used liquid fuels. Liquid rocket fuel is far harder to handle but is a much better propellant. Lindemann's methodology of proceeding from purely theoretical bases multiplied the ill-effects of this blind spot. The solid fuel assumption made for an underestimate of potential rocket power at the same time as the British authorities developed a belief – partly a product of worst-case reasoning – that the rocket's warhead weighed ten tons, instead of one ton as was the case. Lindemann estimated the correct weight of the warhead but tried to go even further and broadcast outright scepticism that any rocket would be impractical.[6] Intelligence estimates of rocket performance tried to square circles and the lack of a single convincing and generally acceptable specification for the rocket did not make for productive debate.

Lindemann was never persuaded that the rocket was a real possibility. Most of the second half of 1943 was occupied by a series of rearguard actions that he conducted against believing that the Germans had a rocket. One broadly neutral observer referred to the grinding meetings on the questions as the disputations of Elijah and the prophets of Baal.[7] By then, it was beyond argument that the Germans were developing something and, on any rational calculation, the British should have focused on disrupting their preparations and preparing civil defence measures to cope with a renewed attack on the country from the air. Instead, Lindemann attempted to hijack the debate and subordinate it to a squabble over whether his scientific judgement might ever be in error. R. V. Jones was soon won over to the verdict that Duncan Sandys advanced in a series of papers that the Germans were developing a powerful rocket. He may have felt that by his initial receptivity to Lindemann's views, he had helped choose King Log. He was sufficiently solicitous of his former patron's standing that he tried to open exit routes for him from an increasingly untenable position, but Lindemann was obstinate. When the British recognised that US experience with liquid fuels demonstrated that that rockets might be far more powerful than first thought, Lindemann attacked the work done to estimate the potential danger from rockets in a spiteful and gratuitous fashion. As evidence mounted that the Germans were also developing a pilotless plane, Lindemann understood that this would be a more effective weapon but treated the news of the V-I as hard evidence for his opinion that the Germans were not developing rockets and were simply feeding false stories of work on rockets as a hoax to obscure the V-I. To begin with, Lindemann could muster the support of a small group of distinguished scientists to support him, but gradually they fell by the wayside as evidence of rocket development mounted. In the end, only the faithful Dr Crow, his ally from the days of Unrotated Projectiles, kept the faith. Lindemann claimed during one especially fraught meeting of a Cabinet committee that 'at the end of the war when we know the full story, we shall find that the rocket was a mare's nest'. Once deliberate deception measures are factored into any intelligence debate, the difficulty expands geometrically. There was a steady trickle of stories in the neutral press that autumn which may have fuelled Lindemann's suspicion.

In this fraught atmosphere, Sir Stafford Cripps was charged with examining the evidence in a small committee. By one of the smaller ironies of wartime politics, Cripps had become Minister of Aircraft Production and proved a thorough and efficient manager, in utter contrast to the way that Lord Beaverbrook had created and shaped the job. Cripps's inquiry was to exclude the scientific evidence in a vain attempt to rescue the assessment of the threat from the morass of theory into which it had been dragged by Lindemann, but the terms of reference to which Cripps's committee worked showed how much Lindemann was able to shape the debate.[8] It was set to answer three points on which Lindemann had challenged the rocket theory: the possibility that this was merely a German hoax, the technical obstacles that they faced and the idea that the objects in reconnaissance photographs or agent reports associated with rockets were, in reality, something quite different.

By November 1943, the chiefs of staff decided that the time had come to treat German secret weapons as a classical, albeit uncertain, military problem. The phase when it deserved to be classed as a 'special intelligence' issue had passed. They had already established a small subcommittee to sift evidence, which Sandys thought would lead to duplication and he asked for a ruling as to whether he or the chiefs of staff's Joint Intelligence Committee should be in charge. Here another specimen of intelligence territoriality had the unintended but helpful result of simplifying the discussion. The chiefs of staff ruled against Sandys; firstly, because Ultra codebreaking was increasingly the prime source of intelligence and they wanted to restrict knowledge of this; secondly, because the intelligence target now included pilotless aircraft as well as rockets; lastly and probably decisively, because the question demanded day-to-day attention from both intelligence and operational staffs. Under the new arrangement, the Joint Intelligence Committee, led by the Assistant Chief of the Air Staff, insisted that they should decide whose scientific advice should be sought. They had the services of three scientists already and the squabbles, over which Lindemann had presided in his drive to persuade the world that rockets were a hoax, had clearly exposed the danger of subordinating a discussion of hard intelligence to one about abstract possibilities.

Drawing a line under the intelligence question did not draw a line under the political issue. Beaverbrook sided with Sandys against Lindemann, although his analysis grotesquely distorted the debate.[9] Beaverbrook's excitement at the prospect of a massive assault by V-weapons revived faint hopes that he might be called upon to replay the role he had played in the summer of 1940.[10] The Labour (and London) politician Herbert Morrison was so frightened by the high estimates of the rocket's power that he seriously called for 1 million people to be evacuated.[11] It took R. V. Jones's calmer and more objective assessment of a lower figure for the size of the rocket to offset this panic.[12] Lindemann had undercut the impact of his own calculations by his high-handed, blanket scepticism.

Lindemann could not be swayed, even though it was no longer a direct fight between him and the Prime Minister's despised son-in-law, which greatly softened the personal edge to the argument. He continued to exploit his privileged position to lobby for his view directly to Churchill. He entirely lost his sense of proportion and subjected the Prime Minister to two of his pet hates: prolixity and Latin tags. Forsaking the half-page memo format of Statistical Section advice, he produced two papers running to several pages each. One included (inaccurately) Tacitus's dictum *omne ignotum pro magnifico est* (everything unknown is immense), which is corrected on Churchill's own copy.[13] It is doubtful whether the improvement in Latin grammar would have made it any more palatable to the Prime Minister. Lindemann delved into minute details, recommending what weapons the aircraft attacking secret weapons sites should use and querying the translation of one cover name for the V-1 so as to question whether it was intended to mislead. Potentially more dangerous, Lindemann downplayed the scale of casualties that secret weapons might inflict. Under other circumstances, his view could have gained more widespread traction. Lindemann's blind optimism was flagged to Bruce Lockhart by Brendan Bracken to counteract the fears that were building of a devastating attack.[14] News of the argument spread far enough to reach the ears of 'Chips' Channon, by then an irrelevant backbencher, who inclined towards Lindemann's view out of his habitual complacency.[15] It was only in July 1944, as the Germans were about to launch the V-2, that Lindemann finally swallowed his pride at R. V. Jones's urging. Typically enough, he then begged Jones to reconsider his then estimate for the weight of the weapon and the warhead which was lower than anyone else's. Lindemann's miscalculation over the V-2 was one of the rare occasions when he fell in Churchill's estimation.[16]

When the Germans launched first V-1s and then V-2s against Britain in the summer of 1944, the days of intelligence speculation were over. The authorities knew the nature of the weapons with which they had to deal in conventional civil defence and military terms. Lindemann proved to have been right to warn of the danger of pilotless aircraft and to decry estimates of a ten-ton payload for the rocket, but he had undermined this by his outright scepticism of the rocket's existence. Admittedly, it did call for a degree of imaginativeness to understand that the Germans were willing to invest massive resources to produce a weapon capable of little more than a conventional bomber aircraft. It was Sandys who took the kudos from the intelligence battle which underpinned his next promotion in the government. Sandys had fought off an intrigue by the Conservative Chief Whip to appoint him to chair the party which would have clipped his wings.[17] He had been lobbying to be made Minister of Housing in succession to Lord Portal who was floundering, overwhelmed by the scale of the task that he faced.[18] It was a large brief and a crucial one for the government's post-war position. Not merely did the government need to avoid a repetition of the toxic failure to deliver 'homes fit for heroes' after the First World War but the damage to the housing stock from air attack had to be made good as well. Churchill was nervous at promoting as unpopular a figure as Sandys.[19] Bracken judged that Sandys's ruthlessness might be effective but unlikely to add to his scant stock of popularity.

35

SCIENCE AND GOLD BRAID

Today's image of the RAF in the Second World War is dominated by the Hurricane and Spitfire fighters that held back the Luftwaffe in the Battle of Britain, but this does not reflect the way that the RAF's Air Staff conceived of the service. To them, fighters were a distasteful if not shameful necessity. Craven and cowardly politicians were too foolish to understand that it was an illusion to suppose that trying to shoot down bombers could provide any defence. The RAF's bombing attacks on German cities (the strategic bomber offensive, as it came to be called) were not, as is often supposed, a response to the turn that the war took after the German conquest of Continental Europe in the summer of 1940 which left Britain with no other method of taking offensive action against Germany. In reality, it was inherent in the doctrine propounded by the RAF's founding father, Sir Hugh (later Lord) Trenchard, that future wars would be bombing contests in which the victor would be the nation which could bomb its enemy's country most effectively. Bombers offered not just safety; they could bring victory on their own, unaided by the other services. In the 1920s, that enemy was expected to be France, but after Hitler's rise to power, Germany took over. When Britain began to rearm to protect itself against the Nazi menace, the RAF's strategy was to build up its bomber force. When Stanley Baldwin made his infamous declaration that 'the bomber will always get through', he continued with words which are far less well-known: 'The only defence is in offence, which means that you have to kill more women and children more quickly than the enemy if you want to save yourselves.'[1] Baldwin was simply expressing the judgement of his professional military advisers.

The expansion of the RAF was both qualitative and quantitative. The Air Staff wanted more and better bombers. Winning the bombing war demanded the largest bombers possible. As the RAF rearmed through the 1930s, the size of its bombers rose from aircraft that could hardly be distinguished from fighters. The standard biplane aircraft of the RAF at the start of the decade, the Hawker Hart and its derivatives, was used both as a fighter and as a bomber. These did not look markedly different to the aircraft of the First World War. Aircraft design underwent a revolution in 1936 which culminated in a generation of multi-engine heavy bombers, including the celebrated Avro Lancaster and Handley Page Halifax bombers and their less successful stablemate, the Short Stirling. The goal of the Air Staff was to convert the RAF's entire bombing force to such aircraft. Their moment came in the panic that followed the Munich crisis of September 1938. The national cheque book was opened wide and the Air Staff set in train the huge industrial and military programme designed to give Britain an air force that could confidently be expected to defeat Germany. This was embodied in Scheme M – the last in the alphabet soup of pre-war RAF expansion schemes. Sir Kingsley Wood, the Air Minister, sought immediate orders for 1,750 heavy bombers, half of his total programme. He foresaw a bomber force of 1,280 heavy bombers with almost no medium bombers by the summer of 1941.[2] The Cabinet discussion of the programme had been inconclusive, but Wood was left with the ammunition to insist on immediate orders for 1,450 bombers, less than one fifth fewer than he wanted. He already had a parliamentary commitment to a frontline air force of 1,750 in his pocket and a working programme of 1,352 bombers in April 1940. Months before the Second World War broke out, the RAF was working towards a large all-heavy bomber force. Unless the government explicitly changed policy, all the Air Staff had to do was keep its nerve and the Trenchardian ideal would be achieved.

The expansion of the RAF was backed by political, financial and military will. What was lacking was time. There was one aspect of this scheme that the Air Staff sedulously left out of the discussion and no politician or civil servant succeeded in bringing to the attention of anyone who mattered: it would take several years to complete this programme. None of the 1936 generation bombers would fly until late in 1939. Until they entered service in 1941, Britain would have to depend on inadequate stopgap bombers. The numerical expansion of RAF Bomber Command was a major task in itself. Even the stopgap bombers featured many new and unfamiliar technologies. This programme was going so badly that the commander of Bomber Command came close to declaring his force unfit for combat in the spring of 1939. The political decision taken on the outbreak of war not to attack inland Germany saved the Air Staff from the most embarrassing or catastrophic consequences of the failure of the expansion programme. When Churchill became Prime Minister, he was determined to fight the war to the utmost with every means at his disposal, but the RAF's bombers were barely ready for the fight, let alone to achieve the victory promised by Trenchardian dogma.

Churchill explicitly endorsed the priority that Lord Beaverbrook gave to fighter production at the Ministry of Aircraft Production, given the imminent threat to Britain, but even at this dark moment, he looked further ahead to when Britain would take the offensive against Hitler. In a brutally frank assessment of how limited Britain's options were, he put the RAF's bombers at the centre of his strategy. Having begun his pitch to rearm Britain by promoting Lindemann's heretical notion that it was possible to defend against German bombers, the accidents of war had transformed him into an advocate of bombing:

But when I look round to see how we can win the war, I see there is only one sure path. We have no continental army which can defeat the German military power. The blockade is broken and Hitler has Asia and probably Africa to draw from. Should he be repulsed here or not try invasion, he will recoil eastward, and we shall have nothing to stop him. *But there is one thing that will bring him back and bring him down, and that is an absolutely devastating, exterminating attack by very heavy bombers from this country upon the Nazi homeland* [author's italics]. We must be able to overwhelm them by this means, without which I do not see a way through. We cannot accept any lower aim than air mastery. When can it be obtained?[3]

Churchill adopted the Air Staff's strategy, but he was soon confronted with the weakness of the weapons at his disposal. When he was making plans for a reprisal raid on Berlin should the Germans bomb the centre of London, he wanted to deploy 'a respectable party' of Short Stirling heavy bombers.[4] This was the first of the 1936 bombers to enter service with the RAF and immense hopes had been held out for it as a potential war-winner which survived until well into the conflict. These hopes had yet to be put to the test of battle. In the summer of 1940, the first squadron of Stirlings was only in the process of formation and Churchill had to content himself with a force of Vickers Wellingtons for the mission to Berlin. Moreover, the Stirling proved a severe disappointment in service, but this lay some months in the future.

The RAF's vision of wreaking total destruction from the air was by far overly ambitious and Churchill discovered this from the embarrassingly public source of *The Times* newspaper. It published aerial reconnaissance photographs of the docks at Dunkirk where the Germans were concentrating barges to be used in the invasion of Britain, Operation Sealion. The pictures showed bomb craters and supposedly bomb-damaged barges, but dozens of barges were intact and moored neatly together. Churchill asked Archie Sinclair the glaringly obvious question of why the bombers had not wrought havoc on such an easy target and urged him to improve the effectiveness of the attacks.[5] It was later estimated that bombing had in fact destroyed 10 per cent of the barges.[6] The Trenchardian purists of the RAF, notably 'Bert' Harris, leapt on this as evidence that Bomber Command and not Fighter Command had prevented Operation Sealion from being launched.

Bomber Command was weak, but the RAF's public relations department was highly effective. Just as the Hurricanes and Spitfires of Fighter Command dominate the legend of the RAF in the summer of 1940 today, it has faded from view just how successful the RAF was in persuading the British public that it had achieved prodigies in the battle of France and that, when it was finally unleashed to attack Germany, it was wreaking devastation. Even as sceptical and well-informed an individual as Sir Alec Cadogan, the professional head of the Foreign Office, could write weeks before the Battle of Britain began that 'whatever happens, RAF have covered themselves with imperishable glory'.[7] The reality was otherwise. In their pre-war planning, the Air Staff had formulated a scheme, WA5 (Western Air 5), for an air attack on the Ruhr, which they fondly deluded themselves into thinking would bring Germany to a halt within weeks. The RAF grossly underestimated the difficulties of bombing accurately and then inflicting meaningful damage when it actually manged to find its targets. The Air Staff had blind confidence that the traditional navigational skills of its officers – astral and dead reckoning – were perfectly adequate for the task of finding small targets at night in the centre of Germany, hundreds of miles from their bases.

The Germans had been just as alert as the British to the menace of air attack and a programme was put in place to inform Goebbels of the effects of British bombing and of any risk to civilian morale that it posed. Through the summer, autumn and winter of 1940, it reported regularly, noting the RAF's occasional successes such as one achieved against a BASF chemical plant, but for the most part, the results were derisory. The vast majority of bombs fell harmlessly in open countryside. At one point, all there was to report was that bombs had killed some cows in a field.

At the same time, the Luftwaffe's night Blitz was devastating British cities. The first crucial step in rethinking the way RAF Bomber Command did its work was to understand how the Germans were doing theirs so much better. The Germans often had a far easier navigational task because the coastal location of many British cities gave visual markers to the attackers, but even inland targets such as Birmingham and, most grievously, Coventry were not spared. The Luftwaffe had the advantage in its night attacks on Britain of radio navigation aids: the *X-Gerät* system of radio beams that intersected over the target area. Their bombers followed one beam until it crossed with the other and they knew that they could drop their bombs. The Germans also had a dedicated, specialist target marking unit, KG 100, which used the beams. The British had been fully aware of this threat since the summer of 1940 and thanks to the efforts of Frederick Lindemann, it was receiving top-level attention. One of his young scientific protégés, Dr R. V. Jones, was working in the air intelligence section of the Secret Intelligence Service (SIS) and had picked up early indications that the Germans were about to deploy the system. Lindemann alerted Churchill to this and he ordered a thorough investigation after a meeting at Downing Street when Jones set out the evidence. Jones later mused that it was by good fortune that he had told Lindemann first and not Henry Tizard, who was more obviously in his chain of command. Tizard was reticent if not downright sceptical at the Downing Street meeting, apparently for no better reason than the fact that it was Lindemann who had raised the matter. Jones imagined that Lindemann would have been the sceptic if the positions had been reversed, which could well have changed the outcome. The venomous personal feud at the heart of British scientific preparations for battle might have done active harm. Tizard did not enjoy a fraction of Lindemann's influence on the Prime Minister. Jones was well aware how much this counted for and he would have wielded Churchill's authority had an uncooperative staff officer who refused to allow RAF flights to track the beams not relented. As it was, the British instituted a programme of research and countermeasures that helped to blunt the Germans' advantage. These were not infallible and Coventry was bombed with the aid of *X-Gerät*, albeit assisted by strong moonlight under clear skies. Lindemann even imagined that it would be possible to sow fields of his and Churchill's cherished aerial mines (then not yet developed) in the path of German bombers using their own beams.[8]

There is no sign that the Germans' successful use of beams spurred the RAF to attempt to imitate them in the short term. Whilst Fighter Command had been avid for any technical assistance that science could give it almost from its inception in 1936, Bomber Command had brusquely rejected the suggestion from Sir Henry Tizard in 1938 that science could help it in its work.[9] In fact, 'Bert' Harris, before he commanded Bomber Command but already an influential figure, showed near delusional confidence in the RAF's ability to navigate by traditional methods when he decried attempts to interfere with German navigation beams:

> We use no beams ourselves but we bomb just as successfully as the Germans bomb, deep into Germany … They are simply aids to navigation, and it is within our experience that such aids are not indispensable to the successful prosecution of bombing expeditions. I would go further and say that they are not even really useful.[10]

Even well into the war, senior officers sniffed at electronic methods, dismissed as 'adventitious aids'.[11]

The next stage in the reform was for the British – certainly Churchill and his circle and probably the RAF Air Staff as well – to discover how miserably Bomber Command was performing. Quite how it came to be known that the RAF's bombing was so inaccurate is unclear. According to one account, a member of Lindemann's Statistical Section happened to be dining at Medmenham, the home of photographic interpretation, and saw reconnaissance coverage of the damage inflicted by RAF raids or, rather, the lack of it.[12] It was learned from a Czech source that a much-vaunted RAF raid on the Škoda arms factory in Pilsen had got no nearer than fifty miles of the target.[13] Lindemann despatched David Bensusan-Butt, one of his economists, to Bomber Command headquarters to investigate further. Sir Charles Portal and the man who succeeded him at Bomber Command, Richard Peirse, were in a weak position as they had conspicuously failed to defeat Germany by bombing, whilst the Luftwaffe was achieving so much, but the forensic investigation by an outside agency of how one of the armed services was performing its job was almost unprecedented. It is inconceivable that this was done without the authority of the Prime Minister. Butt spent an uncomfortable week examining photographs taken by RAF bombers carrying out raids. Perhaps most embarrassingly for the Air Staff, the hard evidence of the RAF's failure was already to hand in the service's files. Butt undertook a detailed statistical analysis. His report delivered in August 1941 made devastating reading. Of those aircraft which were recorded as attacking their targets, only one in three sorties got within five miles; over Germany as a whole, one quarter; and over the Ruhr, one tenth.[14] The results over French ports were far better at two thirds, which shows the relative ease of finding coastal targets. Less than one third of all sorties reached within five miles. For over one year, the efforts of Bomber Command had been nearly wasted. The study is generally called the Butt report but this masks the fact that without Lindemann's standing with Churchill, it would have been impossible.

It is a register of just how high Lindemann stood in the pecking order that he was able to discuss Butt's report personally with both Sir 'Peter' Portal, the chief of the Air Staff, and Peirse, head of Bomber Command. They had some reservations about the reliability of Butt's report but had to accept its core conclusion: that the RAF's bombing accuracy and navigation desperately needed to improve.[15] Lindemann made a number of proposals as to how this might be achieved. The British already had the design for a radio navigation system that had emerged from work at Robert Watson-Watt's radar organisation development and not through any active wish of the RAF's military command. The Gee system of radio navigation, first conceived in 1938 and under live test since the summer of 1940, was to be driven forwards. Lindemann believed that 200 bombers could be fitted with Gee by the end of November and wanted it to be used operationally as soon as 100 sets were available and to accept the risk that the Germans would find countermeasures. He recommended that it would be used by special 'fire-raising' squadrons, which should be created on the pattern of the Luftwaffe's KG 100 with which he was familiar. Further ahead, air-to-surface radar, as had been created for naval use, should be adapted to give ground-following capacity to bombers. The RAF had already anticipated another piece of advice from Lindemann and in September 1941 had set up an operational research group for Bomber Command.

Operational research applied scientific study of data to planning military operations and had already been in use at RAF Fighter and Coastal Commands for over a year. Churchill endorsed Lindemann's prescription to Portal: 'This is a most serious paper, and seems to require your most urgent attention. I await your proposals for action.'[16] Along with the battle of the beams, the Butt report has gone down in legend as one of Lindemann's most important contributions to the war effort. The normally sceptical official history of the strategic bomber offensive for once is hearty in its praise: 'By showing the need for the development of scientific aids to navigation, the scientific study of navigation, and the development of revolutionary tactics, the Butt investigation, carried out under the auspices of Lord Cherwell, had rendered a service to Bomber Command which was second to none.'[17]

The official historians Sir Charles Kingsley Webster and Noble Frankland are echoed by Sir Maurice Dean, one of the leading civil servants in the Air Ministry: 'For his part in these events Lindemann deserves the gratitude of Bomber Command, the Royal Air Force and of Britain.'[18]

Churchill's endorsement had fallen well short, though, of a direct instruction to implement Lindemann's recommendations. Over the months that followed, he accepted Portal's arguments for delaying the introduction of Gee. Churchill was looking at a far bigger picture. In November 1941, Lindemann was still complaining to Churchill of the inaccuracy of the RAF's night bombing and the need to develop pathfinder tactics.[19] This all did something to shake the RAF out of its complacency, but concrete results took some time to come. Portal wanted to reserve his judgement on when and how to roll out Gee.[20] He was confronted not merely by German technological superiority but by the still slow progress that the RAF was making in expanding Bomber Command. Gee was not widely deployed until the middle of 1942. Similarly, the RAF only introduced its own Pathfinder squadrons in the summer of 1942.

As the battle of the beams against the Germans made all too obvious, the advantage conferred by such techniques could only last a relatively brief time. Bomber Command was simply in no state to make effective use of Gee. The emergency switch in priority towards fighters in the summer of 1940 had held back progress towards the heavy bomber force of more than 1,000 aircraft which had been the RAF's target since late 1938. Bomber Command could deploy no more than a few hundred medium bombers. Worse, the Germans were starting to get the measure of the attackers. In the first eighteen days of August 1941, as Butt's report was being written, the RAF lost 107 bombers over Germany, to the distress of the War Cabinet. Things were to get worse: one night in November 1941, a force of 267 aircraft was sent to attack Germany; thirty-seven failed to return, an unsustainable loss rate of 14 per cent. Fighter operations over France were also costly. Churchill minuted Sinclair and Portal: 'Losses which are acceptable in a battle or for some decisive military objective ought not to be incurred merely as a matter of routine ... It is now the duty of both Fighter and Bomber Command to regather their strength for the spring.'[21]

Churchill's instructions were embodied in what came to be known as the conservation directive:

> The War Cabinet ... have stressed the necessity for conserving our resources in order to build a strong force to be available by the spring of next year ...
>
> It was considered undesirable ... that attacks should be pressed unduly especially if weather conditions were unfavourable or if aircraft were likely to be exposed to extreme hazard.[22]

Lindemann had established the principle that the RAF had to accept external oversight of its bombing operations, but the force that was to benefit from this was simply not ready. Far from being a mighty weapon that the British government could use against Germany at any moment, the RAF's striking force needed three years of war before it could even be deployed to any useful effect.

36

THE SIEGE OF
ADASTRAL HOUSE

The RAF's bomber offensive against Germany is one of the most hotly contested elements of Britain's war effort. Much of the debate touches on the ethical dimension: whether the death and suffering inflicted on German civilians can be justified. This was not, though, a dimension that engaged anyone responsible for mounting the offensive or shaping its execution during wartime. The decision-makers focused exclusively on the military questions of avoiding defeat by Germany and of defeating Germany. Churchill himself recognised that morality was not constant and in 1944 stated (not quite accurately) that it had shifted with regard to bombing towns, when he urged the Chiefs of Staff to consider the use of poison gas:

> It is absurd to consider morality on this topic … In the last war the bombing of open cities was regarded as forbidden. Now everybody does it as a matter of course. It is simply a question of fashion changing as she does between long and short skirts of women.[1]

The ethical debate over bombing cities obscures the military one as to whether it would have achieved more by devoting economic resources to other types of weapons. Professor David Edgerton stands at one extreme of the debate here:

> The bulk of aircraft production effort was devoted to strategic bombers, and these failed to bring about the surrender of Germany.

Strategic bombing, while immensely destructive of human life and of buildings, did not destroy civilian morale, or machinery, or sufficient Germans to make a significant difference to war production until the end of the war. Rational, industrial and technological warfare need not work; strategic bombing represented a massive misallocation of resources.[2]

At the start of the war, an absolute commitment to the bombing offensive had been hard-wired into British strategy. The question first arose in the lower ranks of planners at the Ministry of Aircraft Production at the end of 1941, after the entry of the USSR and the USA into the war had radically changed the military and industrial shape of the conflict. One of their number was Alec Cairncross, who went on to be knighted for distinguished work as an economist in academia and public service.

We were by no means happy about the heavy bomber programme since it seemed to us that with America as our ally we ought to change our production programme quite radically in other directions, leaving the production of heavy bombers largely to the United States and concentrating on landing craft, tanks, fighters and other equipment needed for an invasion of Europe …

At the end of 1941 the production of heavy bombers was still quite limited: less than 500 were produced in that year and production had yet to exceed 60 per month. But already the programme envisaged an expansion to over 600 heavy bombers per month by the end of 1943, a figure well above the maximum rate ever reached: only in one month – March 1944 – did output ever exceed 500. Even so, the heavy bomber programme was scheduled to absorb an increasing proportion of the resources at the disposal of the MAP and to account for nearly half the total. So long as this was so, the shape of the aircraft programme was set for the rest of the war and only marginal changes were possible after December 1941.[3]

Cairncross's opinion was echoed by Ely Devons, another government economist:

> The expanded heavy bomber programme was put into effect in the autumn of 1941, when the strategy it implied seemed to give the only possible hope of the United Kingdom defeating Germany on her own. What is astonishing is that this strategy was not reconsidered when the United States entered the war and when it was clear that the Soviet Union would not be overwhelmed 'in a matter of weeks'. Early in 1942 was the crucial period. It was then not too late to change production plans; the inordinate cost of the bomber programme was already apparent, both in its command over economic resources and in depriving other branches of the services of urgently needed aircraft; the technical effectiveness of the heavy bomber in damaging the enemy's productive capacity was beginning to be questioned. But heavy bombing was the sacred cow of British strategy, and the programme went on virtually without question.[4]

As with so much thinking in the realm of economics, Cairncross and Devons were proceeding from a world in which abstract calculation on a (newly) blank sheet of paper are what matter. The political realities of warfare are another. The most powerful imperative was to keep the USSR fighting. Lindemann calculated that this was the most efficient way to kill Germans.[5] No one in Whitehall was under any illusion that Stalin would not strike a separate peace with Hitler if it suited his interests. Closer to the considerations that weighed on Churchill and top-level decision-makers, one of Lindemann's team put his finger on what mattered:

> But more help [than shipping supplies to the USSR] was required and Britain could provide important indirect assistance by attacking the enemy from the air. Thus the case for the bomber offensive was *strengthened* rather than weakened when the Soviet Union was forced

into the war. For in this way, the danger of a Russian defeat or of a separate peace, might be somewhat reduced.[6]

As we have seen, though, in the second half of 1941, Bomber Command was facing a series of crises. It was falling so far behind the results that would have justified Britain's huge investment in it that urgent measures were required. Its difficulties, combined with the dramatic changes in the war itself, set the stage for a debate that went to the heart of the RAF's mission.

The response of the RAF to the failure of its bombing campaign in the year since it was unleashed on Germany had been to ask for a colossal increase in its resources, which was underpinned by an extraordinary volte-face by the other armed services. Following the German attack on the Soviet Union, the chiefs of staff had in July 1941 given the heavy bomber first claim on Britain's resources. The First Sea Lord and the Chief of the Imperial General Staff had put their signatures to a document that would have gladdened the hearts of Trenchard and Newall, who had waged a battle in the final months of peace to elevate the RAF to the status of Britain's premier armed service. The bomber was the 'new weapon in which we must principally depend for the destruction of German economic life and morale'.[7] The only limit on the size of the bomber force would be 'operational difficulties in the United Kingdom'. Any thought that the RAF would be attacking specific industrial plants or infrastructure was quietly forgotten in a new plan that featured the complete destruction of forty-three towns in Germany.[8] The Air Staff estimated that this work would require a force of 4,000 heavy bombers, more than double the total envisaged in Scheme M of 1938. Once Bomber Command had this strength, Portal promised Churchill that Germany could be broken within six months. The 4,000-bomber force was christened 'Target Force E'. Just as Newall and his colleagues had ignored the question of how long it would take to implement Scheme M, Portal was willing to give a timescale for the destruction of Germany but not for creating Force E. At that stage, Bomber Command had approximately 500 medium bombers and a handful of heavies; the industrial plans laid down after the partial adoption of Scheme M had been for rather more than 1,000 heavy bombers. In effect, the Air Staff assumed that Britain could be transformed into a factory complex for heavy bombers. How long this might take and what effect it would have on the rest of the armed forces was left out of the question.

When the rhetoric is peeled away, Force E was never a practical proposition. Even a convinced Trenchardian and personal disciple of the great man himself, Air Marshal John Slessor, then in command of Bomber Command 5 Group, was appalled. He looked at Force E in terms of the trained manpower which it implied; he dismissed it to the head of Bomber Command as 'an opium-smoker's dream'.[9] The First Sea Lord calculated that Force E would increase Britain's need to import aviation fuel more than threefold which could only be achieved by an immense increase in US production of tanker ships.[10] Force E never came close to being adopted as a working programme, but it shaped the debate over grand strategy. It put down a marker that the RAF's bombing strategy held primacy over all other means of waging war. The Air Staff and its allies, including Lindemann, in practice argued that the RAF could never have too much. Lindemann verged on Trenchardian faith in the bombers' ability to win the war, 'if only we could put two or three times as many bombs into Germany as we do at present, we could finish the war quite quickly but [for] the intense jealousy of the circles bound up with anti-U-boat warfare'.[11] They had won the initiative; the other services had no alternative formula for beating Germany outright and so were reduced to sniping from the flanks. Thus was created a two-tier debate: an abstract one over top-level strategy which the bombing lobby won consistently and the mundane one of detailed allocation of men and materials. Both were conducted with comparable ferocity in the hidden parliament of Whitehall which occasionally spilled over into the more visible parliaments of Westminster and public discussion.

It fell, of course, to Churchill himself to make the ultimate choice, but he was prey to ambiguity. On the one hand, he was now fully aware of the inaccuracy of Bomber Command's bombing revealed by the Butt report. He explicitly turned down Portal's claim on behalf of Bomber Command to be able to win the war on its own, but on the other, he knew that Britain was already committed to a huge investment in heavy bombers and was not going to draw back from this:

> We all hope that the Air offensive against Germany will realise the expectations of the Air Staff. Everything is being done to create the Bombing force desired on the largest possible scale, and there is no intention of changing this policy. I deprecate, however, placing unbounded confidence in this means of attack ... Even if all the towns in Germany are rendered uninhabitable, it does not follow that the military control would be weakened or even that war industry could not be carried on.[12]

Lindemann seems to have given as little thought as the air marshals to the practicalities of creating Force E, despite his section's slant towards economics. Even two years later, when the scheme had succumbed to the realities of wartime economics, he bemoaned the fact that 'our promised 4,000 heavy bomber frontline strength by the middle of 1943 has dwindled to 864 today'.[13]

Lindemann did, though, recognise that a rather more objective and quantified basis was needed to justify such a drastic commitment of Britain's war resources than the simplistic Trenchardian faith that bombing on its own could destroy German morale. One Saturday evening in August 1941, he discussed this point with Solly Zuckerman in the senior common room of Christ Church.[14] Zuckerman was a zoologist at Oxford who had been drafted into the war effort to study the physiological effect of bombs on the human body and graduated onto wider topics related to bombing. Zuckerman proposed to Lindemann a study of the overall effects of German bombing on British cities as a starting point. He suggested the cities of Birmingham and Hull as objects for the study, as they were typical industrial and port cities, respectively. The 'Bomb Census' had already garnered comprehensive data on the scale of the attacks that Britain had suffered. Lindemann lent his support to the plan and this opened a trove of data to Zuckerman and his assistants which was otherwise closed. Their work took some months and ran into 1942, but Zuckerman kept Lindemann up to date with information as it emerged.

Zuckerman's work had been commissioned at a relatively low level in the hierarchy and he had not delivered it when the RAF set down what it was going to do with the massive bomber force that it had been building up through the winter of 1941/42. In February 1942, the Air Staff issued a directive that superseded the 'conservation directive': 'The primary object of your operations should now be focussed on the morale of the enemy civilian population and, in particular, of the industrial workers.'[15] This came to be known as the area bombing directive and served as the mandate for the campaign of bombing German cities for the rest of the war. It listed nineteen of Germany's largest cities as 'primary industrial areas'. Although the directive listed specific industrial targets, Portal separately ordered that the aiming points were to be the built-up areas of the cities and not these locations.

The dark days of early 1942, when the British Empire reeled under a series of body blows, invited a rethink of strategy. The area bombing directive triggered the first serious bureaucratic challenge to the primacy of the bomber. The first shot was fired from a predictable quarter – the Royal Navy – which appears to have begun to rue its endorsement of the chiefs of staff report. The admirals seem to have been responding to a new directive to Bomber Command. This came close to embodying the scheme for the wholesale destruction of German cities, which revived the plan from the previous summer to attack German morale. The First Sea Lord, Sir Dudley Pound, did not challenge the strategy of the directive but countered with long shopping lists of RAF squadrons which he wanted transferred to support naval campaigns. The outbreak of war with Japan had expanded the navy's tasks immensely and the assault by U-boats on British shipping had received a huge boost from massive swings in German favour in the codebreaking war.[16] Pound supported his bid for resources in the first sentence of one of his memos: 'If we lose the war at sea, we lose the war.'[17] The Air Staff did not challenge this contention but argued weakly that the RAF could make a more effective contribution to the sea battle by bombing German industry. The strategic choice facing Churchill boiled down to warding off imminent and certain defeat or gambling on uncertain and distant victory.

The next blow to be delivered to the unquestioning faith in the bombing strategy came from a politician. Sir Stafford Cripps, the extreme left-winger, had returned from Moscow with an entirely spurious reputation as the man who had brought Stalin into the war on Britain's side, which he aimed to parlay into solid political influence. He had been brought into the War Cabinet with the non-departmental job of Lord Privy Seal. Cripps questioned

> policy as to the continued use of heavy bombers and the bombing of Germany ... The continued devotion of a considerable part of our effort to the building-up of this bombing force is the best use that we can make of our resources. It is obviously a matter which it is almost impossible to debate in public, but, if I may, I would remind the House that this policy was initiated at a time when we were fighting alone against the combined forces of Germany and Italy, and it then seemed that it was the most effective way in which we, acting alone, could take the initiative against the enemy. Since that time we have had an enormous access of support from the Russian Armies, who, according to the latest news, have had yet another victory over the Germans, and also from the great potential strength of the United States of America. Naturally, in such circumstances, the original policy has come under review and is, indeed, kept constantly under review. I can assure the House that the Government are fully aware of the other uses to which our resources could be put, and the moment they arrive at a decision that the circumstances warrant a change, a change in policy will be made.[18]

Cripps's dubious assertion that the government was seriously rethinking strategy threw the Air Staff into panic.

The hearts of the bombing lobby were then chilled by a minute from Churchill which implied he was getting bored by being bombarded with the Trenchardian doctrine in which he did not believe. He appeared to be lending an ear to the critics of bombing and was even contemplating the heresy of amputating an integral part of the RAF to help in the sea war:

> You need not argue the value of bombing Germany, because I have my own opinion about that, namely, that it is not decisive, but better than doing nothing, and indeed is a formidable method of injuring the enemy …
>
> I hope you realise how very widely the existing policy of the Air Ministry is challenged by opinion. For instance, the Archbishop of Canterbury yesterday spoke to me for half an hour at luncheon on the failure of high-level bombing. He seemed to know a great deal about it, and said these were the opinions he heard on every side in the elevated circles in which he moves …
>
> There are also great complaints that the Navy has not been given a fair share of aircraft, both fighters and torpedo-bombers, and that it has been overlain by the Air Ministry …
>
> The question of putting Coastal Command under the Admiralty is one which will have to be faced in the near future.[19]

Lindemann pitched in on behalf of the Trenchardian lobby with a brief document that came to acquire the status of the scientific manifesto that underlay the RAF's area bombing strategy. Ostensibly, it drew on Zuckerman's work:

> The following seems a simple method of estimating what we could do by bombing Germany:
>
> Careful analysis of the effects of raids on Birmingham, Hull and elsewhere have shown that, on average, 1 ton of bombs dropped on a built-up area demolishes 20–40 dwellings and turns 100–200 people out of house and home.

We know from our experience that we can count on nearly 14 operational sorties per bomber produced. The average lift of the bombers we are going to produce over the next 15 months will be about 3 tons. It follows that each of these bombers will in its lifetime drop about 40 tons of bombs. If these are dropped on built-up areas they will make 4,000–8,000 people homeless.

In 1938 over 22 millions of Germans lived in 58 towns of over 100,000 inhabitants, which, with modern equipment, should be easy to find and hit. Our forecast output of heavy bombers (including Wellingtons) between now and the middle of 1943 is about 10,000. If even half the total load of 10,000 bombers were dropped on the built-up areas of these 58 German towns the great majority of their inhabitants (about one third of the German population) would be turned out of house and home.

Investigation seems to show that having one's home demolished is most damaging to morale. People seem to mind it more than having their friends or even relatives killed. At Hull signs of strain were evident, though only one tenth of the houses were demolished. On the above figures we should be able to do ten times as much harm on each of the 58 principal German towns. There seems little doubt that this would break the spirit of the people.

Our calculation assumes, of course, that we really get one-half of our bombs into built-up areas. On the other hand, no account is taken of the large promised American production (6,000 heavy bombers in the period in question). Nor has regard been paid to the inevitable damage to factories, communications etc. in these towns and the damage by fire, probably accentuated by breakdown of public services.[20]

Even a cursory reading shows the limitations of Lindemann's paper. It is no more than a crude hypothetical model. Nonetheless, it was widely circulated and weighed heavily in the debate over bombing. Seemingly, Lindemann's eminence as a scientist and his closeness to the Prime Minister obscured its flaws. Predictably enough, Sinclair and Portal found this piece of simplistic arithmetical computation 'simple, clear and convincing', although they did not commit themselves to being able to deliver the scenario it embodied. 'Bert' Harris's strategy for Bomber Command consisted of destroying a list of German cities. Equally predictably, Tizard challenged Lindemann on the optimism of his assumptions and a cavalier approach to aircraft production figures. In his replies, Lindemann fell back on a claim that his paper had been intended to say more than the RAF might be able to inflict a great deal of damage on German cities.

Professor Blackett, another government scientist, also looked at Lindemann's paper and concluded that his estimate of what could be achieved was too high by a factor of six.[21] Neither Tizard nor Blackett questioned the vital proposition at the heart of Lindemann's memo and the Trenchardian doctrine itself, that it would be possible to destroy German morale by bombing. Lindemann also escaped unscathed from flagrantly distorting the conclusion from the work of Zuckerman and his colleagues, which he presented as firm evidence. Zuckerman's report demonstrated the exact opposite of Lindemann's claim that bombing could break morale:

THERE IS NO EVIDENCE OF BREAKDOWN OF MORALE FOR THE INTENSITIES OF THE RAIDS EXPERIENCED BY HULL OR BIRMINGHAM.

In neither town was there any evidence of panic resulting either from a series of raids or from a single raid. The situation in Hull has been somewhat obscured, from this point of view, by the occurrence of trekking, which was made possible by the availability of road transport and which was much publicized as a sign of breaking morale, but which in fact can be fairly regarded as a considered response to the situation. In both towns actual raids were, of course, associated with a degree of alarm and anxiety, which cannot in the circumstances be regarded as abnormal, and which in no instance was sufficient to provoke mass anti-social behaviour. There was no measurable effect on the health of either town.[22]

Zuckerman was not aware at the time of Lindemann's distortion; his report was not released until after Lindemann's paper. It only appears to have been examined at low level in the Air Ministry and there is no sign that it reached the exalted spheres of serious decision-making. Tizard saw a copy, but there is no sign that he passed on Zuckerman's verdict that German bombing did not break the morale of Birmingham or Hull. Lindemann's note did not break the deadlock in the debate over the value of bombing. Churchill was again driven to put the question into the hands of Justice Sir John Singleton, just as he had the debate over the estimated strength of the Luftwaffe in late 1940. Singleton's report was entirely inconclusive, but by the time that it appeared, events had moved on.

The turning point for the bombing campaign in Germany came whilst this debate was taking place. The new chief of Bomber Command, Air Marshal Arthur 'Bert' Harris, finally brought some conspicuous results to demonstrate what his force was capable of rather than a stream of hollow press releases. He was ruthless, dynamic and efficient, an unabashedly convinced Trenchardian. Not merely did he believe that bombing could break German morale and win the war but any other form of activity was a waste of energy and resource. Churchill admired Harris's dynamism and commitment to offensive action, but there is no sign that he was swayed by his blind faith in bombing. Harris's first completely successful operation was an attack on the Renault vehicle and weapons factory at Billancourt near Paris. Perversely enough, Harris labelled the operation as anathema on two scores on which it diverged from his prescription for victorious bombing, a 'diversion from the main offensive against Germany but also a precision attack on a key factory'.[23] Billancourt demonstrated to the Cabinet that new target-making techniques could be effective. Far more in line with Harris's view of how the campaign ought to be conducted were raids on the northern cities of Lübeck and Rostock. They were ports and were easy to find; they had many mediaeval timber buildings which were easy to set on fire. The most spectacular of Harris's early victories was Operation Millennium, the 1,000-bomber raid

on Cologne in May 1942. He recognised the importance of showman-
ship in the political environment surrounding the bombing debate
and pulled together the number of aircraft he needed to achieve the
headline force. The city was devastated at the cost of sixty of the attacking bombers.

Harris's achievements went beyond their purely military contribution to the war effort. The bombing of Germany was Britain's most
powerful, early contribution to attacking Nazi Germany directly and
Brendan Bracken understood the powerful propaganda appeal to pat-
riotism in his capacity as Minister of Information. He detected the
fillip to public morale given by the success of Harris's operations when
he was asked to report on home front sentiment which had improved
markedly since the early part of 1942:

> The scale and success of the RAF raids on Cologne and Essen had, of
> course, a profound effect in the stimulation of public confidence ...
> I think that no small part in the great public satisfaction at the recent
> RAF raids was due to the consciousness that they were a blow struck
> directly by this country with its own material and its own forces.
> There is much feeling that the public have been asked for too long to
> admire Russian resistance, American production and Empire fighting
> qualities.[24]

Like many people, Bracken took a more visceral pleasure in the results
of Harris's campaign. He relished the image of the mediaeval timber
houses of Nuremberg, spiritual capital of Nazism, being destroyed by
British bombs.[25] It was a pleasure that he shared with Lindemann,
who also detested the German people and who was disappointed that
the atom bomb was not ready in time to be dropped on Germany.[26]
In a more acerbic mood, Bracken described bombing Germany as 'a
kind of adult educational movement'.[27]

The bombing of Germany gave the British something with which
to counter the Soviet insistence that they were bearing the full brunt of
the war against Germany. Even in the citadel of Trenchardian dogma,

RAF Bomber Command, it was recognised that the bomber offensive against Germany provided ammunition against the call for the Second Front. Gossip there even held that Bert Harris maintained a third copy of his 'Blue Book' of photographs showing air raid damage to Germany in the hands of a wing commander stationed in Moscow, where it could be used to show Stalin how much work the British bombers were doing against the Germans.[28]

* * *

Frederick Lindemann bears a large share of the responsibility for a decision over a technological strategy that left exposed Bomber Command aircraft to the full force of German defences for a year. In common with many scientists, Lindemann had identified the danger that radar was vulnerable to interference by electronic means which could reduce or eliminate its effectiveness of detecting hostile aircraft. He was fully alert to the potential of a crude means of countering radar that had been developed in the winter of 1941/42. This used strips of aluminium foil that could be dropped by aircraft across German radar transmissions, creating a multitude of spurious echoes swamping the echoes produced by authentic bombers. The debate over whether to put this technique into use fell victim to the fact that the mechanism for fighting the scientific war and making sound military use of innovations had lagged far behind the pace at which these innovations were being made. Decisions were shaped by a legacy of the pre-war obsessive fear of disclosing to the Germans even obvious techniques and by the choices and opinions of commanders, who were not necessarily scientifically trained or briefed. A number of active programmes were in hand to defeat German radar, but Lindemann came down against using what came to be known as Windows and, in the American usage, chaff, which is still in use today. He quite correctly pointed out that Windows might be used against British airborne radar and, in yet another demonstration of his blind enthusiasm for his pet weaponry, against the wholly ineffective Turbinlite airborne searchlight, that 'the two great advantages we hold against the enemy in Night Air Defence are [Airborne Interception] and Turbinlite. It seems to be common ground that these will suffer seriously ... [if the Germans deploy Windows].'[29] Lindemann's reasoning was also flawed because he appeared to share the common and erroneous belief in the RAF that the Germans did not have good airborne radar themselves. He pooh-poohed a piece of intelligence pointing to German knowledge of the, ultimately, obvious and uncomplicated nature of Windows. The discussion missed an elementary military equation: the Luftwaffe no longer had the resources to mount a serious attack on Britain, whilst the British ability to execute its strategy of bombing Germany was growing to awesome proportions; technological choices should have given far greater weight to the needs of the attacker. The debate took an entirely surreal turn with the claim that the Germans would be able to paralyse British radar with one ton of Windows whilst the British would need eighty-four tons, or perhaps three times that amount, to achieve anything against the German system.[30] Curiously, the commander of Bomber Command, Harris, came down on Lindemann's side. The debate finally swung in favour of using Windows because of the unexpected support of Sir Trafford Leigh-Mallory, head of Fighter Command, who would have borne the responsibility if the Germans had used the system to defeat British air defences.[31] Operational use was delayed until after the invasion of Sicily in July 1943 on the basis of no consideration that has come down to us, but Windows was finally used to devastating effect in the raids on Hamburg. However, the campaign against the Ruhr was fought without the benefit.

Lindemann came down heavily on the side of Bomber Command in a debate that combined technology, operational security and grand strategic priorities. One of Britain's most valuable developments was short-wave (10cm) radar, which offered far better performance than long-wave radar and could be used equally well in locating surfaced U-boats (under the name ASV) and navigating bombers across ground terrain (under the name H2S). Its key component was a near indestructible cavity magnetron, so use over enemy territory meant that one would inevitably fall into German hands in a bomber that was shot down, alerting them to the technology.[32] The Admiralty thus argued that 10cm radar should only be used over sea, so as to preserve security. Lindemann argued that the potential value of 10cm to the war against U-boats was exaggerated, whilst 'H2S would make a big contribution to our bomber offensive'.[33] Churchill ruled in favour of Bomber Command. Lindemann and Sir Philip Joubert, the head of RAF Coastal Command, went on to argue bitterly over the priority in allocating 10cm radar.[34]

Lindemann supported the Bomber Command position on the other great practical debate between the maritime and the Trenchardian factions: whether to use aircraft to bomb Germany or to patrol the Bay of Biscay. His old arch-foe Sir Henrry Tizard had advocated moving squadrons from Bomber to Coastal Command for use over the bay.[35] Lindemann was alerted that something dubious was afoot: 'Certain people are constantly urging that yet more squadrons should be transferred from Bomber Command to Coastal Command.'[36] Instead, Lindemann believed that Coastal Command should simply use its aircraft more intensively on the basis of a slanted interpretation of statistics. Coastal Command had to content itself with the loan of two squadrons of obsolescent Whitley bombers.

With perfect hindsight, Lindemann's rejection of Admiralty security concerns over the use of 10cm radar over Germany places him unintentionally on the right side of a key aspect of the Battle of the Atlantic. Any indication that the Allies possessed efficient means of detecting U-boats drew the Germans' eyes away from the Allies' true and decisive advantage in the intelligence war of breaking their cyphers. In the event, they made no connection between H2S and ASV, but given their constant suspicion that the Allies were able to find U-boats on the surface through some technological advance, they would probably have found an explanation for Allied ability to locate U-boats in 10cm radar.

Lindemann was firmly Harris's ally in arguing for a strategy aiming to destroy German homes, but he found himself on the opposite side of a furious battle fought within the RAF itself. It will be remembered that one of Lindemann's conclusions after the Butt report was that the RAF should follow the German example and establish a dedicated target-finding and marking unit on the model of KG 100. This scheme was espoused by enthusiasm by the Air Ministry, notably the youthful Director of Bombing Operations Group Captain Bufton, who promoted it directly to Harris. One of the quirks of the RAF's organisation was that comparatively junior officers at the Air Ministry were able to press their views on far more senior commanders of operational units; Hugh Dowding had suffered from this phenomenon at Fighter Command on a number of issues. Harris objected violently on the grounds that he believed that all his crews were equally competent as navigators and that anything that smacked of creating an elite force would hurt the morale of crews not chosen. Behind the scenes, Lindemann deployed all his influence to drive through the proposal.[37] The Singleton report failed to give any guidance of the effects of bombing but did support Bufton. It reported his interviews with two experienced operational officers, both of whom strongly favoured a specialist target-finding unit. Still, Harris resisted the creation of a Pathfinder force using every possible means, but ultimately, the views of Lindemann and Bufton prevailed. Churchill gave a direct order to set up a specialist unit for the task.[38] The Pathfinders were established, soon becoming a highly effective, integral part of Bomber Command. There is no sign that morale elsewhere was at all affected. Harris's only consolation was that he was able to reject the name 'Target Finding Force' proposed by the Directorate of Bombing Operations; his objection was simply that it came from Bufton's organisation.

37

RESCUING A MISBEGOTTEN FREAK

Winston Churchill inherited one especially disastrous administrative legacy from Neville Chamberlain's government: a shambles over preparing for propaganda in war. If Chamberlain paid scant attention to the detail of air rearmament, he paid as good as none whatever to the question of what might be done about propaganda. He turned the question over in its entirety to Sir Horace Wilson, who had no greater interest and treated the whole process as an administrative inconvenience. But for Sir Maurice Hankey's tidy-mindedness, it is more than likely that nothing at all would have been done. As part of routine contingency planning, Hankey had compiled the 'War Book' which featured the creation of a Ministry of Information as had existed during the First World War. The Chamberlain government had simply accepted Hankey's War Book without subjecting it to an examination as to whether it fitted into the tastes and contingencies that ruled the government's thinking. Hankey was the gold standard of bureaucratic propriety and no one was going to get into trouble if they followed his playbook. By the time the possibility of a Ministry of Information (MoI) had become a live one, it was too late for Wilson to have the idea dropped lock, stock and barrel. He personally had a low opinion of propaganda: 'Having been old-fashioned for many years, I find myself unable to show enthusiasm for propaganda by this country & I still cannot bring myself to believe that is a good substitute for calmly getting on with the business of govt including a rational foreign policy.'[1]

Wilson was guided by entirely negative principles: above all, avoiding anything that might provoke Germany. His next goal was to prevent the MoI from developing any kind of life of its own because he feared that an ambitious political or bureaucratic entrepreneur might use it as a power base, in particular Lord Beaverbrook through his ministerial lackey Sir Samuel Hoare.

When the MoI was called into being on the outbreak of war, it was farcically inefficient. Led by amateurs with no aptitude for either propaganda or bureaucratic warfare, it was trapped in a web of structural deficiencies, some intentional. Its failings were so glaring that it was subjected to a debate in Parliament. This was the only vaguely hostile parliamentary moment that Chamberlain faced until the fatal days of the Norway debate. The government's critics made much of the fact that the ministry had precisely 999 staff, a figure that was repeated throughout the debate: not only was it ineffective; it was over-staffed. Ministers and bureaucrats passed though the MoI in a revolving door of despair and frustration. Wars are not, of course, lost by bad propaganda or bad censorship, but the debacle of the Ministry of Information wrung from Chamberlain the admission that his appointment of Lord Macmillan, a Scottish judge, as Minister of Information was 'my one failure and I am not sure that the best plan would not be to abolish the Ministry altogether'.[2] Macmillan's successor, Sir John Reith, former director-general of the BBC, did no better. The failure of the Ministry of Information was emblematic of the policy of a government that did not really want to be fighting a war at all.

When Churchill became Prime Minister, he picked Duff Cooper as the new Minister of Information as his reward for having the moral courage to resign from the Chamberlain government over Munich. It was not, though, a successful appointment and Churchill was confronted by a public shambles over the ministry every bit as bad as anything that Chamberlain had experienced. Cooper's literary skills as the elegant biographer of Talleyrand and Field Marshal Haig did not qualify him for the chaotic and ferocious world of temporary wartime bureaucracy. Cooper's cause was not helped by his junior minister, Harold Nicolson, another ex-diplomat who came out of the same quasi-aristocratic high literary mould. As a former Treasury minister and First Lord of the Admiralty, Cooper was accustomed to having top-flight, highly experienced civil servants prepare answers to parliamentary inquiries; no such support was available at the MoI.[3] Cooper's greatest failure lay in not establishing a good relationship with the major newspaper editors – indeed, he earned their hostility and he was amply punished for the weaknesses in his management of the MoI. He had seemed to endorse outright censorship of news and made hostile comments about newspapers in the House of Commons. His scheme to investigate the state of public morale through paid informants was deemed oppressive and totalitarian. They were labelled 'Cooper's snoopers'. In private, he fought a savage battle with Hugh Dalton, the Labour Minister of Economic Warfare, who had a stake in foreign propaganda operations. He fared no better in internal reforms of his ministry; his selection as its director-general, Frank Pick, former boss of London Transport, simply tried to cut costs and impose discipline, earning the enmity of the MoI's employees.[4] Cooper opened a flank to personal criticism by sending his young son to safety in the US. Wilson's policy of malign neglect had also left the Ministry of Information with two running sores in its structure and remit which Cooper was never able to master. The armed forces jealously guarded their own propaganda operations, in particular the RAF whose mendacious accounts of its success in bombing Germany were fully worthy of Goebbels. The services issued their own communiqués according to their assessment of the balance between kudos obtained and the disclosure of operational intelligence with no reference to the MoI. Cooper issued a semi-public ultimatum to Churchill on this point and was rebuffed. Wilson had also left responsibility for Britain's overseas propaganda divided, with the MoI as only one competitor for authority.

Duff Cooper accurately and pessimistically diagnosed the historical flaws that led the MoI to its desperate pass:

> I have long known that the MOI is a misbegotten freak bred from the unnatural union of Sir Horace Wilson and Sir Samuel Hoare

(considering the progenitors I wonder the offspring is not even more revolting) but I have tried to straighten the freak's limbs and make it serve some useful purpose, as the only alternative was to scrap it and begin again from the beginning which was hardly practical.[5]

But wit and perceptiveness are no substitute for bureaucratic focus and energy. Duff Cooper had practically despaired of the MoI. It was only a matter of time before he was replaced. The question was an irritation to Churchill and not an existential problem. His own speeches were magnificent propaganda and he did not require a bureaucracy to help him with them. In Desmond Morton's words, 'he ... was not interested in propaganda. His attitude towards Duff and Dalton was as follows: he liked Duff but knew that he had failed. Therefore he did not wish to see him. Dalton bored him and no man wants to see bores.'[6] Churchill did not believe in 'killing Hitler with his mouth'. In the words of an MP closely associated with the MoI, his 'dislike of propaganda from any other source than himself was well known'.[7] Churchill could latch on to an effective propaganda campaign such as the 'V for Victory' slogan, but he made it his own through the image of him holding up index and middle finger. When Frederick Lindemann questioned whether it was worth the trouble promoting the V sign in occupied Europe, he flatly turned down the advice.[8]

The failings of the MoI were an embarrassment and a distraction. Beaverbrook entertained notions of making his former employee and confidant Bruce Lockhart minister, but Lockhart did not rise to the bait. This left Brendan Bracken as the next best choice, but it took severe pressure to persuade him to take the job. He was happy and far more comfortable as Churchill's confidant at the centre of power. He took the MoI job only out of loyalty to Churchill. He understood that he was relieving him of an unwanted and unrewarding burden. Even when he was confronted with a near insoluble stand-off amongst ministers a few months later in the dark days of early 1942, he was willing to surrender the MoI's stake in the issue that was being fought over rather than call on Churchill to arbitrate: 'I am not going on with three ministers [all in charge of foreign propaganda]. At the same time I am not prepared to add to the PM's troubles when he has more than he can bear just now.'[9] For good measure, Nicolson was shuffled off onto the BBC board of governors and was replaced by a Labour non-entity, Ernest Thurtle, to appease Labour MPs who wanted one of their own in the ministry.[10]

Bracken had hoped to choose his own candidate to become Church- ill's parliamentary private secretary but Churchill was persuaded to take the man chosen by his newish Chief Whip, James Stuart.[11] Stuart's pick was another former Chamberlain loyalist, George Harvie-Watt, who was unabashed at having resolutely opposed Churchill from the Whips' Office through the appeasement years. He had come to Churchill's notice as the commander of an Unrotated Projectile unit.[12] This was another example of Churchill's pragmatism in working with one-time foes if they could give effective service. Churchill had kept Harvie-Watt's former boss in the Whips' Office, David Margesson, in government under his programme of reconciling his former oppo- nents in the debate over appeasement, but like Lord Halifax he was not going to be a permanent fixture in Churchill's circle of ministers. But Churchill still had to deal with the same 1935 vintage of MPs and needed the knowledge and relations of a man like Harvie-Watt to manage the Conservative benches. Harvie-Watt was utterly differ- ent to Bracken and never became an intimate member of Churchill's circle but served as a quite conventional and efficient parliamentary private secretary, feeding his master with clear weekly reports on the mood of MPs and the party. Bracken continued to feel possessive over the proximity that he used to enjoy to the Prime Minister. Even a year after the change, he was reckoned to be increasingly jealous of Harvie-Watt's position.[13]

Churchill's greatest concern in the media world was to keep down adverse comment, especially directed at him personally. Bracken was not unsympathetic, but his watchword was to permit the maximum to be published. He well understood that there was a distinction be- tween criticism and the disclosure of militarily sensitive material, even if they came close to each other. Bracken's commitment to open comment was thrown on the back foot by some very hostile stories from an Australian journalist about the conduct of senior British officers in London. He found himself fighting a losing battle with Churchill. Bracken was instructed to reverse the previous policy of only barring messages that compromised military security and added messages 'containing speculation as to future operations; or … which might compromise the relations of this country with foreign Powers; or which … calculated to create ill-feeling between the United Nations themselves, or between them … and a neutral country'.[14] Bracken's complaints were rebuffed.

Bracken was more successful in shielding the *Daily Mirror* from Churchill's wrath. The *Daily Mirror* had established itself as the government's most persistent critic in the mainstream press. It lambasted the quality of military officers and its cartoonist Philip Zec had caused particular outage with a cartoon depicting a shipwrecked sailor clinging to a life-raft with the caption, 'The price of petrol has gone up one penny.' It is a measure of Churchill's over-sensitivity at this stage that he took offence. The cartoon could have served to remind the public of the sacrifices made at sea to provide them with the necessities of life. The government had the power under Defence Regulation 2(b) to close down publications inimical to the war effort and Churchill, supported by Labour ministers, wanted to use this against the *Daily Mirror*. Bracken, backed by Beaverbrook, persuaded Churchill against this. When the *Yorkshire Post* criticised Churchill after a squabble over pay for female teachers, Bracken deftly produced the previous day's edition which praised him as 'the greatest Prime Minister Britain ever had', thus disarming Churchill's annoyance.[15]

Bracken did not insist on a formal charter as Minister of Information.[16] He knew that such things were only as good as their execution when a hard decision was needed on a specific case. Bracken was distinctly lower in the formal pecking order than either Dalton or the other minister with a stake in overseas propaganda operations, the Foreign Secretary, Anthony Eden. He knew that tactical manoeuvre would be more important than abstract rulings when push turned to shove. As a step towards resolving the stand-off between the MoI and the service ministries, and as a sop to the concerns of Duff Cooper and Walter Monckton, even before Bracken became minister, the MoI had been given a formal right to see all news items that the service ministries might release. Rather than indulging in complex schemes which divided the issue of news between the MoI and the service ministries that Duff Cooper had played with, Bracken simply insisted on respecting the advance disclosure rule fully; he saw that it was a thin but deep wedge that could be hammered into the crack of service autonomy over news release. Occasionally, he used his clout with Churchill to compel particular items to be released but generally preferred to take a softer line. He caught the Admiralty out in a flagrant breach of the pre-publication rule by failing to disclose to the MoI news of a mutiny amongst sailors on the doomed German battleship *Bismarck*, which was released directly to the *Evening Standard*. Moreover, the navy had not taken photographs of the sinking *Bismarck*, missing an obvious propaganda opportunity. Bracken scored his points but took care not to alienate the First Lord of the Admiralty, A. V. Alexander, whom he took to a genial dinner at the Turf Club. Relations improved markedly. Bracken knew that he would have had Churchill's backing had things come to a fight, but his preferred method was smooth persuasion of the other individuals concerned, larded with intense and utterly insincere flattery. Only with a few hopeless cases did he pursue outright confrontation.

Much as Beaverbrook had inherited a great deal of the groundwork for his success at the Ministry of Aircraft Production, some key moves had already been made before Bracken arrived at the MoI. Admiral Thomson, the new chief censor, was effective and emollient, causing little friction with newspapers by using his powers lightly and wisely. Robert Bruce Lockhart had been given charge of the Political Warfare Executive (PWE) with the rank of Deputy Under-Secretary at the Foreign Office, which explicitly endorsed his appointment. Lockhart shepherded the PWE through a variety of storms for the rest of the war. Bracken's appointment immediately triggered the resignation of its director-general, Sir Walter Monckton, who had been injected into the MoI in the desperate days under Lord Macmillan. Monckton was the archetypal safe pair of hands. His principal value to the government was as the trusted linkman to the Duke of Windsor since the days of the abdication crisis. He had not caused any difficulties at the MoI but had achieved little. Bracken smoothed his departure so as to avoid the impression of crisis, arranging a temporary posting to Cairo. Monckton's deputy Cyril Radcliffe proved a far more effective administrator and he established an excellent working relationship with Bracken. When Monckton attempted to return to his old slot, Bracken turned him away and appointed Radcliffe as full director-general.

The relationship between Bracken and his non-politician partner was one of the keys to the dramatic upswing in the MoI's fortunes. MP Ronald Tree was at the MoI from the early days of Lord Macmillan, through Reith and then Duff Cooper and Bracken and thus was an informed observer of its abjection and redemption:

> Between Radcliffe and Bracken a close friendship sprang up, and in many ways they complemented each other. Both were fundamentally tough and, having the support of the Press behind them, were not prepared to stand any nonsense from their colleagues or from the House of Commons. The result was that the Ministry of Information assumed a new status. Instead of being a whipping boy and a butt for the cartoonist, it began for the first time to feel a sense of pride in its achievements, and to be a force to be reckoned with. It was aware that it had a minister prepared and well able to defend it, and developed morale and self-confidence.[17]

Bracken's lodestar in running the MoI was that it should be run efficiently; he was uninterested in the underlying policy of propaganda.[18] Like most of the new wartime departments, the MoI and its satellites were burdened with chancers and office politicians hungry for power, influence and comfortable billets. Such people were perfectly at home in a world of futile inter-departmental rivalries which be-devilled organisations like the MoI. Bruce Lockhart was reminded of Lord Milner's dictum about the Whitehall infighting during the First World War: 'I could have written a history of the last war without even mentioning the Germans.'[19] At the MoI and the PWE, political infighting between the far left and others added to the mix. This frequently made for a poisonous atmosphere of intrigue and back-biting. Bracken stands out as an exception to this pattern. Ivone Kirkpatrick, the intelligence operative turned diplomat who passed through this world, was not universally admired, but he appears to have been straightforward in his dealings with colleagues. He advised Harman Grisewood, then at the beginning of a distinguished career with the BBC and contemplating with dread the prospect of becoming deeply involved in the interdepartmental world of propaganda, that 'the two people I should treat as friends – the only two – were Brendan Bracken and Bruce Lockhart'.[20] Bracken's conduct of the MoI showed him at his pragmatic best – he was balanced, perceptive and flexible. But signs of the old mythomaniac Adam still showed through disconcertingly to those unfamiliar with his old ways. Almost any discussion of a military engagement brought forth a woeful tale of the heroic and fictional death of Bracken's equally fictional brother on the battlefield concerned.[21]

Bracken's greatest strength as Minister of Information was his success in building good relations with the newspaper editors, then by far the dominant figures in the media world.[22] Here his own familiarity and empathy with the newspaper world was a major plus. He had persuaded Churchill against his will to take two press reporters with him across the Atlantic to his first summit conference with Roosevelt.[23] Bracken made it known he was fully willing to look at complaints from the press about the ministry – large or small – at any time. He also invested time and effort in nurturing personal contact with both proprietors and editors. He had the great advantage of being known to be close to Churchill, so anything he said about top-level policy was rated as 'from the horse's mouth'.[24] Beaverbrook claimed the credit for Bracken pursuing this strategy on his advice from his own time as Minister of Information during the First World War.[25] Bracken was committed to having as free a press as possible. Just as Churchill understood the crucial importance of US political and military support, Bracken courted US reporters. The Beaverbrook newspapers had been amongst Duff Cooper's most savage critics, but Bracken was spared the worst of their attentions. Beaverbrook could not hold back his spirit of mischief sufficiently to stop him publishing the story that Bracken's father had been refused a gun licence because of his Irish republican affiliations.

On at least one occasion, Bracken was able to use his privileged position with Churchill to argue him away from a decision which could have had disastrous consequences, certainly in terms of propaganda and probably worse. The Germans had reacted to the discovery that a few prisoners taken during a commando raid had been shackled and shot when they attempted to escape with the threat to manacle British PoWs in their camps. In turn, German PoWs had actually been shackled in Canada, provoking a serious riot. In a heated and brandy-fuelled discussion, Bracken had argued for magnanimity, but Churchill wanted to maintain a hard line: 'You want me to grovel in the mud to the Nazis?'[26] Bracken astutely played the card of the recent decisive British victory in the desert war at El Alamein: 'No, they're grovelling in the sand to you.' The German prisoners were unshackled.

One of Bracken's notable flaws as a minister was disregard for the importance of secrecy in certain areas. He cheerily blabbed highly confidential details of the planned British–American Torch landings in North Africa to a meeting about radio propaganda.[27]

Bracken gained the respect and affection of his people because of his willingness to protect them from outside pressure to which a time-server would have bowed.[28] He would listen to newspaper complaints at censorship decisions, but he consistently supported the judgement of his chief censor, Admiral Thomson.[29] One of Bruce Lockhart's ablest black propagandists, Sefton Delmer, used his fake clandestine radio station *Gustav Siegfried Eins* to spread stories of orgies with German admirals. Word of this reached Sir Stafford Cripps, who combined prudishness with extreme left-wing politics; he complained to Eden.[30] Bracken faced an even more severe moralistic attack on Delmer's work when an operation to deliver similar black propaganda to France by small balloons miscarried. The balloons were blown back over England and one reached the hands of an MP, J. B. Hynd, who complained directly to the minister. Bracken defused Hynd's complaint with a bravura and entirely extempore performance in which he persuaded Hynd that it would be playing into Goebbels's hands to block the operation.[31] Beaverbrook was impressed by Bracken's handling of the ministry but less sure of the value of black propaganda.[32] Bracken's loyalty to his juniors was not defined by political affiliations either. He defended Labour left-winger Richard Crossman, an able but widely distrusted figure, when he broadcast without authority words by Air Marshal Bomber Harris.[33] Harris had issued a threat that his bombers would attack Germany. Bracken's instinct to protect Crossman may have been reinforced by his sympathy for Harris's strategy.

Bracken found one useful item in the legacy he garnered from Dalton's involvement in propaganda and he seized on it and drove it to become one of Britain's trumps in the propaganda battle and beyond: the Aspidistra high-power radio station on high ground at Crowborough in the Ashdown Forest whose transmissions reached far into occupied Europe. A US domestic political decision to sustain competition by restricting the power of transmitters available to US radio stations made the RCA network, which had commissioned it specially for one New Jersey station, a willing seller of the equipment. It was a project in which Churchill took a personal interest and soon after Bracken became minister, he was pursuing the state of progress.[34] This was the kind of powerful, quasi-military hardware that fascinated him. The question of obtaining replacement valves from the US provided him with an opportunity for the kind of micro-management in which he delighted.[35] One of the early bureaucratic battles over the project gave Bracken a perfect opportunity to undermine Dalton, the Labour Minister of Economic Warfare who was trying to hijack propaganda for himself.[36] Unwisely, Dalton claimed Lindemann's authority for his stance on Aspidistra, which Bracken was easily able to disprove.

Aspidistra came on air in November 1942 and there was keen competition for its services. As well as broadcasting black propaganda supposedly originating from secret transmitters in Europe, Aspidistra broadcast false instructions to German night fighters. When the US counterparts to the PWE set up in Europe, they urgently needed transmitting capacity for their own broadcasts and asked Bracken for his help.[37] Aspidistra was a ready-made answer and after a degree of negotiation, the British were able to provide the Americans with one of the rare specimens of 'Reverse Lend-Lease'. Aspidistra established itself as a major asset and Bracken became possessive of its control and insisted quite wrongly that he was the sole arbiter of its use when the chiefs of staff wanted to use it for military purposes.[38]

* * *

Sir Horace Wilson had stored up a host of problems for the men left to guide Britain's wartime propaganda operations, in particular the deep and long-running feud over who should control foreign propaganda. As a counterweight to the embryonic MoI and its ambitious director-general, Sir Stephen Tallents, Wilson had built up the projects of a lower-profile but no less ambitious figure, Sir Campbell Stuart. Stuart harboured the fantasy that he would be able to replicate the imaginary achievement of British propaganda in the First World War in bringing German morale to a fatal collapse; the Germans, especially General Lu-dendorff, happily promoted this myth to mask their strategic miscalculations and outright defeat on the battlefield. Stuart had been permitted to build up in the deepest secrecy a propaganda department subject to no control but his own. All that mattered to Wilson was that Stuart's operation was out of sight and depended entirely on his goodwill.

Stuart had been eliminated immediately in May 1940 as a Wilsonite relic, but his operation, Electra House, had been renamed SO1 and transferred to the clandestine activities grouped under the Special Operations Executive (SOE), established by Churchill to undertake subversion and sabotage in occupied Europe, to 'set Europe ablaze'. The SOE had been partly inspired by the Labour politician Hugh Dalton, who became Minister of Economic Warfare in Churchill's government.[39] He was rewarded for being one of the few Labour politicians who wholeheartedly supported Churchill's stance on appeasement and it would have affronted the political balance of the coalition if Britain's (new) secret service had been put under the control of a Conservative minister like the other two. With active resistance to Nazi domination still in its infancy, propaganda was the most active component of Dalton's power base and he jealously guarded his power over SO1. Its personnel had been inculcated with Stuart's secret service mentality and it was based at Woburn Abbey, distant from London. Under Duff Cooper's weak regime, this had all combined to foster a state within a state. The demarcation between propaganda operations had been subjected to adjudication by Sir John Anderson, who was becoming established as Churchill's supremo in Whitehall, in May 1941, which gave Dalton unfettered control over 'secret propaganda', although this left open the question of what constituted secret as opposed to open propaganda. Dalton could be confident in far greater political firepower than Cooper.[40]

Bracken's relations with Dalton had been poor since the early days of the Churchill government, when Dalton suspected Bracken of conducting a whispering campaign against Labour ministers, which he tried to counter by spreading word of his suspicions to his senior colleagues.[41] Dalton denigrated Churchill's circle as his 'camarilla'.[*] Even before Bracken was installed, Dalton was trying to work Clement Attlee up against him.[42] Bracken repaid the compliment by broadcasting his desire to get control of SO1's clandestine propaganda operation and to remove Dalton.[43] The battle to control SO1 degenerated rapidly into open warfare with a decidedly personal edge. In one

---

[*] Derogatory term for a small group of favoured individuals around a monarch.

meeting, Bruce Lockhart described Dalton as 'white to the top of his bald head with rage' when Bracken taxed him with the delinquencies of his operations.[44] Dalton denounced Bracken variously as a fool and a nuisance, rude, assertive, ignorant, inconsequent, stupid, angular and unreceptive, with brainless bad manners, who was part lunatic, part showman, part bellhop and an unmannerly cub.[45]

Here Bracken's strong ties to Churchill were the trump card and when the ministers clashed, as they did acrimoniously over an operation in Argentina, Churchill ruled in Bracken's favour.[46] SO1 was extracted from the SOE and placed under the tripartite control the Foreign Office, the MoI and the Ministry of Economic Warfare, with Bruce Lockhart at its head. This did not blunt Dalton's ambitions and the running battles continued to the frustration and perplexity of Lockhart. After one acrimonious meeting to which Bracken 'brought no papers, has studied nothing, is arrogant, rude, inconsequent, critical, purely destructive', Dalton appealed to the Labour Party leader Clem Attlee and badgered him to intervene against Bracken.[47] He tried the same tactics that he had tried against Beaverbrook, by tittle-tattling the story of remarks made by Bracken against Labour ministers. Dalton read the politics wrong in thinking that Attlee would use up political ammunition against Bracken on behalf of a colleague of whom he was actually dubious. Just as Churchill sacrificed Beaverbrook to the need to propitiate Attlee, Attlee did not intervene when Churchill came down firmly on Bracken's side in the battle over propaganda. In the formal ministerial pecking order, Dalton was kicked upstairs to become President of the Board of Trade in March 1942, but he had lost out to Bracken. He was replaced as Minister of Economic Warfare by the Conservative Lord Selborne, who proved far less awkward. Propaganda was dwindling in importance for the Ministry of Economic Warfare; the SOE's originally intended military activities were finally gaining momentum; and Selborne estimated that this now occupied three quarters of his time.

* * *

The problems that Brendan Bracken inherited at the BBC were minor compared to those at the MoI itself and the ambiguous control of foreign propaganda, but they were bad enough. Sir Horace Wilson had given no thought whatever to what the BBC might do in war-time or even once it emerged from the personal dictatorship of its founding father, Sir John Reith. Wilson and his then nominal su-perior, Sir Warren Fisher, head of the civil service, simply wanted to bring the BBC under full state control. Reith himself was happy to leave the future of the BBC to others; he looked to Wilson to install him in some grand government job. Reith had built the BBC into a powerful corporation with a distinct ethos that was proud of its independence of the government, but by some standards, he had been happy to bargain this away for what proved to be a miserable reward: chairmanship of Britain's failing national airline, Imperial Airways. The structure that Reith had built evolved around his position as a strong director-general. Wilson and Fisher stopped short of choosing a civil servant to succeed him. Instead, an ineffectual but high-mind-ed academic, Frederick Ogilvie, who knew something of tourism but nothing of broadcasting was appointed. Reith knew instantly he was the wrong man and even the BBC's official history described Ogilvie's tenure as 'in some ways calamitous'. Even without the peculiar de-mands of wartime, the BBC required major reform.

No one had thought to bring the BBC into wartime contingency planning even though its position as Britain's national broadcaster made it a prime candidate for regulation. The BBC was on the side-lines as the MoI went through the successive agonies of the pre-war shadow regimes and then Macmillan, Reith and Duff Cooper, albeit prey to the terror that the government in one form or another would encroach on its liberties. It was bombarded from all sides with advice and requests as to its content. This was not just a question of how it should broadcast to Britain and the empire. Partly at the government's behest, in 1938, the BBC had started broadcasting in foreign languag-es, including Arabic, French, German and Italian. Duff Cooper had made a tentative step towards imposing some order on the resulting chaos by appointing a home and a foreign adviser as the sole points of contact: a respected newspaper journalist A. P. Ryan and a professional diplomat and First World War intelligence officer, Ivone Kirkpatrick, respectively. This still left open the large question of foreign propaganda.

Soon after he became minister, Bracken was gifted the opportunity to show the BBC that he was not bent on taking control when his Labour under-secretary, Ernest Thurtle, tactlessly told the House of Commons that the BBC's governors served no purpose in wartime. Bracken could assure them publicly that this was not so and, privately, that Thurtle would be muzzled. Thurtle's indiscretion brought the added benefit that he could be replaced by a Conservative minister, leaving the MoI as the only department without a Labour minister.[48] Bracken understood clearly that the BBC's domestic broadcasting operations should be treated in the same way as the newspapers: allowed the maximum possible freedom of expression. Its foreign broadcasts were part of British propaganda, which the government should control. Bracken worked in harmony with the BBC's chairman Sir Allan Powell, a colourless public servant whose role at the wartime BBC is often described as ambiguous. In the words of the BBC's official history, 'confrontation gave way to cooperation'.[49] He avoided open stances on issues of controversy and seems simply to have recognised that Bracken had authority and was a force for good. Between them, they eased out the controller of overseas, Sir Stephen Tallents, who had returned to the BBC, and he was replaced by Kirkpatrick who was better attuned to the operational requirements of the task and the bruising world of wartime bureaucratic infighting. A. P. Ryan was moved to a conventional BBC job as head of the news department. Powell's next target was the director-general, Ogilvie, worthy but ineffectual and ripe for replacement.

By stealth, Bracken orchestrated a renewal of the BBC's top ranks. It was not an outright purge of the Reithian old guard but brought in much-needed new blood. Neither Reith nor Ogilvie had done anything to create a robust administrative or financial structure for the corporation. Bracken's City contacts opened an avenue to a respected utilities manager, Robert Foot, whom he persuaded to take on the task, declaring that he deserved the George Cross for this. Foot proved his worth sufficiently to succeed Ogilvie when he was eased out in 1942. Foot shared the post with a BBC staffer, Cecil Graves, who served as a visible guarantor of the corporation's autonomy. Graves, though, was a sick man and weakened his position with a ludicrous complaint that the BBC bored listeners by playing songs by Vera Lynn, of whom he was only dimly aware but found 'debilitating'. A. P. Ryan had to show him the error of his ways.[50] Foot, with Bracken's support, brought in a provincial journalist, William Haley, to succeed Graves. Here again, Allan Powell's support was crucial in pushing the appointment through against the opposition of high-minded governors, notably Harold Nicolson who felt that Haley was not suited to 'the cultural job we had in mind': proof, if needed, of Nicolson's weakness as a wartime media controller. Haley served until 1952 and proved to be one of the corporation's defining director-generals and astonishingly won the approval of Reith himself.

* * *

By 1943, the MoI had been brought fully under control and the need for hands-on management dwindled. This suited Brendan Bracken well as it left him with time to be with Winston Churchill; he was losing interest in the job.[51] He claimed that Churchill had offered him three other jobs, including the War Office, but this would have been immensely time-consuming and diminished his direct contact with the Prime Minister. He was certainly considered as Dominions Secretary in April 1944.[52] The combination of accumulated stress and losing engagement with the ministry was reflected in heavy drinking and frequent bouts of illness, although Bruce Lockhart suspected that Bracken might have been using his health as a pretext to give up the MoI.[53] Bracken was still capable of epic county walks.[54] His lack of real work to do at the MoI translated into patchy and capricious performance. He indulged in an unnecessary and futile attempt to restage his triumph over Hugh Dalton on the question of control of the PWE, this time at the expense of Anthony Eden as Foreign Secretary.[55] But on this occasion, Churchill backed Eden against Bracken. Bracken doubled down on this with a display of similarly pointless proprietorial wilfulness over Aspidistra, which prompted Hastings Ismay to say he was 'a very nice man, but such a fool and his own worst enemy'.[56]

Bracken had, however, proved his value to Churchill and Clemmie recognised this. Over the years, her initial hostility had softened and finally Bracken was promoted out of the 'terrible Bs' bracket.[57] She inscribed a book which she gave to him, 'To Brendan with love from Clemmie, Christmas 1944.'[58] In particular, she appreciated Bracken's success pleading with Churchill to take rest when he was ill. She had come to realise 'how much [Churchill] owed to the undeviating devotion and friendship of [Bracken]'.[59]

38

PLANNING FOR
POST-WAR BRITAIN

During Lord Beaverbrook's period out of government, Winston Churchill moved Frederick Lindemann up another two spaces on the chessboard of public status and recognition. In July 1942, Lindemann was formally brought into government as Paymaster General, a near complete sinecure and quaint survival of an earlier age. He was no longer merely the Prime Minister's personal adviser. His personal standing in his own right was further boosted in 1943 when, like Brendan Bracken in 1940, he was elevated to the Privy Council. In practice, his work with Churchill was unchanged but, if nothing else, Lindemann's ministerial title served as the anchor for a parody of Gilbert and Sullivan's 'The Modern Major-General's Song' that did the rounds of Whitehall:

> My secretariat scrutinizes memoranda topical,
> Elucidating fallacies in detail microscopical;
> I plumb the depths of strategy, I analyze ballistics;
> Reform the whole of industry, or fabricate statistics;
> My acumen's infallible, my logic irrefutable;
> My slightest proposition axiomatic, indisputable;
> And so in matters vegetable, animal and mineral,
> I am the very model of a good Paymaster General[1]

With Beaverbrook in eclipse and Bracken occupied by his duties at the Ministry of Information, Churchill had all the more need for personal advice from someone he trusted. The issues with which Churchill had to grapple were becoming more diverse and involved as the war progressed. Up to the middle of 1942, almost everything could be subordinated to the direct question of how to obtain victory on the battlefield. The correct choices would depend on mysteries of science and economics which remained a closed book to Churchill. Burdened by the huge questions of how the war should be fought, he had no concentration or energy to spare; when Lindemann presented him with one minute on a peacetime topic, he stated: 'I cannot comprehend the issue and have neither the life nor the strength to learn.'[2] Beaverbrook, Bracken and Lindemann were all Churchill's confidants, but Lindemann came closest to being his adviser in the fullest sense. The growing complexity of the issues on which Churchill sought guidance from Lindemann had ramifications in diplomacy and domestic party politics, not spheres in which Lindemann had any great experience, not that this deterred him from strong opinions.

Britain started to plan for the world once the war had ended remarkably early. Some steps were being taken in 1940, but after the middle of 1942, when the fear of defeat had faded drastically, the process began to gain significant momentum. The abject performance of the government at the end of the First World War, in particular its failure to deliver on the promise 'homes fit for heroes', served as an object lesson, if only of the potential political cost. The presence of Labour in the wartime coalition was another significant drive of change.

Given its focus on economic matters, it was natural that the Statistical Section would be involved in post-war planning. About one third of the minutes that Lindemann sent to Churchill covered this topic. This marked something of an expansion of its remit from navigating through the thickets of Whitehall's existing practices. The timescale was of its nature greater than the immediate questions of wartime. Deliberations were more abstract and hypothetical. They also inevitably featured decisions that were overwhelmingly political.

The first great contribution to the debate about what shape Britain should take when peace returned arose accidentally. It combined the force of one individual's vision and personality with a moment in history when these struck a chord with the nation. William Beveridge was a committed social reformer who had combined public service with academia but had been unable to find a happy niche in the Second World War administration. He was unassailably certain of his own intellectual gifts but lacked a significant political patron such as Lindemann had found in Churchill. He had been shunted into chairing a minor inter-departmental inquiry into coordinating social services, which was not expected to report until the war was over. Beveridge spotted and seized the opportunity to make a powerful statement of his vision. He spent eighteen months studying the existing system, but his true ambition became to present radical proposals of his own. Jessy Mair, his secretary at LSE and later his wife, urged him to 'imbue his proposals with a "Cromwellian spirit" and messianic tone'.[3] Beveridge certainly achieved the latter by casting his goal as slaying the 'five giants of idleness, ignorance, disease, squalor and want'. The report's concrete recommendations perhaps fell short of this vision, but they were sweeping. The key proposal was a universal flat-rate social security scheme that would provide a set minimum income. The hated means testing for benefits was to be practically done away with. Beveridge's only truly novel benefit proposal was for family allowances of eight shillings per child to be paid from general taxation. He also called for a national health service without giving detail. Beveridge sedulously cultivated interest in the report through broadcasts and press articles; he won the support of the trade unions. When it was published in November 1942, the report was a stunning success with the public. Its 300 pages of dense type did not deter people from buying over 100,000 copies in the first month at the admittedly modest price of two shillings (about £4 today). The report is considered with some justice to have been the foundation of the 'welfare state'. A high-level response would be needed.

Even the Statistical Section's economists were on unfamiliar territory, but they set to work to prepare a brief for Lindemann. Lindemann's advice to the Prime Minister was remarkably pragmatic in light of his approach to social class. He knew that the reality of post-war finance would shape what could be achieved and that there was little merit in getting bogged down in detail at this stage. His greatest concern was that the US might see the project as an attempt to pay for British social security from their financial contributions. 'Either, it seems to me, the Government should accept the Report in principle, subject to adjustment of details, and so acquire merit in liberal circles, or it should reserve the position and keep its hands free.'[4]

Lindemann's advice was rejected and the government preferred to take a fiscally low-risk stance in very vaguely endorsing Beveridge's principles in uninspiring speeches by Sir John Anderson and Sir Kingsley Wood, a technocrat and Chamberlainite throwback, respectively. The field was left clear for Labour's Herbert Morrison to welcome Beveridge wholeheartedly. The damage was compounded by a White Paper proposing some form of social security scheme but with so little clarity or detail that it had no impact.

Beveridge had also proposed a national health service which translated into a White Paper in early 1944 by the Conservative Health Minister Henry Willink, one of the forgotten fathers of the NHS. It embodied the principle of providing health service free at the point of delivery. Lindemann advised Churchill to adopt the proposals, although he presciently anticipated opposition from the general practitioners. Here he faced the combined opposition of Beaverbrook and Bracken.[5] Since his return to government the previous autumn, Beaverbrook had been cultivating his contact to Bracken and had developed influence over him.[6]

Beveridge's proposals for a national health service were far less contentious, but here too Churchill and his immediate allies showed their reluctance to countenance major social reform. In February 1944, the Cabinet was willing to take a long stride in the direction of establishing the National Health Service with the publication of Henry Willink's White Paper. The Cabinet had set aside the prescient claim that the scheme would face bitter opposition from some doctors, who would see it as a threat to the whole basis of the medical profession. That evening, Beaverbrook and Bracken came to 10 Downing Street to lobby against the proposals and succeeded in persuading Churchill to reverse his approval.[7] The day afterwards Churchill instructed his de facto deputy, Anthony Eden, to discuss the next steps with Beaverbrook and Bracken, who had both been present at the Cabinet meeting.[8] Churchill described them as 'pretty knowledgeable' on the topic, which suggests that they had already been working on it on his behalf. He himself pleaded his inability to get on top of such a complex area, still less, to give it worthwhile consideration 'under present conditions'. Bracken kept up violent opposition to the last.[9] Churchill's mind was dominated by the vast preparations for D-Day and he was happy to farm out questions of domestic post-war policy to his friends. Eden does not appear to have been swayed and the Cabinet reaffirmed its decision a few days later.

The First World War had been swiftly followed by a surge in inflation as the returning servicemen were absorbed in the economy, which was followed equally swiftly by a slump in activity and a surge in unemployment that persisted through the 1920s. The Great Slump in the early 1930s set the seal on industrial misery which had begun years before. The danger of a repetition of this pattern was firmly in the minds of the statesmen of the Second World War, Churchill included. It was also in the minds of the servicemen fighting the war and Churchill spontaneously endorsed their right to expect work when he and Ernest Bevin, Labour's Minister of Labour, were speaking to troops about to embark for battle: 'Ernie, when we have done this job for you, are we going back on the dole?'[10] Both Bevin and the Prime Minister told them that would not be. Lindemann came early to the discussion on how to ward off this danger. He was aware of the miseries and waste of unemployment and happily supported measures to prevent it.[11] Here he came under the influence of Donald MacDougall, the leading economist in his team, who had studied the problem of trade cycles since before the war.[12] MacDougall overcame Lindemann's hesitations on the Keynesian notions that he advanced.

The outcome was the White Paper on Employment Policy, the first formal government acceptance that one of its jobs was to maintain 'high and stable employment', a commitment that lasted until 1978.

Lindemann also had a small hand in the one major piece of social legislation that came from the wartime government, Rab Butler's 1944 Education Act. Butler was already looking well beyond the politics of the coalition and wanted to position himself in the Conservative Party as it faced an entirely new set of challenges in peacetime.[13] He seized with both hands the opportunity with which Churchill presented him when he moved him to the Board of Education in the government reshuffle of July 1941. In Churchill's eyes, the department might have seemed a convenient dead-end into which to shuffle one of the surviving Chamberlainites and an arch-appeaser to boot, with the fig leaf of a promotion to heading a department. Butler disregarded Churchill's concern at the risk of stirring up religious controversy and embodied a thoroughgoing reform of the existing structures into an Act that gave every child a right to free secondary education. Lindemann urged Butler to make sure that Churchill included educational reform in a speech he was to make on the home front and oversaw Butler's rewriting of that part of the speech.[14] Butler was a thoroughly competent politician, but his colleague in the Ministry of Agriculture, Rob Hudson, had come up with little more than appeasement of the farming lobby as his contribution to the programme. Lindemann knew that Butler held the Prime Minister's credentials as a social reformer in his hands.

Lindemann's advice to Churchill was not entirely in favour of enlightened social policy. Indeed, the issue on which Lindemann took an emphatically reactionary stance marked, by some measures, the first gambit in the battle with Labour which led to the 1945 general election. As Allied victory appeared ever more certain from the middle of 1943 onwards, the issue of coal began to loom large in British political debates. By some standards, Churchill fired the first shot in the campaign for the next general election in October 1943 over the future of the coal mining industry, arguably the most politicised sector of the economy. The British economy was overwhelmingly coal-powered in the 1940s, but coal belonged to the landowners on whose property it had been found and their descendants; many were aristocrats and many had become fabulously wealthy. Technological inventiveness and pioneering capitalism were two facets of the Industrial Revolution, but accidents of geology and land tenure determined how much of the wealth it created was shared. Mine owners held the whip hand over their employees and used it to the full to keep costs – both wage and safety measures – low. The conflict between coal owners and mineworkers made for one of the most important divides in politics with the Conservatives on one side and Labour on the other. Generations of exploitative management left the industry with a ramshackle and inefficient structure. The desperate needs of the wartime economy had given the government the leverage to impose temporary controls, but a huge question mark lay over the industry's future after the war.

The proposal for full state control or ownership of the mines came from within the government and not from the Labour Party. The Minister of Fuel and Power since 1942 was Gwilym Lloyd-George, son of the former Prime Minister and part of his family group of supporters but increasingly a significant and competent political figure in his own right. He argued to the Cabinet that in order to improve coal output, it would be necessary to place all mine management under direct state control with the key and ominous qualification that it 'will fail if it is merely of a temporary character'.[15] Nationalisation of all industry had long been a formal policy of the Labour Party. Churchill turned to Lindemann to frame his answer to this proposal. They worked on Churchill's draft speech the evening before the key debate on the coal industry and to make doubly sure that there were no flaws sent it to MacDougall and his team for urgent inspection.[16] From the start, they warned against the introduction of 'far-reaching social changes by a side-wind' and depicted the coal-mine issue as one important enough on which to a fight general election.[17] The furthest they would go was to offer the continuation of the wartime regime of controls for the first year of peace. Churchill and Lindemann were lining up with high Torydom to preserve a relic of an earlier age.

39

THE PREOCCUPATIONS OF A
PAYMASTER GENERAL

The notion of releasing the energy held within atoms and making weapons with the technology gained widespread currency during the 1920s and 1930s, although the journalists who wrote up the concept were well in advance of science. Winston Churchill was unusual amongst the politicians of his day in being constantly alert to the impact of new scientific knowledge in the development of ever-more potent weapons. In 1924, he wrote a speculative essay entitled 'Shall We All Commit Suicide?' which mused on the possibility that

> a bomb no bigger than an orange [might] be found to possess a secret power to destroy a whole block of buildings – nay to concentrate the force of a thousand tons of cordite and blast a township at a stroke? Could not explosives even of the existing type be guided automatically in flying machines by wireless or other rays, without a human pilot, in ceaseless procession on a hostile city, arsenal, camp, or dockyard?

Frederick Lindemann kept up Churchill's interest in cutting-edge science with the gift of a book on quantum physics in the spring of 1926 which so grabbed Churchill's attention that it distracted him from preparing his upcoming Budget for a few hours.

The recognition in 1939 by two refugee Jewish scientists working at the new Nuffield Laboratory of Birmingham University transformed nuclear weapons from a near-abstract notion to a practical possibility. The prospects that this opened for usable weapons were subjected to the stately process of consideration by a Whitehall committee code-named MAUD. When MAUD finally delivered its report in July 1941, Lindemann summarised its conclusions to Churchill, together with a strong recommendation that Britain should build its own bomb and not throw itself on the help of the greater resources available in the US. Churchill approved and put the project into the hands of Lindemann himself and Sir John Anderson, in title Lord Privy Seal but in practice the government's maestro of the Whitehall machine who had the added unusual qualification of possessing a scientific training. Churchill was enthusiastic at the prospect of a new, highly destructive weapon.[1] From then on, the duo held the strings of Britain's nuclear policy in their hands, subject only to the agreement of Churchill. They were Churchill's only advisers as Churchill and Roosevelt reshaped British–American collaboration on nuclear weapons which had become increasingly contentious. Churchill was fully aware of the importance of the nuclear research, but it was not one of his constant preoccupations. He left the work to Lindemann, seeking updates as he needed. The project was remote enough from his routine considerations that he even forgot the codename, Tube Alloys, which it had been given, at one point simply referring to 'Anderson's affair'.[2] Lindemann's views were coloured by a degree of scepticism over the possibility of nuclear weapons. He thought that the odds of success given by British scientists of 100:1 on were too optimistic by a factor of ten.[3] He was correct in spotting that the Americans were in error to invest heavily in the untested calutron method of enriching uranium and predicted that this would fail outright, but he was far too conservative in estimating that it would take a minimum of three and a half to four years to develop a bomb.[4] His former pupil, R. V. Jones, believed that Lindemann simply did not believe (or hoped) that it would not be possible to release nuclear energy.[5]

Lindemann was positive, though, that Britain should not be left out. Lindemann feared not only that Germany might win the race to nuclear weapons and with it the war but also that after the war, Britain might find itself shut out of a world in which the Soviets might have the bomb.[6] Lindemann knew that cooperation with the US was vital, but he was not satisfied with the agreement that Churchill and Roosevelt struck at the Quebec conference in August 1943. He was sceptical of Churchill's confidence that the mutual veto over the use of nuclear weapons would outlast their terms in office. This provoked the only serious argument between Lindemann and Churchill, in the form of a blazing row in front of the Danish nuclear physicist Niels Bohr, whom the British had exfiltrated from his country to deprive the Germans of his services. Bohr was worried about proliferation of nuclear weapons technology, but Churchill was convinced that his agreement with Roosevelt for a British–American veto removed the possibility. Churchill did fall in with one project of Anderson and Lindemann's which tried to circumvent US hostility. British personnel sent to help with the industrial side of the project in the US were to act de facto as industrial spies.[7] Churchill's rock-solid confidence in his relationship with Roosevelt, which was one of the bedrocks of British strategy, remained untouched. Months later, he was assuring Lindemann that 'our association with the United States must be permanent, and I have no fear that they will maltreat or cheat us', although he admitted that history might prove him wrong.[8] Post-war considerations weighed heavily with the Americans, who had been suspicious when an executive of the British chemicals giant ICI had been involved at an early stage, triggering concerns that British businesses would piggy-back on US-funded research. Lindemann and Anderson picked up this sore spot and advised caution.[9] Many in the US were as sceptical as Lindemann of the Churchill–Roosevelt Quebec agreement and their concerns were impeding progress on the military project to an extent that Lindemann had to ask for Churchill to intervene with Roosevelt.[10] Lindemann was left to battle with the Americans' 'extraordinary ideas of security'.[11] By early 1945, the Americans wanted to prevent any development activity in Britain, ostensibly on security grounds.[12]

The security of the project was a major consideration interlocked with the fear that the Germans might also be developing atomic weapons. Almost from the start, Anderson was concerned not to alert the Germans to the fact that Britain and the US were taking the possibility seriously.[13] He faced a difficult choice over what should be done about the production of heavy water (deuterium oxide) in occupied Norway which potentially could be used in a German programme. He chose to take the risk of flagging to the Germans how important the British took the danger when he initiated an attack on the Norsk Hydro heavy-water plant by special forces in October 1942.[14] One of the most celebrated special forces operations of the Second World War, immortalised in the movie *The Heroes of Telemark*, a staple of Christmas TV movie schedules, was undertaken at the behest of the staidest of bureaucrats. Even once the plant was put out of operation and the stocks of heavy water destroyed, Churchill was still alert to the danger that the Germans might have built a plant to produce uranium. After the D-Day landings, he tasked Lindemann with reviewing any intelligence available and discussing it with the Chief of the Air Staff, presumably with a view to bombing any German plant.[15] Lindemann's preoccupation with security extended beyond the Germans to some of Britain's nominal allies. He spotted that some of the French scientists working on the project had strong links to the communists and he was doubtful of their loyalty. He even went as far as proposing that they be kept in Canada and not allowed to return to France. Here Anderson overruled him.[16]

* * *

Oil from the fields in Iraq was a vital component in the war effort and it passed through the territory that came under the imperial government of India, which charged the British government a financial levy on it. The Statistical Section spotted that the reference oil price used to calculate this duty was artificially and excessively high.

Frederick Lindemann's scepticism toward statistics produced by the government of India extended to their figures for food requirements on the subcontinent and the dire warnings that they issued of impending famine in Bombay in the summer of 1943. It was an episode that showed Lindemann at his worst: high-handed and intolerant of the possibility that local administrators might understand conditions better than he did from a skewed and selective reading of the numbers.

Last December we were told that 600,000 tons of wheat were essential ... It turned out that the harvest was a million tons above the previous year and the emergency vanished.

The annual Indian harvest is nearly 50 million tons of rice, wheat, millet and gram plus some 15 million tons of maize, barley and pulses. Yet we are told failure to provide half a million tons of cereals will result in a reduction of national output, refusal to export food [to Sri Lanka], famine conditions, civil disturbance and subversive activity among the troops of the Indian army. Actually, it appears that the shipment is required not to make good a deficit in grain but in order to deter the Indian profiteers from hoarding by the fact that our imports will cause prices to drop. This seems a roundabout way of tackling the problem. In any event, it is a little hard that the UK, which has already suffered a greater drop in the standard of life than India, should be mulcted because the government of India cannot arrange its affairs in an orderly manner.

In view of the large demand on shipping which will obviously arise if Italy collapses, the diversion of tonnage to India for this purpose scarcely seem justified unless the Ministry of War Transport think this would be the best course.[17]

Lindemann seemed to conflate the artificial and irrelevant imbalance of financial transfers in favour of the government of India account with the real economic and human problem of hunger. He blithely ignored the size of the population and the size of the country with its weak infrastructure, which meant that statistics for the whole subcontinent meant little in the Bengal region where wartime disruption was most acute. Above all, he put the diminution in living standards of a

wealthy and developed country such as Britain on a par with the catastrophic effect of a reduction in food supplies to a region where the
vast bulk of the population lived a fragile subsistence existence under
threat of starvation. Lindemann appeared to have a natural propensity
to downplay the risk of famine and later infuriated Anthony Eden by
denying his (prescient) fears in the autumn of 1944 that Europe faced
starvation.

Even when the famine had actually taken hold in Bengal, Lindemann trotted out the same figures for food production and wrote of
this as though famine was an opinion of the military and the government of India rather than a horrific fact:

> The Government of India assures us and the Chiefs of Staff agree,
> that famine conditions have actually occurred in Chittagong and
> even Calcutta. To what extent this is due to the internal difficulties
> of internal traffic caused by floods, as is now claimed, to what extent
> this is the failure of the India government to extract hoarded wheat
> from the Provinces and to what extent it reflects sheer inefficiency and
> corruption due to Indianising the Civil Service it is impossible to say.
> But if conditions are really as bad as we are told it might be, in view
> of the easier shipping position, to increase the loadings of gain for the
> time being. If this is done I suggest that its continuance should be
> conditional on the Government of India's adopting the necessary steps
>
> (a) to make the Provincial Governments disgorge their surplus and
>   also to extract hoarded gain from the peasants;
> (b) to see that the grain is loaded for ports in the deficiency regions lest
>   we are afterwards told that they were unable to transport it to the
>   famine areas.
>
> Everyone must regret distress in India, even though it be the fault of
> the India Government which have undoubtedly been soft and flabby in
> their administration and their financial arrangements and have thereby
> allowed inflation to occur. On the other hand we must remember that

starvation costs many hundreds of Allied lives every day the war in Europe is prolonged.[18]

Lindemann's last sentence is absurd in stating that hunger was costing a comparable number of lives in Europe, but it captures the brutal question of priorities that underlay the catastrophe. Winning the war against Germany ranked above dealing with a humanitarian problem.

Churchill paid little attention to the famine. It provided him with a pretext to damn his old bête noire General Sir Archibald Wavell with faint praise when he finally removed him from a directly military job as army commander-in-chief for India to become viceroy in India. Wavell was to be informed that Churchill would mention his past military achievements in welcoming him to his new post in October 1943, but 'in the main [Churchill] will speak about the Indian tragedy'.[19] Churchill's own reaction to the famine was chillingly racist and placed the blame on the victims themselves. He was 'obsessed by the tendency of Indians to breed right down to the margin of subsistence'.[20]

* * *

Lindemann's faith in the Trenchardian doctrine never wavered and he gave ample proof of this with his participation in one of the most furious debates over strategy in the run-up to Overlord, the invasion of France in 1944. Here, once again, he showed his capacity for bending statistics to support a pre-existing position rather than feeding an objective analysis of the question.

After the discussion over strategic bombing in 1942 which had culminated in the Singleton report, Solly Zuckerman had moved to the Mediterranean theatre of operations. Here he had supported Air Marshal Arthur Tedder, head of RAF Middle East Command who had spent three years dealing with the realities of deploying air power in a land and sea campaign rather than forcing the air force's activities onto the Procrustean bed of Trenchardian dogma. Tedder, who had toyed with an academic career and written a study of the British

Navy in the late seventeenth century, was an intellectual and open to a truly rigorous study of data in shaping militia operations. Zuckerman returned to Britain convinced of the importance of attacking the enemy's transport network as a preliminary to a land campaign. He was shocked at the inadequate plan for air preparations for Overlord, which appeared to assume blithely that the weather in the two-to-three weeks before the landing would be good enough for full-scale operations. Instead, Zuckerman formulated what came to be called the Transportation Plan, which required an all-out assault on the entire railway network which the Germans could use to reinforce their units in the landing area. Zuckerman was supported by Beaverbrook's tool in the intrigue against the top commanders of the RAF in 1940: McCloughry, now partially rehabilitated as an air commodore and senior staff officer in the Allied Expeditionary Air Force (AEAF), the air section of the Supreme Headquarters Allied Expeditionary Force. This rapidly attracted the opposition of Bomber Command, who saw in it a diversion from their cherished strategy of bombing Germany into submission. Lindemann was firmly in the Trenchardian camp.

The RAF officer with the greatest say on the question was Tedder, who had returned from the Mediterranean, to become General Eisenhower's deputy as Supreme Allied Commander. He saw the truth of Zuckerman's judgement but was sensitive enough to the politics of the debate to play the long game. When Lindemann invited Tedder to dinner at Christ Church, he tried to win him away from heresy over a sweet sherry: 'Well, Tedder, you surely don't believe in this nonsense of Solly's about railways?'[21] For the moment, Tedder refused to become sucked into the controversy, but he did complain that 'the Prof is a *bad* man, really bad man. Yet the PM listens to him.'[22]

The issue was fought out in four separate, gruelling and protracted late-night meetings of the Cabinet Defence Committee, Churchill's 'midnight follies'. These spread over one month and were the last to be held before the invasion itself was launched. The ostensible question that was being debated was not, though, the military value of bombing the railway network versus continuing the bombing of German cities.

Rather, it was the scale of casualties that would be inflicted on the French civilian population by the Transportation Plan. Churchill and most of the other politicians, notably the Foreign Secretary Anthony Eden, genuinely feared that these might create an irreparable breach between France and Britain.[23] They thought it might also be necessary to brief General de Gaulle in advance of the precise invasion plans, which the British and Americans had so far succeeded in avoiding. The first estimate of casualties on which the committee had to work on was 40,000 dead and 120,000 seriously wounded in the space of a dozen or so weeks, comparable to what Bomber Command was inflicting intentionally on Germany. Churchill's visceral Francophilia came to the fore and he repeatedly described the losses as a 'slaughter', warned that the plan might 'build up dull hatred in France ... for many years to come' and inveighed against 'a policy which was not in keeping with British morality and resulting in killing large numbers of our friends in France'.[24] The casualty estimate was ostensibly prepared by the Joint Intelligence Committee, but it was based on data provided by a reliable Trenchardian from the Air Staff. The most blatant thumb on the scales to tilt the figures in the direction that Bomber Command wanted was that they embodied an extremely conservative 'operational factor': the scale of the attack required to carry out the plan was multiplied by the arbitrary figure of three.

Lindemann's attempt to undermine Zuckerman's credibility as the author of the Transportation Plan at the first meeting degenerated into farce. He had not expected Zuckerman to be at the meeting and was surprised that Sir Charles Portal had brought him. He had written what was clearly intended to be a private briefing for the Prime Minister, which described it as 'the brainchild of a biologist who happened to be passing though the Mediterranean'.[25] Lindemann was horrified when Churchill simply read this out verbatim to the committee and seemed to be trying to pluck the paper from his hands. Lindemann rolled out a clutch of arguments against the Transportation Plan – some entirely unsupported by evidence – they included a wild exaggeration of the free capacity in the French railway system and even went so far as to qualify his scepticism on the danger from German V-2 rockets as to suggest that bombers might be needed to bomb their launch sites. The only participant to come close to openly deploying Trenchardian dogma against the Transportation Plan was the Air Minister, Archie Sinclair, and over the course of the meeting, his opposition crumbled; even the Air Staff representative held back.

During the meetings, Portal held steadfastly to his commitment to the Transportation Plan. Churchill stayed hostile to the end and even tried to recruit President Roosevelt to his cause. In Tedder's eyes, even Churchill's energy was low, showing the drain on his resources since 1940.[26] General Sir Alan Brooke, the Chief of the Imperial General Staff, who attended these and other meetings, noted in his diary that Churchill was 'dull and lifeless and missing the main points. He looked old and tired, and in my opinion is failing fast.'[27] Lindemann continued to plead the cause of alternative targets, rolling out fancifully low figures for the weight of bombs needed to cut a bridge. Opposition was undermined by a revision in the casualty estimates driven by Zuckerman to a more realistic figure, supported by actual data of casualties in raids actually undertaken against railway centres in France, where even Vichy figures were below British estimates. The Transportation Plan was finally approved, subject to the preposterous condition that French casualties were not to exceed 10,000, as though accurate ongoing measurement would be possible. By a fluke, the best estimate of French killed and wounded by the Transportation Plan is exactly that figure. Air Marshal Harris obeyed orders to commit Bomber Command to the attack, which achieved remarkably good accuracy. In his memoirs, Churchill admitted that the Transportation Plan had delivered the necessary effect: 'The sealing off of the Normandy battlefield from reinforcement by rail may well have been the greatest direct contribution that the bomber forces could make to "Overlord". The price was paid.'[28]

40

THE RETURN OF A
COURT FAVOURITE

Lord Beaverbrook re-entered the government as part of a broader reshuffle in September 1943 triggered by the death in office of Sir Kingsley Wood, the Chancellor of the Exchequer. The reshuffle marked something of a turning point. Wood had been the last remaining top-rank figure left over from Neville Chamberlain's government. He was replaced by Sir John Anderson, also a Chamberlain appointment but firmly in the technocratic mould of the wartime Cabinet. Anderson had been a senior and highly respected civil servant before the war; as governor of Bengal between 1932 and 1937 when the fight over the India Bill occupied Winston Churchill, he had been firmly on the side of law and order. Whilst Anderson was the Conservatives' candidate in the by-election for the Scottish Universities which brought him into Parliament, he never took the Conservative whip. As Lord President of the Council and chairman of the Home Affairs Committee, he had held an extensive brief over domestic affairs, in practice serving as a counterweight to the influence of the Labour leaders. Clement Attlee succeeded Anderson as Lord President in a small shift of power over domestic affairs to Labour.

Some surprise was expressed that Beaverbrook should reappear in the government given the ferocity and breadth of his campaigns against government policy over the preceding months, but this suggests that observers might not have understood the peculiar dynamics of his relationship with Churchill. Beaverbrook's hobby horse of an early

Second Front in which he had served as Stalin's mouthpiece had faded from view, so the only serious policy issue that had distinguished him no longer mattered. Beaverbrook had served as a useful implement in the early days of Roosevelt's enthusiasm for a quick invasion of France, but after that he had been noisily irrelevant to the military decision. The Anglo-American landings in North Africa in October 1942 and in Italy in 1943 had given positive proof that the Allies were going to conduct a rational strategy. There was no question that France would be invaded in 1944, but the scale of the task involved was light years away from Beaverbrook's propagandist agitation. Brendan Bracken believed that Anthony Eden, who was placating potential enemies to his own rise to power, had smoothed Beaverbrook's return at Bracken's urging.[1] He judged 'that the PM (who is in many ways a lonely man) not only liked Max but found in him a more robust and more fully developed mind than in other ministers. He told Max practically everything. It was therefore better to have him in the government than outside it.'

Beaverbrook was given the non-departmental office of Lord Privy Seal, which conferred status although he remained outside the Cabinet. This choice of office inspired baseless terror throughout Whitehall that Beaverbrook would mimic the power developed by Sir John Anderson as chairman of a network of committees spanning practically every area of policy; Anderson was the committee chairman par excellence, whilst Beaverbrook detested them.[2] Bracken recognised Churchill's need for Beaverbrook: not only did Beaverbrook provide him with stimulation that he could not find from other ministers but he also provided an antidote to his loneliness.[3] Other ministers resented Beaverbrook's return, but Anthony Eden, the de facto number two Conservative in government, understood that it was better to have him subjected to some kind of control as a member of government; Churchill told him everything anyway, so this helped defuse his potential as a critic. Beaverbrook (and Bracken) attended Cabinet meetings so frequently that his exclusion was symbolic rather than anything else. He was installed in the stately Georgian mansion Gwydyr House, a few yards from Downing Street. His staff were his personal followers, with one leavening from the professional civil service. A. J. P. Taylor had described Beaverbrook's twenty-one months as Lord Privy Seal as his happiest time in politics.[4] He had public status that underpinned his role as Churchill's confidant and adviser, which he had never truly lost. He could now claim to be an entirely constructive force and his level of aggression towards colleagues dwindled. There was no recurrence of his stress-related asthma or repetition of the cascade of resignation letters that had marked his first foray into government. His private secretary David Farrer judged, though, that Beaverbrook had permanently damaged his standing by his antics over the Second Front: Churchill 'couldn't do without Beaverbrook either, but Churchill did not lightly forgive the "Second Front" treachery. Beaverbrook returned to England in the doghouse. The dream of high office – perhaps even the highest – vanished into limbo.'[5]

Beaverbrook's standing might have shrunk since 1941, but the suspicion of him and Churchill's other intimates amongst traditional Conservatives had not diminished. Chamberlainite relic 'Chips' Channon reported 'serious unrest' that a 'political harlot' should grow in influence.[6] Suspicions even went far enough to imagine that the 'new triumvirate of Bracken, [Lindemann] and Beaverbrook could rule the country when the Oligarch is abroad, and dominate and fascinate him when he is at home'. The gossips were right to detect an alliance between Bracken and Beaverbrook but well wide of the mark to suppose that the Prof joined in. Beaverbrook and Bracken were close now but maintained a jocular tone. Bracken feigned astonishment at Beaverbrook's newly discovered interested in church patronage after he forwarded a letter begging for a bishopric to him: 'Mr Bracken suggests that you should aid him by telling his Lordship that he thinks there is now a good case for dis-establishing the Church of England. He considers it the ripest of scandals that a bigoted Presbyterian should become a Patron of Church livings.'[7]

The major specific task that was given to Beaverbrook looked forward to the world after the war. He was charged with negotiating an agreement with the US to regulate international civilian air transport.

The advances in aviation technology made during the war meant that the sector would attain a scale and importance undreamed of before the conflict. The British had focused on building bombers, but the US had developed the C-54 and the Constellation, four-motor passenger aircraft, initially as military transports, but they were perfect for use as civilian airliners. A. J. P. Taylor dismisses the episode as 'dead stuff, never to be stirred again except perhaps by some researcher desperate for a subject'; the dossier was a far cry from the vital mission that Churchill had handed Beaverbrook in 1940 of winning the air battle with Nazi Germany.[8] Beaverbrook achieved nothing; he attempted to bypass Assistant Secretary of State Adolf Berle by appealing direct to Harry Hopkins. It was rapidly evident to his private office that he found dealing with the practicalities of a complex, structured international negotiation boring. The discussions were loaded with recondite jargon such as 'cabotage' and even the full-time services of Peter Masefield, an aviation expert, did not transform Beaverbrook into an effective negotiator. It was all quite different to bending the ears of US industrialists with vaulting schemes for war production. Berle was notably anti-British.[9] Beaverbrook tried to persuade Churchill to hand the responsibility over to a series of different departments.[10] When this failed, he first tried to cozen with a misguided and in fact entirely inappropriate personal gift, then to humiliate Berle – neither to any noticeable end. Beaverbrook floated a bilateral deal between Britain and the US with a special place for Canada which proved to be a complete non-starter.[11] The kindest thing that can be said about Beaverbrook's performance is that he did not provoke a stand-up, blazing row as happened to Lord Swinton, who took over the job from him. Only in 1946 did a new generation of politicians and officials – including Masefield – hammer out the Bermuda Agreement which regulated civil flying between Britain and the US. Beaverbrook did no better with the other contentious issue which he attempted to negotiate, the future structure of the oil industry.[12]

Civil aviation was only one of a myriad of facets of what was to happen to the Anglo-American relationship in peacetime. In wartime, the partnership rested on the relationship between Churchill and Roosevelt, which was driven by compatible visions. Roosevelt was committed to defeating the Axis dictatorships beginning with Germany and Churchill knew that Britain could not achieve victory without the military and industrial support of the US. Deciding joint military strategy during the war was not a smooth process; Roosevelt was willing to ignore many strong voices that called for the US to give priority to the war against Japan, but it took agonised debate until Britain and the US decided where and when they would attack Nazi power on Continental Europe. The burgeoning problems of peace presented issues far more diverse and every bit as complex. Behind them all lay the recognition that once the war ended, national interests would resume their position in the debate.

The economist John Maynard Keynes, together with junior Foreign Office minister Richard Law, led the British negotiations with the US on the shape of the world financial system when peace returned. As well as the most immediate questions of helping the British economy transition from its wartime autarkic organisation, Keynes understood the importance of avoiding a repetition of the errors made in the settlement after the First World War, which left a fragile system vulnerable to the financial crashes that occurred in October 1929 and afterwards. Something far more robust and flexible would be required. It was common ground between the US and Britain that some organisation would be needed to coordinate international financial relations, but its exact shape and how it might regulate exchange rates were deeply contentious. In parallel to this, Britain faced the need to give some flesh to Article VII of the 1942 Mutual Aid Agreement with the United States, under which America provided weapons to Britain under Lend-Lease. Article VII set, as a quid pro quo for assistance, 'the elimination of all forms of discriminatory treatment in international commerce, and ... the reduction of tariffs and other trade barriers' in order to meet the vaguely delineated economic goals for the Atlantic Charter signed by Roosevelt and Churchill in August 1941. Keynes recognised that the desperate state of the British economy meant that massive US assistance would be required and was prepared to make concessions accordingly.

By the autumn of 1943, Keynes and Law had thrashed out the Washington Agreement with the US, which contained the origin of the International Monetary Fund (IMF). This was reported to Cabinet together with the outline of what had been discussed about Article VII. An unholy alliance sprang up to oppose Keynes's work. Its most prominent member was Beaverbrook, who scented a return to the gold standard in the IMF plan and, worse, a supposed threat to Imperial Preference in the Article VII talks; the first echoed his lone advice to Churchill as Chancellor of the Exchequer against returning to gold in 1926 and the second embodied his belief – the only principle that can be detected in his public life – in the durability of the British Empire as a trading bloc.[13] His backers included the government's other great imperialist believer, Leo Amery; Robert Hudson, the mouthpiece of the farming lobby; the Bank of England; parts of the Treasury; Labour elements; and theoretical economists hostile to free trade on principle. The politicians kept up a steady bombardment of hostile papers. Beaverbrook latched onto the fight against Keynes with the same enthusiasm that he had pursued the feuds of his past, even though his knowledge and understanding of the plan was superficial at best. He depended on an oral precis of Keynes's document supplied by his secretary Farrer, who confessed to a shaky knowledge of economics, from which he concluded 'if the Government accept these proposals it will be the ruin of the British Empire'[14]. Beaverbrook's strategy was to present the IMF as the gold standard in another guise and to conflate it with free trade and the supposed destruction of Imperial Preference. He submitted a paper to the Cabinet that retold Britain's woes under the gold standard in the language of a newspaper leading article and concluded by telling his colleagues that 'we should not allow the United States to lasso us this time'.[15] Lindemann was firmly willing to accept the threat to Imperial Preference and urged early signature of the deal.[16]

Keynes had borne the brunt of the battle, but now he had a powerful ally. Lindemann was fully aware of the scale of political opposition and the political danger of appeasing the farming lobby.[17] He was especially contemptuous of Amery's hopes for the empire as a boon for the British post-war economy: 'It is no use Amery, etc., talking about our having "a splendid market"; one might as well say that he, Prof., was a great asset to Claridge's merely because he had a splendid appetite.'[18] But Lindemann's proposed solution of stripping Germany and Japan of their pre-war markets was no more realistic. He knew that Churchill leaned towards Beaverbrook's position but saw how much the debate was one of conviction rather than of reason: 'It is no use arguing with a prophet; you can only disbelieve him.' Lindemann set out the simple economic realities to Churchill in February 1944: 'I hope that full Cabinet approval will be given, not only because any weakening on our side would greatly antagonise the Americans, whose aid we shall badly need in the first year after the war, but also because the arrangements being discussed are highly advantageous to us.'[19]

Lindemann did not yield in his opinion, although he did admit to stating his case vigorously a month later: 'On re-reading these notes I feel I must apologise for having succumbed to the revivalist flavour that has recently been imported into the dismal science of economics.'[20] The swipe at the fervour of the debate was aimed equally at his opponents.

In the upshot of the first Cabinet discussion of the proposals, a committee was appointed with both Beaverbrook and Lindemann as members. Lindemann kept Keynes abreast of the political action: 'Complete bedlam ... Ministers are in perpetual session, driving one another crazy with their mutual ravings, the Beaver being mainly responsible, his approach being nothing short of criminal.'[21]

Bracken pitched in on Beaverbrook's side, but Churchill left Beaverbrook and Lindemann to fight it out. He claimed that he could not grasp the abstruse issues of monetary policy that were at stake. More important, the imminence of Overlord dominated his thinking. Churchill grasped the elementary principle that American goodwill was vital to the war effort. His Liberal roots were still deep enough to align him in favour of free trade. He could still trot out the old Liberal mantra that protection meant dear food.

The House of Commons fully lived down to Keynes's worst expectations when it debated the scheme, described as 'a loonies picnic or an idiots' day out, where lunatic Members who on other occasions would be doomed to a decent restraint have a chance, for once, of catching the Speaker's eye'.[22] MP after MP assailed the proposal for no better reason than that it came from the US. But they did not succeed in blocking it. When it was Keynes's turn to speak in the Lords (he had been ennobled shortly before), it was a triumph. Mercifully, Beaverbrook held his tongue.

41

THE ROAD TO A LANDSLIDE

There had been a general election in 1935 and, under normal circumstances, there would have been another one in 1939 or 1940 but special legislation had been passed every year since 1940 to remove the need during wartime. The existence of the wartime all-party coalition under Winston Churchill greatly limited the task and influence of the House of Commons, but no one expected this to be a permanent or even a long-lasting state of affairs. Full-scale democratic political activity would resume at some point; the only question was when and how. Above all, there would have to be elections for a new House of Commons.

After D-Day, Churchill lapsed into a state of lethargy and near hopelessness. Frederick Lindemann was nearly in despair at his failure to tackle the complex financial issues that Britain was facing.[1] Brendan Bracken and Duncan Sandys also tried to persuade him to take more interest in the home front and managed to flush out from him a commitment to take on the Conservative back benches over the controversial Town and Country Planning Bill which offered compensation to owners of land requisitioned by the government only at the prices of 1939 before wartime inflation.[2] Lindemann provided the economic backing here, for once in agreement with Lord Beaverbrook.[3] Bracken's enthusiasm for winning Churchill over to engagement with domestic issues was soon swamped by Beaverbrook's malign influence. The strain to which Bracken had been exposed showed through in an accentuation of his erratic tendencies. On one occasion, even Churchill struggled to stem the flow of Bracken's loquacity and was reduced to delivering a vivid account of the German offensive of March 1918 which he witnessed himself in order to silence him.[4]

Churchill was roused from this torpor by the civil war in Greece, which gave him an opening for his dramatic mid-winter flight to Athens to broker a settlement between the opposing parties, which he seemed to treat as a military operation and criticised John Colville, who was still an RAF officer, for not having carried a weapon.[5] It was as though conflict was Churchill's true vocation. He was already musing about the prospect of a general election which would follow victory. He was braced for a fight and believed that he had a 'full armoury of mud' to sling back if the opposition brought up the past.[6]

The autumn of 1944 and the following winter have the feel of a calm on the political home front before a storm. Positions were already being taken, not least a burgeoning axis between Beaverbrook and Bracken. Beaverbrook had been cultivating contacts with Bracken since the autumn of 1944, dining regularly on Mondays.[7] Some of the period's manifestations were trivial, such as Bracken and Beaverbrook trying to prevent Churchill from going to France for 1944 Armistice Day. But the more professional politicians saw danger ahead. Anthony Eden complained that 'Max and Cherwell have produced crises daily'.[8] The wider political discontent at the influence of Bracken and Beaverbrook penetrated Lindemann's consciousness and he foresaw the danger that they would trigger a 'crushing defeat' at the next election which might threaten the future of the Conservative Party itself.[9] He reported 'much annoyance' at their 'using their influence with the PM, to sabotage of measures such as the new health service about which they are hopelessly ignorant'.

Otherwise, the multitude of domestic issues with which Churchill was confronted evinced no such response. He left the home front to his two trusted friends, Bracken and Beaverbrook, who had ample spare time for such matters. This did not make for a happy functioning of government. At the turn of the year, Clem Attlee, the Labour leader, was so furious that he personally drafted a highly confidential letter of complaint to the Prime Minister, provoked by the proceedings at a meeting where both Beaverbrook and Bracken were present. The topic is uncertain but was probably the future of the distribution of industry, on which Beaverbrook and Bracken had submitted a paper attacking Hugh Dalton's proposals. They accused him of going far beyond the policy set down in a White Paper to extend state control over industry.[10]

Attlee wrote:

> I have for some time had it in mind to write to you on the method or rather lack of method of dealing with matters requiring Cabinet decision ... I consider the present position inimical to the successful performance of the tasks imposed on us as a government and injurious to the war effort.[11]

Attlee's particular concern was Churchill's lack of preparation for discussion on civil affairs, which he accused led to ineffective debate and simply wasted time. Attlee also took issue with Churchill's reliance on Beaverbrook and Bracken for advice, as both ministers were outside the War Cabinet:

> The conclusions agreed upon by a Committee on which have sat five or six members of the Cabinet and other experienced ministers are then submitted with great deference to the Lord Privy Seal [Beaverbrook] and the Minister of Information [Bracken], two ministers without Cabinet responsibility, neither of whom has given any serious attention to the subject. When they state their views it is obvious that they do not know anything about it. Nevertheless an hour is consumed in listening to their opinions. Time and again important matters are delayed or passed in accordance with the decision of the Lord Privy Seal. The excuse is given that in him you have the mind of the Conservative Party. With some knowledge of opinion in the Conservative Party as expressed to me on the retirement from and re-entry into the Government of Lord Beaverbrook, I suggest that this view would be indignantly repudiated by the vast majority.

Churchill sensed that he was getting bogged down in a profitless fight and advised his staff they should 'not bother Atler or Hitlee [*sic*]'. He thought better of sending his inflammatory reply. Not merely did Clemmie think that Attlee's letter was 'both true and wholesome' but Beaverbrook himself, despite the letter's criticism of him, thought it was a good one.[12] He contented himself with a brief and possibly insincere if not downright sarcastic acknowledgement: 'I have to thank you for your Private and Personal letter of January 19. You may be sure I shall always endeavour to profit by your counsels.'

Beaverbrook might have seen some justice in Attlee's letter, but neither he nor Bracken were moved to adopt a more constructive approach. Attlee had opened a vulnerable flank to his adversaries. The Lord President's committee had been losing ground in the pecking order of Whitehall since Attlee had taken over the office from Sir John Anderson, who had made it the bedrock of his domination of home front administrative matters. Attlee had first tried to improve attendance be reinstituting a firm weekly slot for its meetings.[13] This seems to have brought no improvement and he resorted to outright insistence that 'responsible ministers' attend.[14] Beaverbrook and Bracken gleefully brought Attlee's discomfiture to Churchill in a flippant letter to the Prime Minister a few days afterwards:

> Our attention has been drawn to the lament of Mr Attlee in his Paper L. P. (45) 17 that Ministers do not attend his committee.
>
> We now offer to fill two of the vacant places.
>
> We are moved by the sad plight of the Lord President:
>
> 'Alone, alone, all, all alone
>
> Alone on the wide, wide sea,'
>
> Yours ever,
>
> B.
>
> B. B.
>
> P. S. Our offer depends on the approval of the Lord President

Churchill's response to this from Yalta in the Crimea, where he had gone for a summit conference with Roosevelt and Stalin, suggests that he felt that it was more his job to orchestrate teasing the Labour leader:

> All the Bs.
> Wait till I return please.

Ernest Bevin opened party political hostilities at the beginning of April whilst the war in the west had still a month to run. Previous speeches by Attlee and Herbert Morrison had highlighted economic differences between the parties and called for cooperation until Germany was defeated. In Bevin's words, bricks could fly after the dissolution of Parliament. He had been goaded by suggestions in Beaverbrook's newspapers that he was about to turn his back on the Labour Party, which he denied emphatically. He and other union leaders had hopes of extending the coalition government into peacetime. Bevin riposted with a firm point-by-point affirmation of all his party's positions, beginning with its declaration in the previous November that it would fight the coming election. He drew a distinction between Churchill as national leader and the Conservatives whose record on rearmament in the long years it held power before the Second World War he savaged. He endorsed the Labour commitment to nationalise coal mines and utilities.

When he read Bevin's speech, Churchill said that 'if the Labour Party were going ahead on those lines he thought the time had come for him to *brusquer les affaires* – i.e. to hasten the departure of the Opposition groups from the Government'.[15] It fell to Bracken to deliver a 'slashing' reply, which repeatedly portrayed Labour's goals as totalitarian:

> Mr Bevin's Blitz on the Conservatives … Mr Bevin is very cross with us. When I heard a summary of his speech on the BBC it sounded so lively and full of invective that I thought it was wrongly attributed.

I thought it was made by Mr Aneurin Bevan. But when I read the authoritarian sentences in the full report I knew that they could only come from a forceful trade union leader – one who was used to trumping disagreeable ideas by a couple of million card votes.[16]

Bracken excavated a comment from March 1939 in which Ernest Bevin queried whether war would come, 'blissfully forgetting the campaign conducted by the Socialist Party against rearming Britain'. Bracken praised Churchill's warnings against the danger from Germany, 'In so far as he found any support for these warnings it came from Conservatives.' He devoted much of his speech to a ringing affirmation of the power of private sector industry, with digs at wartime controls thrown in for good measure:

Surely a Government had enough to do without meddling directly in the management of our trades and industries ...

Britain would never accept the sort of totalitarian State desired by the Socialists ...

Britain has prospered by daring. What sort of future lies ahead of us if under State control risk-taking is abolished or controlled by that excellent body, the Public Accounts Committee of the House of Commons?

Our scientists, our workers, our industrialists, our financial institutions are the best in the world. What folly it would be to crib, cabin or continue them in monopolies controlled by the State, employers or labour monopolies. As a nation of enterprisers our future is boundless. As a nation of form-fillers and restrictionists we have the bleakest of futures. Fears and doubts of our future seem to hagride the Socialists towards a lop-sided totalitarianism. Why should we be timid in facing the future? Our only need is the breath of life.[17]

A fortnight later, the government suffered the last in the long list of by-election defeats that had punctuated public discontent at the lack of an outlet for opposition. In normal circumstances, Chelmsford was a rock-solid Conservative seat, but the vaguely utopian Common Wealth Party won with a healthy majority in a contest between two serving RAF officers. It was described as a 'smashing' victory. The winner had the rather more distinguished war record, but, ominously for the government, this was the first English constituency to vote on a new electoral register. Men and women serving overseas and returned PoWs also voted. Churchill summoned a crisis group of government figures to discuss the implications: Beaverbrook and Bracken from his inner circle and James Stuart, the Chief Whip, and Ralph Assheton, the party chairman, from the Conservative Party leadership. Churchill was not going to entrust the coming general election campaign to the machine of a party which he had never truly adopted. As the election campaign got seriously under way, Bracken neglected his admittedly not very onerous duties at the Ministry of Information in favour of his political work.[18]

The first tactical decision facing Churchill was whether to hold the election as soon as possible or to wait until the autumn. Labour feared that an election soon after VE Day would favour the Conservatives with the aura of the architects of victory. Contrary to Churchill's later claim that a large majority of Conservative ministers preferred an early election, the balance actually lay in favour of proposing to Labour an extension of the coalition until Japan were defeated.[19] The most vocal advocate of delay was Rab Butler, who had only recently been elevated to the Cabinet and who was almost alone in being definitely cautious about Conservative prospects at the election. He received the rough end of Beaverbrook's tongue for his pains afterwards. To the end, Beaverbrook was firmly convinced the Conservatives would win.

Beaverbrook said to Butler, 'Young man [he was forty-two], if you speak to the Prime Minister like that, you will not be offered a job in the next Conservative government.'

Butler replied, 'That doesn't really affect me; for if we have an early election, there is not going to be a Conservative government.'[20]

Confronted with Clemmie's preference for postponement and an opinion poll by Beaverbrook's operation which showed a much larger majority of respondents (and an even greater one amongst Conservative voters) in favour of an autumn election, Churchill offered to prolong the coalition.

Churchill left it to Labour to choose whether to extend the wartime coalition beyond victory in Europe. Handled otherwise, this might have been made to appear as if the opposition was turning against national unity in the face of enormous challenges: Japan had yet to be defeated and huge damage from German bombing had to be made good. But this would only have been a question of presentation. There is no sign that Churchill genuinely hoped or expected to be a unifying peacetime leader. He was the Conservative Party's only serious electoral asset. Equally, he never gave serious thought to the idea of withdrawing into retirement, with his lustre as war leader untarnished by party politics; he told Duncan Sandys that he was not 'yet ready to be put on a pedestal'.[21] When the news arrived that Labour had definitively pulled the plug, Churchill threw himself into the fray enthusiastically: 'At once all was swept aside and electioneering became the only topic.'[22] Churchill had composed his reply to Attlee with some advice from Randolph and Harold Macmillan, who happened to be there. He concluded the first draft of his letter with a courtly acknowledgement of Labour's contribution and an affirmation of underlying national unity:

> I should not like to end this letter without assuring you once again how grateful I am to you and your Labour colleagues for the grand support they have given to the Island and its Empire in their struggle for life out of which we have all risen victorious, but still beset by dangers and crowned with new responsibilities. Whatever hard words may be used in the warfare of Party politics roughly at Elections – we must never forget that the underlying ties that have united us all may well prove indestructible.[23]

Churchill expected that this letter would be published as a swansong of the coalition. Beaverbrook, though, rejected its positive dimensions and persuaded Churchill to omit any such kindly references. The final version accused Attlee of playing to party advantage and wanting something that was not in the national interest. The tone was set for the coming campaign.

Before the campaign got fully under way, Beaverbrook held a weekend gathering at Cherkley that gave a flavour of how he was going to approach the operation. He began by presenting himself and Bracken as true men of quality who had had to make their own way in life whereas men such as Anthony Eden had got as far as they did through the accident of birth. The established leaders of the Conservatives, Assheton and Stuart, were both Etonians and the latter was positively aristocratic. Beaverbrook attacked Bevin and praised Morrison. Churchill's secretary Colville judged that 'the evening was fun, with a real buccaneering, racketeering atmosphere. Of course, they are both utterly mischievous and will do the Conservatives countless harm, at this election and afterwards.'[24]

The campaign did not get off to a happy note. In keeping with his practice of reducing questions to a fight between his own superior wisdom and lesser individuals, Beaverbrook accused Assheton of being insufficiently aggressive. Even Churchill felt the need to call him to order, but there was another problem:

As Lord Beaverbrook is being too high-handed about the Tory Party and the coming election, the PM saw him before dinner and protested. He then had a political dinner party, to discuss election propaganda to which, in addition to Lord B. Oliver Lyttelton, James Stuart and Ralph Assheton were bidden. Brendan was not included, as the PM is well aware that people, and particularly the Tory Party, are beginning to look askance at the Brendan–Beaver combination.[25]

Beaverbrook even went as far as trying to turn Bracken against Churchill by insinuating that he had been ungrateful towards him. Colville feared that Beaverbrook's influence was poisoning Bracken's judgement: 'Brendan's advice becomes less sound as Lord Beaverbrook's influence grows more enveloping.'[26] Bracken started defending Bea-verbrook against accusations that he was a bad influence on Church-ill.[27] Beaverbrook had taken to promoting the utterly fanciful idea that Bracken should lead the Conservatives as a rival to Eden. It lay so far out of the realm of the possible that conventional Conservatives would accept Bracken as a leader that it casts serious doubts on Beaverbrook's understanding of politics at that point. Bracken had a poor opinion of Eden's supposed lack of political courage since the days of tripartite control of propaganda and was now openly contemptuous of Eden, whom he called 'Robert Taylor' after an American film star, noted for his good looks and little else, but there is no sign that he did anything active to further this particular whimsy of Beaverbrook.[28] Beaverbrook insinuated to Bracken that Churchill's supposed ingratitude embraced not making him Chancellor of the Exchequer, a job for which he was barely suitable.[29] Beaverbrook praised Bracken in public speeches, including one in which he described him as the 'greatest First Lord after Winston Churchill', which could have referred to his position as First Lord of the Admiralty or even First Lord of the Treasury (i.e. Prime Minister). This prompted the hilarity that it deserved, although the tale that Beaverbrook predicted Bracken would be 'the greatest First Lord of the Admiralty since Nelson' is apocryphal. Beaverbrook was suspected of using Leslie Hore-Belisha, who had never managed to return to office, to spread propaganda for the idea of Bracken as Prime Minister.[30]

The most conspicuous contribution that Beaverbrook made to the campaign was through his newspapers. Initially, he had resisted Churchill's attempt to keep him in the purely Conservative caretaker government that was to manage the country until the result of the election was out. He felt that he could be more effective using his press empire as a propaganda tool on behalf of the Conservatives. When he had been in government – and sometimes outside – he had maintained the fiction that his newspapers operated independently and that he had no input into their coverage. This provided a conven-ient tool to disclaim responsibility for articles that provoked protests from the victims; they were almost invariably abusive or mischievous. But as his secretary wrote: 'Dropped now was all pretence that as a Minister he took no part in the conduct of his newspapers. He master-minded their every story, their every leading article, their every attack on those opponents who had so recently been Beaverbrook's colleagues.'[31]

Beaverbrook had long detested Clem Attlee and Ernest Bevin, but the dictates of maintaining the coalition government had forced him to bite his tongue. Attlee had shown exceptional loyalty to Churchill throughout the war and given no opportunity to the Conservatives to attack him. Attlee's understated calm approach to affairs was anathema to Beaverbrook. Bevin had steadily blocked all of Beaverbrook's moves to extend his influence over war production, providing him with a handy scapegoat for deeper structural problems in the same way that the bureaucracy of the Air Ministry had provided a perma-nent target for his ire at the Ministry of Aircraft Production. Now that he was off the leash, he could attack his foes to his heart's content. It was doubtless satisfying but of dubious electoral value, as Colville suspected: 'Brendan and the Beaver are firing vast salvos which mostly, I think, miss their mark. Labour propaganda is a great deal better and is launched on a rising market.'[32] Beaverbrook with Bracken in tow were pressing Churchill to hold the election as soon as possible.[33]

As well as assailing Labour's top leaders, Beaverbrook set out to demonise Harold Laski, the Marxist chairman of the Labour Party. Then, as now, the Labour executive was further left than the leader-ship. Laski was a tempting target, providing Beaverbrook's newspapers with a stream of copy which could be used to support an image of the Labour Party controlled by extremists. Churchill invited Attlee to accompany him to the Potsdam summit conference, which took place during the election campaign, to demonstrate the democratic continuity of British government. Laski had tried to force a declara-tion from Attlee that he would not be bound by any decisions taken at the conference. Attlee ignored him, but the affair came into public knowledge. When a Conservative councillor accused Laski of having advocated violent revolution, he sued for libel. Beaverbrook specially thanked the long-standing editor of his *Daily Express*, Arthur Christiansen, for publicising a statement by Laski calling for 'Socialism by force'.[34] Churchill even named Laski as the man who would control a Labour government through the national executive in a radio broadcast.

Neither Beaverbrook nor Bracken was present at Chequers when Churchill composed the infamous speech in which he claimed that a Labour government would automatically be totalitarian:

> No Socialist Government conducting the entire life and industry of the country could afford to allow free, sharp or violently worded expression of public discontent. They would have to fall back on some form of Gestapo, no doubt very humanely directed in the first instance. And this would nip opinion in the bud; it would stop criticism as it reared its head, and it would gather all the power to the supreme party and the party leaders, rising like stately pinnacles above their vast bureaucracies of civil servants, no longer servants and no longer civil.[35]

Clemmie spotted immediately the folly of the mention of a Gestapo and vainly begged her husband to remove it. He paid far less attention to delivering a positive message on the benefits that a renewed Conservative government would bring the country. Neither Beaverbrook nor Bracken was directly involved, but according to one source, Beaverbrook did have a small input: persuading Churchill to remove a reference to Bevin.[36] Even if Beaverbrook and Bracken bore no direct responsibility for the broadcast, one of Beaverbrook's closest collaborators saw it as being of a piece with their flawed strategy for the campaign.[37] Beaverbrook grasped that the Gestapo comment was damaging to the Conservatives' cause and tried to turn this to his advantage in his battle to undermine the official party hierarchy. He told Colville, entirely falsely, that James Stuart, the Chief Whip, had seen and approved the speech.[38]

Few doubted that the mention was a grave error and the broadcast that Attlee made in reply the following evening was on the wireless at a dinner attended by Churchill, Rab Butler, Oliver Lyttelton and James Stuart.[39] Attlee's riposte might have fallen wide of the mark in identifying the actual author of the words, but it struck home nonetheless: 'The voice we heard last night was that of Mr Churchill, but the mind was that of Lord Beaverbrook.' Beaverbrook tried to comfort Churchill by telephoning round his men in the provinces and reporting to the Prime Minister that they judged Attlee's broadcast to have been a failure, in an obvious exercise of wishful thinking and self-delusion. The Prime Minister was aware that his words had provoked a damaging storm. Self-pityingly, he bemoaned the demise of a tradition of political invective, in which harsh words were dealt and taken in a collegial spirit.

It was not just the negative and aggressive tone of the broadcast that struck Churchill's minister and long-standing sparring partner Leo Amery, who saw a huge missed opportunity:

I am afraid I was greatly depressed by [the broadcast]. The whole strategy of the campaign I should have thought would have been to lay stress on the external situation and urgent measures of demobilisation and housing etc., and to have insisted on putting the issue of Socialism versus Individualism in the background ... Instead of that Winston jumped straight off his pedestal as world statesman to deliver a fantastical exaggerated onslaught on Socialism which, while cheering a good many of our supporters, will put off a lot of those who might otherwise have voted for us. I fear Max and Brendan have completely collared him ...

We all listened to Attlee's broadcast, a very adroit quiet reply to Winston's rodomontade. Julian [Amery's son, later a notably right-wing Conservative] was considerably impressed and I fear had considerable searchings of heart as to whether he was really on the Right side.[40]

For all the criticism, Churchill doubled down and in his next election broadcast a fortnight afterwards foretold a dictatorship backed by force: 'The natural change of parties in office from time to time would necessarily come to an end, and a political police would be required to enforce an absolute and permanent system upon the nation.'[41]

In the immediate run-up to the campaign, Lindemann was practically acting as a private secretary to Churchill, struggling to help Colville clear his overflowing inbox. He and Colville had to impose a more sensible bedtime on the Prime Minister: 1.30 a.m.[42] Lindemann appears not to have played an active part in the campaign, but he did monitor malevolently Beaverbrook's contribution: 'It is difficult to detect a coherent policy in Lord Beaverbrook's Bradford speech or in his subsequent letters to the Press.'[43] He skewered Beaverbrook's shaky understanding of elementary economics and pointed out the contradiction between his claim that 'the policy of Imperial Preference saved the world. Of all policies that policy must be furthered and extended' and his advocacy of Article VII. According to Lindemann, when it came to agriculture, Beaverbrook 'indulges in a great deal of irresponsible demagogy about higher wages, higher standards of living by international agreement and so on'. Lindemann accused Beaverbrook of trying to present his own views as those of the party. It is unclear whether Lindemann actually offered this analysis to the Prime Minister, but Beaverbrook certainly struck at Lindemann. He had compiled a substantial dossier of the occasions on which Lindemann had been proved to be in the wrong, beginning with the V-2 which he showed to Churchill's secretary, albeit taking care that Colville had no opportunity to make a copy but doubtless hoping to poison his mind.[44]

The official slogan for Churchill's campaign – 'Help him finish the job' – seemed to prioritise the military defeat of Japan, which few expected before 1946 or even 1947. The speed of Japan's surrender after the atom bombs on Hiroshima and Nagasaki, combined with the Soviet declaration, came as a surprise. The exhortation 'Vote National' was hollow to the point of falsehood; the Liberals were reunited in opposition and the moribund National Labour Organisation had dissolved itself; Churchill was purely a Conservative candidate. The Labour poster with pictures of members of each fighting service and the slogan 'Help Them Finish Their Job! Give Them Homes and Work' was infinitely better attuned to voters' interests, albeit mildly illogical.

The polls closed on 5 July 1945, but this was followed by an odd interval of three weeks, during which the votes cast by servicemen and women overseas were sent back to Britain and onwards to the relevant constituencies. Churchill took his first real holiday since the war began at Hendaye in south-west France near the Spanish border. The count itself followed the traditional overnight pattern, with the results being declared in the course of the following day. The results were catastrophic for the Conservatives. The result of the 1935 victory was almost exactly reversed. Labour won 393 seats whilst the number of Conservative MPs was more than halved to 210. The Labour majority of 146 was the largest for any post-war government. The damage was especially great in Churchill's immediate circle. Out of respect, none of the opposition parties put up a candidate against him in the new constituency of Woodford, which took in much of his old Epping constituency, but Alexander Hancock, a local farmer, stood as an independent, describing himself as a philosophical communist. Hancock polled over 10,000 votes compared to nearly 28,000 for the Prime Minister. This was a pure protest vote; when Hancock stood against Churchill again in 1951 in a fully contested poll, he received 851 votes. Bracken was on the verge of tears when he learned he had been defeated in North Paddington by Sir Noel Mason-Macfarlane – a general of no political experience who held a grudge against Churchill for his dismissal during the war, was almost confined to a wheelchair by a series of sporting and car accidents and was rumoured to drink two bottles of whisky a day.[45] He was barely classed as a no-hope candidate by the Labour Party. Sandys and Randolph lost to more conventional opponents.

The scale of the Labour victory took most senior politicians aback. Attlee had thought that a majority of thirty-odd seats was possible. In the higher ranks of the government, only Bracken and Lindemann had an inkling of the danger.[46] It was more junior figures such as Labour's

Nye Bevan and the Conservative Rab Butler who foresaw the severity of the punishment that the voters would dish out. Beaverbrook
was sublimely confident to the last.[47] Intriguingly, one prescient voice
warning Churchill came from a general rather than a politician. The
commander of the British Army in Burma, Bill Slim, told him bluntly: 'My troops won't be voting for you.' This might help explain how
the result came as a surprise. Traditionally, professional servicemen
tended to vote Conservative, but Slim understood that the mass army
of conscripts would follow the more class-based pattern of civilian life.
With only narrow experience of the forces overseas, the politicians
based in Britain might have overlooked this factor and focused on
home-based voters.

Bob Boothby, who held his seat, derived a perverse pleasure from
his party's humiliation, claiming to have sung the 'Red Flag' in the
House of Commons.[48] He judged that the combination of Beaverbrook and Bracken had cost the Conservatives 100 seats and singled
Bracken out for special criticism.

Many factors contributed to Labour's victory and it is now seen as
having been inevitable. Even without the inept and aggressive campaign championed by Beaverbrook, few believe that the result would
have been fundamentally different. As Beaverbrook understood,
memories of the Baldwin and Chamberlain governments elected in
1935 were long and bad enough to inspire a reaction; Beaverbrook just
drew the wrong conclusion. Many saw the socially levelling effect of
war socialism in a positive light. The bulk of the electorate, who saw
little of the realities of negotiating with Stalin, may have seen socialism in the roseate, pro-Soviet glow of the fight against the German in-
vaders. On a more mundane level, Labour had devoted much effort to
building up its local machinery, whilst the Conservative apparatus was
traditionally elderly and ex-officer class. Not only was it in a creaky
state after wartime neglect but Beaverbrook can have done nothing
to motivate it. In the aftermath of defeat, Beaverbrook was reluctant
to discuss the campaign, which Bruce Lockhart took as showing that
Beaverbrook understood his own responsibility for it.[49]

AFTERWORD

Brendan Bracken returned to Parliament through a by-election in November 1945, but his political career was over. He disapproved of the drift of the Conservative Party towards the centrist stance of Rab Butler and Harold Macmillan. He had remained faithful to the dream of the Raj until the bitter end, sorrowfully claiming that 'we have been chattered out of India', as though idle parliamentary manoeuvre had destroyed something that would otherwise have remained intact.[1] He resisted Winston Churchill's blandishments to return to government after he won the 1951 election and returned to power. Churchill made him a viscount, but he never took his seat in the House of Lords. He remained a good friend of Lord Beaverbrook and they conducted a long gossipy correspondence about political developments. Bracken returned to the world of business and financial publishing full-time and saw through the merger of his *Financial News* with his larger rival, the *Financial Times*. The merged paper kept the competitor's name, but he controlled the business and it continues to thrive as one of the world's leading financial newspapers. Its offices have returned to the now magnificently restored Bracken House, which keeps his name alive to the wider world. He died of throat cancer in 1958.

Duncan Sandys returned to Parliament when Randolph gave up a promising constituency in his favour. Sandys had three children with Diana Churchill, but they divorced in 1960. He became Minister for Supply in the 1951 government and he led the life of a prominent albeit second-rank Conservative politician into the Edward Heath era. His name featured in the series of sex scandals which destroyed Harold Macmillan's government in the early 1960s, as one of the (numerous)

candidates to be the 'headless man' photographed being fellated by
the Duchess of Argyll. He was ennobled and moved into business,
where his private, tax-efficient pay arrangements at 'Tiny' Rowland's
Lonrho conglomerate were stigmatised by Prime Minister Ted Heath
as showing 'the unpleasant and unacceptable face of capitalism'.

Frederick Lindemann left the smallest mark of the friends on the
wider world after the war. His relationship with Churchill was sub-
stantially unaltered and he was once again Paymaster General in the
1951 government. His contribution was much the same as in the wartime government: the Prime Minister's personal adviser rather than a
minister in the full sense. He was given a seat in the Cabinet, which
allowed him to resume his feud with Sandys full-bloodedly. He was a
student of Christ Church until his death in 1957.

Bob Boothby rebuilt his career as both a politician and a natural and
an effective TV presenter, both roles firmly outside Churchill's orbit.
His business and, by one account at least, sexual life were incautious,
but British defamation law favours heavily the plaintiff and Boothby's
involvement with the London gangsters the Kray twins was only very
briefly brought to public attention. The relationship between Churchill
and Boothby was ambiguous to the end and seems to have mattered
more to Boothby, even after his intervention on Churchill's side in the
Tobruk debate had practically marked the last act of their friendship.
Boothby asked Hastings Ismay, whom he regarded as a great friend, why

> [Churchill] bothered, at intervals, to hate me, when I was so unim-
> portant. He replied: 'Because you wrote him one or two tactless letters
> which angered him, and because you were apt to tell things he didn't
> want to hear. But, most of all, because you were one of the very few
> people he was ever fond of.'[2]

Ismay advised Boothby simply to accept Churchill's wishes if he
thought they were right. Boothby heeded and was favoured with a
knighthood and a part in the Conservatives' nascent policy towards
the European Community. Boothby confessed, 'I never really liked

him. I simply could not take the element of brutality ... in his nature.'
Privately, he even accused Churchill of having tried to destroy him.[3]

In the run-up to the 1951 election, Lord Beaverbrook obeyed
Churchill and killed off a promising lead to the story of the Duke
of Windsor's flirtation with Nazi Germany in 1940.[4] Churchill did
not want reminders of his own embarrassing support for the Duke
during the abdication crisis. But Beaverbrook was not called back into
government after Churchill won the election; it is unsure whether he
wanted to be or was disappointed not to be, but later that year he
discontinued his membership of the Conservative Party and formally
renounced his British citizenship. Beaverbrook has a firm place in the
popular story of Churchill's first premiership. If they hear his name
today, the vast majority of those British people who have heard of him
at all will know of him as the Minister of Aircraft Production and a
major contributor to the victory in the Battle of Britain by bringing a
dramatic increase in the production of Hurricanes and Spitfires just in
time to fight the battle. This is still repeated even by professional historians. The National Trust, custodians of Churchill's Chartwell and
thus keeper of the flame, credits Beaverbrook with increasing fighter
production by 300 per cent in four months.[5] It is a key part of the
Churchill victory in the Battle of Britain myth but rests heavily on the
mythomaniac accounts that Beaverbrook himself gave.

Randolph Churchill's life after the war was a repetition of his
pre-war life: a succession of failures to regain a seat in Parliament;
spasmodic journalism; boorish, drunken behaviour; arguments with
his parents; and an unstable personal life. After his father's death, he
began to write his biography, just as Winston had written his own father's biography. He had only completed the first two volumes, which
are generally highly regarded, when he died of a heart attack at the age
of fifty-seven. It was left to a professional historian, Martin Gilbert,
to complete the project. Randolph's volumes embody the flourish his
father brought to his biographies of the 1st Duke of Marlborough, but
perhaps inevitably, the eight thick volumes of the complete work tend
more towards monument or reference work than portrait.

In later life, Beaverbrook dedicated effort and money to history and the curation of history, but this focused on his own past. The Beaverbrook library, under the stewardship of his satellite A. J. P. Taylor and originally situated in the offices of his *Daily Express*, served to feed his own memory and the books he wrote, steered or planned focused on his vendettas, above all his lifelong hatred of Stanley Baldwin.[6]

Duncan Sandys indulged in the retired politician's predilection for sustaining his own reputation and refighting parochial feuds, but his contribution represents the many fights which Lindemann inspired in his lifetime. In the early 1960s, the tale of the intelligence battle over the V-2 broke in public and Sandys mounted an offensive to set out his side of the story. Lindemann had died in 1957, so was unable to respond. Sandys gave a full briefing to the historian David Irving. The book that arose, *The Mare's Nest*, was well received, though it is today overshadowed by Irving's now evil reputation. Sandys had better luck in the world of fiction, where he collaborated extensively in the production of a movie covering the battle against the V-2, *Operation Crossbow*. Here the draft script featured Sandys as the Whitehall dynamo of the fight against the V-2, with an obstructive and sceptical 'Professor Bird', played by Trevor Howard, trying to hold him back for honest but obstinate motives. When the fictionalised Sandys helps plan the RAF air raid on Peenemünde, he hopes it will 'bomb to hell all the Professor Birds who are living there', hinting at rather more vengeful feelings.[7] In the movie itself, the pseudonym was dropped and the Professor was given his real name: Lindemann.

Ambiguous towards Churchill as ever, Boothby made full play of their association in his memoirs but famously complained of Churchill's 'streak of cruelty'.[8] He relished the additional sales of the book that the ensuing furore generated; his publishers estimated that the comment trebled the sales of the book.[9]

Neither of Churchill's most loyal friends did anything to record their glory days helping him fight appeasement and then Hitler. Lindemann preserved his papers, which are one of the most useful sources for a historian, but Bracken ordered that his own papers be destroyed

entirely, which they were. Bracken deprived history of much potential gold, but he did support John Colville's project to commemorate
Churchill with a college of Cambridge University that was to bear his
name. Appropriately enough, he left the residue of his estate to provide the master of the college with a suitable wine cellar and furniture
for his rooms.[10] As Bracken wrote to the chancellor of the university
very shortly before he died in 1958: 'In distant times the comforts and
dignity of the Masters' Lodges encouraged all sorts of useful people
to seek their hospitality. And so I hope the Churchill College will not
only be acclaimed as a house of learning but one of discerning hospitality.' It was a fitting dedication from one who shared an appreciation
of good company and the finer things in life with Churchill himself.

NOTES

Introduction: Friendship and Churchill (ppxxxiii–xxxviii)

1 'Right and Consistent', International Churchill Society, https://winstonchurchill.org/resources/quotes/right-and-consistent/

2 John Colville, *Footprints in Time*, 1976, p197

1: Return Trip to the Wilderness (pp1–5)

1 Richard Toye, *Lloyd George and Churchill: Rivals for Greatness*, 2007, pp169f

2 Ibid., p180

3 Thomas Jones (ed. Keith Middlemas), *Whitehall Diary: Volume 2, 1926–1930*, 1969, 26 April 1926

2: The Two Ronin (pp7–15)

1 Churchill to Clemmie, 4 January 1922 quoted in Mary Soames (ed.), *Speaking for Themselves: The Personal Letters of Winston and Clementine Churchill*, 1998, p246

2 Hilton Young diary, 18 November 1924, quoted in Philip Williamson and Edward Baldwin (eds), *Baldwin Papers*, 2004, p166

3 Robert Rhodes James, *Victor Cazalet*, 1976, p115

3: An Australian on the Make (pp17–22)

1 'Brendan Bracken: The Fantasist Whose Dreams Came True', International Churchill Society, https://winstonchurchill.org/publications/finest-hour/finest-hour-113/brendan-bracken-the-fantasist-whose-dreams-came-true/; Martin Gilbert, *Winston S. Churchill: Volume 5, The Prophet of Truth, 1922–1939*, 1976, p45

2 Robert Bruce Lockhart (ed. Kenneth Young), *The Diaries of Sir Robert Bruce Lockhart: Volume 2, 1939–1965*, 1980, p356

3 Colville, *Footprints in Time*, p315

4 Andrew Boyle, *Poor, Dear Brendan*, 1974, pp87ff

5 CAC BBKN 4, interview with Patrick Buchan-Hepburn

6 Cecil King, *With Malice Toward None*, 1970

7 Boyle, *Poor, Dear Brendan*, p141

8 Charles Edward Lysaght, *Brendan Bracken*, 1979, pp72f

4: A Ducal Professor (pp23–9)

1 Henry 'Chips' Channon (ed. Simon Heffer), *Henry 'Chips' Channon: The Diaries, Volume 2, 1938–1943*, 2022, p585

2 Richard Davenport-Hines and Adman Sisman (eds), *One Hundred Letters from Hugh Trevor Roper*, 2014, p31

3 Channon diaries, vol. 2, p667

4 'The Professor and the Prime Minister: Frederick Lindemann and Winston Churchill', International Churchill Society, https://winstonChurchill.org/publications/finest-hour/finest-hour-195/the-professor-and-the-prime-ministerfrederick-lindemann-and-winston-Churchill/

5 Roy Harrod, *The Prof*, 1959, p142

6 Ibid., p98

7 Earl of Birkenhead, *The Prof in Two Worlds*, 1961, p119

8 Ibid., p127

9 Gilbert, *Winston S. Churchill: Volume 5*, p301

10 Cherwell papers E23 draft 'letter to national press', 1926

11 Gilbert, *Winston S. Churchill: Volume 5*, pp158, 166

5: A Golden Youth (pp31–6)
1 Boothby papers, Boothby to Churchill, 9 October 1926
2 Lord Boothby, *Recollections of a Rebel*, 1978, p45
3 Boothby papers, Churchill to Boothby, 10 August 1926
4 CAC BBKN 4, interview with Mary Links
5 Harold Macmillan, *Winds of Change, 1914–1939*, 1966, p204
6 Ibid., p204; for Beaverbrook, Gilbert, *Winston S. Churchill: Volume 4*, p99
7 Boothby papers, Churchill to Boothby, 6 February 1932
8 Ibid., Churchill to Boothby, 10 August 1926
9 Ibid., Churchill to Boothby, 7 December 1928
10 'At Home with Lloyd George', *Picture Post*, 20 April 1940 quoted in Toye, *Lloyd George and Churchill*, p346
11 Nicholas Davenport, *Memoirs of a City Radical*, 1974
12 Boothby papers, Churchill to Boothby, 6 February 1932

6: Chartwell (pp37–44)
1 Sarah Churchill, *A Thread in the Tapestry*, 1967, pp36f
2 Gilbert, *Winston S. Churchill: Volume 5*, p126
3 Churchill, *A Thread in the Tapestry*, pp36f
4 Mary Soames, *A Daughter's Tale: The Memoir of Winston and Clementine Churchill's Youngest Child*, 2011, p45
5 Cherwell papers, K63, Churchill to Lindemann, 31 May 1928
6 Gilbert, *Winston S. Churchill: Volume 5*, p442
7 Information terminal at Chartwell, National Trust
8 Churchill, *A Thread in the Tapestry*, p38
9 Ronald Tree, *When the Moon was High*, 1975, p139
10 Jones (ed. Middlemas), *Whitehall Diary: Volume 2*, p67
11 Gilbert, *Winston S. Churchill: Volume 5*, p299
12 Brian Roberts, *Randolph*, 1984, p36
13 Jones, *Whitehall Diary*, p176
14 Cherwell papers, K75, Randolph to Cherwell, 1 May 1928
15 Ibid., Randolph to Cherwell, 27 November 1934
16 Martin Gilbert (ed.), *The Churchill Documents, Volume 12: The Wilderness Years, 1929–1935*, 1981, pp269, 244
17 Roberts, *Randolph*, p107. Sadly, if Channon was keeping a diary at this point, it has disappeared
18 Bruce Lockhart diaries, vol. 1, p269. Beaverbrook told a slightly different version of the story; David Kynaston, *The Financial Times*, 1988, p123
19 Bruce Lockhart diaries, vol. 1, p229
20 CAC BBKN 4, interview with Randolph Churchill
21 Churchill papers, Churchill to Randolph, 29 December 1929
22 Bruce Lockhart diaries, vol. 1, p229

7: The Financial Publisher (pp45–50)
1 Boyle, *Poor, Dear Brendan*, p119
2 Lysaght, *Brendan Bracken*, pp80f
3 Lord Drogheda, *Double Harness*, 1978, p45
4 *The Times*, 31 July 1928
5 Kynaston, *The Financial Times*, p107
6 Ibid., 106f
7 Bruce Lockhart diaries, vol. 1, p192
8 Ibid., p275
9 Beaverbrook papers, BBK/C/59

8: The Winstonians (pp51–60)
1 *The Times*, 24 February 1931
2 Gilbert, *Winston S. Churchill: Volume 5*, p421 n421
3 Ibid., p422
4 William Percival Crozier (ed. A. J. P. Taylor), *Off the Record: Political Interviews, 1933–1943*, 1973, p319
5 J. C. C. Davidson (ed. Robert Rhodes James, *Memoirs of a Conservative: J. C. C. Davidson's Memoirs and Papers, 1910–1937*, 1969, p385
6 John Ramsden, *The Age of Balfour and Baldwin, 1902–1940*, 1978, p304

7   Graham Stewart, *Burying Caesar: Churchill, Chamberlain and the Battle for the Tory Party*, 2000, p187
8   Ibid., pp153, 158, 152, 167
9   Ibid., p167
10   Lord (Rab) Butler, *The Art of the Possible*, 1973, p51
11   Baldwin papers, Baldwin to Davidson, 13 November 1930
12   Quoted at Stewart, *Burying Caesar*, p161
13   Rhodes James, *Memoirs of a Conservative*, p385
14   Tom Jones diary, 11 March 1931, in Williamson and Baldwin (eds), *Baldwin Papers*, p258
15   Baldwin to Duchess of Atholl, 23 February 1933, in Williamson and Baldwin (eds), *Baldwin Papers*, p306
16   Stewart, *Burying Caesar*, quoting Hoare
17   Ibid., p160
18   Rhodes James, *Memoirs of a Conservative*, p385
19   Butler, *The Art of the Possible*, p49
20   Stewart, *Burying Caesar*, p195
21   Rhodes James, *Memoirs of a Conservative*, p384
22   Stewart, *Burying Caesar*, p163
23   Patrick Donner, *Crusade*, 1984, p135
24   Stewart, *Burying Caesar*, p188

9: The Disciple (pp61–7)
1   David Lough, *No More Champagne*, 2015, p207
2   Gilbert (ed.), *The Churchill Documents, Volume 12*, p349
3   Ibid., p269
4   Ibid., p458
5   Ibid., p448
6   CAC BBKN 4/2, from Hodge's notebook
7   Gilbert, *Winston S. Churchill: Volume 5*, p460
8   Ibid., p513
9   Crozier, *Off the Record*, p25
10   Churchill to Randolph, 7 February 1931, documents p264
11   Gilbert (ed.), *The Churchill Documents, Volume 12*, p1,133
12   Timothy S. Benson, 'David Low and Lord Beaverbrook: The Case of a Cartoonist's Autonomy', Political Cartoon Society, https://www.original-political-cartoon.com/cartoon-history/low-and-lord-beaverbrook-case-cartoonists-autonomy/
13   Gilbert (ed.), *The Churchill Documents, Volume 12*, p1,045
14   Ibid., p1,063
15   Stewart, *Burying Caesar*, p185
16   *The Times*, 8 March 1935
17   Roberts, *Randolph*, p140
18   Stewart, *Burying Caesar*, p191
19   Roberts, *Randolph*, pp140ff
20   Gilbert (ed.), *The Churchill Documents, Volume 12*, p1,181

10: Apprenticeship in Survival (pp69–73)
1   Kynaston, *The Financial Times*, p114
2   Collin Brooks (eds N. J. Crowson and Royal Historical Society), *Fleet Street, Press Barons and Politics: The Journals of Collin Brooks, 1932–1940*, 1998, p29
3   Ibid., p29
4   Kynaston, *The Financial Times*, p117
5   Brooks, *Press Barons and Politics*, p23
6   Ibid., p45f
7   Ibid., p45
8   Kynaston, *The Financial Times*, p123
9   Ibid., 124
10   Lysaght, *Brendan Bracken*, p145
11   Bruce Lockhart diaries, vol. 1, p305
12   Drogheda, *Double Harness*, p41

13 Lysaght, *Brendan Bracken*, p146
14 Ibid., p146
15 CAC BBKN 4, interview with Einzig
16 Logue, *No More Champagne*, p7

11: Parrying the Knock-Out Blow (pp75–84)
1   Gilbert, *Winston S. Churchill: Volume 5*, p408
2   Ibid., p409
3   Ibid., p451
4   Hansard, 23 November 1923
5   Gilbert, *Winston S. Churchill: Volume 5*, pp446f
6   Ibid., p450
7   Ibid., p457
8   Boothby papers, Boothby to Churchill, 22 January 1932
9   Hansard, 1 March 1933
10 Boothby, *Recollections of a Rebel*
11 Robert Rhodes James, *Bob Boothby*, 1991, p152
12 Barbara Cartland, *My Brother, Ronald*, 1942, p181
13 Macmillan, *Winds of Change*, pp238ff
14 Lyttelton, *The Memoirs of Viscount Chandos*, p194
15 D. Kendall and K. Post, 'Reminiscences and discoveries: The British 3-Inch Anti-Aircraft Rocket. Part One: Dive-Bombers', *Notes and Records of the Royal Society of London*, vol. 50, no. 2, 1996, pp229–39
16 Channon diaries, vol. 1, p402
17 Ibid., p405
18 Clementine Churchill to Churchill, 27 December 1937 in Soames (ed.), *Speaking for Themselves*
19 CAC BBKN 4, interview with Einzig
20 Channon diaries, vol. 3, p290. Channon is probably wrong to include Beaverbrook
21 Cartland, *My Brother, Ronald*, p115
22 Adrian Phillips, *Fighting Churchill, Appeasing Hitler*, 2019, Chapter 7
23 Cartland, *My Brother, Ronald*, p123

12: Into the Labyrinth of Committees (pp85–101)
1   NA CAB 16/67
2   Stephen Roskill, *Hankey: Man of Secrets, Volume 2, 1919–1931*, 1972, p406
3   NA CAB 16/67, Lindemann note to committee, 2 June 1925
4   Ibid., minutes, 5 July 1926
5   *The Times*, 8 August 1934
6   Cherwell papers, F5/2, Lindemann to Londonderry, 3 December 1934
7   Ibid., F6/1, Lindemann to Churchill, 9 December 1934
8   H. Montgomery Hyde, *British Air Policy Between the Wars 1918–1939*, 1976, pp322ff
9   Cherwell papers, Lindemann to Churchill, 22 January 1935
10 Ibid., F7/1, Address to the 1922 Committee, 18 February 1935
11 Ibid., F7/1 Address to the 1922 Committee, 18 February 1935
12 Ibid., F7/1, Lindemann to O'Connor, 8 March 1935
13 Ibid., F6/1, Lindemann to Chamberlain, 11 June 1935
14 Ibid., F/10, Air Defence (1939) diary
15 Birkenhead, *The Prof in Two Worlds*, p202
16 NA CAB 16/33/48
17 NA CAB 16/33/48/51
18 NA CAB 16/133/53A
19 Cherwell papers, Lindemann to Wood, 3 January 1939
20 R. V. Jones, *Most Secret War*, 1978, p36
21 NA AIR2/4484, Watson-Watt to DSR and DSS, 9 May 1937
22 Birkenhead, *The Prof in Two Worlds*, p185
23 NA PREM 1/253, Hankey to Chamberlain, 24 June 1938
24 Birkenhead, *The Prof in Two Worlds*, p147
25 Ibid., p153

26 Ibid., p152
27 Churchill to Wood, 9 June 1938; Gilbert (ed.), *The Churchill Documents, Volume 12*, p1,057
28 Churchill to Wood, 6 September 1938; Gilbert (ed.), *The Churchill Documents, Volume 12*, pp13, 1,149
29 Churchill to Wood, 28 July 1938; Gilbert (ed.), *The Churchill Documents, Volume 12*, p1,111; Cherwell papers, F20, Lindemann to Churchill, 7 November 1938
30 NA PREM 1/253, Churchill to Wood, 30 October 1938
31 NA PREM 1/253, Syers to Chamberlain, 2 November 1938
32 Ronald Clark, *Tizard*, 1965, pp177ff
33 Gilbert, *Winston S. Churchill: Volume 5*, p1,052
34 Clark, *Tizard*, p179
35 Boothby papers, Harrod to Boothby, 4 October 1975
36 Adrian Phillips, *Rearming the RAF for the Second World War*, 2022, pp245–8
37 Ibid., pp190–95

13: In League with the League (pp103–12)
1 Gilbert, *Winston S. Churchill: Volume 5*, pp702f
2 Cherwell papers, Lindemann to Churchill, 17 January 1936
3 Hansard, 13 July 1934, col. 671
4 Austen Chamberlain diary letters, p500
5 Rhodes James, *Boothby*, p163
6 Colin R. Coote, *The Other Club*, 1971, pp87f
7 Churchill to Cecil, 9 April 1936; John Colville, *The Fringes of Power: Downing Street Diaries, 1939–1955*, 1985, pp13, 93f
8 Lesley, *The Life of Noël Coward*, 1976, p210
9 Helen Hardinge, *Loyal to Three Kings*, 1967, p102
10 E. C. Blanche Dugdale (ed. Norman Rose), *Baffy: The Diaries of Blanche Dugdale, 1936–1947*, 1973
11 Lord Beaverbrook (ed. A. J. P. Taylor), *The Abdication of King Edward VIII*, 1966, p65
12 Churchill papers, CHAR 2/326; Coote, *The Other Club*
13 Gilbert, *Winston S. Churchill: Volume 5*, p360
14 *Sunday Times*, 26 April 1964
15 Churchill to Clementine, 27 November quoted in Gilbert *Winston S. Churchill: Volume 5*
16 Adrian Phillips, *The King Who Had to Go*, 2016, pp205–8

14: Alluring but Fateful (pp113–18)
1 Churchill to Boothby, 12 December 1936
2 Churchill papers, 2/264, Boothby to Churchill, 11 December; de Courcy memorandum, 10 December
3 BBK G/6/13, Megan Lloyd George to David Lloyd George, 14 December
4 Crathorne papers, 'Kakoo' Rutland to Peggy Wakehurst n.d.; Dugdale diaries, 13 December
5 Boothby papers, Boothby to Churchill, 11 December 1936
6 Harold Nicolson (ed. Nigel Nicolson), *Harold Nicolson: Diaries and Letters, 1930–1939*, 1971, p284, 9 December
7 Dugdale diaries
8 Channon diaries, vol. 2, 10 December 1936
9 Leo Amery diary quoted in Gilbert, *Winston S. Churchill: Volume 5*, p827
10 Duff Cooper (ed. John Julius Norwich), *The Duff Cooper Diaries, 1915–1951*, 2005
11 Nicolson, *Harold Nicolson*, p284, Nicolson to Vita Sackville-West, 9 December
12 Macmillan, *Winds of Change*, p479
13 Bruce Lockhart diary, vol. 2, 10 December 1936
14 Viscount Stuart, *Within the Fringe*, 1967, p132

15: A New Way to Deal with Dictators (pp119–26)
1 Winston Churchill, 'The Truth about Hitler', *Strand Magazine*, November 1935
2 Heidemarie Uhl, 'Of Heroes and Victims: World War II in Austrian Memory', *Austrian History Yearbook*, vol. 42, 2011, pp185–200
3 Hansard, 24 March 1938
4 Kenneth Young, *Churchill and Beaverbrook*, 1966, p124
5 Ibid., pp124–7
6 Lough, *No More Champagne*, p245
7 Bruce Lockhart diaries, vol. 2, p277

16: Bandits Snipe at the Prime Minister (pp127–34)

1 Macmillan, *Winds of Change*, pp548ff
2 Rhodes James, *Boothby*, p174
3 Hansard, 22 February 1938
4 Channon diaries, vol. 1, p894
5 Cadogan diary, 23 June 1938
6 Chamberlain to Hilda, 25 June 1938
7 Channon diaries, vol. 1, p895
8 Hansard, 23 June 1938
9 Duff Hart-Davis, *Man of War*, 2012, Chapter 8
10 Chamberlain to Hilda, 25 June 1938
11 Frederick Pile, *Ack-Ack*, 1956, pp77–80
12 Chamberlain to Ida, 4 July 1938
13 Chamberlain to Ida, 16 July 1938
14 BBKN 4, from F. M. Lord Ismay
15 NA CAB 23/94 Meeting of 22 June 1938
16 Harvey diary, 6 September 1938, p167
17 Templewood papers, XIX, talk with Lord Home, 12 March 1952
18 Quoted at A. J. P. Taylor, *Beaverbrook*, 1972, p498
19 Rhodes James, *Boothby*, p185

17: The Dark at the End of the Rainbow (pp135–40)

1 Macmillan, *Winds of Change*, p573
2 CAC, Sandys papers
3 Roberts, *Randolph*, p183
4 CAC, Sandys papers, Bracken to Sandys, 12 December 1938
5 Macmillan, *Winds of Change*, pp587f
6 Chamberlain to Hilda, 5 March 1939
7 R. A. C. Parker, *Churchill and Appeasement*, 2000, pp193f
8 Colin Thornton-Kemsley, *Through Wind and Tides*, 1974
9 Chamberlain to Ida 12 February 1939
10 Cadogan diary, 10 March 1939
11 Chamberlain to Hilda, 19 March 1939
12 Chamberlain to Ida, 9 April 1939
13 Cadogan diary, 15 March 1939
14 NA CAB 23/98/1
15 Chamberlain to Hilda, 15 April 1939
16 Nicolson diaries, 20 April 1939

18: The Most Squalid Form of Appeasement (pp141–53)

1 Kynaston, *The Financial Times*, p128
2 CAC BBKN 4, interviews with Einzig and Alexander
3 Kynaston, *The Financial Times*, p129
4 Hansard, 26 May 1939
5 NA T273/210, Waley to Wilson, 3 August 1939
6 NA T273/210, Padfield memorandum, 5 August 1939
7 NA T273/210, Wilson memorandum, 8 August 1939
8 NA T273/210, manuscript note to Wilson memorandum, 8 August 1939

19: Every Crime in the Calendar (pp155–9)

1 Channon diary, 3 April 1939
2 Chamberlain to Ida, 8 July 1939
3 Maisky diary, 5 July 1939
4 Churchill papers, 2/367, Churchill to Lord Rothermere, 19 July 1939
5 Chamberlain to Hilda, 30 July 1939
6 Chamberlain to Hilda, 30 July 1939
7 Chamberlain to Ida, 5 August 1939

8   'Radio Address by Neville Chamberlain, Prime Minister, September 3, 1939', Avalon Project, https://avalon.
     law.yale.edu/wwii/gb3.asp

20: A Real War in Whitehall (pp161–71)

1   Winston Churchill, *The Second World War, Volume 1: The Gathering Storm*, 1948, p317
2   Roskill, *Hankey*, p413
3   Ibid., p419
4   Duff Cooper diary, 3 September 1939
5   Boyle, *Poor, Dear Brendan*, p241
6   Lysaght, *Brendan Bracken*, p170
7   Chamberlain to Ida, 30 March 1940
8   Crozier, *Off the Record*, pp123f, 156
9   Paul Einzig, *In the Centre of Things*, 1960, pp205f
10   Roberts, *Randolph*, p188
11   Tree, *When the Moon was High*, p94
12   Chamberlain to Ida, 27 January 1940
13   Harvey diary p326; Anne Chisholm and Michael Davie, *Lord Beaverbrook: A Life*, 1992, p372
14   *Evening Standard*, 23 April 1940
15   Cherwell papers, K22, Lindemann to Beaverbrook, 24 April 1940; Harrod, *The Prof*, p32
16   Cherwell papers, K22, Beaverbrook to Lindemann, 26 April 1940
17   Rhodes James, *Boothby*, p234
18   Ibid., p236
19   Bruce Lockhart diaries, vol. 2, 2 May 1940

21: Muddle and Scandal (pp173–7)

1   Phillips, *Rearming the RAF*, p289
2   NA CAB 65/1 WM (39) 15
3   NA CAB, cover notes to WP(39) 102 and WP(40)7
4   Cherwell papers, F95, Lindemann to Churchill, 18 October 1939
5   Cherwell papers, F95, Lindemann to Churchill, 18 October 1939
6   Cherwell papers, F95, Lindemann to Churchill, 11 January 1940
7   NA CAB WP(40) 7
8   NA CAB 65/11/14
9   NA CAB 65/11/14
10   NA CAB 65/11/14
11   NA CAB 65/11/14
12   NA CAB 83/5/2, note by secretary
13   NA CAB 65/11/10
14   Cadogan diary, 19 May 1940
15   NA CAB 83/3/6
16   Martin Gilbert, *Winston S. Churchill: Volume 6, Finest Hour, 1939–1941*, 1983, p458

22: An Enthusiastic Believer (pp179–82)

1   CHAR 25/18, War Office memorandum, 31 January 1939
2   CHAR 25/18, Lindemann memorandum n.d.
3   Cherwell papers, D136/1, Bolton-King to Lindemann, 8 August 1938 and subsequent correspondence
4   NA CAB 120/363, unsigned memorandum, 9 September 1941
5   Cherwell papers, G376, First Lord minute, 14 November 1939
6   CHAR 19/7, Lindemann to Churchill n.d.
7   NA CAB 101/239/4, First Lord minute, 14 March 1940
8   Stephen Roskill, *Churchill and the Admirals*, 2004, p152 footnote
9   Sir John Martin, *Downing Street: The War Years*, 1991, p40
10   Cherwell papers, G550/2-4

23: The Scum Surrounding Winston (pp183–92)

1   Lysaght, *Brendan Bracken*, pp172f
2   Taylor, *Beaverbrook*, p553

3   Cadogan diary, pp286ff
4   Bruce Lockhart diaries, vol. 2, p75
5   Crathorne papers, Nancy to Tommy Dugdale, 18 June 1940
6   Colville, *Footprints in Time*, p104
7   Ibid., p194
8   Ibid., p303
9   Phillips, *Fighting Churchill, Appeasing Hitler*, p24
10 Hugh Dalton (ed. Ben Pimlott), *The Second World War Diary of Hugh Dalton, 1940–1945*, 1985; Bruce Lockhart diaries; W. J. Brown, *So Far*, 1943, p222
11 Hugh Dalton, *The Fateful Years: Memoirs, 1931–1945*, 1957, p260
12 Tree, *When the Moon was High*, p127
13 Colville, *Footprints in Time*, p308
14 Ibid., p311
15 CAC BBKN 4, interview with Harold Macmillan
16 Stuart, *Within the Fringe*, pp106f
17 Colville, *Footprints in Time*, p156
18 Cadogan diary, p281
19 Crathorne papers, Nancy to Tommy Dugdale, 18 June 1940
20 Colville, *Footprints in Time*, p96
21 Alan Lascelles (ed. Duff Hart-Davis), *King's Counsellor*, 2006, p417
22 Hardinge, *Loyal to Three Kings*, pp147, 151, 162f; Colville, *The Fringes of Power*
23 Gilbert, *Winston S. Churchill: Volume 6*, p316
24 Lysaght, *Brendan Bracken*, p177
25 Ibid.
26 Dalton diary, p36
27 John Colville, *The Churchillians*, 1980, p79
28 Colville, *Footprints in Time*, p107
29 Channon diaries, vol. 2, p386

24: Controlling Figures (pp193–200)
1   Birkenhead, *The Prof in Two Worlds*, p215
2   NA CAB 101/239, First Lord minute, 9 October 1939
3   Harrod, *The Prof*, p186
4   Thomas Wilson, *Churchill and the Prof*, 1997, p14
5   Chamberlain to Ida, 8 October 1939
6   Donald MacDougall, *Don and Mandarin*, 1987, pp30f
7   Cherwell papers, F66, Lindemann to Bridges, 24 September 1940
8   Cherwell papers, F66, Harrod to Bridges, 27 September 1940
9   Lord Chandos quoted in Birkenhead, *The Prof in Two Worlds*, pp214f
10 Hastings Ismay, *The Memoirs of General the Lord Ismay*, 1960, p173
11 Birkenhead, *The Prof in Two Worlds*, p216
12 BBKN 4, from F. M. Lord Ismay
13 MacDougall, *Don and Mandarin*, pp27ff
14 Ibid., p32
15 Harrod, *The Prof*, pp187f
16 Ibid., p193
17 MacDougall, *Don and Mandarin*, p26
18 Channon diaries, vol. 2, pp384, 585
19 Ismay, *The Memoirs of General the Lord Ismay*, p113
20 Charles Richardson, *From Churchill's Secret Circle to the BBC: The Biography of Lieutenant General Sir Ian Jacob*, 1991, p52
21 Ibid., p95
22 Roskill *Hankey: Volume 3*, p487
23 Butler, *The Art of the Possible*, p110
24 Bernard Katz, 'Archibald Vivian Hill. 26 September 1886–3 June 1977', *Biographical Memoirs of Fellows of the Royal Society*, vol. 24, 1978, pp71–149

25: Short-Fused (pp201–7)

1   NA CAB 101/240, Prime Minister personal minute to Ismay, 18 May 1940
2   NA CAB 101/240, Prime Minister personal minute to Lindemann, 7 June 1940, and to Ismay, 4 August 1940
3   CAB 120/363, First Sea Lord to Vice Admiral Dover, 29 July 1940
4   NA PREM 33/450/1
5   NA CAB 21/1098, Elliot memorandum, 18 May 1940
6   Colville, *Footprints in Time*, p165
7   NA CAB 101/240, Prime Minister personal minute to Ismay, 4 August 1940
8   Harold Macmillan, *The Blast of War*, 1967, p129
9   NA CAB 101/239, First Lord minute, 24 March 1940
10 'World War II – Churchill's Aerial Mines Project', War Over Britain 1939–45, http://airwargreatbritain.blogspot.com/2015/03/world-war-ii-churchills-aerial-mines.html
11 Cherwell papers, G152, Beaverbrook to Sinclair, 9 July 1940
12 NA CAB 66/13 WP(40) 469
13 NA AIR 8/324, Churchill to Sinclair, 19 November 1940
14 Cherwell papers, G152, Beaverbrook to Churchill, 8 October 1940
15 Cherwell papers, G152, Beaverbrook note, 11 October 1940, 'Long Aerial Mines and Mine Laying Aircraft'
16 NA CAB 101/240, personal minute, 18 September 1940
17 Beaverbrook papers, D/42 Helmore to Beaverbrook, 20 May 1941
18 CHAR 1/355, Sandys to Churchill, 2 June 1940
19 Colville, *Footprints in Time*, p175
20 NA CAB 101/240, Prime Minister personal minutes, 19 and 23 September 1940
21 NA CAB 120/363, note of phone conversation, 26 October 1940
22 NA CAB 120/363, report on the proximity fuse, 13 September 1940
23 Kendall and Post, 'Reminiscences and discoveries', pp229–39
24 NA CAB 120/363, Elliot to Ismay, 7 February 1941
25 Colville, *Footprints in Time*, p360
26 Roberts, *Randolph*, p193
27 'Sandys, (Edwin) Duncan, Baron Duncan-Sandys', Oxford Dictionary of National Biography, https://doi.org/10.1093/ref:odnb/39858; Channon diaries, vol. 2, p606
28 George Harvie-Watt, *Most of My Life*, 1980, p101
29 Colville, *The Fringes of Power*, p461
30 Colville, *Footprints in Time*, p127

26: An Inspired Brigand (pp209–22)

1   David Farrer, *G for God Almighty*, 1969, p35
2   Cadogan diary, p291
3   Winston Churchill, *The Second World War, Volume 2: Their Finest Hour*, 1948, p12
4   Anthony Furse, *Wilfrid Freeman*, 1999, Chapter 8
5   Farrer, *G for God Almighty*, p50
6   Beaverbrook papers, BBK/D/415, Beaverbrook to Churchill, 2 December 1940 and BBK/D/416, 3 January 1941
7   NA CAB 101/240, minute number 418
8   Evelyn Waugh, *Scoop*, 1938, p14
9   Crozier, *Off the Record*, pp195–7
10 Beaverbrook papers, BBK/D/415, Beaverbrook to Churchill, 10 November 1940
11 Dalton diary, pp24f
12 Sholto Douglas and Robert Wright, *Years of Command*, 1966, pp119f
13 Tree, *When the Moon was High*, p124
14 Furse, *Wilfrid Freeman*, Appendix IV
15 For instance James Holland, *The Story of the RAF: 1918–2018*, 2018, pp100f
16 Gilbert, *Winston S. Churchill: Volume 6*, p391
17 Ibid., p460
18 Ibid., pp655f
19 John Slessor, *The Central Blue: Recollections and Reflections*, 1956, p307; Douglas, *Years of Command*, p119
20 John Terraine, *The Right of the Line: The Royal Air Force in the European War, 1939–1945*, 1985, pp191f. See also Douglas, *Years of Command*, p119; Slessor, *The Central Blue*, pp307f

21 Sebastian Ritchie, *Industry and Air Power*, 1997, pp174f; Brian Brinkworth, 'On the planning of British aircraft production for the Second World War and reference to James Connolly', *Journal of Aeronautical History*, paper no. 2018/09, 2018, p40
22 Furse, *Wilfrid Freeman*, pp110–14
23 Ibid., pp135f
24 NA AIR 8/480, No. 40 Group – Equipment Depots
25 Furse, *Wilfrid Freeman*, pp137–41
26 NA CAB 79/4/63
27 Farrer, *G for God Almighty*, p39
28 Ibid.
29 NA CAB 65/7/54, conclusion of 9 June
30 Cadogan diary, pp285f
31 NA CAB 66/8/41, 19 June 1940
32 NA PREM 3/38
33 Beaverbrook papers, BBK/D/416, Beaverbrook to Churchill, 6 January 1941
34 Beaverbrook papers, BBK/D/416, Beaverbrook to Churchill, 15 April 1941
35 NA AIR 2/7068, Newall to Ismay, 20 May 1940
36 Farrer, *The Sky's the Limit*, p28
37 NA AIR 19/485, note by A. M. S. O., 30 December 1940
38 Ibid.
39 NA AIR 19/485, draft note on Cabinet paper (40)489
40 Churchill, *The Second World War, Volume 2*, pp286f; also Crozier, *Off the Record*, p298
41 Arthur William Tedder, *With Prejudice*, pp14f
42 Maurice Dean, *The Royal Air Force and Two World Wars*, 1979, pp137f
43 Young, *Churchill and Beaverbrook*, p185
44 Lord Brabazon of Tara, *The Brabazon Story*, 1956, pp202f
45 Dalton diary, p105

27: Defending a Private Empire (pp223–9)
1 NA AIR 19/477, McKeen to Newall
2 NA AIR 19/477, Churchill to Eden, Churchill to Sinclair, 13 October 1940
3 NA AIR 19/477, Beaverbrook to Churchill, 13 October 1940
4 Beaverbrook papers, BBK/D/414, Churchill to Beaverbrook, 27 August 1940
5 Dalton diary, p86, NA CAB66/12 WP(40) 386
6 Gilbert, *Winston S. Churchill: Volume 6*, p409
7 Bruce Lockhart diaries, vol. 1, p91
8 Colville, *The Churchillians*, p74
9 NA AIR 8//464 Sinclair to Beaverbrook, 1 October 1940
10 NA AIR 8/464 Dowding to Sinclair, October 1940
11 Beaverbrook papers, BBK/D/35, Beaverbrook to Sinclair, 22 September 1940
12 Beaverbrook papers, BBK/D/35, Sinclair to Beaverbrook, 25 September 1940
13 Taylor, *Beaverbrook*, p585 n1
14 'The Dispersal (1940–1941)', The Supermariners, https://supermariners.wordpress.com/the-places/southampton/the-dispersal-1940-1941/
15 David Farrer, *The Sky's the Limit*, 1943, p51
16 Bruce Lockhart diaries, vol. 2, pp666f
17 NA AVIA 38/778, Wilson to Beaverbrook, 27 July 1940, Packard deal
18 Farrer, *The Sky's The Limit*, pp44f
19 Beaverbrook papers, BBK/D/46, undated, unheaded transcript of phone call

28: Intriguing Against the Air Marshals (pp231–42)
1 CAB 106/1193
2 Taylor, *Beaverbrook*, p535
3 NA CAB 118/11, Norris to Attlee, 14 August 1940
4 Solly Zuckerman, *From Apes to Warlords*, 1988, p225
5 Denis Richards, *Portal of Hungerford*, 1977, p168 and note 36
6 NA PREM 4/3/6, 'A Weak Link' n.d.
7 NA PREM 3/20//9, Churchill to Sinclair, 17 July 1940

8 NA PREM 4/3/6, Ward to Churchill, 17 August 1940
9 NA CAB 118/11, 'The Technical Direction of the RAF'
10 NA CAB 118/11, 'Facts Concerning the Higher Direction of the Royal Air Force…'
11 Beaverbrook papers, BBK/D/35, Beaverbrook to Sinclair, 8 and 14 August 1940; Sinclair to Beaverbrook, 13 August 1940 and 18 September 1940
12 Zuckerman, *From Apes to Warlords*, p225
13 NA CAB 118/11, Norris CV, 3 August 1940
14 Trenchard to Portal quoted in S. Ritchie, 'A Political Intrigue Against the Chief of the Air Staff: The Downfall of Air Chief Marshal Sir Cyril Newall', *War & Society*, vol. 16, issue 1, 1998, pp83–104
15 Vincent Orange, *Dowding of Fighter Command*, 2008, p210
16 Ibid.
17 NA AIR 8/464 Dowding to Sinclair, October 1940
18 Salmond to Trenchard, 25 September 1940, quoted in Ritchie, 'A Political Intrigue Against the Chief of the Air Staff'; Orange, *Dowding of Fighter Command*, p210
19 NA PREM 2/7341, Newall to Beaverbrook, 14 September 1940
20 NA AIR 2/7341, draft note of meeting on 1 October 1940
21 NA AIR 2/7341, Dowding to Air Ministry, 27 September 1940
22 NA AIR 14/225, Group Captain Plans to Ludlow-Hewitt, 28 September 1938
23 Colville, *The Fringes of Power*, p216
24 Farrer, *G for God Almighty*, pp54f
25 Bruce Lockhart diaries, vol. 2, p256
26 Dalton diary, p109
27 NA AIR 8/339, Portal to Beaverbrook, 28 January 1941
28 NA AIR 8/339, Beaverbrook to Portal, 31 January 1941
29 Beaverbrook papers, BBK/D/34, Sinclair to Beaverbrook, 5 February 1941
30 Beaverbrook papers, BBK/D/34, Beaverbrook to Sinclair, 6 February 1941
31 Taylor, *Beaverbrook*, p601
32 Ibid., p602
33 Dalton diary, p313
34 Ibid., p44
35 Taylor, *Beaverbrook*, p591

29: Czech Assets (pp243–9)

1 Dalton diary, p16
2 Rhodes James, *Boothby*, p250
3 Ibid., p251
4 Ibid., p261
5 Toye, *Lloyd George and Churchill*, Chapter 10
6 NA KV 2/2856
7 NA T273/218, Waley to Wilson, 2 October 1940
8 NA T273/218, Wyatt to Wilson, 1 October 1940
9 NA T273/218, Wilson manuscript memorandum, 10 October 1940
10 NA T273/218, Wilson to Wood, 10 October 1940
11 NA T273/218, memorandum by Treasury Solicitor Wilson manuscript annotation
12 NA T273/218, Wilson to Wood, 8 October 1940
13 NA T273/218, draft letter to Boothby for Churchill
14 NA PREM 4/83/1B, Wood and Somervell to Churchill, 10 October 1940
15 NA PREM 4/83/1B, Churchill to Wood, 11 October 1940
16 NA PREM 4/83/1B, Churchill to private office, 11 October 1940
17 Dalton diary, p94
18 Rhodes James, *Boothby*, pp274 and 277
19 Ibid., p276
20 Colville, *The Fringes of Power*, p99
21 *Truth*, 29 October 1940 (copy in Boothby's MI5 file)
22 Dalton diary, p96
23 NA KV 2/2856, Janetta Oppenheimer to Clementine Churchill, 22 November 1940
24 NA PREM 4/83/1B
25 Macmillan, *Winds of Change*, p597

30: Churchill's Gestapo (pp251–60)
1   CHAR2/434, Colville to Churchill, 18 June 1941; Colville, *Footprints in Time*, p339
2   CAC JACB, Jacob papers, Riviera – unofficial diary entry 3 August 1941
3   Martin, *Downing Street*, p56
4   CAB 120/41, Churchill to Lindemann, 17 October 1941
5   Birkenhead, *The Prof in Two Worlds*, pp216f
6   Harrod, *The Prof*, pp190f
7   Colville, *Footprints in Time*, p100
8   Harrod, *The Prof*, p192
9   Cherwell papers, F66, Harrod to Bridges, 25 October 1940
10 Cherwell papers, F81/3/7, minute, 3 February 1942
11 Cherwell papers, F155, Lindemann to Churchill, 24 March 1942
12 Colville, *The Fringes of Power*, p375
13 Churchill papers, CHA 20/258A, Lindemann to Churchill
14 Cherwell papers, F155/6, Cherwell to Churchill, 24 March 1942
15 Churchill papers, CHA 20/258A, Lindemann to Churchill, 27 February 1941
16 Churchill papers, CHAR 20/258A/34, Lindemann to Churchill, 27 February 1941
17 Birkenhead, *The Prof in Two Worlds*, p215
18 F. H. Hinsley, *British Intelligence in the Second World War: Volume 1*, 1979, p177
19 Cherwell papers, G 26/1, Churchill to Sinclair and Portal, 9 December 1940
20 Harrod, *The Prof*, p196
21 Wilson, *Churchill and the Prof*, p205
22 Ibid., p112
23 Birkenhead, *The Prof in Two Worlds*, p227; Cherwell papers, G138/6, papers unsigned to Godfrey, 2 March 1944 and Godfrey to Clarke, 1 March 1944
24 Harrod, *The Prof*, pp202f
25 Katz, 'Archibald Vivian Hill', pp71–149
26 Colville, *Footprints in Time*, p218
27 Churchill papers, CHAR 20/13, Lindemann to Churchill, 15 July 1940
28 Churchill papers, CHAR 20/258A, Lindemann to Churchill, 7 March 1941
29 Lindemann to Churchill, 25 July 1941 CHAR 20/258C/361
30 Harrod, *The Prof*, pp201–12
31 Ibid., p202
32 Wilson, *Churchill and the Prof*, p98
33 Cherwell papers, F/156, Lindemann to Churchill, 7 May 1942
34 Colville, *The Fringes of Power*, p554
35 John Reith (ed. Charles Stuart), *The Reith Diaries*, 1972, p271
36 Tree, *When the Moon was High*, p113
37 Reith diaries, p325
38 Birkenhead, *The Prof in Two Worlds*, p224
39 Dalton diary, pp84–6
40 Ibid., p109
41 Cherwell papers, D/146, Charles Lindemann to Lindemann, 15 October 1942
42 Birkenhead, *The Prof in Two Worlds*, p216
43 Hansard, 11 November 1940
44 Harvie-Watt, *Most of My Life*, p63
45 Channon diaries, vol. 2, p667
46 Harvie-Watt, *Most of My Life*, p76
47 Macrae, *Winston Churchill's Toyshop*, pp132ff
48 NA PREM 4/11/1, Lindemann to Churchill, 19 February 1942

31: A Deliberate Act of Promotion (pp261–72)
1   Colville, *The Fringes of Power*, p526
2   Ibid., p296
3   Ibid., p342
4   Gilbert, *Winston S. Churchill: Volume 6*, p1,227
5   Farrer, *G for God Almighty*, p65
6   Crozier, *Off the Record*, p287

7   Beaverbrook to Churchill, 17 March 1942 quoted in Young, *Churchill and Beaverbrook*, pp235f
8   Beaverbrook to Hoare, 2 May 1941 quoted in Young, *Churchill and Beaverbrook*, pp187
9   Dalton diary, p223
10 Ibid., pp227, 238
11 Ibid., p238
12 Colville, *Footprints in Time*, p335
13 Beaverbrook to Churchill, 3 June 1941; Hoare quoted in Young, *Churchill and Beaverbrook*, p187
14 Colville, *Fringes of Power*, p254
15 Bruce Lockhart diaries, vol. 2, p108
16 Farrer, *G for God Almighty*, p73
17 NA PREM 4/11/1, Beaverbrook to Lindemann, 6 September 1941
18 NA PREM 4/11/1, Churchill to Ismay and Bridges, 8 September 1941
19 Ibid.
20 NA PREM 4/11/1, Bridges to Churchill, 29 September 1941
21 NA CAB 120/363, Sandys to Churchill, 1 October 1941
22 Ibid.
23 NA CAB 120/363, Lindemann to Churchill, 7 October 1941
24 Ibid.
25 NA CAB 120/363, Bridges to Churchill, 15 October 1941
26 NA CAB 120/363, Churchill to Bridges, 17 October 1941
27 NA CAB 120/363, Bridges to Brown, 17 October 1941
28 NA PREM 4/11/1, Lindemann to Churchill, 29 October 1941 with annotation by Churchill, 31 October 1941
29 Colville, *The Churchillians*, p79; Farrer, *G for God Almighty*, p55
30 Bruce Lockhart diaries, vol. 2, p483
31 Ibid., p107
32 Dalton diary, p117
33 Martin, *Downing Street*, p39
34 Colville, *Footprints in Time*, p372
35 Young, *Churchill and Beaverbrook*, pp201f
36 Sally Bedell Smith, *Reflected Glory*, 2006, p108
37 Beaverbrook papers, BBK/C/87, Beaverbrook to Churchill, 7 October 1942
38 B. T. White, *Valentine, Infantry Tank Mk III*, 1969
39 Dalton diary, p297
40 Bruce Lockhart diaries, vol. 2, p157
41 Ibid., p123
42 Cadogan diary, p408
43 Bruce Lockhart diaries, vol. 2, p157
44 Ibid.
45 Ibid., p176
46 Cherwell papers, F144, Lindemann to Churchill, 13 September 1941
47 Keith Middlemas and John Barnes, *Baldwin: A Biography*, 1969, p1,061. A. J. P. Taylor exonerates Beaverbrook, but more recent writers – Middlemas and Barnes, David Cannadine, Geoffrey Fry and Philip Williamson – hold him guilty. As with Cato's *Guilty Men*, this author finds it hard to believe that Beaverbrook was not actively involved. In both cases, the venom and brutality of the writing provided ample motive for Beaverbrook to hide any part in the work.

32: Filial Impiety (pp273–84)

1   Oliver Lyttelton, Viscount Chandos, *The Memoirs of Lord Chandos*, 1964, 195
2   Roberts, *Randolph*, p193
3   Channon diaries, p395
4   CHAR 20/65, Randolph to Cassandra , 3 March 1942
5   Hansard, 28 January 1942
6   Colville, *Footprints in Time*, p224
7   Alan Hoe, *David Stirling*, 1992, p50
8   CHAR 1/362, Randolph to Churchill, 14 March 1941
9   Artemis Cooper, *Cairo in the War, 1939–1945*, 1989, p90; Roberts, *Randolph*, p203
10 Channon diaries, vol. 2, p487
11 CHAR 20/33, Randolph to Churchill, 5 July 1941

12   CHAR 1/362, Randolph to Churchill, 31 March 1941
13   CHAR 20/33, Randolph to Churchill, 5 July 1941; CHAR 1/362, Randolph to Churchill, 26 September 1941
14   Roberts, *Randolph*, p211
15   Quoted in Cooper, *Cairo in the War*, p97
16   Roberts, *Randolph*, p204
17   CHAR 20/33, Randolph to Churchill, 5 July 1941
18   Boothby papers, Boothby to Blake, 8 January 1977
19   Martin, *Downing Street*, pp18f
20   Bruce Lockhart diaries, vol. 2, p104
21   Peter Coats, *Of Gardens and Generals*, 1976; CHAR 1/362, Randolph to Churchill, 6 April 1941
22   CHAR 20/33, Randolph to Churchill, 5 July 1941
23   CHAR 1/362, Randolph to Churchill, 20 October 1941
24   Colville, *The Fringes of Power*, p353; Chandos, *The Memoirs of Lord Chandos*, p223
25   Lyttelton, *The Memoirs of Lord Chandos*, p192
26   CHAR 1/362, Randolph to Churchill, 26 September 1941
27   CHAR 20/33, Churchill to Lyttelton, 11 July 1941; Lyttelton to Churchill, 13 July 1941
28   CHAR 1/362, Randolph to Churchill, 26 September 1941
29   NA CAB 101/241, personal minute to Margesson and Stuart, 13 December 1941
30   Alan Moorehead, *A Year of Battle*, 1944, p203
31   Cooper, *Cairo in the War*, p124
32   CHAR 1/362, Randolph to Churchill, 3 December 1941
33   Bruce Lockhart diaries, vol. 2, p159
34   Channon diaries, vol. 2, p715
35   Leo Amery (eds John Barnes and David Nicholson), *The Empire at Bay: The Leo Amery Diaries, 1929–1945*, 1988, p766
36   Boothby papers, Boothby to Gilbert, 27 September 1977
37   CHAR 1/369, Randolph to Churchill, 22 April 1942
38   Christopher Ogden, *Life of the Party*, 1994, p152
39   Channon diaries, vol. 2, p826
40   Bruce Lockhart diaries, vol. 2, p352

33: Beaverbrook's Useful Idiocy (pp285–98)

1   Chisholm and Davie, *Lord Beaverbrook*, p428; Averell Harriman and Elie Able, *Special Envoy to Churchill and Stalin*, 1975
2   F. H. Hinsley, *British Intelligence in the Second World War: Volume 2*, 1981, p187
3   Mary Soames, *Clementine Churchill*, 1979, pp351f
4   CHAR 20/52, Bracken to Churchill, c. 17 February 1942
5   CAC HARV 4/1, Harvie-Watt to Churchill, 20 February 1942
6   NA PREM 4/11/1, Lindemann to Churchill, 19 February 1942
7   NA PREM 4/11/1, Churchill to Lindemann, Bridges and Ismay, 10 March 1942
8   Taylor, *Beaverbrook*, p661f
9   Ibid., p662. Kenneth Young places this letter before the meetings of the evening.
10   Bruce Lockhart diaries, vol. 2, p147; Harvie-Watt, *Most of My Life*, p79
11   Crozier, *Off the Record*, p298
12   Ibid., p283
13   Bruce Lockhart diaries, vol. 2, p150
14   Farrer, *G for God Almighty*, pp90ff
15   Bruce Lockhart diaries, vol. 2, p252
16   Taylor, *Beaverbrook*, p686
17   Bruce Lockhart diaries, vol. 2, p252
18   Ibid., pp176, 214 and 225
19   Ibid., p253
20   Chisholm and Davie, *Lord Beaverbrook*, pp493f
21   Taylor, *Beaverbrook*, pp814f, 889
22   Harvie-Watt, *Most of My Life*, pp73f
23   Bruce Lockhart diaries, pp102, 176, 189
24   Ibid., p189

25 David Farrer, 'The Old Bastard' in Logan Gourlay (ed.), *The Beaverbrook I Knew*, 1984, p49
26 Bruce Lockhart diaries, vol. 2, p186
27 Young, *Churchill and Beaverbrook*, p246
28 Harriman and Able, *Special Envoy to Churchill and Stalin*
29 Bruce Lockhart diaries, vol. 2, p186 and p252
30 Hansard, 23 February 1943
31 Cherwell papers, K22, Beaverbrook to Lindemann, 28 January 1943
32 Harvie-Watt, *Most of My Life*, p85
33 Ibid.
34 Bruce Lockhart diaries, vol. 2, p223
35 BBK/C/59, Foot to Beaverbrook, 22 April 1943
36 Beaverbrook papers, BBKC/56, Bracken to Beaverbrook, 23 June 1942
37 Farrer, *G for God Almighty*, p100
38 Bruce Lockhart diaries, vol. 2, p185
39 Taylor, *Beaverbrook*, p696
40 Farrer, *G for God Almighty*, p101
41 Ibid., p108
42 Ibid., p62

34: The Unassailable Weapon (pp299–306)

1 'Adolf Hitler', Der Fuehrer, https://der-fuehrer.org/
2 Jones, *Most Secret War*, pp64ff
3 F. H. Hinsley, *British Intelligence in the Second World War: Volume 3, Part 1*, 1984, pp360ff
4 Ibid., p363
5 Jones, *Most Secret War*, p335
6 Colville, *The Fringes of Power*, p480
7 Richardson, *From Churchill's Secret Circle to the BBC*, p193
8 NA CAB 120/748 Fol 236/866
9 Taylor, *Beaverbrook*, p714
10 Farrer, *G for God Almighty*, p134
11 Jones, *Most Secret Warp*, p445
12 Ibid., p449
13 NA PREM 3/110 COS (O)715(O)
14 Bruce Lockhart diaries, vol. 2, p334
15 Channon diaries, vol. 3, p83
16 Bruce Lockhart diaries, vol. 2, p322
17 Colville, *The Fringes of Power*, p497
18 Ibid., pp499 and 502
19 Harvie-Watt, *Most of My Life*, p169

35: Science and Gold Braid (pp307–16)

1 Hansard, 10 November 1932, col 632
2 NA CAB 24/279/18
3 NA CAB 101/240, personal minute to Beaverbrook, 8 July 1940
4 NA CAB 101/240, personal minute to Sinclair and Newall, 20 July 1940
5 NA CAB 101/240, personal minute 125, 23 September 1940
6 'How Bomber Command Helped Win the Battle of Britain', Imperial War Museum, https://www.iwm.org.uk/history/how-bomber-command-helped-win-the-battle-of-britain
7 Cadogan diary, 18 May 1940
8 Cherwell papers, G152, Lindemann to Churchill, 20 November 1940
9 Phillips, *Rearming the RAF for the Second World War*, pp245–8
10 Harris to Joubert, 1 February 1941 quoted in Jones, *Most Secret War*, p169
11 Jones, *Most Secret War*, p217
12 Boothby papers, Harrod to Boothby, 3 February 1967
13 Jones, *Most Secret War*, p210
14 C. K. Webster and N. Frankland, *The Strategic Air Offensive Against Germany, 1939–1945, Volume 4*, 1961, pp205–15
15 NA AIR 8/1356, Lindemann to Churchill, 2 September 1941

16 NA CAB 101/241, personal minute to Newall, 3 September 1941
17 Webster and Frankland, *The Strategic Air Offensive Against Germany, Volume 1*, p180
18 Dean, *The Royal Air Force and Two World Wars*, pp268f
19 Cherwell papers, F148, Lindemann to Churchill, 11 November 1941
20 NA AIR 8/1356, Newall to D. B. Ops, 3 September 1941
21 NA CAB 101/241, personal minute Churchill to Portal and Sinclair marked action this day, 11 November 1941
22 Bottomley to Peirse, 13 November 1941 quoted in Webster and Frankland, *The Strategic Air Offensive Against Germany, Volume 4*, p142

36: The Siege of Adastral House (pp317–33)
1 Churchill to Ismay, 6 July 1944 quoted in Farmelo, *Churchill's Bomb*, p269
2 David Edgerton, *England and the Aeroplane*, 1991, p130
3 Alexander Cairncross, *Planning in Wartime: Aircraft Production in Britain, Germany and the USA*, 1991, p9
4 E. Devons, 'Review of British War Production by M. M. Postan', *Economica*, vol. 20, no. 79, 1953, pp279–82
5 Cherwell papers, F144/9, Lindemann to Churchill marked read by Churchill, 13 September 1941
6 Wilson, *Churchill and the Prof*, p67
7 C. O. S. memo, 31 July 1941 quoted in Webster and Frankland, *The Strategic Air Offensive Against Germany, Volume 1*, p181
8 Webster and Frankland, *The Strategic Air Offensive Against Germany, Volume 1*, p182
9 Slessor, *The Central Blue*, p385
10 Webster and Frankland, *The Strategic Air Offensive Against Germany, Volume 1*, p341
11 Cherwell papers, D14, Lindemann to his brother, 7 February 1943
12 NA CAB 101/241, personal minute Churchill to Portal, 7 October 1941
13 Cherwell papers, F180, Lindemann to Churchill, 23 June 1943
14 Zuckerman, *From Apes to Warlords*, pp139ff
15 Bottomley to Baldwin in Webster and Frankland, *The Strategic Air Offensive Against Germany, Volume 4*, pp143ff
16 Hinsley, *British Intelligence in the Second World War: Volume 2*, p179
17 Pound to Defence Committee, 6 March 1942 quoted in Webster and Frankland, *The Strategic Air Offensive Against Germany*, p327
18 Hansard, 25 February 1942
19 NA CAB 101/241, personal minute to Sinclair and Portal, 13 March 1942
20 NA CAB 69/4, Lindemann to Churchill, 30 March 1942
21 Ronald Clark, *Tizard*, 1965, p311
22 'Quantitative Study of the Total Effects of Air Raids', Ministry of Home Security, Research and Experiments Department, 2770, 8 April 1942, reproduced in Zuckerman, *From Apes to Warlords*, p405
23 Arthur Travers Harris, *Bomber Offensive*, 1947, p104
24 NA CAB 66/25/30
25 Harman Grisewood, *One Thing at a Time*, 1968, p146
26 Colville, *Footprints in Time*, p99
27 BBKN 4, from Hodge's notebook
28 Zuckerman, *From Apes to Warlords*, p218
29 Cherwell papers, G345, Cherwell to Freeman, 21 May 1943
30 Jones, *Most Secret War*, pp290–92
31 Ibid., p296
32 NA AIR 8/327 C. O. S. (42) 446 (o), C. O. S. (42) 197 the meeting memorandum to Prime Minister, 17 December 1942
33 NA CAB 79/58/54 C. O. S. (42) 204th meeting
34 Philip Joubert de la Ferté, *The Third Service*, 1955, p160
35 NA AIR20/867, Joubert to Bottomley, 16 November 1941
36 NA PREM 3/971/1, Lindemann to Churchill, 4 June 1942
37 Wilson, *Churchill and the Prof*, p69 and note 31
38 Donald Bennett, *Pathfinder*, 1958, p162

37: Rescuing a Misbegotten Freak (pp335–52)
1 NA PREM 1/272, Wilson to Chamberlain, 18 January 1938
2 Chamberlain to Ida, 24 October 1939

3   Tree, *When the Moon was High*, p119
4   Ivone Kirkpatrick, *The Inner Circle*, 1959, pp149f
5   NA INF 1/857, Duff Cooper to Monckton, 27 May 1941
6   Bruce Lockhart diaries, vol. 2, p89
7   Tree, *When the Moon was High*, pp169 and 183
8   Harrod, *The Prof*, p12
9   Bruce Lockhart diaries, vol. 2, p146
10   Dalton diary, p252
11   Stuart, *Within the Fringe*, p103
12   Harvie-Watt, *Most of My Life*, pp37f
13   Channon diaries, vol. 2, p820
14   NA CAB 65/25/35
15   Bruce Lockhart diaries, vol. 2, p295
16   Ibid., p109
17   Tree, *When the Moon was High*, p173
18   Bruce Lockhart diaries, vol. 2, p155
19   Ibid., p84
20   Grisewood, *One Thing at a Time*, p143
21   Tree, *When the Moon was High*, p112
22   George Thomson, *Blue Pencil Admiral*, 1947, p132
23   Colville, *Footprints in Time*, p360
24   BBKN 4
25   Bruce Lockhart diaries, vol. 2, p225
26   Ibid., p202
27   Ibid., p190
28   Ibid., II p300
29   Thomson, *Blue Pencil Admiral*, p132
30   Bruce Lockhart diaries, pp26 and 178
31   Boyle, *Poor, Dear Brendan*, p306
32   Bruce Lockhart diaries, vol. 2, p217
33   Bruce Lockhart diaries, vol. 2, p185
34   NA CAB 101/241, personal minute to Bracken, 31 August 1941
35   Bruce Lockhart diaries, vol. 2, p197
36   Bruce Lockhart diaries, vol. 2, p138
37   Kirkpatrick, *The Inner Circle*, pp165ff
38   Bruce Lockhart diaries, vol. 2, pp342, 445
39   M. R. D. Foot, *SOE: An Outline History of the Special Operations Executive, 1940–46*, 1984, pp18–22
40   Dalton diary, p69
41   Ibid., pp162ff, p166
42   Ibid., p252
43   Bruce Lockhart diaries, vol. 2, p110
44   Ibid., p125
45   Dalton diary, vol. 2, p292f, 309; Bruce Lockhart diaries, vol. 2, p139
46   Lord Gladwyn (Hubert Gladwyn Jebb), *The Memoirs of Lord Gladwyn*, 1972, p104
47   Dalton diary, pp316, 319, 329, 296, 350
48   Bruce Lockhart diaries, vol. 2, p192
49   Asa Briggs, *Governing the BBC*, 1979
50   Boyle, *Poor, Dear Brendan*, p274
51   Bruce Lockhart diaries, vol. 2, p265
52   Colville, *The Fringes of Power*, p462
53   Bruce Lockhart diaries, vol. 2, p372
54   Ibid., p355
55   Bruce Lockhart diaries, pp198, 130, 198, 247, 315f
56   Ibid., p344
57   Soames, *Clementine Churchill*, pp280f
58   Lysaght, *Brendan Bracken*, pp233f
59   CAC BBKN 4, interview with Marquesa de Casa Maury

38: Planning for Post-War Britain (pp353–9)

1   'Frederick Alexander Lindemann, Viscount Cherwell, 1886–1957', Royal Society, https://doi.org/10.1098/rsbm.1958.0005

2   MacDougall, *Don and Mandarin*, p36

3   Quoted in Wilson, *Churchill and the Prof*, p149

4   Cherwell papers, H257, Lindemann to Churchill, 11 February 1943

5   Wilson, *Churchill and the Prof*, p157

6   Bruce Lockhart diaries, p291, 356

7   Colville, *The Fringes of Power*, p462

8   NA PREM 4/36/3, Churchill to Eden, 10 February 1944

9   Colville, *The Fringes of Power*, p453

10 Wilson, *Churchill and the Prof*, p159

11 Ibid., p160

12 MacDougall, *Don and Mandarin*, pp35f

13 Nigel Middleton, 'Lord Butler and the education act of 1944', *British Journal of Educational Studies*, vol. 20, no. 2, 1972, pp178–91

14 Butler, *The Art of the Possible*, p109

15 NA CAB 66/42 WP 446

16 CHAR 9/192 C, Brown to Clarke, 13 October 1943

17 CHAR 9/192 C, fols 290–306

39: The Preoccupations of a Paymaster General (pp361–70)

1   Graham Farmelo, *Churchill's Bomb*, 2013, p188

2   NA PREM 3/139/11A, Churchill to Lindemann, 10 January 1944

3   NA PREM 3/139/8A, Lindemann to Churchill, 7 April 1943

4   Ibid.

5   Jones, *Most Secret War*, p474

6   Farmelo, *Churchill's Bomb*, pp234f

7   NA PREM 3/139/8A, Lindemann to Churchill, 19 October 1943

8   NA PREM 3/139/11A, Churchill to Lindemann, 27 May 1944

9   NA PREM 3/139/8A, Lindemann to Churchill, 28 July 1943

10 NA PREM 3/139/11A, Lindemann to Churchill, 30 June 1944

11 NA PREM 3/139/11A, Lindemann to Churchill, 25 July 1944

12 NA PREM 3/139/11A, Lindemann to Churchill, 26 January 1945

13 NA PREM 3/139/11A, Brook minute, 27 November 1941

14 NA CAB 121/443, notes on Operation Freshman, 17 October 1942

15 NA PREM 3/139/11A, Lindemann to Churchill, 24 November 1944

16 NA PREM 3/139/11A, Anderson to Churchill, 26 October 1944

17 Cherwell papers, F131, Lindemann to Churchill, 3 August 1943

18 Cherwell papers, H290, Lindemann to Churchill, 23 September 1943

19 CHAR 20/99B/168, private office note initialled WSC, 5 October 1943

20 Dalton diary, p668

21 Zuckerman, *From Apes to Warlords*, p236

22 Bruce Lockhart diaries, vol. 2, p307

23 Ibid., p483

24 NA CAB 69/6

25 Zuckerman, *From Apes to Warlords*, p248

26 Tedder, *With Prejudice*, p552

27 Field Marshal Lord Alanbrooke (eds Alex Danchev and Dan Todman), *War Diaries, 1939–1945*, 2001, p542

28 Gilbert, *Winston S. Churchill: Volume 5*, pp466–8

40: The Return of a Court Favourite (pp371–78)

1   Bruce Lockhart diaries, vol. 2, pp264f

2   Ibid., p263

3   Ibid., p264

4   Taylor, *Beaverbrook*, p702

5   Farrer, 'The Old Bastard', p49

6   Channon diaries, vol. 3, p65

7   Beaverbrook papers, BBK/C/59, Hodge to Hogg, 22 June 1944
8   Taylor, *Beaverbrook*, p713
9   Alan P. Dobson, 'The Other Air Battle: The American Pursuit of Post-War Civil Aviation Rights', *Historical Journal*, vol. 28, no. 2, 1985, pp429–39
10   Farrer, *G for God Almighty*, p128
11   Christopher Brewin, 'British Plans for International Operating Agencies for Civil Aviation, 1941–1945', *International History Review*, vol. 4, no. 1, 1982, pp91–110; Farrer, *G for God Almighty*, p128
12   Bruce Lockhart diaries, vol. 2, p330
13   MacDougall, *Don and Mandarin*, p39
14   Farrer, *G for God Almighty*, p136
15   NA CAB 66/46/45
16   MacDougall, *Don and Mandarin*, p37
17   Colville, *The Fringes of Power*, pp456f
18   Ibid., p530
19   Quoted in Wilson, *Churchill and the Prof*, p175
20   Quoted in ibid., p176
21   Quoted in Robert Skidelsky, *John Maynard Keynes*, 2003, p750
22   Quoted in ibid., p753

41: The Road to a Landslide (pp379–94)

1   Colville, *The Fringes of Power*, p487
2   Ibid., p501
3   Dalton diary, p758
4   Colville, *The Fringes of Power*, p543
5   Ibid., p523
6   Ibid., p485
7   Farrer, *G for God Almighty*, p123
8   Bruce Lockhart diaries, vol. 2, pp366f
9   Colville, *The Fringes of Power*, p456
10   NA CAB 66/58 WP (44) 652
11   CAC Attlee papers, ATLE 2/2/16-21 quoted in Allen Packwood, *How Churchill Waged War*, 2018, p233
12   Colville, *The Fringes of Power*, p526
13   NA CAB 21/284 LP (43) 281, Attlee memorandum, 9 December 1943
14   NA CAB 71/20 LP (44) 281
15   Colville, *The Fringes of Power* pp554f
16   *The Times*, 10 April 1945
17   Ibid.
18   Bruce Lockhart diaries, vol. 2, p426
19   Packwood, *How Churchill Waged War*, p243
20   Butler, *The Art of the Possible*, p127
21   Soames, *Clementine Churchill*, p420
22   Colville, *The Fringes of Power*, p567
23   CHAR 2/550 fols 25–27
24   Colville, *The Fringes of Power*, p570
25   Ibid., p562
26   Colville, *The Churchillians*, p48
27   Bruce Lockhart diaries, vol. 2, pp356
28   Ibid., p148
29   Colville, *Footprints in Time*, pp197f
30   Bruce Lockhart diaries, vol. 2, p449
31   Farrer, *G for God Almighty*, p143
32   Colville, *The Fringes of Power*, p573
33   Bruce Lockhart diaries, vol. 2, p424
34   Arthur Christiansen, *Headlines All My Life*, 1961, p240
35   Quoted in Richard Toye, 'Winston Churchill's "Crazy Broadcast": Party, Nation, and the 1945 Gestapo Speech', *Journal of British Studies*, vol. 49, no. 3, 2010, pp655–80
36   Lascelles, *King's Counsellor*, p331
37   Bruce Lockhart diaries, vol. 2, p468

38 Colville, *The Churchillians*, p83
39 Butler, *The Art of the Possible*, p127
40 Amery diaries, p1046
41 *The Times*, 14 June 1945
42 Colville, *The Fringes of Power*, p464
43 Cherwell papers, H265, Lord Beaverbrook's public statements draft
44 Colville, *The Churchillians*, p40
45 Bruce Lockhart diaries, vol. 2, p174
46 Colville, *The Churchillians*, p43
47 Farrer, *G for God Almighty*, p146
48 Bruce Lockhart diaries, vol. 2, pp477f
49 Ibid., p482

Afterword (pp395–9)
1   Monckton papers, Bracken to Monckton, 29 April 1946
2   Boothby papers, Boothby to Gilbert, 27 September 1977
3   Boothby papers, Boothby to Blake, 8 January 1977
4   Adrian Phillips, *The First Royal Media War*, 2023, pp162f
5   @ChartwellNT, https://twitter.com/ChartwellNT/status/1627623446262824960. The source of the figures is mysterious.
6   Chisholm and Davie, *Lord Beaverbrook*, pp501–11
7   Sandys papers, DSND 2/11, script for *Operation Crossbow*
8   Boothby, *Recollections of a Rebel*, p55
9   Boothby papers, Boothby to Wasserman, 31 December 1978
10 Charles Edward Lysaght, 'The Legacy of "Winston's Chela" Lasted Far Longer Than He Expected', Brendan Bracken Memorial Lecture at Churchill College, Cambridge, 9 May 2009, reproduced in Gilbert, *Winston S. Churchill: Volume 6*, p113, https://winstonchurchill.org/publications/finest-hour/finest-hour-113/brendan-bracken-the-fantasist-whose-dreams-came-true/

BIBLIOGRAPHY

GOVERNMENT ARCHIVES

National Archives (TNA)

OTHER UNPUBLISHED MATERIAL AND ARCHIVES

Beaverbrook, Parliamentary Archives (BBK)
Boothby, National Library of Scotland
Cherwell, Nuffield College, Oxford (CSAC)
Churchill, Churchill Archives Centre, Cambridge (CHUR and CHAR)
Crathorne (Dugdale), private collection
Harvie-Watt, Churchill Archives Centre, Cambridge (HARV)
Jacob, Churchill Archives Centre, Cambridge (JACB)
Monckton Deposit, Balliol College, Oxford
Sandys, Duncan, Churchill Archives Centre, Cambridge (DSND)
Sinclair, Sir Archibald Churchill Archives Centre, Cambridge (THRS)

PUBLISHED COLLECTIONS OF DOCUMENTS

Cockett, Richard (ed.), *My Dear Max*, 1990
Davenport-Hines, Richard and Sisman, Adman (eds), *One Hundred Letters from Hugh Trevor-Roper*, 2014
Gilbert, Martin (ed.), *The Churchill Documents, Volume 12: The Wilderness Years, 1929–1935*, 1981

Gilbert, Martin (ed.), *The Churchill Documents, Volume 13: The Coming of War, 1936–1939*, 1982

Hunter, Ian, *Winston and Archie: The collected correspondence of Winston Churchill and Sir Archibald Sinclair 1915–1960*, 2005

Minney, R. J. (ed.), *The Private Papers of Hore-Belisha*, 1960

Soames, Mary (ed.), *Speaking for Themselves: The Personal Letters of Winston and Clementine Churchill*, 1998

Williamson, Philip and Baldwin, Edward (eds), *Baldwin Papers*, 2004

NEWSPAPERS

The Times, London

PUBLISHED DIARIES AND LETTERS

Alanbrooke, Field Marshal Lord (eds Danchev, Alex and Todman, Dan), *War Diaries, 1939–1945*, 2001

Amery, Leo (eds Barnes, John and Nicholson, David), *The Empire at Bay: The Leo Amery Diaries, 1929–1945*, 1988

Brooks, Collin, (eds Crowson, N. J. and Royal Historical Society), *Fleet Street, Press Barons and Politics: The Journals of Collin Brooks, 1932–1940*, 1998

Bruce Lockhart, Robert (ed. Young, Kenneth), *The Diaries of Sir Robert Bruce Lockhart: Volume 1, 1915–1938*, 1973

Bruce Lockhart, Robert (ed. Young, Kenneth), *The Diaries of Sir Robert Bruce Lockhart: Volume 2, 1939–1965*, 1980

Chamberlain, Neville (ed. Self, Robert), *The Neville Chamberlain Diary Letters, Volume 4: The Downing Street Years, 1934–1940*, 2005 (references given as 'Chamberlain to Hilda' or 'Chamberlain to Ida')

Channon, Henry 'Chips' (ed. Heffer, Simon), *Henry 'Chips' Channon: The Diaries, Volume 1, 1918–1938*, 2021

Channon, Henry 'Chips' (ed. Heffer, Simon), *Henry 'Chips' Channon: The Diaries, Volume 2, 1938–1943*, 2022

Channon, Henry 'Chips' (ed. Heffer, Simon), *Henry 'Chips' Channon: The Diaries, Volume 3, 1943–1957*, 2022

Colville, John, *The Fringes of Power: Downing Street Diaries, 1939–1955*, 1985

Cooper, Duff (ed. Norwich, John Julius), *The Duff Cooper Diaries, 1915–1951*, 2005

Dalton, Hugh (ed. Pimlott, Ben), *The Second World War Diary of Hugh Dalton, 1940–1945*, 1985

Dugdale, Blanche E. C. (ed. Rose, Norman), *Baffy: The Diaries of Blanche Dugdale, 1936–1947*, 1973

Harvey, Oliver (ed. Harvey, John), *The Diplomatic Diaries of Oliver Harvey, 1937–1940*, 1970

Harvey, Oliver (ed. Harvey, John), *The War Diaries of Oliver Harvey, 1941–1945*, 1978

Ironside, Sir Edmund (eds Macleod, Roderick and Kelly, Denis), *The Ironside Diaries, 1937–1940*, 1962

Jones, Thomas, *A Diary with Letters, 1931–1950*, 1954

Jones, Thomas (ed. Middlemas, Keith), *Whitehall Diary: Volume 2, 1926–1930*, 1969

Lascelles, Alan (ed. Hart-Davis, Duff), *King's Counsellor*, 2006

Macmillan, Harold, *War Diaries: Politics and War in the Mediterranean, January 1943–May 1945*, 1984

Maisky, Ian (ed. Gorodetsky, Gabriel), *The Maisky Diaries: Red Ambassador to the Court of St James's, 1932–1943*, 2015

Martin, Sir John, *Downing Street: The War Years*, 1991

Nicolson, Harold (ed. Nicolson, Nigel), *Harold Nicolson: Diaries and Letters, 1930–1939*, 1971

Nicolson, Harold (ed. Nicolson, Nigel), *Harold Nicolson: Diaries and Letters, 1939–1945*, 1967

Pownall, Sir Henry (ed. Bond, Brian), *Chief of Staff: The Diaries of Lieutenant-General Sir Henry Pownall*, 1972

Reith, John (ed. Stuart, Charles), *The Reith Diaries*, 1972

MEMOIRS AND AUTOBIOGRAPHIES

Attlee, Clement, *As It Happened*, 1954
Babington Smith, Constance, *Evidence in Camera*, 1957
Balfour, H. H., *Wings Over Westminster*, 1973
Beaverbrook, Lord (ed. Taylor, A. J. P.), *The Abdication of King Edward VIII*, 1966
Bennett, Donald, *Pathfinder*, 1958
Boothby, Lord, *My Yesterday, Your Tomorrow*, 1962
Boothby, Lord, *Recollections of a Rebel*, 1978
Brabazon of Tara, Lord, *The Brabazon Story*, 1956
Bright Astley, Joan, *The Inner Circle*, 1971
Brooks, C., *Devil's Decade: Portraits of the Nineteen-Thirties*, 1948
Brown, W. J., *So Far*, 1943
Bruce Lockhart, Robert, *Comes the Reckoning*, 1947
Bruce Lockhart, Robert, *Giants Cast Long Shadows*, 1960
Butler, Lord (Rab), *The Art of Memory: Friends in Perspective*, 1982
Butler, Lord (Rab), *The Art of the Possible*, 1973
Carrington, Charles, *Soldier at Bomber Command*, 1987
Cartland, Barbara, *My Brother, Ronald*, 1942
Cazalet-Keir, Thelma, *From the Wings*, 1967
Christiansen, Arthur, *Headlines All My Life*, 1961
Churchill, Sarah, *A Thread in the Tapestry*, 1967
Citrine, Lord, *Men and Work*, 1963
Coats, Peter, *Of Generals and Gardens*, 1976
Colville, John, *Footprints in Time*, 1976
Cooper, Duff, *Old Men Forget*, 1954
Coote, Colin R., *Editorial*, 1965
Coote, Colin R., *The Other Club*, 1971
Dalton, Hugh, *The Fateful Years: Memoirs, 1931–1945*, 1957
Davenport, Nicholas, *Memoirs of a City Radical*, 1974

Davidson, J. C. C. (ed. Rhodes James, Robert), *Memoirs of a Conservative: J. C. C. Davidson's Memoirs and Papers, 1910–1937*, 1969

Donner, Patrick, *Crusade*, 1984

Douglas, Sholto and Wright, Robert, *Years of Command*, 1966

Drogheda, Lord, *Double Harness*, 1978

Einzig, Paul, *In the Centre of Things*, 1960

Farrer, David, *G for God Almighty*, 1969

Frankland, Noble, *History at War: The Campaigns of an Historian*, 1998

Gladwyn, Lord (Gladwyn Jebb, Hubert), *The Memoirs of Lord Gladwyn*, 1972

Grigg, P. J., *Prejudice and Judgement*, 1948

Grisewood, Harman, *One Thing at a Time*, 1968

Hanfstaengl, Ernst, *Hitler: The Missing Years*, 1957

Hardinge, Helen, *Loyal to Three Kings*, 1967

Harriman, Averell and Abel, Elie, *Special Envoy to Churchill and Stalin*, 1975

Harris, Arthur Travers, *Bomber Offensive*, 1947

Harrod, Roy, *The Prof*, 1959

Harvie-Watt, George, *Most of My Life*, 1980

Hoare, Samuel, Viscount Templewood, *Nine Troubled Years*, 1954

Hollis, Leslie, *One Marine's Tale*, 1956

Home of the Hirsel, Alec Douglas-Home, *The Way the Wind Blows*, 1978

Howard, Peter, *Innocent Men*, 1941

Ismay, Hastings, *The Memoirs of General the Lord Ismay*, 1960

Jones, R. V., *Most Secret War*, 1978

Joubert de la Ferté, Philip, *The Fated Sky: An Autobiography*, 1952

Joubert de la Ferté, Philip, *Rocket*, 1957

King, Cecil, *With Malice Toward None*, 1970

Kirkpatrick, Ivone, *The Inner Circle*, 1959

Leasor, James and Hollis, Leslie, *War at the Top: Based on the Experiences of General Sir Leslie Hollis*, 1959

Loelia, Duchess of Westminster, *Grace and Favour*, 1961

Low, David, *Low's Autobiography*, 1956

Lyttelton, Oliver, Viscount Chandos, *The Memoirs of Lord Chandos*, 1964

MacDonald, Malcolm, *People and Places*, 1969

MacDougall, Donald, *Don and Mandarin*, 1987

Macmillan, Harold, *The Blast of War*, 1967

Macmillan, Harold, *A Man of Law's Tale*, 1952

Macmillan, Harold, *Winds of Change, 1914–1939*, 1966

Marshall-Cornwall, James, *Wars and Rumours of Wars*, 1984

Moorehead, Alan, *A Year of Battle*, 1944

Moran, Lord, *The Anatomy of Courage*, 1966

Pile, Frederick, *Ack-Ack*, 1956

Reith, John Charles Walsham, Baron Reith, *Into the Wind*, 1949

Riley, Norman, *999 and All That*, 1940

Rowe, A. P., *One Story of Radar*, 1948

Sandys, Celia, *Churchill's Little Redhead*, 2021

Slessor, John, *The Central Blue: Recollections and Reflections*, 1956

Soames, Mary, *A Daughter's Tale: The Memoir of Winston and Clementine Churchill's Youngest Child*, 2011

Strong, Kenneth, *Intelligence at the Top*, 1968

Stuart, Campbell, *Opportunity Knocks Once*, 1952

Stuart, Viscount, *Within the Fringe*, 1967

Swinton, Lord (Greame, Philip Lloyd), *I Remember*, 1948

Swinton, Lord (Greame, Philip Lloyd), *Sixty Years of Power*, 1966

Tedder, Arthur William, *With Prejudice*, 1966

Thomson, George, *Blue Pencil Admiral*, 1947

Thornton-Kemsley, Colin, *Through Wind and Tides*, 1974

Tree, Ronald, *When the Moon was High*, 1975

Watson-Watt, Robert Alexander, *Three Steps to Victory*, 1958

Zuckerman, Solly, *From Apes to Warlords*, 1988

WORKS BY CONTEMPORARIES OR DRAWN ESSENTIALLY FROM CONTEMPORARY SOURCES

Churchill, Winston, *The Second World War, Volume 1: The Gathering Storm*, 1948

Churchill, Winston, *The Second World War, Volume 2: Their Finest Hour*, 1948

Colville, John, *The Churchillians*, 1981

Crozier, William Percival (ed. Taylor, A. J. P.), *Off the Record: Political Interviews, 1933–1943*, 1973

Dean, Maurice, *The Royal Air Force and Two World Wars*, 1979

Farrer, David, *The Sky's the Limit*, 1943

Foot, M. R. D., *SOE: An Outline History of the Special Operations Executive, 1940–46*, 1984

Gourlay, Logan (ed.), *The Beaverbrook I Knew*, 1984

Hyde, H. Montgomery, *British Air Policy Between the Wars, 1918–1939*, 1976

James, Robert Rhodes, *Victor Cazalet*, 1976

Joubert de la Ferté, Philip, *The Third Service*, 1955

Low, David, *Low Again: A Pageant of Politics*, 1938

Low, David, *The World at War*, 1942

Pitts, Denis, *Clem Attlee: The Granada Historical Records Interview*, 1967

Roskill, Stephen, *Hankey: Man of Secrets, Volume 2, 1919–1931*, 1972

Roskill, Stephen, *Hankey: Man of Secrets, Volume 3, 1931–1963*, 1974

Templewood, Samuel John Gurney Hoare, *Empire of the Air: The Advent of the Air Age, 1922–1929*, 1957

Williams, Edward Francis, *A Prime Minister Remembers*, 1961

Wilson, Thomas, *Churchill and the Prof*, 1997

Wrench, John Evelyn Leslie, *Geoffrey Dawson and Our Times*, 1955

SECONDARY WORKS

Addison, Paul, *Churchill on the Home Front, 1900–1955*, 1992

Addison, Paul, *The Road to 1945*, 1977

Aster, Sidney, *1939: The Making of the Second World War*, 1973

Beckett, Francis, *Clem Attlee*, 2000

Bedell Smith, Sally, *Reflected Glory*, 2006

Bew, John, *Citizen Clem*, 2016

Birkenhead, Lord, *Walter Monckton*, 1969

Bond, Brian, *British Military Policy Between the Two World Wars*, 1980

Bourne, Richard, *Lords of Fleet Street: The Harmsworth Dynasty*, 1990

Boyle, Andrew, *Montagu Norman: A Biography*, 1968

Boyle, Andrew, *Poor, Dear Brendan*, 1974

Boyle, Andrew, *Trenchard*, 1962

Briggs, Asa, *Governing the BBC*, 1979

Briggs, Asa, *The History of Broadcasting in the United Kingdom*, 1995

Bullock, Alan, *The Life and Times of Ernest Bevin: Volume 1, Trade Union Leader*, 1960

Bungay, Stephen, *The Most Dangerous Enemy: A History of the Battle of Britain*, 2001

Cairncross, Alexander, *Planning in Wartime: Aircraft Production in Britain, Germany and the USA*, 1991

Cato, *Guilty Men*, 1940

Charmley, John, *Chamberlain and the Lost Peace*, 1989

Charmley, John, *Churchill: An End to Glory*, 1993

Charmley, John, *Lord Lloyd and the Decline of the British Empire*, 1987

Chisholm, Anne and Davie, Michael, *Lord Beaverbrook: A Life*, 1992

Churchill, Randolph, *Winston S. Churchill: Volume 2, Young Statesman, 1901–1914*, 1967

Clark, Ronald, *Tizard*, 1965

Collier, B., *The Defence of the United Kingdom*, 1957

Collier, B., *Leader of the Few*, 1957

Cooper, Artemis, *Cairo in the War, 1939–1945*, 1989

Cross, J. A., *Lord Swinton*, 1982

Day, David, *Menzies and Churchill at War*, 1986

Deighton, Len, *Fighter*, 1979

D'Este, Carlo, *Warlord*, 2008

Edgerton, David, *Britain's War Machine*, 2011

Edgerton, David, *England and the Aeroplane*, 1991

Evans, Sir Trevor Maldwyn, *Bevin*, 1946

Farman, Christopher, *The General Strike: May 1926*, 1974

Farmelo, Graham, *Churchill's Bomb*, 2013

Field, Leslie, *Bendor: The Golden Duke of Westminster*, 1983

Flint, Peter, *Dowding and Headquarters Fighter Command*, 1996

Foot, Michael, *Aneurin Bevan*, 1975

Fort, Adrian, *Prof*, 2003

Franks, Norman L. R., *RAF Fighter Command, 1936–1968*, 1992

Fry, Geoffrey, *The Politics of Crisis*, 2001

Furse, Anthony, *Wilfrid Freeman*, 1999

Garnett, David, *The Secret History of PWE: The Political Warfare Executive*, 2002

Gilbert, Martin and Gott, John, *The Appeasers*, 1963

Gilbert, Martin, *Winston S. Churchill: Volume 5, The Prophet of Truth, 1922–1939*, 1976

Gilbert, Martin, *Winston S. Churchill: Volume 6, Finest Hour, 1939–1941*, 1983

Gough, J., *Watching the Skies*, 1993

Harris, Kenneth, *Attlee*, 1982

Hart-Davis, Duff, *Man of War*, 2012

Hastings, Max, *Bomber Command*, 1981

Hennessy, Peter, *Whitehall*, 1990

Hinsley, F. H., *British Intelligence in the Second World War: Volume 1*, 1979

Hinsley, F. H., *British Intelligence in the Second World War: Volume 2*, 1981

Hinsley, F. H., *British Intelligence in the Second World War: Volume 3, Part 1*, 1984

Hoe, Alan, *David Stirling*, 1992

Holland, James, *The Story of the RAF: 1918–2018*, 2018

Horne, Alistair, *Macmillan, 1894–1956*, 1988

Hough, Richard, *Winston and Clementine*, 1990

Howard, Anthony, *Rab: The Life of R. A. Butler*, 1987

Irving, David, *The Mare's Nest*, 1964

Jago, Michael, *Clement Attlee: The Inevitable Prime Minister*, 2014

James, T. C. G., *The Growth of Fighter Command, 1936–1940*, 2002

Jeffrey, Keith, *MI6: The History of The Secret Intelligence Service, 1909–1949*, 2010

Jenkins, Roy, *Churchill*, 2001

Kavanagh, Dennis and Seldon, Anthony, *The Powers Behind the Prime Minister*, 1999

Keegan, John (ed.), *Churchill's Generals*, 1991

Kershaw, Ian, *Making Friends with Hitler: Lord Londonderry and Britain's Road to War*, 2005

Kynaston, David, *The Financial Times*, 1988

Kynaston, David, *Till Time's Last Sand*, 2017

Lacey, Robert, *Ford*, 1986

Lesley, Cole, *The Life of Noël Coward*, 1976

Lough, David, *No More Champagne*, 2015

Lysaght, Charles Edward, *Brendan Bracken*, 1979

McDonald, Iverach, *A Man of the Times*, 1976

McDonough, Frank, *Neville Chamberlain, Appeasement and the British Road to War*, 1998

McKinstry, Leo, *Spitfire: Portrait of a Legend*, 2007

McLaine, Ian, *Ministry of Morale*, 1979

Macleod, Iain Norman, *Neville Chamberlain*, 1961

Maiolo, Joseph A., *Cry Havoc*, 2011

Middlemas, Keith, *Diplomacy of Illusion*, 1972

Middlemas, Keith and Barnes, John, *Baldwin: A Biography*, 1969

Montgomery Hyde, H., *Baldwin: The Unexpected Prime Minister*, 1973

Mosley, Leonard, *On Borrowed Time: How World War II Began*, 1971

Murphy, John Thomas, *Labour's Big Three: A Biographical Study of Clement Attlee, Herbert Morrison and Ernest Bevin*, 1948

Naylor, John F., *A Man and an Institution*, 1984

Ogden, Christopher, *Life of the Party*, 1994

O'Halpin, Eunan, *Head of the Civil Service: A Study of Sir Warren Fisher*, 1989

Orange, Vincent, *Dowding of Fighter Command*, 2008

Overy, Richard, *The Birth of the RAF, 1918: The World's First Air Force*, 2018

Overy, Richard, *The Bombing War: Europe, 1939–1945*, 2013

Packwood, Allen, *How Churchill Waged War*, 2018

Parker, R. A. C., *Chamberlain and Appeasement*, 1993

Parker, R. A. C., *Churchill and Appeasement*, 2000

Peden, G. C., *British Rearmament and the Treasury*, 1979

Perkins, Anne, *A Very British Strike: 3 May–12 May*, 1926

Phillips, Adrian, *Fighting Churchill, Appeasing Hitler*, 2019

Phillips, Adrian, *The First Royal Media War*, 2023

Phillips, Adrian, *The King Who Had to Go*, 2016

Phillips, Adrian, *Rearming the RAF for the Second World War*, 2022

Postan, M. M., *British War Production*, 1952

Postan, M. M., Hay, D. and Scott, J. D., *Design and Development of Weapons*, 1964

Powers, Barry Douglas, *Strategy Without Slide-Rule*, 1976

Probert, Henry, *Bomber Harris: His Life and Times*, 2001

Ramsden, John, *The Age of Balfour and Baldwin, 1902–1940*, 1978

Read, Donald, *The Power of News: The History of Reuters*, 1992

Rees, Laurence, *WWII: Behind Closed Doors*, 2008

Rhodes James, Robert, *Bob Boothby*, 1991

Richards, Denis, *Portal of Hungerford*, 1977

Richards, Denis, *The Royal Air Force, 1939–1945: Volume 1, The Fight at Odds*, 1952

Richardson, Charles, *From Churchill's Secret Circle to the BBC: The Biography of Lieutenant General Sir Ian Jacob*, 1991

Ritchie, Sebastian, *Industry and Air Power*, 1997

Roberts, Andrew, *Eminent Churchillians*, 1994

Roberts, Brian, *Randolph*, 1984

Roskill, Stephen, *Churchill and the Admirals*, 2004

Sayers, Richard Sidney, *The Bank of England, 1891–1944*, 1976

Schneer, Jonathan, *Ministers at War*, 2015

Self, Robert C., *Neville Chamberlain: A Biography*, 2006

Sellar, Walter and Yeatman, Robert, *1066 and All That*, 1930

Seymour-Ure, Colin, *David Low*, 1985

Shay, Robert P., *British Rearmament in the Thirties*, 1977

Sinnott, Colin, *The RAF and Aircraft Design, 1923–1939*, 2001

Sisman, Adam, *A. J. P. Taylor: A Biography*, 1994

Skidelsky, Robert, *John Maynard Keynes*, 2003

Smith, Frederick, Earl of Birkenhead, *The Prof in Two Worlds*, 1961

Smith, Frederick, Earl of Birkenhead, *Walter Monckton: The Life of Viscount Monckton of Brenchley*, 1969

Smith, Malcolm, *British Air Strategy Between the Wars*, 1984

Soames, Mary, *Clementine Churchill*, 1979

Stewart, Graham, *Burying Caesar: Churchill, Chamberlain and the Battle for the Tory Party*, 2000

Storr, Anthony, *Churchill's Black Dog*, 1990

Taylor, A. J. P., *Beaverbrook*, 1972

Terraine, John, *The Right of the Line: The Royal Air Force in the European War, 1939–1945*, 1985

Thomas-Symonds, Nicklaus, *Attlee*, 2010

Thompson, J. Lee, *Politicians, the Press and Propaganda*, 1999

Thompson, Neville, *The Anti-Appeasers: Conservative Opposition to Appeasement*, 1971

Timmins, Nicholas, *Five Giants*, 1995

Toye, Richard, *Lloyd George and Churchill: Rivals for Greatness*, 2007

Vysny, Paul, *The Runciman Mission to Czechoslovakia, 1938*, 2002

Wark, W. K., *The Ultimate Enemy: British Intelligence and Nazi Germany, 1933–1939*, 1986

Webster, C. K. and Frankland, N., *The Strategic Air Offensive Against Germany, 1939–1945*, 1961

Williams, Charles, *Max Beaverbrook: Not Quite a Gentleman*, 2019

Williams, Edward Francis, *Ernest Bevin: Portrait of a Great Englishman*, 1952

Williamson, Philip, *Stanley Baldwin*, 1999

Wykeham, Peter, *Fighter Command: A Study of Air Defence, 1914–1960*, 1960

Young, G. M., *Stanley Baldwin*, 1952

Young, Kenneth, *Churchill and Beaverbrook*, 1966

Zimmerman, David, *Britain's Shield: Radar and the Defeat of the Luftwaffe*, 2013

ARTICLES

Brewin, Christopher, 'British Plans for International Operating Agencies for Civil Aviation, 1941–1945', *International History Review*, vol. 4, no. 1, 1982, pp91–110

Brinkworth, Brian, 'On the planning of British aircraft production for the Second World War and reference to James Connolly', *Journal of Aeronautical History*, paper no. 2018/09, 2018, pp233–99

Devons, E., 'Review of British War Production by M. M. Postan', *Economica*, vol. 20, no. 79, 1953, pp279–82

Dobson, Alan P., 'The Other Air Battle: The American Pursuit of Post-War Civil Aviation Rights', *Historical Journal*, vol. 28, no. 2, 1985, pp429–39

Katz, Bernard, 'Archibald Vivian Hill. 26 September 1886–3 June 1977', *Biographical Memoirs of Fellows of the Royal Society*, vol. 24, 1978, pp71–149

Kendall, D., and Post, K., 'Reminiscences and discoveries: The British 3-Inch Anti-Aircraft Rocket. Part One: Dive-Bombers', *Notes and Records of the Royal Society of London*, vol. 50, no. 2, 1996, pp229–39

Middleton, Nigel, 'Lord Butler and the education act of 1944', *British Journal of Educational Studies*, vol. 20, no. 2, 1972, pp178–91

Ritchie, S., 'A Political Intrigue Against the Chief of the Air Staff: The Downfall of Air Chief Marshal Sir Cyril Newall', *War & Society*, vol. 16, issue 1, 1998, pp83–104

Thomson, George Paget, 'Frederick Alexander Lindemann, Viscount Cherwell, 1886–1957', *Biographical Memoirs of Fellows of the Royal Society*, vol. 24, 1978, pp71–149

Toye, Richard, 'Winston Churchill's "Crazy Broadcast": Party, Nation, and the 1945 Gestapo Speech', *Journal of British Studies*, vol. 49, no. 3, 2010, pp655–80

Uhl, Heidemarie, 'Of Heroes and Victims: World War II in Austrian Memory'. *Austrian History Yearbook*, vol. 42, 2011, pp185–200

ACKNOWLEDGEMENTS

My huge thanks for their help in making this book possible for the staff at the archives in which I found the documents that told the story. The magnificent Churchill Archives at Cambridge were the hub for my research, where Andrew Riley was unstinting with his time, efforts and advice and Katharine Thomson applied her forensic knowledge of the handwriting of Churchill and his circle to one special conundrum. Cherish Watton and Nicole Allen masterminded the provision of photos to use as illustrations. Everyone at Nuffield College, Oxford, notably Emma Quinlan, were a joy to work with on my inspections of the Cherwell papers and afterwards. Dr Bethany Hamblen of the Balliol College, Oxford, archive helped me navigate the otherwise baffling twists and turns of Walter Monckton's papers. All at the National Library of Scotland, especially Heidi Egginton, gave immense assistance with Bob Boothby's papers. Annie Pinder gently guided me through the mysteries of the Parliamentary Archives' new booking procedures for what, sadly, will be my last visits before the collection migrates to the National Archives at Kew. Most generously, Lord Crathorne has given me access to his parents' papers.

Both before and, most especially, after the devastating cyber-attack, everyone at the British Library offered vital resource. I am sure that I was not the only one to throw extra demands on the London Library to help fill some of the gaps done to the British Library's services. My thanks to all.

My exploration of less familiar aspects of the bandits' lives were greatly helped by the kind efforts of individuals willing to gift time and energy to this project which fell firmly outside their normal concerns.

Semecký Leoś of the Hispano-Suiza and Classic Club shared his ency-clopaedic knowledge of the marque to help me track down the model of Brendan Bracken's trademark limousine, as well as providing pho-tographs. Jacqueline Thalmann, curator of the Christ Church Picture Gallery, Oxford, gave vital advice on Frederick Lindemann's taste in paintings.

I am very grateful to Dr Allen Packwood of the Churchill Archives who was willing to discuss the project with me at an early stage and share his unsurpassed knowledge of Winston Churchill's world when we met in Edinburgh. David Blaazer and Neville Wylie each provided vital guidance on the Czech gold affair. The opinions and judgements expressed in the book are, of course, entirely my own.

My agent Robert Dudley was an inexhaustible source of wise coun-sel and encouragement. Thank you to everyone at Biteback, for their enthusiasm and support all along the way, most especially my editor Ella Boardman.

Lastly, this book would not have been possible without the help of my wife Sheila, whom I wish to thank for her advice, patience and support, both in looking after me and in a myriad pieces of practical help with the book, from turning her shrewd eye to the text to leading grandchildren – Jessica, William and George – in a highly delicate phase of the research operation.

INDEX